Springer Series on Behavior Therapy and Behavioral Medicine

Series Editors: Cyril M. Franks, Ph.D.
Frederick J. Evans, Ph.D.

Advisory Board: John Paul Brady, M.D.,
Robert P. Liberman, M.D., Neal E. Miller, Ph.D.,
and Stanley Rachman, Ph.D.

Barbara G. Melamed is Professor of Clinical Psychology in the Departments of Clinical Psychology, Psychiatry, and Dentistry at the University of Florida, and is Director of the Psychophysiological Laboratory for Stress Management and Behavioral Medicine. She received her Ph.D. from the University of Wisconsin. Dr. Melamed's contributions to the field include numerous articles and book chapters, film media to help surgeons and dentists prepare children and adults psychologically for stressful medical procedures, and curriculum development for the training of health care professionals. A recipient of several National Institutes of Health research awards for the study of fear, anxiety, and pain-related problems, Dr. Melamed has also given invited lectures at the Maudsley Psychiatric Institute in London, the Max Planck Institute in Munich, and the University of Tubingen.

Lawrence J. Siegel is both Assistant Professor of Psychology and Psychiatry and the Director of the Psychological Clinic at the University of Missouri, Columbia. Among his research interests are stress- and pain-reduction procedures in medical settings and the behavioral treatment of somatic disorders in children. A past Director of Children's Services at Mid-Missouri Mental Health Center, he is currently a consultant in the Department of Family and Community Medicine at the University of Missouri Medical School. Dr. Siegel received his Ph.D. from Case Western Reserve University and completed his internship at Rutgers Medical School.

BEHAVIORAL MEDICINE

Practical Applications in Health Care

Barbara G. Melamed, Ph.D.
Lawrence J. Siegel, Ph.D.

SPRINGER PUBLISHING COMPANY
New York

Copyright © 1980 by Barbara G. Melamed and Lawrence J. Siegel

Springer Publishing Company, Inc.
200 Park Avenue South
New York, New York 10003

80 81 82 83 84 / 10 9 8 7 6 5 4 3 2 1

Library of Congress Cataloging in Publication Data

Melamed, Barbara G
  Behavioral medicine.

  (Springer series in behavior modification; 6)
  Includes bibliographies and indexes.
  1. Behavior therapy. 2. Medicine and psychology.
I. Siegel, Lawrence J., joint author. II. Title.
[DNLM: 1. Behavior therapy. W1 SP685M v. 6 / WM425
M517b]
RC489.B4M45   615.8'51   80-13418
ISBN 0-8261-2170-5
ISBN 0-8261-2171-3 (pbk.)

Printed in the United States of America

To Frances and Al, Jodi and Douglas
B.G.M.

To Marcia and Daniel
L.J.S.

Contents

vii

Part II. Applications of Behavior Therapy to Health Care Problems

Foreword

Behaviorism at the Bedside

Behavioral medicine is a broad discipline, representing an intersection of rapidly expanding behavioral science with the science and practice of medicine. It includes parts of sociology, psychology, education, psychophysiology, and many other subfields that have relevant knowledge, actual or potential, that can assist health care and illness prevention. This book does not pretend to cover such a vast terrain. It focuses on a segment of this field—it describes new applications of experimental psychology to medical practice, or more specifically, it shows how techniques of behavior therapy and behavior modification can be used to facilitate general health care. This emphasis is very appropriate for one of the first books in such a rapidly developing discipline. Behavioral treatment is, in a sense, the practical focus of behavioral medicine. It is a body of knowledge and associated procedures, already successful on the psychopathology testing ground, that seems ready for application in the everyday practice of medicine.

The authors of this book are experienced behavior therapists, and this book reflects a thorough knowledge of the research literature and extensive practical clinical experience in the medical setting. The reader who is a physician or other health-care worker will recognize the problems being addressed as familiar aspects of medical practice. Furthermore, the authors' development of the theoretical rationale, their presentation of the research literature, and their description of procedures are clear and concise. Thus, providing the prologue is easy. I only have to set the stage, place the work in historical and cultural context, and give some inkling of events to come. In addition, because the book presents a novel perspective on treatment and the health care worker–patient relationship, I shall try to elucidate the underlying philosophy of this proposed alliance between psychological science and the more venerable art and science of medicine.

It is common practice for many physicians and other care givers to divide the patient population into two groups: the truly medically ill and those who are at first accepted as ill but for whom, after examination, no explanatory organic defect can be found. The former remain in treatment with the physician and his allies in physical care, while the latter are relabeled as psychiatrically or psychologically disordered, given palliative-only or placebo treatments if the condition is not too severe, or when the behavior deviates markedly from the norm or their persistent requests for care become too troublesome, are passed on to psychiatry, for what mysterious mental aid the general practitioner may not possess.

For many practicing physicians, a psychiatric referral represents a judgment that the case is not one that will respond to physical medicine. This implies that the physician is indeed practicing only physical medicine, that the categories of physical and psychological medicine are nonoverlapping, and that it is the job of others to take care of psychological problems. From this not uncommon perspective there are two main types of illness: one type involves a defect of the physical organs and is therefore the concern and responsibility of the medical care team; the other type involves the "mind," and presumes that troubled spirits are a physical disease that normal medical interventions may not be expected to cure. Of course, there is the tradition of a third, mixed type, so-called psychosomatic disorder, where the illness includes palapable organic detritus, but in which the psychological factors are so prominent that their influence cannot be ignored. However, the latter are generally given no more than a chapter in the volumes of medical practice and are considered the focus of a minor specialty.

The position taken by the authors of this book differs importantly from the view that physical and psychological medicine are wholly separate disciplines. If the reader normally sees the relationship between psychology and medicine as nonoverlapping, the full use of the information presented in this book requires some adjustment of perspective. First, the authors do not hold that there is a fundamental, epistemological difference between psychological and physiological phenomena. Both are held to be objective and to be understood within the metaphysical structure of natural science. That is, it is held that the only relevant observations are those which can in principle be reduced to quantities and be shared among a community of observers. An explanation of a phenomenon is achieved when a parsimonious, logical model (ideally mathematical) of relationships between observations has been described and tested by experiment. Furthermore, while there is always an art in medicine—individual sensitivity, and skill of treatment—the basis of good practice is the application of the technological fruit of a self-correcting scientific enterprise. This book shuns the idea that there are two data bases for medical practice serving the Cartesian dualism of mind and body. Psychology and psychiatry may use a different set of facts from internal medicine, even interpret them differently, but there should be no disagreement as to what constitutes a fact. Thus, the practitioner of ophthalmology, orthopedics, or occupational therapy will not find allusions to a mysterious "psyche" and unconscious processes that defy objective inquiry. Instead, he will find a straightforward discussion of observable events, procedures designed to deal with them directly, and methods for evaluating change that are methodologically similar to those used in the basic sciences that already serve medicine.

Secondly, the authors clearly do not hold that behavioral analysis and psychological interventions are relevant only for the mentally ill. An underlying theme of this book is that experimental psychology is potentially one of the scientific pillars of modern general medicine, as are now her sister disciplines—physiology, anatomy, and pharmacology. It may be argued that it is high time that psychology assisted in this caryatidian role. Psychological factors have been viewed as fundamentally important in medicine since the time of Hippocrates. "Galen estimated that sixty percent of his patients had symptoms of emotional rather than physical origin. This number is close to the contemporary estimate of fifty to eighty percent" (Shapiro, 1978). Psychological treatment and cure are equally ubiquitous. It is difficult to deny the importance of managing behavior at every stage of the patient–care worker relationship, including encouraging behavior consistent with illness prevention, assuring compliance with examination and treatment regimes, psychological intervention (e.g., placebo drugs), and coping with the anticipation and emotional aftereffects of medical stress.

All of these behavioral-management tasks are routinely carried out by physicians and paramedical personnel. For most health workers, efforts at behavioral management are not the conscious application of a scientific technology. Rather, they follow the traditions of the medical setting, extending back over centuries. These have been remarkably effective, and psychologists should be wary of presumptuous claims to do better. Indeed, if we can credit historians who hold that cinchoma bark (quinine), used in the treatment of malaria, was the first specific nonplacebo drug, and that truly effective surgery began with the control of sepsis by Lister (in the last half of the 19th century), then physicians practiced psychological medicine almost exclusively throughout the period prior to these discoveries and, despite this limitation, maintained an important, even venerated position in the structure of society and clearly met many needs of the sick.

The last several decades have seen unprecedented growth in the technology of physical medicine. With the expansion of scientific knowledge, physicians have deployed a new and powerful armamentarium on the terrain of patient care. The effect has been dramatic. Diseases that were the scourge of whole peoples are now wholly absent from the earth. Nevertheless, in these advances psychological science made almost no contribution. Despite agreement that psychological factors are paramount at every stage of illness and its treatment, experimental psychology has heretofore generated no potent technology for health care. Why not?

Compared with chemistry and physics, psychology is very much a newcomer to the sisterhood of sciences. In 1979, psychology's centennial year just came to a close. In 1879 Wilhem Wundt founded in Leipzig what most scholars believe was the first formal laboratory for the exclusive study of psychology. The beginnings of physics are less easy to date. However, the tradition of the physics laboratory, developing out of alchemy, certainly existed long before Galileo started rolling balls down inclined planes. Thus, it would be easy to argue that psychology is too young, and as no fundamental work has been accomplished, it is too early to expect a technological product. The argument has some substance. Psychology's diversity of method and topic betrays a lack of integrating theory. There are major disagreements between its scientists even as to the fundamental issues of the field. It is a discipline in active ferment. Nevertheless, empirical psychology has been applied successfully. The field of tests and measurement has provided important, practical tools for education and occupational selection; engineering psychologists have an increasing place in industry in the design of man–machine environments. Thus, while psychology's immaturity may have retarded its impact on medicine, this is not the whole story. Also important was medicine's embrace of a different view.

At about the same time that Wundt began his laboratory, the master clinician of Vienna, Sigmund Freud, began formulating a theory of psychology which, with its variants and modifications, came to dominate the field of psychopathology and the psychology of medicine generally. Freud's theory was not based on the data of the laboratory, but on the unique, clinical interactions that he had with his patients. Furthermore, despite protestations to the contrary, it was not a scientific theory, but a theory of human experience. It was part of a developmental line extending from Descartes and Brentano, rather than from Newton, Helmholtz, or Pasteur. Nevertheless, its impact on the field of medicine was profound. Agreeing with the theory meant that understanding and treating mental illness required the acceptance of radical new rules of evidence. Subjective experience, previously understood to be forever private, could now be observed by the skilled analyst. Physicians were alternately skeptical and tolerant of this view, but with dramatic reports of the psyche's exploration and no compelling alternative, dynamic theory came to dominate both psychiatry and medical psychology.

This dominance continued unaltered until the late 1950s and early 1960s. The new approach began where psychodynamics had started—with the treatment of neurosis. Psychiatrists and clinical psychologists had become dissatisfied with the marginally effective, often interminable therapies then in vogue. A physician, Joseph Wolpe, began experimenting with a clinical treatment for neurosis which derived from the experimental psychology of conditioning and learning. I was amazed by his book, *Psychotherapy by Reciprocal Inhibition* (1958), which described treatments based on animal models and related human experimentation, more in the tradition of applied physiology than what we had come to understand as clinical psychology. I remember traveling with a colleague from Pittsburgh to Virginia to eagerly confront Dr. Wolpe, who had recently arrived from South Africa. We would evaluate his ideas critically, put them to laboratory test, and soon prove him wrong. We failed only in the latter goal. Wolpe's method of systematic desensitization of phobias proved to be an efficient and economical treatment. A second behavioral revolution was underway, now in clinical application, paralleling the earlier Watsonian movement in laboratory science.

At about the same time as Wolpe began his work, clinical psychologists first applied B. F. Skinner's reinforcement theory to problems in psychopathology. From early studies of the bar-pressing behavior of psychotic patients and efforts to shape language in the interview, the work evolved to experimental treatments. These methods had the advantage of objective description. They could be evaluated and improved through experiment, and were readily communicated to the practitioner. Behavior therapy found a name and prospered. Its new ascendency in clinical research was illustrated by changes in the allocation of grant funds. The number of applications approved by the National Institute of Mental Health for the study of behavior therapy went from zero in 1959 to a level in which almost all research funded by that agency for the study of psychological treatments involved behavioral forms in intervention. In clinical work behavior modification and therapy methods are close to becoming the standard nondrug treatment of anxiety and other aversive emotional states.

It is not surprising that in this atmosphere of success, behaviorists would offer their wares to the field of general health care. It is even possible that behavior therapy may be more effective in general medicine than it has been in the treatment of mental illness. Experimental-behavioral psychology is primarily a psychology of the intact central nervous system and the neuro-chemically normal brain. The tradition of experimental psychology is the study of normal human beings and animals, in search of general principles which can explain and sytematize all behavior. Thus, most of our information concerns how people in general learn, perceive, are motivated, and so forth. Instances of serious psychopathology represent deviations from the norm, which are by definition less readily predicted from our knowledge of human action and, indeed, represent inconsistencies with the principles of behavior in which psychologists have confidence. Thus, it is reasonable to expect that behavior modification methods will be more effective with the psychologically normal individual (who happens to be suffering from illness) than with people afflicted by a fundamental disturbance of behavior. The application of behavioral engineering to such tasks as psychological preparation for surgery, encouraging behavior consistent with disease prevention, or maintaining a drug regime is more straightforward, more within the bounds of present knowledge, than the cure of a serious psychopathological defect.

The greatest barrier to behavioral applications in health care lies in the lack of information about psychology currently available to both professionals and patients. The crowded medical school curriculum does not include courses in experimental psychology or its applications. Many physicians may hold that the elaborate psychological treatment summarized by the term, "a good bedside manner," cannot be systematized or improved through scientific inquiry and that his physically ill patients have enough to worry about without being troubled by psychology (paradoxical thought!). It is even more likely that resistance will be found among patients. They have learned to be wary of psychology and presume that any mention of it implies that they "must be crazy." Like many health care workers, patients make the distinction between illnesses which are "all in the mind" and "true diseases" for which they are not morally culpable. We all need to see that behavior is no less objective than physiology and that the stress of physical illness calls for the consideration of both kinds of data.

The introduction of behavioral methods into general medicine in no way implies a reduction in patient responsibility for his own care. On the contrary, behavioral interventions require that the patient participate more actively in his own treatment. Nearly all of us, as patients, covet the hope that the physician will magically deliver us from disease without effort on our part. However, patients are always asked to do some of the work—to take a drug on schedule. The newer psychological treatments, such as biofeedback, demand an even greater investment of resources by the patient. The task of learning to control a visceral system through the use of an exteroceptive display is more similar to that of the Olympic athlete perfecting his sport than to our vision of a passive patient magically cured. If this kind of cooperation is to be forthcoming, we will need to share more information with patients. They will need to know more about their bodies, how they function, and what behaviors are in the best interest of optimal health. Perhaps we should anticipate some modification of the traditional doctor–patient relationship. We might expect more of an alliance against disease, rather than the sometime patient role of supplicant seeking protection from a superpower. Patients may come more often to consult health care workers, rather than seek to turn over to them all responsibility for care.

In a recent book Susan Sontag (1979) confronts the metaphors of illness. She shows that disease imagery alters self-conceptions, pervades political rhetoric, confuses the patient, and complicates his struggle against disease. Thus, the nineteenth century aesthete almost welcomed consumption as a confirmation of his sensitive, artistic spirit. In our century man cringes in fear under the evil scourge of cancer. We see the carcinoma visited on an unjust head of state as a symbolic manifestation of his malignant influence. Like so many portraits of Dorian Gray, our bodies give physical representation to the secrets of our souls. The metaphoric psychology of disease is rampant in all cultures, and it is more often the enemy than the friend of health. This tendency has been given further fuel by the psychology of the unconscious, which often has represented disease as the expression of hidden instincts, distorted expressions of our desires and fears.

This book will not add to the dark poetry of illness. Behavioral psychology does not hold that disease is predestined by our personalities or that we are physical victims of our basest desires. It is not wholly free of metaphor, but it is an optimistic metaphor. Arguing that the psychology as well as the physiology of illness can be understood in the objective terms of scientific inquiry, the authors choose reason over magic. While there is a good measure of common sense here, and much that will be changed with practice, there is also a rational, humanistic spirit and considerable technological promise. Already we can see these tools being used against disease and some signs of a new patient–care worker alliance.

The authors of this book would not want me to close on a note of unreasoned optimism. I know them both personally, and they are serious and cautious scientists, as well as able practitioners. They would join me in encouraging the reader to remain skeptical and to question while reading and evaluating this book, and to be cautious and deliberate in attempting its application. Scientific theories and their technological fruit are not made to last for the ages. Science is a protean and opportunistic servant. New data nullify the most robust-appearing explanation, and new explanations may spawn technological innovation beyond our present expectation. Such fields as human information processing, the psychophysiology of thought and emotion, are in active development within psychology, and new discoveries could profoundly influence forms of therapeutic intervention. Indeed, it would be discouraging if ten years from now our clinical procedures were not better than they are now, or if many or all are not replaced by improved methods generated by an advancing science. Thus, it is in this spirit of pleasure at these first accomplishments and in the hope that you will take part in the task of bettering them that I commend this book to the reader.

Peter J. Lang, Ph.D.
Clark Hull Professor of Psychology
University of Wisconsin—Madison

References

Shapiro, A. K. Placebo effects in medical and psychological therapies. In S. L. Garfield & A. E. Bergin (Eds.), *Handbook of psychotherapy and behavior change: an empirical analysis* (2nd Edition). New York: John Wiley & Sons, 1978, pp. 369–410.

Sontag, Susan. *Illness as metaphor.* New York: Vintage Books, 1979.

Wolpe, J. *Psychotherapy by reciprocal inhibition.* Stanford: Stanford University Press, 1958.

Preface

This book is about helping patients cope with stress. The stress reaction is a breakdown in the normal adaptive process. It may occur in any overwhelming life circumstance, such as job loss or marital disappointment. It is also a common reaction to illness.

People normally respond to difficult life events with coping strategies learned early in life. The child generally learns to deal with separation from the parents, problems with peers, and the other normal life stresses without serious consequences. However, illness, injury, and their treatment can create special problems that exceed a person's ability to adapt: fear of unknown pain, facing a major operation, the crippling effects of injury, the dismal prospect of chronic disease, the terrifying fact of a terminal illness. These situations require the considered attention of health care specialists. Patients and their families need help in adjusting to the many practical, personal, and social problems presented by illness and disease. It is the members of allied health professions—physicians, nurses, social workers, psychologists, dentists, rehabilitation specialists—who take up this challenge, and it is to these professionals and their students that this book is addressed.

Our main objective is to provide you with a sample of behavioral approaches that can be used in the context of medical treatment. Applications of behavioral management methods to dysfunctions of physical illness or to the psychological and behavioral problems associated with illness are now available (e.g., see Gambrill, 1977; Katz & Zlutnick, 1975; Knapp & Peterson, 1976; Walen, Hauserman, & Lavin, 1977; Williams & Gentry, 1977). Rachman (1977) and others (Epstein, Katz, & Zlutnick, 1979; Pomerleau & Brady, 1975; Rachman & Philips,

1978) have noted the contributions that behavioral science has already made to such diverse areas as doctor–patient communication; preparation for surgery; treatment of chronic pain; problems in rehabilitation of the paralyzed, burned, or chronically ill; and problems in patient compliance with medical regimens.

Specialized applications have been demonstrated in mental retardation (Whitney, 1966), public health (Pomerleau, Bass, & Crown, 1975), psychiatric nursing (Aiken, 1970; Ayllon & Azrin, 1965; Ayllon & Michael, 1959; Berni, Dressler, & Baxter, 1971; Berni & Fordyce, 1973; Layton, 1966; LeBow, 1973; Marks, Hallam, Connolly, & Philpott, 1977), pediatric nursing (Coyne, Peterson, & Peterson, 1968), geriatric care (MacDonald & Butler, 1974), and dentistry (Ayer & Hirschman, 1972; Wright, 1975).

The groundwork for behavioral medicine has been laid. Nevertheless, despite this growing literature pointing to the effective use of behaviorally oriented methods in the treatment of health problems, few physicians or other clinical workers systematically employ behavioral interventions. The aim of this textbook is to develop a curriculum for the health care professions from this literature, in the hope that a wider application of these methods will be stimulated.

The purpose of Part I is to define the main strengths of the behavioral approach. The experimental foundations of these treatments are described in the first two chapters. Chapter 3 provides the necessary steps in a behavioral treatment program. A treatment program outline is developed that is helpful in defining the presenting problems and elucidating the situations that maintain them. It details strategies for identifying problem behaviors in such a way that patient and therapist can monitor progress throughout the intervention program. This will be used to describe in detail one functional analysis of a patient's problem within each of the applied chapters. It forms a problem-oriented guide for decision making. Treatment recommendations take into consideration the practical realities (time, personnel, and equipment limitations) of the clinical setting. Specific topics include engaging the patient in treatment, educating the staff, and eliciting family participation.

The book focuses on interdisciplinary programming since the problems of illness involve many fields. Part II addresses the specific concerns in pediatric management; psychiatric care; internal medicine; occupational, physical, and vocational rehabilitation; social services; surgery; dentistry; and many other areas of patient care. Chapter 4 deals with patient management issues common to all areas that involve promoting the patient's adherence to medical or behavioral regimens.

Fears associated with medical procedures that prevent a person from seeking or receiving effective medical care are addressed. The behavioral implications of the "sick-role" concept are reviewed. Health risk factors such as weight control, exercise, and illness-prone behavior patterns are discussed.

The focus of Chapter 5 is on the collaboration between health care providers and parents in the management of childhood disorders associated with developmental problems. The interaction between physical and psychological processes underlying psychiatric disturbances is emphasized in Chapter 6 to help in the selection of appropriate treatment foci. A broad range of illnesses including anorexia nervosa, headaches, muscular tics, sexual dysfunctions, insomnia, and obsessive-compulsive medical concerns are viewed in the context of the relaxation procedures and operant contingency programs applied in their treatment. The evaluation of physiological, behavioral, and verbal components are important considerations in treatment selection.

Rehabilitation, as defined in Chapter 7, involves helping patients to relearn or compensate for skills and abilities lost through impairment due to illness, injury, or the aging process. Examples are provided for retraining neuromuscular control, treating problems associated with wheelchair and prosthetic devices, and teaching skills necessary for independent daily living. Motivation, anxiety, depression, and tolerance of pain are important aspects of the behavioral treatment program for *all patients*. They are discussed here in great detail.

Part III addresses the issues of research and prevention. The orientation throughout this book involves an emphasis on accountability. Research means evaluating what works when, how, and in which problem situations. To this extent, we are all engaged in research. It is important to evaluate whether a particular strategy is therapeutic. One should never assume beneficial effects of any preparation without an empirical basis. The behavioral approach allows one to do this without deviating from the practitioner's primary service role. Research has contributed to our basic understanding about methods to allay anxiety in patients facing medical experiences. How much preparatory information does an individual need in face of an impending stressful medical intervention? When should this information be imparted? These questions should be considered in work with patients. Chapters 8 and 9 demonstrate the contributions of behavioral research in preparation of patients for surgery, childbirth, and dentistry.

Chapter 8 provides a format for dealing with many of the issues common in evaluation research:

1. the need to define the population for whom the therapy is intended,
2. the importance of controlling for other factors that may contribute inadvertently to the treatment's effectiveness, such as age, sex, and socioeconomic or educational level of the individual,
3. the need to consider patients' previous experience in the impending situation, as well as their prehospital adjustment,
4. personality styles which may affect individuals' ability to cope with information provided in advance of the stressful event,
5. the need to compare the treatment with appropriate control groups so as to identify the effective components of therapy,
6. the importance of limiting conclusions to the situations in which the procedures have been evaluated until generalization is demonstrated.

This process is further illustrated in studies of the behavioral preparation for childbirth. Reductions have been found in the actual length of labor and the amount of analgesic medication of the mothers using these methods.

Behavioral scientists must communicate their findings to the health care professionals as practical recommendations. Chapter 9 translates the empirical findings of research in dental settings (Melamed, 1979) into practical suggestions for patient management. It provides a curriculum for dental personnel in the application of psychological principles in dentistry.

In all the chapters, the patient is considered part of the health care team. The emphasis is on the patient's responsibility to learn new skills that can be applied prophylactically, if similar problems arise when the patient is no longer in the medical setting. Examples are provided of treatment failure as well as success, so that a realistic view of the pitfalls of behavioral treatment can be appreciated. It will be seen that problems and treatments are similar in different health care settings, and that common principles underlie both medical and psychological applications. Recognition of this fact will help us to work more effectively as an interdisciplinary team.

In this regard, Katz and Zlutnick (1975) have aptly noted that:

In conjunction with already established medical technology, behavioral techniques allow for a more comprehensive approach to patient care. In contrast, lack of attention to the environmental, behavioral, and social components of health problems may result in a less than satisfactory treatment outcome. Clearly, the patient profits from the collaboration between medical practitioners and behavioral scientists [p. 15].

References

Aiken, L. H. Patient problems are problems in learning. *American Journal of Nursing*, 1970, *70*, 1916–1918.

Ayer, W., & Hirschman, R. *Psychology and dentistry.* Springfield, Ill.: Charles C Thomas, 1972.

Ayllon, T., & Azrin, N. H. The measurement and reinforcement of behavior of psychotics. *Journal of Experimental Analysis of Behavior*, 1965, *8*, 357–383.

Ayllon, T., & Michael, J. The psychiatric nurse as a behavioral engineer. *Journal of the Experimental Analysis of Behavior*, 1959, *2*, 323–334.

Berni, R., Dressler, J., & Baxter, J. Reinforcing behavior. *American Journal of Nursing*, 1971, *71*, 2180–2183.

Berni, R., & Fordyce, W. *Behavior modification and the nursing process.* St. Louis: C. V. Mosby, 1973.

Coyne, P., Peterson, L., & Peterson, R. The development of spoon feeding behavior in a blind child. *The International Journal for the Education of the Blind*, 1968, *18*, 108–112.

Epstein, L. H., Katz, R. C., & Zlutnick, S. Behavioral medicine. In M. Hersen, R. M. Eisler, & P. M. Miller (Eds.), *Progress in behavior modification*, Vol. 7. New York: Academic Press, 1979.

Gambrill, E. *Behavior modification: Handbook of assessment, intervention, and evaluation.* San Francisco: Jossey Bass, 1977.

Katz, R. C., & Zlutnick, S. (Eds.), *Behavior therapy and health care: Principles and applications.* New York: Pergamon Press, 1975.

Knapp, T., & Peterson, L. Behavioral management in medical and nursing practice. In W. E. Craighead, A. Kazdin, & M. Mahoney (Eds.), *Behavioral modification: Principles, issues, and applications.* Boston: Houghton Mifflin, 1976.

Layton, M. Behavior therapy and implications for psychiatric nursing. *Perspective Psychiatric Care*, 1966, *4*, 38–52.

LeBow, M. *Behavior modification: A significant method in nursing practice.* Englewood Cliffs, N.J.: Prentice Hall, 1973.

MacDonald, M. L., & Butler, A. K. Reversal of helplessness: Producing walking behavior in nursing home wheelchair residents using behavior modification procedures. *Journal of Gerontology*, 1974, *29*, 97–101.

Marks, I. M., Hallam, R., Connolly, J., & Philpott, R. *Nursing in behavioral therapy: An advanced clinical role for nurses.* London: Royal College for Nursing, 1977.

Melamed, B. G. Behavioral approaches to fear in dental settings. In M. Hersen, R. M. Eisler, and P. M. Miller (Eds.), *Progress in behavior modification,* Vol. 7. New York: Academic Press, 1979.

Pomerleau, O., Bass, F., & Crown, V. Role of behavior modification in preventative medicine. *New England Journal of Medicine,* 1975, *292,* 1277–1282.

Pomerleau, O., & Brady, J. P. Behavior modification in medical practice. *Pennsylvania Medicine,* 1975, *78,* 49–59.

Rachman, S. J. (Ed.), *Contributions to medical psychology.* Oxford: Pergamon Press, 1977.

Rachman, S. J., & Philips, C. *Psychology and medicine.* Middlesex, England: Penguin, 1978.

Walen, S., Hauserman, N., & Lavin, P. (Eds.), *Clinical guide to behavior therapy.* Baltimore, Md.: Williams & Wilkins, 1977.

Whitney, L. Behavioral approaches to the nursing of the mentally retarded. *Nursing Clinics of North America,* 1966, *1,* 641–650.

Williams, R., & Gentry, N. (Eds.), *Behavioral approaches to medical treatment.* Cambridge, Mass.: Ballinger, 1977.

Wright, G. *Behavioral management in dentistry for children.* Philadelphia: W. B. Saunders, 1975.

Acknowledgments

In an effort to make the material presented in this book as relevant as possible to our readers, we sought the expertise of a number of colleagues from the various health care disciplines. We would like to express our appreciation to Cynthia Belar, Ph.D.; Carroll Bennett, D.D.S.,M.S.; Douglas Bernstein, Ph.D.; Jan Dally, R.N., M.P.H.; Suzanne Johnson, Ph.D.; Audrey Kalafatich, R. N., Ed.D.; Dan Kivlahan, M. A.; Lewis Leavitt, M. D.; Isaac Marks, M. D., F.R.A.C.P.; William McReynolds, Ph.D.; Ferol Menks, M.S., O.T.R.; Georgia Nolph, M.D.; Paul Peters, D.D.S.; Clare Philips, Ph.D.; Stanley Rachman, Ph.D.; Helene Siegel, O.T.R.; Matthew Speltz, M.A.; Craig Twentyman, Ph.D.; Kristi Twitchell, M.S.W.; and all the hospital staff at Case Western Reserve Medical School; J. Hillis Miller Health Center, University of Florida; Mid-Missouri Mental Health Center and the University of Missouri Medical School, who have worked with us in our effort.

The authors' research and clinical practice in the area of behavioral medicine began as a collaborative effort between student and teacher and has continued as one of colleague and friend. Dr. Cyril Franks gave us the opportunity and guidance to create a textbook translating our empirical work into a practical contribution for health care professionals. This book represents equal contributions of both authors. Dr. Peter Lang, who was mentor of the first author, has contributed greatly in the realization of this book. He has critically reviewed the manuscript and contributed new thoughts and ideas. Dr. W. Stewart Agras has reviewed the manuscript for its specific relevance for medical practitioners. The loving support and the patience of Nancy Davidson and Jodi and Doug Melamed was freely given and gratefully accepted.

We wish to acknowledge the support of grants from the Cleveland Foundation, the National Institute of Dental Research (DE-04243), the Division of Maternal and Child Health, U.S. Public Health Service (MCR-0290412010), and the University of Missouri Institutional Biomedical Research Support Grant from the National Institutes of Health (RR-07053). The ideas of our students, colleagues, and patients have provided the impetus for this endeavor. Finally, we would like to thank Pat Klitzke, Ann Lang, Betty Rich, and Joyce Winn, who contributed to various stages of the manuscript typing and editing.

Part I

THEORETICAL AND EMPIRICAL FOUNDATIONS OF BEHAVIORAL MEDICINE

1

Behavior Therapy in Health Care

What Is Behavior Therapy?

Interest in using behavioral methods in medical practice is growing rapidly. Unfortunately, as Brady (1973) has pointed out, there are few opportunities to learn about behavioral principles in most medical schools and residency training programs. Furthermore, most texts seem to equate behavior modification with a set of procedures (e.g., systematic desensitization, reinforcement procedures, flooding, modeling, or token economies) without a rationale for when they should be used. It is difficult for most practitioners to see how these techniques may be applied directly in their work. However, what is essential and distinctive about behavior therapy is the way in which clinical problems are analyzed. Behavior therapy is a system for collecting, organizing, and evaluating clinical data and then designing individual treatment programs tailored to specific presenting problems.

Behavior therapy aims to modify current symptoms that interfere with an individual's adaptive functioning. It focuses attention on observable behavioral manifestations of these problems. These may include the person's self-report statements, actual avoidance or maladaptive behaviors, and/or somatic arousal responses. There are many diverse approaches that compose the behavior therapies. All have in common the application of learning principles. Learning theories assume that both genetic and environmental factors are important in determining abnormal behavior. The acquisition, maintenance, and alteration of those behaviors labeled as troublesome are thought to follow the same laws as those behaviors which are adaptive. This opens up the way toward changing "sick" behavior without assuming that there is an underlying disease. Instead, maladaptive behaviors, such as overeating, encopresis, anorexia, or sexual dysfunctions, are viewed as bad habits or faulty learning patterns. Following a physical illness it is not uncommon for patients to experience sleep, eating, or bowel disturbances that may impede their recovery. The behavior therapist might help individuals to modify these troublesome habits and to form new, more adaptive patterns of behavior.

Maladaptive behavior has effectively been altered without an extensive search into the patient's past history. There is no need to postulate an unconscious, intrapsychic cause or to find the original source of the problem. There have been many documented applications of learning techniques to a variety of psychiatric and medical problems. These methods have been successful in altering the dysfunctional behaviors without producing additional symptoms. This lends credence to the behavioral approach. The responsible behavior therapist does not "remove" the maladaptive behavior without helping the patient to replace it with more adaptive skills.

Rationale for Behavior Therapy

The most distinctive feature of behavior therapy is in the command it gives to the therapist in both implementing therapy and in evaluating the progress of treatment. When one approach fails to accomplish change, another is tried according to objective indications, each variation being an application of an experimentally established principle.

Behavioral therapies offer several advantages in working with health care problems. Outcomes of behavioral treatment indicate that it is often possible to alter the symptom associated with organic dysfunction without medical intervention. For instance, biofeedback has been used in the treatment of a case of severe fecal incontinence (Engel, Nikoomanesh, & Schuster, 1974), in which the patient learned to defecate by learning how to monitor his sphincter activity. Similarly, Patel (1976) used relaxation and biofeedback to decrease blood pressure and serum cholesterol levels without drugs in patients with hypertension.

There are distinct advantages in applying nonpharmacological approaches in altering behavior problems associated with organic dysfunction. Often, it is difficult to get patients to comply with medication regimens. Although prescribed by the physician, drugs may not reliably be taken by the patient. Furthermore, some antihypertensive drugs, for instance, are associated with fatigue, depression, and stomach upset. Therefore, the patient may choose to increase the serious long-term risks of the disease by neglecting his medication for short-term relief from the drug's side effects. Another disadvantage of medicating patients who need to learn new skills to cope with their disease is that the learning process may be adversely affected by certain drugs. There is evidence that information learned while under the effects of a drug does not necessarily transfer to the nondrugged state (Overton, 1966; Turner & Young, 1966). This can be a serious problem since the goal of any behavioral treatment is to enable the new behaviors to transfer to the real-life situation. There is also data suggesting that individuals who attribute a change in their behavior to the effects of a drug are less likely to maintain this behavior than if they attribute change to their own efforts (Davison & Valins, 1968; Kopel & Arkowitz, 1975).

There have, however, been studies in which the use of a relaxing drug has aided the therapeutic process. Wolpe (1958) recommended the use of a tranquilizer during systematic desensitization therapy. Marks, Viswanathan, Lipsedge, and Gardner (1971) found that diazepam (Valium) enhanced the effectiveness of a procedure to reduce phobic behavior. The drug increased the probability that the patients would continue to expose themselves to the frightening situations. Often, pharmacological agents may be employed to permit chronically withdrawn schizophrenics or hyperkinetic children to become more receptive to behavioral intervention (Hersen, Edelstein, Turner, & Pinkston, 1975; Safer & Allen, 1976).

Behavior therapy is more economical than traditional therapies in that it can be learned easily by paraprofessionals, including family members, teachers, and auxiliary nursing and dental personnel. This is due to the fact that most behavioral technology is relatively simple; a practical understanding of its procedures does not depend on an extensive scientific education. Often, behavioral treatment can accomplish goals in a shorter period of time, thus costing less in terms of both expense for the patient and professional time of the health care provider. These therapies deal with strengthening the patients' already adaptive behavior, eliminating maladaptive habits, or helping them to adjust to their illness or handicap. Because the patient is likely to see some immediate improvement for a given problem, he or she is further encouraged to cooperate.

The limitations and problems in the application of learning principles to changing dysfunctional behaviors should also be noted. In treating patients outside of a hospital setting, social interactions are very complex. The therapist cannot effectively manipulate all the factors in the environment that would help alleviate the patients' distress. Therefore, important individuals in the patient's life must be involved to facilitate cooperation with the treatment program. It is also necessary to evaluate the secondary gains of the "sick role." If the patient is receiving increased attention or being allowed to get out of responsibilities in the home, family members must be directed to make more appropriate demands upon the patient and reward adaptive behaviors. In some families, the persons providing the patient with care are being reinforced for the caretaker role and may be reluctant to see the patient improve and become independent of them. In addition, problem behaviors persist because they may be anxiety-reducing in that they allow the patient to avoid situations (social interactions, sexual intercourse) that might be stressful. Therefore, the individual needs to be taught other, more socially approved ways of dealing with stress. The ultimate goal of any behavioral program is to enable patients to regain control over those situations which first brought them into treatment.

Contributions of Behavioral Specialists in Medicine

Although the term "behavioral medicine" is currently in wide use, often referring to any application of psychology to health-related problems, the discipline of behavioral medicine is only beginning to be defined. A conference held at Yale University in 1977 brought together experts in both biomedical and behavioral sciences. The Academy of Behavioral Medicine was established and a working definition of behavioral medicine was developed:

> Behavioral medicine is the field concerned with the development of behavioral-science knowledge and techniques relevant to the understanding of physical health and illness and the application of this knowledge and these techniques to prevention, diagnosis, treatment, and rehabilitation. Psychosis, neurosis, and substance abuse are included only insofar as they contribute to physical disorders as an end point [Yale Conference on Behavioral Medicine, 1977].

The discipline combines the expertise of people with a diverse range of professional orientations, including physicians, psychologists, sociologists, and other social scientists, and the health care professionals who provide primary patient care. The area now has its own journals, *The Journal of Behavioral Medicine* and *Behavioral Medicine Abstracts,* which will help define the scope of the problems within the field.

Any new discipline achieves its identity through what the pioneers in the field actually do. It is evident that behavior therapists have already had an impact in medically related areas. The last decade has witnessed an increased productivity in the collaboration between medical specialists and behavioral clinicians. This book emphasizes the contribution of behavior theorists and therapists to the developing discipline of behavioral medicine. Significant contributions have already been made in patient management, pain management, pediatric management, psychosomatic disorders, psychiatric disorders, rehabilitation, geriatrics, and preventive health practice. A brief review of these efforts is presented here. In subsequent chapters many of these problems are readdressed, and details of methods and procedures are provided.

Patient Management

Many health professionals have been trained to believe that if the patient understands the reasons for taking pills, maintaining a balanced diet, and exercising regularly, that this provides sufficient motivation to assure that these regimens will be followed. In most cases, the assumption that understanding alone changes behavior is erroneous. Sackett, Haynes, Gibson, Hackett, Taylor, Roberts, and Johnson (1975) found that knowledge of causes and treatment of hypertension did not insure compliance with the medication programs. Even when physician care was readily available in the industrial plant where the patients were employed, they failed to stay on their prescribed regimens. Despite scientific evidence and scare tactics that indicate that cigarette smoking, overeating, and lack of physical exercise may be harmful to their well-being, patients cannot easily change old habits. The behavioral scientist offers expertise regarding the modification of these reinforcing, but self-destructive behaviors. After an evaluation of the patient's strengths as well as his or her weaknesses in self-control, the therapist can instruct him or her in more effective problem-solving strategies. For instance, the obese individual may learn to limit eating behavior to the kitchen area only, and to control the rate of eating, as well as the quality of the food. Depression may accompany the feeling of lack of control over problem behaviors. Unfortunately, many inpatient medical settings inadvertently encourage dependency behaviors in the patient. The patient's reestablishment of control permits greater independence and often results in a concomitant increase in self-confidence.

Pain Management

Psychologists are spending a great deal of both clinical and research effort in helping people cope with chronic pain (Fordyce, 1976; Sternbach, 1978). Regardless of the cause of the pain—back injury, spinal cord defects, cancer treatments—patients must learn to tolerate the discomfort and continue to carry on with their daily responsibilities. Certain behavioral procedures and self-management routines can be taught that may alleviate their symptoms. For example, Gannon and Sternbach (1971) demonstrated that alpha conditioning through biofeedback devices effectively reduced the frequency and the severity of migraine symptoms. Other biofeedback instruments focusing on finger temperature increases, training in vasomotor constriction, and reducing electromyographic activity have also been effective. Procedures that do not involve complex mechanical devices have also achieved similar success. Thus, relaxation instruction or simple meditation procedures have been used (Benson, 1976). Philips (1977) pointed out, however, that reduced autonomic arousal does not necessarily lead to reduced use of pain medication. Thus, the whole complex of pain behaviors must be examined.

Fordyce and his colleagues (1968, 1973) have focused more on environmental factors that contribute to maintaining pain behaviors. They have identified the social gains that may accrue to the pain-complaining patient. Relatives become sympathetic, compensation and disability benefits are often available, and the individual may learn to avoid resuming a responsible adult role. This may inadvertently lead to a vicious cycle: the patient expresses feelings of hopelessness, is reassured by others; this in turn reinforces the patient's dependency and complaint behaviors; the sympathizer may be reinforced by a temporary termination of depressive behavior; the sick role is rewarded. Fordyce uses the environmental contingencies available to reverse this cycle. For instance, patients are rewarded with rest after improved walking behavior, instead of being allowed to quit when the frustration becomes overwhelming. Family and friends who interact with the patient are told to reward and encourage success attempts and to ignore complaining behaviors.

Pediatric Management

Wright (1975) stated that almost all children with medically involved conditions have psychological needs. These emotional problems may exacerbate medical symptoms and cannot be ignored. For instance, hospitalization itself may lead to a sense of isolation as well as a reduced opportunity to develop appropriate peer interactions. Wright (1977) convincingly argues for a broadening of the concept of psychosomatic disorders to include all behavioral concomitants of illness. This conception would encompass problems of development, such as encopresis, childhood phobias, and hyperactivity. Psychological disturbances created indirectly by physical illness (e.g., diabetes, hemophelia, epilepsy) such as failure to cooperate, social withdrawal, aggressive behavior, and so forth, should also be the focus of treatment.

Behavioral strategies such as systematic desensitization have helped asthmatic children cope with their fears of dying or separation from the nebulizer (Creer, 1970; Purcell, 1975). Alexander (1972) has used biofeedback directly to increase peak respiratory flow or to decrease muscle tension levels by providing asthmatic children with information regarding these physiological responses. The role of environmental factors in the development and maintenance of asthma was illustrated clearly in a case that resulted in the reduction of number of bedtime wheezing episodes merely by instructing the parents consistently to ignore the child's wheezing (Neisworth & Moore, 1972).

In many cases, it is the parent who needs assistance in implementing the child's special diets, exercise, and medication regimens. Too often, the parents of a chronically ill child may reinforce infantile behavior, thus contributing to delays in cognitive, emotional, and social development (Creer & Christian, 1976). It is also important not to overlook the stresses placed on well children who must live with sick siblings. Mixed emotions, including guilt for being healthy, fear of developing the disorder, embarrassment in front of friends, or anger at the parents' preferential treatment of the ill child, also need to be a focus of intervention. It is possible for the well child to begin to model sick behaviors or to act inappropriately in order to gain attention. The family process must be understood since role demands change when illness strikes. The increased demands on the parents to tend to illness behavior results in less time available to reward appropriate behaviors, not only in the patient, but in other siblings. Thus, behaviors most likely to result in attention are rewarded. This may manifest itself in high-intensity maladaptive behaviors (e.g., complaining, yelling, fighting).

Behavioral consultants have been used widely in advising parents, teachers, and pediatricians how to handle developmental problems such as enuresis (Foxx & Azrin, 1975), aggressiveness (Wahler, 1969), and excessive fears (Johnson & Melamed, 1979). Medically related problems, such as hyperkinesis (Christensen & Sprague, 1973), tracheostomy addiction (Wright, Nunnery, Eichel, & Scott, 1968), fear of hypodermic needles (Turnage & Logan, 1974), and refusal to take oral medication (Wright, Woodcock, & Scott, 1969), have also been amenable to behavioral approaches.

Adult Psychosomatic Disorders

Katz and Zlutnick (1975) have presented a series of adult cases in which such diverse symptoms as anorexia nervosa, spasmodic torticollis, migraine headaches, and seizure activity have been successfully reduced with behavioral methods. A variety of operant procedures have successfully modified seizure activity of both organic and nonorganic origin. By applying a mild electric shock or a loud noise, or by imposing a cognitive task during the early phase of a seizure, frequency of episodes has been reduced (Zlutnick, Mayville, & Moffat, 1975). Sterman and Friar (1972) controlled the involuntary seizures of a 28-year-old woman by using a biofeedback device to produce brain wave patterns incompatible with seizure. Behavioral scientists have discovered that autonomic activity in humans can be brought under operant control. This has had exciting implications for patients suffering from increased blood pressure (Benson, Shapiro, Tursky, & Schwartz, 1971) and premature ventricular contractions (Weiss & Engel, 1971). Blanchard and Young (1974), however, after a critical review of the literature, have cautioned against premature clinical use of biofeedback.

Psychiatric Patients

The psychiatric setting has been the most widely used arena for the application of behavioral principles. The pioneers in the field focused on altering the environments and response repertoires of inpatient psychiatric patients by use of token economies (Ayllon & Azrin, 1965; Schaefer & Martin, 1969). Hersen and Bellack (1977), Kazdin (1975, 1977), and Stahl and Leitenberg (1976) have adequately reviewed this area. Paul (1969) reviewed the prerequisites that must be taught to chronic mental patients to resocialize them, reinstate occupational skills, and reduce bizarre behavior to enable them to readjust outside the hospital. Outpatient treatment approaches have been summarized by Leitenberg (1976). The case illustrations provided in Walen, Hauserman, and Lavin (1977) demonstrate behavioral approaches used with neurotic distrubances, including those having medical as well as psychiatric symptoms.

Rehabilitation

The needs of recently disabled individuals include learning new skills, adjusting to their physical and cognitive losses, and relearning previous skills or abilities that have been impaired. A number of studies have reported treatment programs that have been used to enable the patients to maximize their potential abilities despite an illness or disability (e.g., Sand, Trieschmann, Fordyce, & Fowler, 1970). This intervention often prevents further complications that can be associated with their disorders. Goodkin (1966), for example, increased the speed with which a patient with Parkinson's disease propelled his wheelchair merely by providing praise and attention for the desired behavior. Similar techniques were effective in helping patients with spinal cord injuries to shift their body position more frequently in order to prevent pressure sores (Rottkamp, 1976). Azrin and his colleagues (Azrin, Rubin, O'Brien, Ayllon, & Roll, 1969) demonstrated the effectiveness of a portable operant conditioning apparatus in developing postural control in patients. Birbaumer, Dworkin, & Miller (1979) are evaluating a feedback device that may prevent the further deterioration of spinal curvature in scoliosis victims.

Geriatric Patients

The application of behavioral principles to the problems of aging is not in itself unique. The treatment of difficulties, including incontinence, fears of ambulation or sexual dysfunction, dependency, and so on, have much in common with other problem areas reviewed in this book. While some of the problems exhibited by the elderly, such as decreased physical and cognitive activity, poor motor coordination, decreased motivation to engage in activities, may have a physical or biological basis, the changes observed with advancing age may also be affected by environmental and social factors (Lester & Baltes, 1978; Lindsley, 1964). Behavior therapists have dealt with specific behaviors, such as increasing social interactions (McClannahan & Risley, 1973) and reducing the overuse of wheelchairs (MacDonald & Butler, 1974). By devising appropriate prosthetic environments, Lindsley found that older people could maintain more independence.

Preventing Stress and Reducing Health Risk Factors

If one can recognize potential stress situations, it would seem possible to prevent more serious disturbances by teaching patients adaptive coping responses. Holmes and Rahe (1968) and Cline and Chosy (1972) have pointed out the relationship between normal life stresses and the development of physical symptoms. Illness is just one factor that may precipitate life crises if it occurs too frequently or in conjunction with other stresses (e.g., death of a close relative, divorce or separation, loss of job, moving to a new location).

Medical practitioners can prepare patients properly for medical procedures, thereby reducing the threat of the unknown and providing coping skills. Johnson and Leventhal (1974) found that instructions about what to expect during an endoscopic examination were most successful in reducing emotional reactions when combined with descriptions about what sensations the patient would experience.

Vernon and Bailey (1974) and Melamed and Siegel (1975) used film modeling in preparing children for anesthesia and surgery. They demonstrated that having information about what to anticipate decreased physiological indices of arousal as well as self-reported concerns. In addition, the patients cooperated more with the medical procedures. These modeling techniques can be applied successfully to a variety of situations in which procedures are unfamiliar and distressing (e.g., heart catheterization, dental surgery). The literature on preparing children for dental treatment by behavioral strategies is also expanding (Melamed, 1979). Similarly, Beck and Siegel (in press) have reviewed the behavioral strategies used to alleviate the stress associated with labor and delivery in childbirth.

Other behavioral scientists try to prevent medical problems by decreasing the risk factors that contribute to disease (Pomerleau, Bass, & Crown, 1975). Behavioral procedures used to prevent obesity (Wilson, 1978), smoking (Brengelmann, 1978; McFall, 1978), and addiction to drugs (Nathan & Lansky, 1978) are increasing in number. Social psychologists are continuing to explore the use of behavioral principles in getting people to increase oral hygiene (Evans, Rozelle, Lasseter, Dembroski, & Allen, 1970), receive inoculations (Leventhal, Singer, & Jones, 1965), and maintain preventive visits to their physicians. Specific prevention of risk factors in cardiovascular disease has been addressed (Meyer & Henderson, 1974; Suinn, 1974).

This is just a small sample of medically related problems that have benefited from the collaboration between medical and behavioral scientists and practitioners. The following chapters will provide you with the knowledge to make the transition from theory to practice. The motivation to apply these methods should come from the success of early attempts in work with your own patients.

Summary

The behavior therapies consist of an approach to problematic behaviors that involves the systematic application of learning principles. Individuals who have suffered loss because of physical illness, injury, or emotional disturbance are taught to regain control over those situations which elicit anxiety and/or behavioral deficit. Health care professionals are already using a wide variety of behavioral interventions in patient management in obtaining compliance with medical regimens and in helping patients maintain a high level of activity despite pain and discomfort associated with their illness or disability. In pediatric medicine, internal medicine, and psychiatry, patients with a broad range of psychophysiological disorders, including anorexia nervosa, asthma, seizures, and migraine headaches, have benefited from behavioral approaches. The elderly have achieved greater independence through procedures directed at improving their social interactions, reducing the use of the wheelchair, and restructuring the physical environment in accordance with their needs. Patients within a rehabilitation setting have learned adaptive skills or reacquired old skills through programs that emphasize rewards for successive approximations to self-care. Psychiatric conditions secondary to health problems, including patient motivation, depression, and pain tolerance, have been treated within a behavioral framework. The focus of behavioral scientists and practitioners on prevention of disease by reducing risk factors such as obesity, excessive smoking, and drug addiction has provided innovative programs. The continued need for encouraging patients to maintain good health habits, receive inoculations, and have regular medical and dental examinations has also been recognized as an area of importance. Psychological preparation for surgery and other stressful medical procedures has led to a reduction of medical fears in these patients. This provides additional support for those individuals reluctant to seek necessary health care because of fears and misinformation.

References

Alexander, A. B. Systematic relaxation and flow rates in asthmatic children; relationship to emotional precipitants and anxiety. *Journal of Psychosomatic Research,* 1972, *16,* 405–410.

Ayllon, T., & Azrin, N. H. The measurement and reinforcement of behavior in psychotics. *Journal of Experimental Analysis of Behavior,* 1965, *8,* 357-383.

Azrin, N. H., Rubin, H., O'Brien, F., Ayllon, T., & Roll, D. Behavioral engineering: Postural control by a portable operant apparatus. *Journal of Applied Behavior Analysis,* 1969, *1,* 99–108.

Beck, N. S., Siegel, L. J. Preparation for childbirth and contemporary research on pain anxiety and stress reduction. *Psychosomatic Medicine,* in press.

Benson, H. *The relaxation response.* With M. Klipper. New York: Morrow, 1976.

Benson, H., Shapiro, G., Tursky, B., & Schwartz, G. Decreased systolic blood pressure through operant conditioning techniques in patients with essential hypertension. *Science,* 1971, *73,* 740–742.

Birbaumer, N., Dworkin, B., & Miller, N. E. Biofeedback in scoliosis patients. Paper presented at the European Congress of Behavior Therapy, Paris, 1979.

Blanchard, E. B., & Young, L. D. Clinical applications of biofeedback training: A review of evidence. *Archives of General Psychiatry,* 1974, *30,* 573–589.

Brady, J. P. The place of behavior therapy in medical student and psychiatric resident training. *Journal of Nervous and Mental Disease,* 1973, *157,* 21–26.

Brengelmann, H. Cited in S. J. Rachman & C. Philips, *Psychology and medicine.* Middlesex, England: Penguin, 1978.

Christensen, P., & Sprague, R. Reduction of hyperactive behavior by conditioning procedures alone and combined with methylphenidate (Ritalin). *Behaviour Research and Therapy,* 1973, *11,* 331–334.

Cline, D. W., & Chosy, J. J. A prospective study of life changes and subsequent health changes. *Archives of General Psychiatry,* 1972, *27,* 51–53.

Creer, T. L. The use of a time-out from positive reinforcement procedure with asthmatic children. *Journal of Psychosomatic Research,* 1970, *14,* 117–120.

Creer, T. L., & Christian, W. P. *Chronically ill and handicapped children: Their management and rehabilitation.* Champaign, Ill.: Research Press, 1976.

Davison, G., & Valins, S. On self-produced and drug-produced relaxation. *Behaviour Research and Therapy,* 1968, *6,* 401–402.

Engel, B., Nikoomanesh, P., & Schuster, M. Operant conditioning of recto-sphincteric responses in the treatment of fecal incontinence. *New England Journal of Medicine,* 1974, *290,* 646–649.

Evans, R., Rozelle, P., Lasseter, R., Dembroski, T., & Allen, B. Fear arousal persuasion, an actual versus implied behavior change: New perspective utilizing a real life dental program. *Journal of Personality and Social Psychology,* 1970, *16,* 220–227.

Fordyce, W. E. An operant conditioning method for managing chronic pain. *Postgraduate Medicine,* 1973, *53,* 123–128.

————. *Behavioral methods for chronic pain and illness.* St. Louis: Mosby, 1976.

Fordyce, W. E., Fowler, R. S., Lehman, J. F., & LeLateur, B. J. Some implications of learning in problems of chronic pain. *Journal of Chronic Diseases,* 1968, *21,* 179–190.

Foxx, R., & Azrin, N. *Toilet training the retarded.* Champaign, Ill.: Research Press, 1975.

Gannon, L., & Sternbach, R. A. Alpha enhancement as a treatment for pain. A case study. *Journal of Behavior Therapy and Experimental Psychiatry,* 1971, *2,* 209–213.

Goodkin, R. Case studies in behavioral research in rehabilitation. *Perceptual and Motor Skills,* 1966, *23,* 171–182.

Hersen, M., & Bellack, A. S. Assessment of social skills. In A. R. Ciminero, K. S. Calhoun, and H. E. Adams (Eds.), *Handbook for behavioral assessment.* New York: John Wiley & Sons, 1977.

Hersen, M., Edelstein, B., Turner, S., & Pinkston, S. Effects of phenothiazines and social skills training in a withdrawn schizophrenic. *Journal of Clinical Psychology,* 1975, *31,* 588–594.

Holmes, T. H., & Rahe, R. H. The social readjustment rating scale. *Journal of Psychosomatic Research,* 1968, *11,* 213–218.

Johnson, J., & Leventhal, H. Effects of accurate expectations and behavioral instructions on reactions during a noxious medical examination. *Journal of Personality and Social Psychology,* 1974, *29,* 710–718.

Johnson, S., & Melamed, B. G. Assessment and treatment of fear in children. In B. Lahey and A. Kazdin (Eds.), *Advances in clinical child psychology,* Vol. 2. New York: Plenum, 1979.

Katz, R. C., & Zlutnick, S. (Eds.), *Behavior therapy and health care: Principles and applications.* New York: Pergamon Press, 1975.

Kazdin, A. *Behavior modification in applied settings.* Homewood, Ill.: Dorsey Press, 1975.

————. *The token economy: A review and evaluation.* New York: Plenum, 1977.

Kopel, S. A., & Arkowitz, H. The role of attribution and self-perception in behavior change: Implications for behavior therapy. *Genetic Psychology Monograph,* 1975, *92,* 175–212.

Leitenberg, H. Behavioral approaches to treatment of neuroses. In H. Leitenberg (Ed.), *Handbook of behavior modification.* Englewood Cliffs, N.J.: Prentice-Hall, 1976.

Lester, P. B., & Baltes, M. M. Functional interdependence of the social environment and the behavior of the institutionalized aged. *Journal of Gerontological Nursing,* 1978, *14,* 23–27.

Leventhal, H., Singer, R., & Jones, S. Effects of fear and specificity of recommendations on attitude and behavior. *Journal of Personality and Social Psychology,* 1965, *2,* 20–29.

Lindsley, O. R. Geriatric behavior prosthetics. In R. Kastenbaum (Ed.), *New thoughts on old age.* New York: Springer, 1964.

McClannahan, L. E., & Risley, T. R. A store for nursing home residents. *Nursing Homes,* 1973, *22,* 10–11.

MacDonald, M. L., & Butler, A. K. Reversal of helplessness: Producing walking behavior in nursing home wheelchair residents using behavior modification procedures. *Journal of Gerontology,* 1974, *29,* 97–101.

McFall, R. Smoking-cessation research. *Journal of Consulting and Clinical Psychology,* 1978, *46,* 703–712.

Marks, I. M., Viswanathan, R., Lipsedge, M., & Gardner, R. Enhanced extinction of fear by flooding during waning diazpam effect. *British Journal of Psychiatry,* 1971, *119.*

Melamed, B. G. Behavioral approaches to fear in dental settings. In M. Hersen, R. Eisler, and P. M. Miller (Eds.), *Progress in behavior modification,* Vol. 7. New York: Academic Press, 1979.

Melamed, B. G., & Siegel, L. J. Reduction of anxiety in children facing hospitalization and surgery by use of filmed modeling. *Journal of Consulting and Clinical Psychology,* 1975, *43,* 511–521.

Meyer, A. J., & Henderson, J. B. Multiple risk factor reduction in the prevention of cardiovascular disease. *Preventative Medicine,* 1974, *3,* 225–236.

Nathan, P., & Lansky, D. Common methodological problems in research on the addictions. *Journal of Consulting and Clinical Psychology,* 1978, *46,* 712–726.

Neisworth, J., & Moore, F. Operant treatment of asthmatic responding with the parent as therapist. *Behavior Therapy,* 1972, *3,* 95–99.

Overton, D. A. State-dependent learning produced by depressant and atropine-like drugs. *Psychopharmacologia,* 1966, *10,* 6–31.

Patel, C. Reduction of serum cholesterol and blood pressure in hypertensive patients by behavior modification. *Journal of the Royal College of General Practitioners,* 1976, *26,* 211–215.

Paul, G. Chronic mental patient: Current status—future directions. *Psychological Bulletin,* 1969, *71,* 81–94.

Philips, C. A psychological analysis of tension headache. In S. Rachman (Ed.), *Contributions to medical psychology.* London: Pergamon, 1977.

Pomerleau, O., Bass, F., & Crown, V. Role of behavior modification in preventative medicine. *New England Journal of Medicine,* 1975, *292,* 1277–1282.

Purcell, K. Childhood asthma: The role of family relationships, personality, and emotions. In A. Davids (Ed.), *Child personality and psychopathology: Current topics* (2). New York: John Wiley & Sons, 1975.

Rottkamp, B. C. A behavior modification approach to nursing therapeutics in body positioning of spinal cord-injured patients. *Nursing Research,* 1976, *25,* 181–186.

Sackett, D. L., Haynes, R. B., Gibson, E. S., Hackett, B. C., Taylor, D. W., Roberts, R. S., & Johnson, A. L. Randomized clinical trial of strategies for improving medication compliance in primary hypertension. *Lancet,* 1975, *1,* 1205–1207.

Safer, D. J., & Allen, R. P. *Hyperactive children: Diagnosis and management.* Baltimore: University Park Press, 1976.

Sand, P., Trieschmann, R., Fordyce, W. E., & Fowler, R. J. Behavior modification in the medical rehabilitation setting: Rationale and some applications. *Rehabilitation and Practice Review,* 1970, *1,* 11–24.

Schaefer, H., & Martin, P. *Behavior therapy.* New York: McGraw-Hill, 1969.

Stahl, J. R., & Leitenberg, H. Behavioral treatment of the chronic mental hospital patient. In H. Leitenberg (Ed.), *Handbook of behavior modification.* Englewood Cliffs, N.J.: Prentice-Hall, 1976.

Sterman, M. B., & Friar, L. Suppression of seizures in an epileptic following sensorimotor EEG feedback training. *Electroencephalogy and Clinical Neurophysiology,* 1972, *33,* 89–95.

Sternbach, R. A. (Ed.), *The psychology of pain.* New York: Raven Press, 1978.

Suinn, R. M. Behavior therapy for cardiac patients. *Behavior Therapy,* 1974, *5,* 569–571.

Turnage, J., & Logan, D. Treatment of a hypodermic needle phobia by in vivo systematization desensitization. *Journal of Behavior Therapy and Experimental Psychiatry,* 1974, *5,* 67–69.

Turner, R. K., & Young, G. C. CNS stimulant drugs and conditioning treatment of nocturnal enuresis: A long-term follow-up study. *Behaviour Research and Therapy,* 1966, *4,* 225–228.

Vernon, D., & Bailey, W. The use of motion pictues in the psychological preparation of children for induction of anesthesia. *Anesthesiology,* 1974, *40,* 68–72.

Wahler, R. Oppositional children: A quest for parental reinforcement control. *Journal of Applied Behavior Analysis,* 1969, *2,* 159–190.

Walen, S., Hauserman, N., & Lavin, P. (Eds.), *Clinical guide to behavior therapy.* Baltimore: Williams & Wilkins, 1977.

Weiss, T., & Engel, B. Operant conditioning of heart rate in patients with premature ventricular contractions. *Psychosomatic Medicine,* 1971, *33,* 301–321.

Wilson, T. G. Methodological considerations in treatment outcome research on obesity. *Journal of Consulting and Clinical Psychology*, 1978, *46*, 703–712.

Wolpe, J. *Psychotherapy by reciprocal inhibition*. Stanford, Calif.: Stanford University Press, 1958.

Wright, L. Outcome of a standardized program for treating psychogenic encopresis. *Professional Psychology*, 1975, *6*, 453–456.

————. Conceptualizing and defining psychosomatic disorders. *American Psychologist*, 1977, *52*, 625–628.

Wright, L., Nunnery, A., Eichel, B., & Scott, R. Application of operant conditioning principles to problems of tracheostomy addiction in children. *Journal of Consulting and Clinical Psychology*, 1968, *32*, 603–606.

Wright, L., Woodcock, J., & Scott, R. Conditioning children when refusal of oral medication is life-threatening. *Pediatrics*, 1969, *44*, 969–972.

Yale Conference on Behavioral Medicine. U. S. Department of Health, Education, & Welfare, DHEW Publication No. (NIH) 78–1424, 1977.

Zlutnick, S., Mayville, W. J., & Moffat, S. Modification of seizure disorders: The interruption of behavioral chains. *Journal of Applied Behavior Analysis*, 1975, *8*, 1–12.

2

Theoretical and Experimental Foundations of Behavior Therapy

A unique feature of a behavioral treatment approach is that patient and therapist join together in objectively defining the problem and developing a viable treatment plan. The assumption of this method is that most disordered behavior results from faulty learning experiences or insufficient motivation to change.

A *functional analysis* is the framework within which behavioral assessment is undertaken. Its purpose is to identify the problem area in such a way that treatment can be clearly prescribed and objectively evaluated. This includes the assessment of strengths and weaknesses and careful analysis of events preceding and following the occurrence of the maladaptive behavior. The focus is on the here and now. The goal is to make the unpredictable predictable. This is achieved by defining changes to be made by the patient or changes to be made in the social environment that can improve the patient's ability to function effectively and cope with the illness.

This approach through a functional analysis is illustrated by the following case. A twenty-three-year-old high school teacher complained of an acute case of hives that had begun "inexplicably" six weeks earlier. Although she had consulted several physicians, submitted to allergy tests and injections, and had sought relief through a private warehouse of prescription and nonprescription drugs, including antihistamines, Tylenol, Midol, cortisone, Sinequan, Seconal, and Chlor-Trimeton, there was no relief of the symptoms. When the behavior therapist had the patient keep a daily diary of events and thoughts that regularly preceded the skin eruptions, the predictability of these attacks was established. The main complaint of the patient was swelling and itching over her entire body. This occurred daily, gradually reaching a peak in the early evening and interfering with sleep as well as intimacies with her husband. Wheals also erupted following arguments with the husband about spending and saving money, visiting his father, and inviting his relatives into their house. She would react with rage and verbal outbursts to any sympathy her husband expressed toward his own family. His calm demeanor on such occasions augmented her reaction, and hives inevitably followed (Daniels, 1973). The functional analysis had identified several situations that reliably preceded attacks.

The next goal in the functional analysis is to determine what therapies can be used to change a patient's behavior in the desired manner. The behavioral clinician turns to the principles of behavior that have been well-documented by experimental psychology and tried out in laboratory and clinical settings. Three basic questions are addressed:

1. What behavior is maladaptive?
2. What is maintaining the maladaptive behavior?
3. How can we change the behavior?

In the patient with urticaria, it became apparent that her marital relationship was intensifying her skin eruptions. Yet her husband's insensitivity to her problems made it unlikely that marital therapy would be acceptable. During their marriage, the patient had suffered headaches and other somatic complaints, but she was basically satisfied with their lives. Therefore, her own excessive arousal reaction to stressful situations became the treatment focus. She was trained in relaxation techniques. The therapist and the patient developed a hierarchy of situations associated with the onset of hives, such as "You are with your father-in-law and husband in a restaurant." These situations were practiced in imagery and in real life, while the patient remained in a calm, relaxed state. This procedure permitted the patient to control her anger, and the hive episodes subsided without further medication.

The following brief review of learning theory is presented to show the basic learning mechanism underlying this systematic desensitization approach and to illustrate alternative strategies that can be used with a variety of medical problems.

Learning Theory

Behavior may be thought of as the ways people *react* to their environment and what they *do* in their environment. There are at least two types of behaviors. The first type, *respondent behavior,* is similar to involuntary, elicited, or autonomic responding. For example, salivating to food, startling at a loud or sudden noise, and sweating profusely while exercising are elicited responses. Emotional responses such as fear, anxiety, and anger experienced in reaction to physical illness can come to be elicited in a similar automatic way under certain stressful circumstances.

In contrast to respondent behaviors, *operant behaviors* are similar to "purposeful" responses. They are mediated by the central nervous system and include those behaviors which interact with and have an effect upon the individual's environment. Operants are "doing" behaviors, including walking, talking, taking medication, crying, scratching, and so on. Thoughts may also be considered as operants in that they influence what a person does. Operant behaviors encompass much of the ongoing daily behaviors of an individual as he or she interacts with others and with the environment (Mikulas, 1972).

How are these respondent and operant behaviors acquired and modified?

Respondent (Classical) Conditioning

The basis for applying learning theory to the treatment of anxiety and stress-related disorders grew out of laboratory demonstrations on conditionability of fears. Watson and Raynor (1920) demonstrated that a severe rat phobia could be induced in an eleven-month-old child named Albert. It was first demonstrated that Albert was totally unafraid of furry animals such as a rabbit or white rat. However, when presented in association with a loud noise (unconditioned stimulus), Albert reacted with a startle and began to cry and shake (unconditioned response). When the unconditioned stimulus (loud noise) was presented at the same time the youngster reached for the white rat, he came to react to the animal with the same fearful response. This is an example of respondent (classical) conditioning, in which the presentation of a previously neutral stimulus (white rat) becomes a conditioned stimulus that elicits a startle reaction (conditioned response). The fear also generalized in that Albert was also afraid of rabbits, cotton, and his mother's white fur coat.

Thus, for example, patients who have had unpleasant experiences in the physician's office may respond toward the physician and his or her setting, assistants, and instruments with an aversive emotional response. Similarly, it is often noted that cancer patients in need of repeated noxious medical procedures respond with nausea, fear, and discomfort to many events unrelated to the actual treatment, such as being in the waiting room or driving to the hospital, because these events have occurred repeatedly in association with their experienced pain. This type of learning paradigm, in which one stimulus, by being paired with a second stimulus, comes to elicit a response similar to the response previously elicited only by the second stimulus, is called *respondent conditioning.* Conditioning takes place because of the contiguity of the conditioned and unconditioned stimuli. Pairing of stimuli can occur in time, space, or proximity. This paradigm provides the behavioral clinician with several strategies for altering maladaptive behavior acquired or maintained in this manner.

Therapies Based on Respondent Conditioning

The behavioral clinician has two basic procedures for changing respondently conditioned responses: extinction and counterconditioning. They have in common a focus on breaking the maladaptive associations that have occurred by classical conditioning.

Extinction. The extinction procedure consists of continually presenting the conditioned stimulus without its being paired with the unconditioned stimulus until it no longer elicits the conditioned response. A variant of this procedure has been called implosive therapy or flooding (Stampfl & Levis, 1967). In this technique, the patient is presented with a feared object or an imaginary representation of a feared situation in a safe setting until these cues no longer elicit fear (Marshall, Gauthier, & Gordon, 1979)

The physician may find that visceral responses accompanying fear (e.g., palpitations, sweating, and nausea) may have become conditioned to previously painful or distressing experience so that the very thought of these events leads to avoidance behaviors. Patients with dental fears, for example, often avoid treatment until a painful abcess can no longer be tolerated. Even when such patients come for treatment, gagging, breathing difficulties, and profuse sweating may be noted by the observant practitioner and often may interfere with necessary procedures.

One approach based on flooding that a physician can use with patients having extreme fears of injections or necessary blood tests is to encourage them to imagine that they are looking at the hypodermic needle, that they are receiving repeated injections, and so on until imagining these events no longer elicits anxiety. This procedure has been used successfully with a variety of phobic and obsessive behaviors (Marks, 1975). However, there are many learning theorists and behavioral clinicians who suggest caution in the use of these procedures. For instance, it is difficult to predict or identify all the cues that may be associated with the original anxiety. It is also difficult to get individuals to remain in intense anxiety-provoking situations when their avoidance responses are very strong. Furthermore, in some cases there may be a sensitization effect in which even more situations become associated with the anxiety. There are several alternative strategies that provide the patient with a more gradual way of dealing with evoked anxiety.

Counterconditioning. A more widely used technique for the extinction or elimination of fears is systematic desensitization, based on the principle of counterconditioning. This procedure involves the respondent conditioning of a more adaptive response to the fearful or unpleasant situation. For example, Jones (1924) documented deconditioning of children's fears by bringing the feared object in association with a pleasant stimulus. Thus, while feeding three-year-old Peter, who had a fear of rabbits, she gradually brought the animal closer and closer until he no longer reacted with fear. A new response, the pleasant experiences from eating, had replaced the fear associated with seeing the rabbit, and he now felt more comfortable in its presence.

More typically, with adult anxiety states, induced muscle relaxation is the response chosen to replace anxiety. Systematic desensitization involves three basic components:

1. training in a response that will compete with anxiety, such as deep muscle relaxation (Jacobson, 1938),
2. construction of a hierarchy of situations ranked by the patient from least to most anxiety-evoking, and
3. counterposing relaxation while the patient imagines that the actual hierarchy situation is taking place.

Thus, a pregnant woman who has an extreme fear of childbirth may be taught relaxation and breathing exercises prior to delivery. The therapist helps her to pinpoint the situations that cause her worry and fear. For example, feeling contractions, driving to the hospital, being placed in the stirrups on the delivery table, and feeling the passage of the infant through the birth canal are ranked in increasing order of their anxiety-provoking capacity for the woman. The patient is then told to imagine each of these events while remaining in a calm, relaxed state. The Lamaze (1970) prepared childbirth method makes use of this type of procedure in the real-life situation. The prospective mother is taught to respond to different phases of childbirth with breathing and relaxation responses that have been preconditioned to different patterns of muscular contractions that will accompany the birth process.

Wolpe (1958) assumed that the process responsible for systematic desensitization was "reciprocal inhibition." If a response inhibitory to anxiety can be made to occur in the presence of anxiety-evoking stimuli so that it is accompanied by a complete or partial suppression of the anxiety response, the bond between those stimuli and the anxiety response will be weakened. Wolpe postulated that the relaxation brings about predominantly parasympathetic responses under the individual's control and inhibits the sympathetic responses that mediate the fear response. Physiological evidence for this theory is equivocal, although reduction of fear is often associated with reduced autonomic activity. The stepwise progression of substituting relaxation for fear generalizes from low-anxiety situations to higher-anxiety situations, so that eventually the patient is able to think about undertaking the most feared activity with little concern. The generalization to real-life fear situations is facilitated by assigning the patient between-sessions tasks involving the performance of those activities imagined without fear during the preceding therapy session. Thus, the pregnant woman who feared childbirth may be encouraged to drive to the hospital, visit the labor room, and imagine that she has just delivered her child.

It is often reported that once the patient has completed more than half the hierarchy items he or she can spontaneously succeed in carrying out some of the higher items without further desensitization. For instance, an agoraphobic patient initially had difficulty driving alone to the therapy sessions. By the time she had completed the lower third of her anxiety hierarchy with the therapist, she was able to drive alone on crowded highways to familiar places, return purchases to a downtown shopping area, and visit her son in a different state.

The systematic desensitization technique reportedly has been successful in the treatment of a wide variety of problems including phobias, anxiety symptoms such as palpitations, fear of heart attack, sexual problems, unassertive behavior, personal devaluation, fear of authority figures, anorexia nervosa, and psychogenic seizures. Case illustrations are provided thoughout this book.

Variations of Systematic Desensitization. There are additional procedures that can be used other than Jacobson's (1938) progressive relaxation to produce responses incompatible with anxiety. The patient can be taught to have pleasant imagery accompany a cue word, such as "relax," at the time that the fearful situations are presented. In children, "emotive imagery" that arouses feelings of pride, affection, and self-assertion has been used (Lazarus & Abramovitz, 1962). For example, a ten-year-old boy, who was afraid of the dark, was able to remain alone in the bathroom with all the lights off, awaiting a communication from Superman.

In addition to imagery, hypnotic states, eating, and assertive and sexual responses have been used to countercondition anxiety. Biofeedback training procedures have also been used as an adjunct in desensitization to lessen autonomic arousal or to monitor the effectiveness of relaxation training.

The patient's cooperation during the construction of the hierarchy is a necessary ingredient in the treatment process. Training manuals on relaxation and hierarchy construction are readily available (Bernstein & Borkovec, 1973; Goldfried & Davison, 1976).

While the use of imagery has the advantage of flexibility when a fear is complex (e.g., personal evaluation or public speaking anxiety), not all patients can be taught to visualize vividly, and not all situations lend themselves well to imagined representations. In vivo desensitization involves exposing the patient to the actual feared situation. Thus, a person who is afraid of having a venipuncture may first be encouraged to hold the syringe, draw water from a cup into the syringe, observe other individuals having their blood drawn, and practice having a tourniquet placed around the arm prior to the blood test.

Another successful variant of desensitization is "contact desensitization," a combination of in vivo and participant modeling (Ritter, 1969). This procedure involves:

1. having the patient observe another individual (usually the therapist) approach the feared situation or object,
2. followed by the therapist-model helping the patient approach the feared object, and finally

3. gradually fading out the therapist's assistance as the patient approaches the feared situation.

This method is often employed by doctors and dentists with children when they first demonstrate the instruments or procedures on themselves and then permit the child to examine the instruments prior to actually undertaking the medical or dental intervention.

Desensitization is economical in that group therapy as well as automated variants have produced successful coping. Medical patients benefit from participating in a supportive group in which fears of impending surgery or anesthesia induction, childbirth fears, postmastectomy concerns, and postcoronary bypass breathing procedures are not merely discussed, but where other patients model nonfearful, adaptive responses to anxiety and embarrassment. These sessions often include specific practice in breathing and relaxation techniques with spouse participation being encouraged. Patients learn not only what to expect, but what they can do to handle their fears and discomforts. The interpretation of events as painful is thought to be minimized when anxiety is reduced (Melzack, 1973).

The effectiveness of desensitization components is further substantiated by the fact that the process can be specified with enough precision that automated desensitization devices have been shown to produce changes similar to those achieved by a live therapist (Lang, Melamed, & Hart, 1970; Wish, Hasazi, & Jurgela, 1973). The use of audiotapes to supplement relaxation training has become a standard component of the therapy experience.

The interpretations of the success of systematic desensitization have varied from counterconditioning explanations to the idea that the patient is learning a very general coping strategy (Goldfried, 1971). Thus, self-control procedures have been developed in which patients are instructed in a variety of cognitive methods for dealing with impending stress (Meichenbaum, 1974). For instance, an asthmatic woman who had become excessively dependent upon nebulizers because of her persistent fear of attacks was able to reduce her use of inhalants through a combination of relaxation cues and self-induced instructions to forestall using them for as long as possible in any given situation (Sirota & Mahoney, 1974).

Bandura (1977) attributes behavioral change as due to an individual's expectations of personal efficacy. Although he states that expectations determine whether or not coping is initiated or sustained in the face of obstacles and aversive experiences, empirical evidence is still lacking. Self-control strategies will be discussed more thoroughly in a later section.

Aversive Counterconditioning. This is a special form of counterconditioning that is used to condition an aversive response to stimuli that previously elicited self-rewarding but undesirable conditions, such as alcoholism, smoking, overeating, sexual deviance, and self-destructive behaviors. It should not be confused with punishment, a procedure to be discussed later. Counterconditioning involves eliciting a response incompatible with the response to be altered, not merely presenting aversive events contingent on the undesirable behavior. Because these methods are unpleasant and raise some ethical questions, they are usually restricted to behaviors that are resistant to other forms of treatment. The appropriate application of this method does, however, often result in dramatic elimination of life-threatening behaviors.

The case of a nine-month-old infant with ruminative vomiting illustrated a dramatic use of aversive counterconditioning (Lang & Melamed, 1969). The vomiting was considered a maladaptive response that could be specified in terms of the physiological concomitants that accompanied it. A mild electric shock was applied contiguously with the appearance of electromyographic responses indicating the onset of vomiting. This produced crying, a response incompatible with vomiting, and led to a cessation of the problem behavior within three sessions. Figure 2.1 illustrates the usefulness of the physiological responses in making the decision for correct timing so as not to interfere with healthy sucking responses. Figure 2.2 shows the change in appearance of this child 13 days after treatment. Figure 2.3 shows weight gains concomitant with treatment.

Practitioners have relied primarily on two classes of stimuli for eliciting the aversive response: chemicals that induce nausea and electric shock. In treating alcoholism, for example, the taste of a martini might be paired with Antabuse (disulfiram), a drug that causes the patient to feel nauseated. This procedure would be continued until the mere thought of taking a drink produces a nauseous feeling.

The general results of aversive counterconditioning have been encouraging because they deal with behaviors that are difficult to treat by any other technique. However, one must be cautious about removing maladaptive self-rewarding behaviors, such as excessive alcohol consumption, without considering whether or not this behavior serves to reduce anxiety about other life stresses. Often, retraining an individual in alternative strategies for coping with distressing situations must accompany aversive procedures. It is also necessary to have the

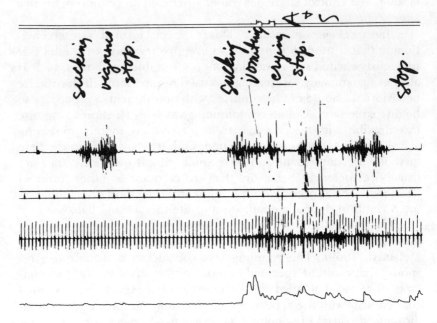

Figure 2.1   Three channels of electromyographic activity are presented. The nurse-observer's comments are written above the first channel. The intense muscle activity on this line is associated with sucking behavior, recorded from the underside of the chin. The lowest line indicates esophagus recordings where rhythmic pulsing of vomiting can be seen. The top line shows the point at which two brief shocks were administered. It may be noted that they follow closely on the first pulse of vomiting. The actual treatment involved only five conditioning sessions.

From P. J. Lang and B. G. Melamed, Avoidance conditioning therapy of an infant with chronic ruminative vomiting. *Journal of Abnormal Psychology*, 1969, *74*, 1–8. Copyright © 1969 by the American Psychological Association. Reprinted by permission.

patient return for additional conditioning sessions (booster treatment) in order to minimize extinction of the conditioned aversion. The objections that are sometimes raised with the use of these procedures has led to the development of a procedural variant referred to as *covert sensitization,* which utilizes an imagined scene as the aversive event (Cautela, 1966). For example, smoking has sometimes been reduced by aversive procedures that involve actual satiation with smoky air as in the rapid-smoking technique (Grimaldi & Lichtenstein, 1969). How-

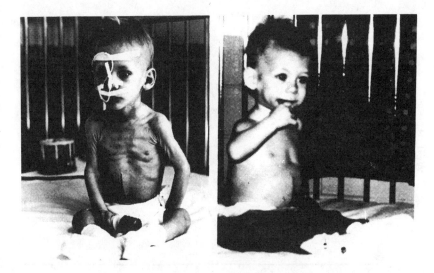

Figure 2.2 The photograph at the left was taken during the observation period just prior to treatment. It clearly illustrates the patient's debilitated condition—the lack of body fat and the skin hanging in loose folds. The tape around the infant's face holds tubing for the nasogastric pump. The photograph at the right was taken on the day of discharge from the hospital, thirteen days after the first photo. The 26 percent increase in body weight already attained is easily seen in the full, more infant-like face, the rounded arms, and more substantial trunk.

From P. J. Lang and B. G. Melamed, Avoidance conditioning therapy of an infant with chronic ruminative vomiting. *Journal of Abnormal Psychology*, 1969, *74*, 1–8. Copyright © 1969 by the American Psychological Association. Reprinted by permission.

ever, one could use covert sensitization, in which the patient would imagine that he or she is in a high-probability smoking situation, while simultaneously imagining negative sensations such as burning or irritated eyes, nausea, and sore throat.

Operant (Instrumental) Conditioning

Behaviors that are modified or maintained by the consequences that follow them are called *operants.* Operant behaviors are so called because they operate on or influence the environment, which results in

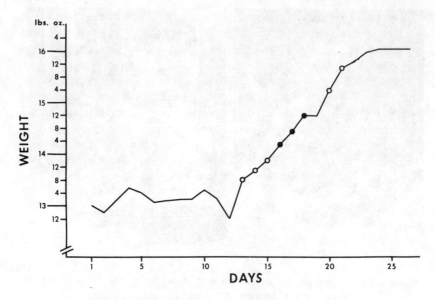

Figure 2.3   The infant's body weight as determined from the nursing notes is plotted over time, from well before conditioning therapy was instituted to the day of discharge from the hospital. Days on which conditioning sessions occurred are marked by circles on the curve. Reinforcers were delivered only on days marked by open circles. The decline in body weight in the few days just prior to therapy was probably occasioned by the discontinuance of the nasogastric pump, in favor of normal feeding procedures. The marked weight gain from Day 13 to Day 18 is coincident with the first six days of therapy. The temporary reduction in weight increase, associated with a resumption of emesis, is apparent at Day 19. The additional conditioning trials appear to have acted immediately to reinstate weight gain.

From P. J. Lang and B. G. Melamed, Avoidance conditioning therapy of an infant with chronic ruminative vomiting. *Journal of Abnormal Psychology,* 1969, *74,* 1–8. Copyright © 1969 by the American Psychological Association. Reprinted by permission.

additional consequences that strengthen or weaken the behavior. As noted earlier, operant behaviors include much of the ongoing daily behavior of individuals as they interact with others and their environment. Operants constitute what a person *does* or *says* as he or she interacts with the environment. Behavior therapists are primarily concerned with operants that are maladaptive—that lead to an individual's feelings of distress or discomfort or that are problematic and troublesome for others. Examples of operants that would be of particular interest to health care practitioners might include: excessive alcohol consumption, overeating, frequent headache complaints, refusal to take medication, or inactivity in geriatric and chronic pain patients.

Operant or instrumental conditioning is a learning situation in which certain events or consequences are made contingent (i.e., conditional) on specified behaviors. Every response that is made by an individual has some consequences. The operant conditioning procedures, which are based on the laboratory investigations of Skinner (1953), suggest that it is more important to explore the effect of consequences on behavior than to know what caused the behavior in the first place. Consequences may be either pleasant or aversive for an individual. In operant conditioning, positive or pleasant consequences are used to increase the frequency of desired behaviors, while negative or aversive consequences generally are used to decrease the frequency of undesirable behaviors.

The application of operant conditioning in the management of the quantity of fluid intake in patients following surgery, illness, or spinal injury (Fowler, Fordyce, & Berni, 1969) is one such illustration. Patients are instructed to self-monitor their daily fluid intake. These records are publicly displayed in the form of a graph. Increases in fluid intake are rewarded by the nursing staff through positive social attention and comments to the patients regarding their compliance with this task. At the same time, noncompliance with instructions for increased fluid intake is systematically ignored. In this manner, the ways in which the hospital staff respond to the patient can facilitate or impede physical recovery. As these authors note, "The way staff give attention to patients is as powerful as medicine and should be planned as carefully" (p. 1226).

Health practitioners can learn to use a variety of operant strategies for changing patient behaviors that interfere with medical treatment or impede recovery by understanding the different behavioral principles that underlie the various procedures: positive reinforcement, negative reinforcement, token economies, contingency contracting, biofeedback, extinction, and punishment.

Methods for Increasing Behavior

Positive Reinforcement. A procedure in which a positive event contingently follows a behavior and increases the frequency of that behavior is called positive reinforcement. An event is a positive reinforcer only if it has the effect of increasing the frequency of a behavior that it follows. Therefore, a positive reinforcer is defined by its effect on the behavior.

For example, in many hospital or nursing care settings, staff shortages result in the tendency of nurses to pay attention to the loudest, most-complaining patients to achieve momentary quiet. This attention, paradoxically, increases the likelihood that the patient will make future demands. The nurses' attention, whether it be a reprimand or an alleviation of the patient's discomfort, even if it merely provides an infrequent social interaction, serves to increase and, thereby, reinforce the patient's bid for attention. Thus, the contingent use of positive reinforcement must be carefully planned so as to immediately follow desirable patient behaviors rather than to maintain inappropriate responses. It would be more beneficial to reward the patient with attention or special privileges following his or her attempts to improve mobility or independently undertake a strenuous task within the rehabilitation program.

There are two basic types of positive reinforcers. *Primary* or *unconditioned reinforcers* are naturally occurring or unlearned reinforcers that are biologically based. Food, water, and sex are examples of primary reinforcers. The majority of reinforcers for humans, however, are *secondary* or *conditioned reinforcers*. Secondary reinforcers acquire their reinforcing properties through repeated associations or pairings with primary or already established secondary reinforcers. Money and a variety of social reinforcers such as praise, attention, and physical contact are examples of secondary reinforcers.

Positive reinforcement is probably the most frequently used operant conditioning procedure in behavioral intervention programs. In addition, positive reinforcement is typically used in conjunction with several closely related procedures such as shaping, prompting, and extinction.

Negative Reinforcement. A second method for increasing behavior is negative reinforcement. Negative reinforcement is a procedure in which an aversive or unpleasant event is terminated or postponed contingent on the performance of a particular behavior. The behavior is increased in frequency through the removal or postponement of the aversive stimulus. Behaviors that are maintained by negative reinforcement are referred to as escape or avoidance behaviors.

This operant conditioning procedure is illustrated in the case of a parent who attends to a child who is screaming, crying, and kicking. These tantrum behaviors are aversive or unpleasant for the parent who intervenes to terminate them. As a result, the parent's behavior is negatively reinforced by removing an aversive event. Other examples of negative reinforcement include taking aspirin to avoid or terminate pain, closing a window to avoid or terminate a draft, and driving within the speed limit to avoid receiving a fine.

Negative reinforcement may also be used as a therapeutic strategy to increase the frequency of desirable behaviors. For example, by using a conditioning apparatus that sounded a loud noise, Malament, Dunn, and Davis (1975) were able to increase the frequency of push-ups performed in their wheelchairs by paralyzed patients in order to reduce skin problems. Push-up behavior was negatively reinforced, since performing a specified number of push-ups terminated or postponed the aversive noise.

What Is Reinforcing? Reinforcers must be capable of maintaining an individual's motivation and responsiveness. They constitute any events that are needed or desired by the person, including tangible rewards such as money, praise, opportunities to engage in enjoyable activities, or satisfaction from doing a good job.

With many patients, particularly those in psychiatric, rehabilitation, and geriatric settings, one of the most difficult tasks facing the staff is finding something that motivates them to participate in therapeutic activities. A frequent complaint of health care personnel who work in these settings is, "Nothing seems to work; I can't get this patient out of bed or away from the television set."

Strategies for finding effective reinforcers for a particular patient are described in Chapter 3. One particularly useful but simple principle for assessing reinforcers has been developed by Premack (1965). This principle states that a more probable behavior can be used to reinforce a less probable behavior. Therefore, positive reinforcers may be determined for each patient by noting what he or she likes to do when given the opportunity. Does the patient enjoy listening to the radio or taking walks? Does the patient enjoy playing cards or visiting friends? These activities may serve as reinforcers for behaviors that occur less often. For example, with a rehabilitation patient who spends considerable time in bed, rest periods can be used to reinforce the patient's participation in physical therapy. If a child spends most of his or her time playing outside and little or no time in completing homework assignments, playing outside can be made contingent on doing the homework.

In health care settings, it is particularly important to be aware of events or experiences that may serve as reinforcers for patients. Often, these reinforcing events serve to increase and maintain undesirable behaviors. A patient, for example, may receive attention and sympathy from others contingent on behaviors indicating discontent, discomfort, pain, or sadness. Since attention and sympathy are reinforcers for most individuals, these undesirable behaviors may be maintained. Many health care settings inadvertently reinforce dependency behaviors by having staff take over activities such as bathing and dressing the patient and administering medication, rather than rewarding the patient for self-care. This can make the posthospital adjustment more difficult for patients and other family members who must assist them in their recovery from illness.

Enhancing the Effectiveness of Reinforcement. There are several factors that influence the effectiveness of a reinforcer. The delay between the response and the reinforcer should be as short as possible, as this promotes better learning. In general, the more immediate the reinforcement, the better. This insures that the specific behavior to be established is rewarded, rather than some unspecified behavior.

The various relationships between a behavior and the occurrence of a reinforcer are called *schedules of reinforcement.* There are two basic schedules of reinforcement. *Continuous reinforcement* involves the reinforcement of every desirable response. This schedule is the most effective for initiating or establishing a response. Once a behavior is occurring at a sufficient frequency, it is best to gradually fade to an *intermittent reinforcement* schedule. In intermittent reinforcement, only some desired responses are reinforced. This schedule is generally more effective in producing behaviors that persist once the therapeutic reinforcement contingencies are terminated and naturally occurring reinforcers take over.

Shaping. A patient recovering from a stroke or a debilitating accident must often relearn complex behaviors once taken for granted. Learning to walk again must be broken down into component parts that the patient can manage, such as balancing on crutches. The partial successes on the simpler steps motivate the patients' continued progress toward accomplishing their goal. Shaping is a useful procedure for initiating or reinstating complex behaviors in a patient's repertoire. In this procedure, the therapist begins by reinforcing a behavior that the patient is already capable of performing and that is similar in some way to the desired behavior. The behavior is broken down into small, manageable units, and the therapist reinforces small steps or approximations that increasingly resemble the desired behavior. As the patient successfully performs the behavior at each step, the criteria for reinforcement are gradually changed so that the required behavior more closely resembles the treatment goal.

A patient may sometimes have difficulty performing a particular response during a shaping procedure. There are several techniques that a therapist may use to *prompt* or guide a behavior more directly to assist the patient in performing the desired response. For example, the therapist can provide *instructions* on how to perform the behavior, or the therapist can *model* or demonstrate the various steps in performing the behavior while the patient observes. The therapist might also *physically guide* the patient through the various steps. Once the patient is able to perform the behavior unassisted, the therapist gradually *fades out* the various behavioral prompts.

Frequently, several prompting procedures are used in combination to teach a behavior. For example, Horner and Keirlitz (1975) used verbal instructions, modeling, and physical guidance along with social reinforcement to teach mentally retarded adolescents to brush their teeth.

At this point, a brief discussion of several special operant conditioning procedures that utilize reinforcement principles is in order. These procedures are token economies, contingency contracting, and biofeedback.

Variants of Operant Programs

Token Economy Programs. A systematic and highly complex reinforcement program in which tokens are used as a reinforcer is referred to as a token economy. Tokens are secondary or conditioned reinforcers, such as money, points, poker chips, or stars, that can later be exchanged for an infinite variety of backup reinforcers. The patient is directly reinforced with tokens for desirable behavior, and these tokens can be used to purchase desired reinforcers such as food, consumables, and activities.

An effective token economy requires that the target behaviors on which tokens are contingent and the number of tokens that will be administered for performing each behavior be clearly specified. In addition, the rate of exchange of tokens for backup reinforcers must be made explicit. This program is frequently necessary with patients with limited cognitive abilities and patients who are not initially responsive to more naturally occurring social reinforcers. Therefore, token programs have been used with retarded individuals, chronic brain syndrome patients, geriatric patients, and patients with severe thought disorders or depression.

Table 2.1 lists some jobs for which psychiatric patients could earn tokens in a token economy described by Ayllon and Azrin (1968). The tasks involved in each job were clearly specified, as were the time

Table 2.1　A Token Economy Program in an Institutional Setting—Several Jobs for Which Tokens Can Be Earned

Type of Jobs	Number of Jobs	Duration	Tokens Paid
WAITRESS			
1. Meals 　　Empties trays left on tables 　　and washes tables between 　　each of four meal groups.	6	10 min.	2
2. Commissary 　　Cleans tables, washes cups and 　　glasses used at commissary. 　　Places cups and glasses in rack 　　ready for automatic dishwasher.	3	10 min.	5
SECRETARIAL ASSISTANT			
1. Tooth Brushing 　　Assists with oral hygiene. 　　Writes names of patients 　　brushing teeth.	1	30 min.	3
2. Exercises 　　Assists recretational assistant 　　with exercises. Writes names of 　　patients participating in 　　exercises.	2	30 min.	3
3. Commissary 　　Assists sales clerk assistant. 　　Writes names of patients at 　　commissary, records number of 　　tokens spent. Totals all 　　tokens spent.	3	10 min.	2

From T. Ayllon and N. H. Azrin, The measurement and reinforcement of behavior of psychotics. *Journal of the Experimental Analysis of Behavior,* 1965, *8,* 357–383. Copyright © 1965 by the Society for the Experimental Analysis of Behavior, Inc. Reprinted by permission.

required to perform the job and the number of tokens earned for successfully completing the task. Patients could exchange the tokens for opportunities to leave the ward, privacy, social interactions with the staff, recreational activities, and canteen items. Some of the backup reinforcers used in this program and the token exchange rates are presented in Table 2.2.

　　Token programs have been used in a wide range of treatment and rehabilitation settings (Kazdin, 1977), and have been particularly useful in motivating patients with longstanding behavior problems. Such programs have been effective in teaching appropriate behaviors and

Table 2.2 A Token Economy Program in an Institutional Setting—A Partial
List of Reinforcers Available for Tokens

Activity	Cost in Tokens
I. Leave from the Ward	
20-minute walk on hospital grounds (with escort)	2
30-minute grounds pass (3 tokens for each additional 30 minutes)	10
Trip to town (with escort)	100
II. Recreational Opportunities	
Movie on ward	1
Opportunity to listen to a live band	1
Exclusive use of radio	1
Television (choice of program)	3

From T. Ayllon and N. H. Azrin, The measurement and reinforcement of behavior of psychotics. *Journal of the Experimental Analysis of Behavior,* 1965, *8,* 357–383. Copyright © 1965 by the Society for the Experimental Analysis of Behavior, Inc. Reprinted by permission.

reducing maladaptive behaviors with psychiatric patients (Ayllon & Azrin, 1965), predelinquent youth (Phillips, 1968), children in special classrooms (O'Leary & Drabman, 1971), and institutionalized retarded residents (Girardeau & Spradlin, 1964).

There are several advantages to using a token program:

1. Tokens can be given immediately without concern in advance as to what each patient will buy with the tokens.
2. The therapist can individualize reinforcers, which is particularly important when working with more than one patient in the treatment program.
3. Tokens may be used anywhere and at anytime without satiation. They do not lose their reinforcing value through repeated use, because a variety of backup reinforcers are available.
4. With tokens, no delay in reinforcement is required. They can be delivered without interfering with ongoing desirable behaviors.
5. Token systems are particularly effective where social reinforcers such as praise and attention are not adequate incentives for the patient to respond in appropriate ways.

Token programs are usually regarded as a *temporary* method for promoting behavior change where other procedures are ineffective. Since token reinforcers are not a typical system of reinforcement found in the natural environment, it is important to begin weaning the patient from the program once the desirable behaviors occur at an acceptable rate. The token program is gradually withdrawn and replaced with more naturally occurring reinforcers such as praise, approval, and a sense of accomplishment.

Contingency Contracting. Reinforcement contingencies may be specified as a *behavioral contract* between several individuals. A contingency contract is an agreement (often in writing) negotiated between the parties desiring behavior change. The contract clearly specifies the conditions under which certain behaviors will occur. In addition, positive reinforcers for compliance with the contract and punishing consequences for failure to comply with the agreement are stated in the contract. The reinforcers for compliance should not be available to the individuals outside the contract and should have a value that is consistent with the effort required by the behavior. Because the contract requires that the individuals involved agree on the nature of the desired behaviors and consequences, contingency contracting can be a useful strategy for teaching problem-solving and negotiation skills.

Contracts have been successfully applied in a number of different settings and with various patient populations. In particular, contingency contracting has been used most often to modify dysfunctional patterns of interaction in marital and family relationships (Azrin, Naster, & Jones, 1973; Jacobson & Martin, 1976; Stuart, 1971; Weathers & Liberman, 1975). In addition, classroom behaviors (Homme, Csanyi, Gonzales, & Rechs, 1970), obesity (Mann, 1972), and alcoholism (Miller, Hersen, & Eisler, 1974) have been treated with contingency contracts.

Miller (1972) demonstrates the use of a contract with a couple experiencing marital difficulties related to the husband's excessive drinking. Baseline records indicated he was consuming an average of eight drinks each day. A contract was negotiated between the couple that stated that the husband could have no more than three drinks each day prior to the evening meal. Any other drinking resulted in the husband paying his wife $20, which she could spend "as frivolously as possible on a nonessential item." The contract further stated that the wife was required to refrain from any negative comments regarding her husband's drinking. If she failed to comply, she paid her husband $20. In addition, both the husband and wife agreed to provide attention and affection to each other when they engaged in the desired behaviors. Shortly after this contract was implemented, the husband's drinking was reduced to an acceptable level, and the marital relationship improved. These behavioral improvements were maintained at a six-month follow-up assessment.

Biofeedback. Until recently, it was believed that autonomic responses were involuntary and could be modified only through respondent conditioning. However, clinical and research evidence has indicated that autonomic responses such as heart rate (Bleecker & Engle, 1973), blood pressure (Shapiro, Tursky, & Schwartz, 1970), and skin temperature (Sargent, Greene, & Walters, 1973) are subject to voluntary control through operant conditioning.

Biofeedback training teaches an individual to monitor and control physiological responses such as heart rate, blood pressure, muscle tension, skin temperature, and electrical activity of the brain. This is accomplished by means of highly specialized instrumentation that converts physiological activity into a bioelectric signal, which in turn provides the patient with continuous external feedback regarding a particular autonomic response. When the patient alters a visceral state so that it correctly matches a predetermined criterion, the patient is immediately provided with visual or auditory feedback indicating that an appropriate response has been made. This feedback information is often used in conjunction with social or tangible reinforcers for desired changes in the physiological response. While the exact mechanism for the effectiveness of this procedure is not entirely understood, it is clear that an individual can learn to monitor and alter certain visceral responses by receiving precise information from biofeedback techniques. The many types of feedback procedures make it difficult to define the effective component. Also, comparisons of this method with other approaches suggest that relaxation training and attention-placebo conditions may be equally effective. However, the scientific nature of this apparatus may provide stronger suggestive power to promote the patient's confidence in the technique. Several applications of its use in bronchial asthma, neuromuscular disorders, headaches, insomnia, seizure disorders, and fecal incontinence are presented in this book.

It should be noted with caution, however, that those patients who might benefit from such feedback training are often unable to. For instance, patients with ischemic heart disease were less able to modify heart rate than age-matched controls or college students (Lang, Troyer, Twentyman, & Gatchel, 1975). Also it must be clearly established that laboratory training generalizes to real life.[1]

[1]Lang (1977) argued against the use of biofeedback as a routine treatment for anxiety: "Methods such as instructed muscle relaxation and meditation exercises are much less expensive and are likely to be equally effective" (p. 328).

The continued encouragement of practitioners in the use of biofeedback devices is justified in that the monitoring of physiological responses accompanying stress, anger, or fear may lead researchers to a clearer understanding of the nature of these emotions. Thus, data gathered during clinical applications, if available, may provide the basis for scientific prediction of the appropriateness of feedback training with a given patient.

Methods for Decreasing Behavior

There are basically two operant conditioning procedures for reducing or eliminating undesirable behaviors. These procedures are *extinction* and *punishment.*

Extinction. Operant extinction (distinguished from respondent extinction discussed earlier) is a procedure in which reinforcement is withheld from a behavior that has been previously reinforced, resulting in a decrease in the frequency of that behavior. Therefore, this procedure requires that the reinforcing events that maintain the undesirable behavior first be identified. While extinction can be an effective technique for reducing or eliminating the frequency of a behavior, its effect on the behavior is often a slow, gradual process (Kazdin, 1975). As a result, extinction may not be an appropriate procedure for use with self-injurious or highly disruptive behaviors that necessitate a more rapid reduction in the behavior's occurrence. Since extinction does not teach new behaviors, it is typically used in conjunction with a reinforcement program. Desirable behaviors are reinforced that are incompatible with the behavior to be eliminated. In essence, the patient is taught alternative methods for obtaining reinforcement in a more acceptable manner.

The therapeutic use of extinction is illustrated in the case of a twenty-year-old woman with a two-year history of neurodermatitis that was exacerbated by her persistent scratching. There was evidence that she was being reinforced for the scratching behavior by the attention and concern that she was receiving from her family and fiancé for the skin condition. For example, her fiancé frequently assisted her in applying ointments to the inflamed areas. The patient's family and fiancé were instructed to ignore all aspects of the neurodermatitis such as her scratching, not to apply the ointment, and to cease all discussions with her about the skin problem. This procedure eliminated the scratching behavior, and within three months the neurodermatitis had disappeared completely. A four-month follow-up indicated that her skin condition remained normal with no recurrence of the scratching behavior.

Ayllon and Michael (1959) used an extinction procedure to reduce the frequency of a patient's visits to the nurses' office in a psychiatric hospital. The patient had been entering the nurses' office on the average of sixteen times a day for over two years, and this behavior had interfered with the nurses' duties. When she entered the office, the nurses usually paid attention to her and on occasion tried to push her back onto the ward. The nurses were informed not to give the patient any attention when she entered the office. It was found that soon after this extinction procedure was introduced, there was a gradual reduction in the frequency of office visits until by the seventh week she was entering the office only twice each day.

Punishment. A procedure in which the presentation of an aversive event or the removal of a positive event, contingent on a behavior, decreases the frequency of that behavior is defined as punishment. It is important to note that punishment is defined solely by the effect that the procedure has on the behavior. Therefore, spanking a child, which is assumed by most parents to be "punishment," may not necessarily decrease the frequency of the undesirable behavior; in fact, for some children it may serve as a positive reinforcer by providing negative attention.

One form of punishment involves the presentation of aversive events contingent on the occurrence of an undesirable behavior. There are two kinds of aversive events that may serve as a punisher for an individual. *Primary aversive stimuli* are naturally aversive to an organism, and include such things as electric shock, loud noises, extreme changes in temperature, and physical pain. *Secondary (conditioned) aversive stimuli,* on the other hand, acquire their aversive properties through repeated associations with events that are already aversive to the individual. Fines, reprimands, statements of disapproval such as "No!" and facial expressions such as frowns are all examples of secondary or learned aversive stimuli.

The use of an aversive stimulus to reduce an undesirable behavior is illustrated by Risley (1968). Electric shock was used to suppress dangerous climbing behavior in a six-year-old girl who had been diagnosed as having brain damage. She had suffered severe physical injuries by falling. Previous efforts at eliminating the behavior through isolation (e.g., time out) and extinction through ignoring the behavior had failed. Shock was delivered to the leg of the child and paired with a loud "No!" whenever she began to climb objects in the treatment setting or at home. This procedure eliminated the dangerous climbing behavior in both settings. A similar procedure has been used in controlling seizure disorders by contingently punishing (shaking patient, shouting "No!") the first signs of preseizure activity (Zlutnick, Mayville, & Moffat, 1975).

The second form of punishment involves the removal of positive events contingent on the performance of the undesirable behavior. For example, a child might lose an opportunity to watch television or to play outside for fighting with other children. In treating anorexic patients, activity and social visits are usually withheld if the patient refuses to eat (Bachrach, Erwin, & Mohr, 1965). There are basically two behavioral procedures that involve the removal of positive events. *Time out* (also referred to as time out from positive reinforcement) is a procedure in which the individual is removed from the opportunity to engage in reinforcing activities contingent on the occurrence of an undesirable behavior. Typically, the individual is removed, for a short period of time, to an area where reinforcing events, including interaction with others, are not available. Time out can be an effective strategy for decreasing undesirable behaviors because it removes the individual from situations or events that may be reinforcing and, therefore, maintaining the problem behavior. However, if the time-out period is too long the procedure loses its effectiveness. The patient should be returned to the social environment and given another opportunity to show appropriate behaviors that then can be reinforced.

A second punishment procedure that involves the removal of positive events is *response cost*. In this procedure, a penalty or fine is imposed (e.g., a ticket for driving beyond the speed limit) or reinforcers are removed (e.g., loss of privileges, forfeiting tokens earned) contingent on undesirable behaviors.

As with extinction, punishment procedures should not be used as the only intervention strategy. Punishment provides the patient with feedback about what he or she is doing wrong. It does not teach the individual how to behave in a desirable manner. Therefore, punishment should be used concurrently with the reinforcement of alternative, adaptive behaviors. There is some evidence that punishment suppresses rather than eliminates a response. This provides the therapist with an opportunity to condition other responses that are more desirable. If the desirable responses are also incompatible with the punished response, the likelihood that the maladaptive behavior will recur in the future is decreased.

Punishment techniques have been effective in decreasing a number of undesirable behaviors (Azrin & Holz, 1966; Kazdin, 1975). Because punishment procedures tend to produce a rapid decrease in the frequency of behavior, they have been particularly useful in the management of self-injurious behaviors and behaviors that are highly dangerous or disruptive to others. Unless one is dealing with such problematic behaviors, however, it is best to try other intervention strategies prior to using punishment. There are unpredictable side effects that may result from punishment procedures that should caution against their injudicious use (Johnston, 1972). The potential side effects are:

1. Punishment elicits motor and emotional responses such as fear that may become conditioned to the situation or punishing agent and, thereby, interfere with the performance of desirable behaviors.
2. Termination of punishment reinforces escape behaviors such as withdrawing from the punishing situation or agent.
3. The individual may learn to avoid the situation and thus have no opportunity to be reinforced for desirable behaviors.
4. If the problem behavior is already an avoidance response (e.g., alcohol consumption), punishment may increase its frequency.
5. Attempted punishment may be a reinforcer for the individual (e.g., negative attention).
6. Punishment might actually result in the modeling of an undesirable behavior (e.g., a child hit by parents may exhibit aggressive behavior when frustrated). Bandura (1969) has shown that aggressive behaviors can be learned from adult models.

Observational Learning

In the previous sections of this chapter, the relationship between environmental stimuli or events and the performance of a response has been emphasized. However, through the process of observational learning (also referred to as vicarious learning or modeling), an individual may acquire a response without having previously performed the behavior (Bandura, 1969). Learning by observing or imitating the behavior of others is an important process in the acquisition of many behaviors. There is considerable evidence that modeling is an effective procedure for helping patients acquire, strengthen, or weaken a variety of behaviors (Thelen, Fry, Fehrenbach, & Frautschi, 1979).

In observational learning, the patient (or observer) is exposed to a model's behavior and the consequences that may accrue to the model's behavior. It is not essential that the patient actually engage in any overt responses or that he or she receive direct consequences for that behavior. The model may be physically present, as in contact desensitization, or may be presented to the patient through filmed or imaginal (i.e., symbolic) techniques.

Bandura (1971) makes a distinction between the acquisition and performance of a response. According to Bandura, a response is learned by observing the model's behavior. The observer forms symbolic responses (imaginal representations) similar to those responses performed by the model; these symbolic mediators have cue producing properties that modify and guide the behavior of the observer (Bandura, 1971). Whether an individual actually performs the modeled behaviors depends on a number of factors, such as the consequences to the model's behavior and whether there are adequate incentives for the observer to perform the behavior.

Observational learning can produce a number of behavioral changes. Through observing a model's behavior, an individual:

> . . . may learn new, appropriate behavior patterns, and modeling may thus serve an *acquisition* function. More likely, the observation of a model's behavior in various situations may provide social *facilitation* of appropriate behaviors by inducing the client to perform these behaviors, of which he was previously capable, at more appropriate times, in more appropriate ways, or toward more appropriate people. Modeling may lead to *disinhibition* of behaviors that the client has avoided because of fear or anxiety. And, while disinhibiting behaviors, modeling may promote *vicarious* and *direct extinction* of the fear associated with the person, animal, or object toward which the behavior was directed [Rimm & Masters, 1974, p. 126].

Modeling procedures have been particularly effective in reducing or eliminating fears and avoidance behaviors. The patient is typically exposed to one or several models who calmly encounter the feared situation without any adverse consequences. As a result, the fear-provoking capacity of the situation is reduced, permitting the patient to approach the feared situation. For example, Bandura, Grusec, and Menlove (1967) exposed dog-phobic preschool children to a fearless peer model who petted and fed a dog while the children enjoyed a party-like atmosphere. These children showed a greater reduction in dog-avoidance behaviors following treatment than children who were exposed to a party alone or to the dog and a party without a model. The use of modeling procedures to reduce fears and prepare patients for potentially stressful medical and dental treatment is presented in Chapters 8 and 9.

A particularly potent modeling treatment approach called participant modeling or modeling with guided practice has been developed by Bandura (1976). This procedure involves the guided practice of the problem behavior during or following the patient's observation of the model's performance. Participant modeling is a graduated and carefully structured procedure in which the modeled performances by the therapist are immediately imitated and practiced by the patient under gradually more difficult and real-life conditions. During this treatment strategy, the therapist provides extensive encouragement, physical or verbal prompts, and positive reinforcement for the patient's practice attempts. Chapter 4 discusses the use of participant modeling in the treatment of patients with severe needle and injection phobias.

Several characteristics of the model's behavior have been shown to facilitate a modeling treatment effect (Marlatt & Perry, 1975). Generally, the greater the perceived similarity between the observer and model, the greater the imitation by the observer (Flanders, 1968). In addition, the use of multiple models may increase modeling effectiveness (Rachman, 1972). Meichenbaum (1971) has found that coping models who are initially anxious but subsequently overcome their fears and complete the task in a competent manner are more effective in reducing anxiety and avoidance behavior than are mastery models who exhibit no fear or concern. Jabichuk and Smeriglio (1976) also found coping models improved social responsiveness in children. However, in studies of preparatory modeling for dental restorations, the differential effectiveness of coping and mastery models was not found (Klorman, Hilpert, Michael, Arata, & Sveen, in press; Melamed, 1979). In fact, patients with previous experience did not improve as much in their cooperation after seeing the model as did patients new to the situation. Laboratory based studies also failed to support clear-cut differences between coping and mastery modeling (Hill, Liebert, & Mott, 1968; Kornhaber & Schroeder, 1975).

It is likely that modeling will continue to play an important therapeutic role within medical practice. Films have already been developed to prepare patients for endoscopic examinations, cardiac catheterization, and coronary bypass surgery. More empirically based research is necessary to identify the effective components of the modeling situation. Information is needed regarding different applications depending on the age, previous experience, and the arousal state of the patient.

Assertion Training

Many individuals are shy, easily hurt, overly self-conscious, passive, and easily manipulated. Patients suffering from interpersonal anxiety often show deficits in assertiveness skills. It is a fact that many patients seen in health care settings exhibit problems such as migraines, angina pectoris, ulcerative colitis, alcohol or drug addiction, and sexual dysfunction, all of which may be influenced by a lack of ability to express themselves effectively. Behaviorally, the nonassertive individual may exhibit problems in the following areas:

1. maladaptive cognitions (e.g., "I don't have the right to be assertive"),
2. inhibited verbal expression, or
3. inappropriate nonverbal communication.

These problems are not always mediated by anxiety. Some individuals simply may never have learned the appropriate social skills. The patient may lack an adequate verbal repertoire or may nonverbally disclaim the meaning of the communication by using poor eye contact and gestures or inappropriate facial expressions. The individual who has difficulty in expressing anger in an appropriate manner also has assertive problems in modulating his or her feelings.

Assertion training programs have recently demonstrated that individuals can learn basic social skills that can be used in a variety of situations to help them express themselves more effectively (Eisler, Hersen, & Miller, 1973; Galassi, Galassi, & Litz, 1974; McFall & Marston, 1970; Twentyman & Zimering, 1979). These programs involve a set of procedures in which the patient acquires the ability to express feelings in an honest and straightforward manner.

An important component of assertion training is a modeling procedure. First, the therapist helps the patient to identify problematic social interactions and skill deficits. To facilitate the acquisition of assertive behaviors, a procedure called *behavioral rehearsal* is used. Using modeling and role-playing techniques, the therapist demonstrates appropriate assertive behaviors. The patient then practices the modeled behavior, after which the therapist provides feedback regarding the positive and negative aspects of the patient's performance. Once patients are capable of engaging in the target behaviors, they are encouraged to use the newly acquired skills in real-life situations. Health-related applications have been employed to teach adolescents to refuse cigarettes and other harmful drugs by use of modeling of assertive responses. A number of books have been written in this area dealing with treatment and evaluation aspects of assertion training (Alberti, 1977; Alberti & Emmons, 1974; Bower & Bower, 1976; Gambrill & Richey, 1975; Lange & Jakubowski, 1976).

Cognitions and Behavior Modification

Several behavioral clinicians and researchers have emphasized the relationship between cognitive processes and behavior (Ellis, 1962; Ellis & Abrahms, 1978; Lazarus, 1976; Mahoney, 1974; Meichenbaum, 1974). Cognitive processes such as thoughts, expectations, attitudes, and beliefs can affect how an individual behaves and his physiological state.

Medical practitioners depend on patients' self-reports about their symptoms to make important clinical decisions, such as what medication to prescribe and what diagnostic procedures to recommend. It is, therefore, imperative to evaluate the role played by the patient's thoughts about his illness. There are many ways in which thoughts have been shown to affect patient's behavior. For instance, a patient who does not believe that his life is endangered by health risk factors involved in smoking, overeating, or drug-taking is not likely to alter these habits. Similarly, recommendations for preventive inoculations are more likely to be heeded if enforced by work requirements, school prerequisites, or insurance policy clauses rather than if the patient's own intentions are relied upon. Leventhal, Singer, and Jones (1965) found that the availability of facilities to receive tetanus inoculations was more important than the patient's specific health-related attitudes. On the other hand, even when medication and treatment are readily available, patient compliance is not assured (Sackett et al., 1975).

Medical researchers studying psychosomatic disorders have found evidence for a strong association between specific emotional attitudes and physiological disturbances, such as hives and hypertension (Graham, Kabler, & Graham, 1962). The research on coronary-prone personality styles further supports the idea that patients' expectations and attitudes may effect their health adversely (Freedman & Rosenman, 1974; Suinn, 1974). Studies in chronically ill asthmatic patients found that hypnotically induced attitudes of fear or anger (Clarke, 1970) as well as suggestions that inert drugs contain bronchoconstrictors (Luparello et. al., 1968) produced asthmatic wheezing in the absence of any allergen or physiological airway obstruction.

There is empirical evidence that patients chronically ill with asthma or tuberculosis who have a tendency to exaggerate or react to their symptoms (as measured on a Panic-Fear dimension of the Minnesota Multiphasic Personality Inventory) increased the length of their hospitalization and the frequency with which they receive medication (Dahlem, Kinsman, & Horton, 1977; Melamed & Johnson, in press). More important, it has been demonstrated that these subjective statements of discomfort influence the physician's prescription of medication. Physicians prescribed more intensive steroid regimens for patients responding with complaints, regardless of objective indices of pulmonary functioning. This has important implications for the influence of the person's coping style on their illness. Both sensitizers and minimizers may be using maladaptive strategies. Patients who tend to minimize or deny their symptoms fail to monitor their symptoms early enough to receive appropriate medication and often are rehospitalized with acute symptoms, whereas patients who overattend to symptoms may be overmedicated (Kinsman, Dahlem, Spector, & Staudenmayer, 1977).

In responding to the threat of serious loss due to amputation or terminal illness, patients exhibit a broad range of cognitive reactions. Kübler-Ross (1969) opened this area to research investigation, and has stimulated health care providers to attend to patient attitudes that accompany illness, such as denial, anger, guilt, and acceptance. There is preliminary data (Safer, Tharp, Jackson, & Leventhal, in press) that important decisions that cancer patients face about whether or not to undergo severe chemotherapy or radiation treatments depend on their concepts of the illness. Emotional attitudes may influence the patients' resistance to debilitating effects of cancer and multiple sclerosis.

The reactions of patients to therapeutic interventions and drugs are also affected by their beliefs. Rachman and Philips (1978) elaborate on the power of the placebo. They conclude that rather than view this as a control condition or as an ethical problem, an attempt should be made to understand what factors influence a person's ability to improve following suggestions or placebo drugs. They recommend that these factors be exploited. If the doctor-patient relationship promotes the patient's acceptance of a drug, they suggest this relationship should be maximized. If the elaborate medical devices employed in biofeedback help to alter the patient's perception of headache pain, it may be useful even in the absence of hard evidence that it alters physiological indices.

The material presented in this section on cognitive control procedures addresses the issue of how inappropriate congnitions may enhance illness. Behavior therapists hold that covert responses can be altered in a manner similar to overt responses. This approach assumes that maladaptive behaviors can be mediated by maladaptive cognitions such as unrealistic or irrational attitudes and beliefs and self-defeating thoughts. It follows, therefore, that in order to change maladaptive behavior patterns or help in the recovery process of illness, one must also modify any disordered or faulty thinking the patient may experience.

Several intervention strategies, generally included under the rubric of *cognitive restructuring,* have been used to modify a patient's maladaptive thought processes. Ellis (1962), an early proponent of this approach, developed a treatment strategy that he termed *rational-emotive therapy.* The primary focus of this procedure is to change the patient's irrational and illogical self-statements, which Ellis feels underly most problem behaviors. Once patients are made aware of their self-defeating irrational thoughts, they are taught to evaluate them in a more objective manner and to replace them with more adaptive and realistic thinking. Beck (1967, 1976) has developed a treatment program for depressed patients based on this formulation of behavior disorders. Depression often accompanies illness. According to Beck, depressed patients distort their perceptions of events and experiences and use illogical thinking to interpret these experiences. Therefore, patients are taught to challenge the basis for their persistent negative cognitive patterns that lead to the depression and to appraise more realistically their behavior and experiences.

Another cognitive strategy for modifying problem behaviors, called *self-instructional training,* has been investigated by Meichenbaum (1974). In self-instructional training, patients are literally taught to "talk to themselves." The patient basically learns to use self-directed verbal commands (overt or covert) when approaching a particular task. Through this procedure, patients are able to gain verbal control over their behavior to perform tasks more effectively. Self-instructional training has been successfully applied to a number of problem behaviors and patient groups. This cognitive strategy has been found to reduce impulsive responding in hyperactive children (Meichenbaum & Goodman, 1971) and to improve the performance of schizophrenic patients on cognitive and perceptual tasks (Meichenbaum & Cameron, 1973). Self-instructional training is discussed further in Chapter 5 in relation to childhood problems.

Behavioral Self-Control

From a behavioral perspective, self-control may be defined as "behavior initiated by the individual and whose controlling variables are *relatively* absent of external constraints" (O'Leary & Wilson, 1975, p.

471). Rather than postulate some inner state to account for an individual's capacity for self-control, the behavioral clinician is concerned with defining specific behaviors in which individuals engage in order to influence their own behavior. Kanfer (1975) further elaborates:

> The concept of self-control implies that an individual can be taught to rearrange powerful contingencies that influence behavior in such a way that he experiences long-range benefits, even though he may have to give up some satisfaction or tolerate some discomforts at first [p. 317].

While most behavioral intervention programs initially involve external, therapist-managed procedures in order to facilitate behavior change, the long-range goal of treatment is to have patients learn to control their own behavior in the absence of the therapist. In essence, patients are taught to become their own therapists (Richards, 1976). This is accomplished by helping patients to learn self-control techniques that they can use to modify their problem behavior. When patients become more skilled in the use of self-control strategies, the therapist gradually withdraws from the intervention process. As discussed in Chapter 3, self-control procedures provide a means for facilitating the maintenance of behavior change when contact between the patient and therapist has been terminated.

Self-control strategies involve the same systematic manipulation of environmental events as do externally managed behavioral procedures; the only difference is that the patient is responsible for the control of these events. Furthermore, self-control procedures follow the same principles of learning and behavior change as do the other intervention strategies discussed in this chapter (Kazdin, 1975).

One advantage of self-control procedures is that they permit patients to engage in a variety of responses to modify problem behaviors in the specific settings in which the behaviors occur. This is particularly useful for maladaptive behaviors that may not be readily accessible to the therapist. Such behaviors might include excessive eating, obsessive-compulsive behaviors, and sexual problems.

Mahoney and Arnkoff (1978) have noted that most of the behavior problems to which self-control strategies have been applied involve responses that require a reversal of a "consequence gradient." That is, maladaptive behaviors, such as overeating, result in immediate reinforcing consequences for the individual, whereas the negative consequences (e.g., obesity, health problems) are more long term. On the other hand, desirable behaviors such as daily physical exercise may have more immediate aversive consequences (e.g., physical discomfort), but have more long-term consequences that are beneficial to the individual. Self-control strategies can be used to reverse this consequence gradient so that the therapeutically desired delayed consequences can be made more immediate for the patient.

Self-Control Techniques

There are a variety of self-control techniques that are used either alone or in combination with other procedures in behavioral intervention programs. Most self-control procedures, including those discussed below, fit within an operant conditioning paradigm. However, a number of treatment strategies presented earlier in this chapter may also be considered within a self-control framework in that they teach a specific skill that can be used by the patient to manage problem behaviors in the settings where the problems occur. Relaxation training, assertion training, and many of the cognitive strategies such as self-instructional training are examples of behavioral procedures that can serve as self-control techniques. More detailed discussions of behavioral self-control can be found in Goldfried and Merbaum (1973), Kanfer (1975), Mahoney and Thoresen (1974), and Thoresen and Mahoney (1974).

Thoresen and Mahoney (1974) suggest that there are three basic self-control strategies. These include: self-observation, environmental planning, and behavioral programming.

Self-Observation

Before patients can effectively change their behavior, they need to know how frequently the behavior occurs and what settings and events are associated with it. This is accomplished through the process known as *self-monitoring,* in which patients systematically observe and record their behavior. In addition to its use as a procedure for assessing treatment effectiveness (see Chapter 3) , self-monitoring also has value as a therapeutic strategy. First, by virtue of the feedback that the patient receives through systematic observation of the relationship between the problem behavior and the environment, the behavior becomes less habitual or automatic (Kazdin, 1975). Second, and more significant, self-monitoring has therapeutic value as a result of its reactive nature; that is, it may alter the frequency of occurrence of the behavior that is observed (Kazdin, 1974; Lipinski & Nelson, 1974; McFall, 1970; Nelson, Lipinski, & Black, 1975). However, research suggests that the accuracy of self-monitoring as an assessment procedure and its reactivity as a treatment strategy are easily affected by numerous factors, such as presence of others and situational demands. In addition, its effects on behavior change are often short-lived (Kazdin, 1974; Lipinski & Nelson, 1974; Romancyzk, 1974; Siecke & McFall, 1976). Therefore, it appears that self-monitoring will only alter behavior under certain conditions and that its effects are not always consistent. As a result, this procedure typically is used along with other intervention strategies. Self-monitoring has been found to modify such problem behaviors as obesity (Romancyzk, 1974), cigarette smoking (Lipinski, Black, Nelson, & Ciminero, 1975), scratching behavior (Maletzky, 1974), and excessive alcoholic drinking (Sobell & Sobell, 1973).

Environmental Planning

The second basic self-control strategy is environmental planning. This process involves the systematic rearrangement of environmental events associated with the problem behavior *prior* to its occurrence.

Patients can be taught to modify their physical or social environment through a strategy called *stimulus control* in order to change an undesirable behavior. Specifically, this procedure involves an alteration of environmental cues that elicit or signal the occurrence of the behavior. Ferster, Nurnberger, and Levitt (1962) first noted that if certain behaviors are repeatedly associated with certain environmental stimuli, those stimuli may eventually come to elicit or cue the behavior's occurrence. Therefore, changing environmental stimuli may produce a concomitant change in the maladaptive response pattern.

There are two forms of stimulus control. The first is known as response prevention. Examples of this are avoiding specific persons or places that may elicit the undesirable behavior. This strategy is particularly useful with events that are highly reinforcing for the patient and, therefore, difficult to resist when present. For example, it may be easier for alcoholics to keep from drinking by avoiding a bar than by standing outside the bar and watching friends inside who are drinking.

Response restriction, in which the patient is trained to narrow the range of stimuli that elicit the undesirable behavior, is a second method of stimulus control. This procedure is beneficial when the goal of treatment is to reduce, rather than completely eliminate, the frequency of occurrence of the behavior. The behavior is reduced by restricting the eliciting stimuli to specific places or times. Examples include restricting one's eating only to the kitchen table or smoking only while sitting in a specific chair.

Stimulus control as an intervention strategy is illustrated in the treatment of insomnia (Borkovec & Boudewyns, 1976). Patients with this problem frequently think about the day's events at the time when they are trying to fall asleep. This behavior, which is incompatible with sleeping, becomes associated with sleeping cues such as the bedroom, the bed, and evening time. The goal of treatment is to reverse this process and return appropriate sleeping behavior to the control of stimuli associated only with sleeping. Therefore, if patients are unable to fall asleep within ten minutes, they are instructed to leave the bedroom and engage in activities that are not typically associated with sleeping. They are to return to the bedroom only when they are sufficiently sleepy and to continue this process until they eventually fall asleep.

Behavioral Programming

A third method of self-control, referred to as behavioral programming, is concerned with the *consequences* contingent on the problem behavior. It is possible for patients to change their behavior by altering the behavior's consequences. There are two forms of consequences that are the focus of self-control programs: self-reinforcement and self-punishment.

In the *self-reinforcement* procedure, the patient self-administers reinforcing consequences contingent on a desired behavior. Reinforcing consequences can take the form of tangible items, pleasant activities, or verbal reinforcers such as self-praise.

There is considerable research evidence that self-reward is an effective self-control strategy for modifying a number of clinical problems (cf., Fuchs & Rehm, 1977; Gulanick, Woodburn, & Rimm, 1975; Mahoney, Moura, & Wade, 1973). Self-reward is assumed to have an effect on behavior similar to external reinforcement (i.e., it increases the probability of occurrence of the behavior) (Kanfer, 1975).

This procedure was used in the treatment of chronic scratching behavior in a young woman with a long history of neurodermatitis (Watson, Tharp, & Krisberg, 1972). The scratching had resulted in inflamed and infected skin. When the patient engaged in behaviors that were incompatible with scratching (e.g., patting her skin) she earned a daily bath that was soothing to her skin condition. After twenty days of this program, the scratching behavior was completely eliminated. Two recurrences of the scratching behavior during an 18-month follow-up were quickly suppressed when the self-reinforcement contingency was reinstituted.

Self-punishment is a procedure in which a person self-administers an aversive or unpleasant stimulus or removes a positive reinforcer contingent on the occurrence of an undesirable behavior. In contrast to self-reinforcement, there has been little research on the efficacy of self-punishment in the treatment of behavior problems. The few studies that have investigated self-punishment suggest that it is not very effective when used as a single treatment strategy (cf., Thoresen & Mahoney, 1974). These results may reflect the fact that self-punishment is less apt to be used consistently when compared to externally applied punishment procedures since patients may find it less than desirable to self-punish their behavior voluntarily (Mahoney & Arnkoff, 1978).

A self-punishment procedure was used in a case study reported by Mahoney (1971). The patient was depressed and engaged in a high frequency of obsessive thoughts that involved negative self-statements. A self-punishment procedure was introduced in which the patient wore a heavy rubber band on his wrist. He was instructed to snap the rubber band contingent on the occurrence of the obsessive thoughts. This procedure was effective in reducing the obsessive thoughts; behavioral improvements were maintained at a four-month follow-up.

Summary

Learning principles used in behavioral interventions are described. Clinical examples illustrate the behavior therapies derived from these principles. The advantages and disadvantages of counterconditioning, punishment, positive reinforcement, contingency-contracting, observational learning, biofeedback procedures and cognitive and self-control strategies are discussed. Although these techniques are described separately, they are often used together in the course of behavioral treatment. The goal of any behavioral program is to increase desirable behaviors and reduce undesirable behaviors.

References

Alberti, R. E. *Assertiveness: Innovations, applications, issues.* San Luis Obispo, Calif.: Impact Press, 1977.

Alberti, R. E., & Emmons, M. L. *Your perfect right.* San Luis Obispo, Impact Press, 1974.

Ayllon, T., & Azrin, N. H. The measurement and reinforcement of behavior of psychotics. *Journal of Experimental Analysis of Behavior,* 1965, *8*, 357–383.

––––––. *The token economy: A motivational system for therapy and rehabilitation.* New York: Appleton, 1968.

Ayllon, T., & Michael, J. The psychiatric nurse as a behavioral engineer. *Journal of the Experimental Analysis of Behavior,* 1959, *2*, 323–334.

Azrin, N. H., & Holz, W. Punishment. In W. N. Honig (Ed.), *Operant behavior: Areas of research and application.* New York: Appleton-Century-Crofts, 1966.

Azrin, N. J., Naster, B. J., & Jones, R. Reciprocity counseling: A rapid-learning-based procedure for marital counseling. *Behaviour Research and Therapy,* 1973, *11,* 365–382.

Bachrach, A. J., Erwin, W. J., & Mohr, J. P. The control of eating behavior in an anorexic by operant conditioning. In L. P. Ullmann, & L. Krasner (Eds.), *Case studies in behavior modification.* New York: Holt, Rinehart & Winston, 1965.

Bandura, A. *Principles of behavior modification.* New York: Holt, Rinehart & Winston, 1969.

––––––. Vicarious and self-reinforcement processes. In R. Glaser (Ed.), *The nature of reinforcement.* New York: Academic Press, 1971.

––––––. Effecting change through participant modeling. In J. D. Krumboltz and C. E. Thoresen (Eds.), *Counseling methods.* New York: Holt, Rinehart & Winston, 1976.

––––––. Self-efficacy: Toward a unifying theory of behavioral change. *Psychological Review,* 1977, *84,* 191–195.

Bandura, A., Grusec, J. E., & Menlove, F. L. Vicarious extinction of avoidance behavior. *Journal of Personality and Social Psychology,* 1967, *5,* 16–23.

Beck, A. T. *Depression: Clinical, experimental, and theoretical aspects.* New York: Harper & Row, 1967.

––––––. *Cognitive therapy and the emotional disorders.* New York: International Universities Press, 1976.

Bernstein, D. A., & Borkovec, T. D. *Progressive relaxation: A manual for therapists.* Champaign, Ill.: Research Press, 1973.

Bleecker, E. R., & Engle, B. T. Learned control of cardiac rate and cardiac conduction in Wolff-Parkinson-White syndrome. *Seminars in Psychiatry,* 1973, *5,* 475–479.

Borkovec, T. D., & Boudewyns, P. A. Treatment of insomnia with stimulus control and progressive relaxation procedures. In J. D. Krumboltz and C. E. Thoresen (Eds.), *Counseling methods.* New York: Holt, Rinehart & Winston, 1976.

Bower, G. H., & Bower, S. *Asserting yourself: A practical guide for positive change.* Reading, Mass.: Addison-Wesley, 1976.

Burstein, S., & Meichenbaum, D. The work of worrying in children undergoing surgery. *Journal of Abnormal Child Psychology,* 1979, *1,* 127–132.

Cautela, J. R. Treatment of compulsive behavior by covert sensitization. *Psychological Record,* 1966, *16,* 33–41.

Clarke, P. S. Effects of emotion and cough on airway obstruction in asthma. *Medical Journal of Australia* 1970, *1*, 535.

Dahlem, N. W., Kinsman, R. A., & Horton, D. J. Requests for as-needed (PRN) medications by asthmatic patients: Relationships to prescribed oral corticosteroid regimens and length of hospitalization. *Journal of Allergy and Clinical Immunology*, 1977, *60*, (5), 295–300.

Daniels, L. K. Treatment of urticaria and severe headache by behavior therapy. *Psychosomatics*, 1973, *14*, 347–351.

Eisler, R. M., Hersen, M., & Miller, P. M. Effects of modeling on components of assertive behavior. *Journal of Behavior Therapy and Experimental Psychiatry*, 1973, *4*, 1–6.

Eisler, R. M., Miller, P. M., & Hersen, M. Effects of assertive training on marital interaction. *Archives of General Psychiatry*, 1974, *30*, 643–649.

Ellis, A. *Reason and emotion in psychotherapy.* New York: Lyle Stuart, 1962.

Ellis, A., & Abrahms, E. *Brief psychotherapy in medical and health practice.* New York: Springer, 1978.

Ferster, C. B., Nurnberger, J. I., & Levitt, E. B. The control of eating. *Journal of Mathetics*, 1962, *1*, 87–109.

Flanders, J. A review of research on imitative behavior. *Psychological Bulletin*, 1968, *69*, 316–337.

Fowler, R. S., Fordyce, W., & Berni, R. Operant conditioning in chronic illness. *American Journal of Nursing*, 1969, *69*, 1226–1228.

Freedman, M., & Rosenman, R. H. *Type A behavior and your heart.* New York: Knopf, 1974.

Fuchs, C. Z., & Rehm, L. P. A self-control behavior therapy program for depression. *Journal of Consulting and Clinical Psychology*, 1977, *45*, 206–215.

Galassi, J. P., Galassi, M. D., & Litz, M. C. Assertive training in groups using video feedback. *Journal of Counseling Psychology*, 1974, *21*, 390–394.

Gambrill, E. D., & Richey, C. A. An assertion inventory for use in assessment and research. *Behavior Therapy*, 1975, *6*, 550–561.

Gannon, L., & Sternbach, R. A. Alpha enhancement as a treatment for pain: A case study. *Journal of Behavior Therapy and Experimental Psychiatry*, 1971, *2*, 209–213.

Girardeau, F. L., & Spradlin, J. E. Token rewards in a cottage program. *Mental Retardation*, 1964, *2*, 345–351.

Goldfried, M. R. Systematic desensitization as training in self-control. *Journal of Consulting and Clinical Psychology*, 1971, *37*, 228–234.

Goldfried, M. R., & Davison, G. C. *Clinical behavior therapy.* New York: Holt, Rinehart & Winston, 1976.

Goldfried, M. R., & Kent, R. N. Traditional versus behavioral personality assessment: A comparison of methodological and theoretical assumptions. *Psychological Bulletin*, 1972, *77*, 409–420.

Goldfried, M. R., & Merbaum, M. (Eds.), *Behavior change through self-control.* New York: Holt, Rinehart & Winston, 1973.

Graham, D. T., Kabler, J. D., & Graham, F. K. Physiologic response to the suggestion of attitudes specific for hives and hypertension. *Psychosomatic Medicine*, 1962, *24*, 159–169.

Grimaldi, K. E., & Lichtenstein, E. Hot, smoky air as an aversive stimulus in the treatment of smoking. *Behaviour Research and Therapy*, 1969, *7*, 275–282.

Gulanick, N., Woodburn, L. T., & Rimm, D. Weight gain through self-control procedures. *Journal of Consulting and Clinical Psychology*, 1975, *43*, 536–539.

Hill, J. H., Liebert, R. M., & Mott, D. E. Vicarious extinction of avoidance behavior through film: An initial test. *Psychological Reports*, 1968, *12*, 192.

Homme, L., Csanyi, A. P., Gonzales, M. A., & Rechs, J. R. *How to use contingency contracting in the classroom.* Champaign, Ill.: Research Press, 1970.

Horner, D., & Keirlitz, I. Training mentally-retarded adolescents to brush their teeth. *Journal of Applied Behavior Analysis*, 1975, *8*, 301–309.

Jabichuk, T., & Smeriglio, U. The influence of symbolic modeling on the social behavior of preschool children with low levels of social responsiveness. *Child Development*, 1976, *47*, 838–841.

Jacobson, E. *Progressive relaxation.* Chicago: University of Chicago Press, 1938.

Jacobson, N. S., & Martin, B. Behavioral marriage therapy: Current status. *Psychological Bulletin*, 1976, *83*, 540–556.

Johnston, J. M. Punishment of human behavior. *American Psychologist*, 1972, *27*, 1033–1054.

Jones, M. C. The elimination of children's fears. *Journal of Experimental Psychology*, 1924, *7*, 382–390.

———. A laboratory study of fear: The case of Peter. *Journal of Genetic Psychology*, 1924, *31*, 308–315.

Kanfer, F. H. Self-management methods. In F. H. Kanfer & A. P. Goldstein (Eds.), *Helping people change.* New York: Pergamon Press, 1975.

Kanfer, F. H., Karoly, P., & Newman, A. Reduction of children's fear of the dark by competence-related and situational threat-related verbal cues. *Journal of Consulting and Clinical Psychology*, 1974, *43*, 251–258.

Kazdin, A. E. Self-monitoring and behavior change. In M. J. Mahoney & C. E. Thoresen (Eds.), *Self-control: Power to the person.* Monterey, Calif.: Brooks/Cole, 1974.

———. *Behavior modification in applied settings.* Homewood, Ill.: Dorsey Press, 1975.

———. *The token economy: A review and evaluation.* New York: Plenum, 1977.

Kinsman, R. A., Dahlem, N. W., Spector, S., & Staudenmayer, H. Observations on patterns of subjective symptomatology of acute asthma. *Psychosomatic Medicine*, 1977, *39*, 102–119.

Klorman, R., Hilpert, P., Michael, R., Arata, C. L., & Sveen, O. Effects of coping and mastery modeling on experienced and inexperienced pedodontic patients' disruptiveness. *Behavior Therapy*, in press.

Kornhaber, R., & Schroeder, H. Importance of model similarity on extinction of avoidance behavior in children. *Journal of Consulting and Clinical Psychology*, 1975, *43*, 601–607.

Kübler-Ross, E. *On death and dying.* New York: Macmillan, 1969.

Lamaze, F. *Painless childbirth, psychoprophylactic method.* (L. R. Celestin, trans.) Chicago: Regnery, 1970.

Lang, P. J. Research on the specificity of feedback training: Implications for the use of biofeedback in the treatment of anxiety and fear. In J. Beatty & H. Legewie (Eds.), *Biofeedback and Behavior.* New York: Plenum, 1977.

Lang, P. J., & Melamed, B. G. Avoidance conditioning therapy of an infant with chronic ruminative vomiting. *Journal of Abnormal Psychology,* 1969, *74,* 1–8.

Lang, P. J., Melamed, B. G., & Hart, J. Automating the desensitization procedure: A psychophysiological analysis of fear modification. *Journal of Abnormal Psychology,* 1970, *76,* 220–234.

Lang, P. J., Troyer, W. G., Twentyman, C., & Gatchel, R. J. Differential aspects of heart rate modification training on college students, older males and patients with ischemic heart disease. *Psychosomatic Medicine,* 1975, *37,* 429–446.

Lange, A. J., & Jakubowski, P. *Responsible assertive behavior: Cognitive/behavioral procedures for trainers.* Champaign, Ill.: Research Press, 1976.

Lazarus, A. (Ed.), *Multi-modal behavior therapy.* New York: Springer, 1976.

Lazarus, A., & Abramovitz, A. The use of "emotive imagery" in the treatment of children's phobias. *Journal of Mental Science,* 1962, *108,* 191–195.

Leventhal, H., Singer, R., & Jones, S. Effects of fear and specificity of recommendations on attitude and behavior. *Journal of Personality and Social Psychology,* 1965, *2,* 20–29.

Lipinski, D. P., Black, J. L., Nelson, R. O., & Ciminero, A. R. Influence of motivational variables on the reactivity and reliability of self-recording. *Journal of Consulting and Clinical Psychology,* 1975, *43,* 637–648.

Lipinski, D., & Nelson, R. O. The reactivity and unreliability of self-recording. *Journal of Consulting and Clinical Psychology,* 1974, *42,* 118–123.

Luparello, T., Lyons, H. A., Bleecker, E. R., & McFadden, Jr., E. R. Influences of suggestion on airway reactivity in asthmatic subjects. *Psychosomatic Medicine,* 1968, *30,* 819.

McFall, R. M. Effects of self-monitoring on normal smoking behavior. *Journal of Consulting and Clinical Psychology,* 1970, *38,* 135–142.

McFall, R. M., & Marston, A. R. An experimental investigation of behavioral rehearsal in assertive training. *Journal of Abnormal Psychology,* 1970, *76,* 295–303.

Mahoney, M. J. The self-management of covert behavior: A case study. *Behavior Therapy,* 1971, *2,* 575–578.

———. *Cognition and behavior modification.* Cambridge, Mass.: Ballinger, 1974.

Mahoney, M. J., & Arnkoff, D. B. Cognitive and self-control therapies. In S. L. Garfield & A. E. Bergin (Eds.), *Handbook of psychotherapy and behavior change* (2nd ed.) New York: Wiley, 1978.

Mahoney, M. J., Moura, N. G., & Wade, T. C. Relative efficacy of self-reward, self-punishment, and self-monitoring techniques for weight loss. *Journal of Consulting and Clinical Psychology,* 1973, *41,* 404–407.

Mahoney, M. J., & Thoresen, C. E. (Eds.), *Self-control: Power to the person.* Monterey, Calif.: Brooks/Cole, 1974.

Maletzky, B. M. Behavior recording as treatment: A brief note. *Behavior Therapy*, 1974, *5*, 107–111.

Malament, I. B., Dunn, M. E., & Davis, R. Pressure sores: An operant conditioning approach to prevention. *Archives of Physical Medicine and Rehabilitation*, 1975, *56*, 161–165.

Mann, R. A. The behavior-therapeutic use of contingency contracting to control an adult behavior problem: Weight control. *Journal of Applied Behavior Analysis*, 1972, *5*, 99–109.

Marks, I. Behavioral treatments of phobic and obsessive-compulsive disorders: A critical appraisal. In M. Hersen, R. M. Eisler, & P. M. Miller (Eds.), *Progress in behavior modification*, Vol. 1. New York: Academic Press, 1975.

Marlatt, G. A., & Perry, A. Modeling methods. In F. H. Kanfer and A. P. Goldstein (Eds.), *Helping people change.* New York: Pergamon Press, 1975.

Marshall, W. L., Gauthier, J., & Gordon, A. The current status of flooding therapy. In M. Hersen, R. M. Eisler, & P. M. Miller (Eds.), *Progress in behavior modification*, Vol 7. New York: Academic Press, 1979.

Meichenbaum, D. Examination of modeled characteristics in reducing avoidance behavior. *Journal of Personality and Social Psychology*, 1971, *17*, 298–307.

———. *Cognitive behavior modification.* Morristown, N.J.: General Learning Press, 1974.

———. *Cognitive-behavior modification: An integrative approach.* New York: Plenum Press, 1977.

Meichenbaum, D., & Cameron, R. Training schizophrenics to talk to themselves: A means of developing attentional controls. *Behavior Therapy*, 1973, *4*, 515–534.

Meichenbaum, D., & Goodman, J. Training impulsive children to talk to themselves: A means of developing self-control. *Journal of Abnormal Psychology*, 1971, *77*, 115–126.

Melamed, B. G. Behavioral approaches to fear in dental settings. In M. Hersen, R. M. Eisler, & P. M. Miller (Eds.), *Progress in behavior modification*, Vol. 7. New York: Academic Press, 1979.

Melamed, B. G., & Johnson, S. B. Behavioral assessment of chronic illness: Asthma and juvenile diabetes. In E. Mash & E. Terdal (Eds.), *Behavioral assessment of childhood disorders.* New York: BMA Guilford Press, in press.

Melzack, R. *The puzzle of pain.* Middlesex, England: Penguin, 1973.

Mikulas, W. *Behavior modification: An overview.* New York: Harper & Row, 1972.

Miller, P. M. The use of behavioral contracting in the treatment of alcoholism: A case report. *Behavior Therapy*, 1972, *3*, 593–596.

Miller, P. M., Hersen, M., & Eisler, R. M. Relative effectiveness of instructions, agreements, and reinforcement in behavioral contracts with alcoholics. *Journal of Abnormal Psychology*, 1974, *83*, 548–553.

Nelson, R. O., Lipinski, D. P., & Black, J. L. The effects of expectancy on the reactivity of self-monitoring. *Behavior Therapy,* 1975, *6,* 337–349.

O'Leary, K. D., & Drabman, R. C. Token reinforcement programs in the classroom: A review. *Psychological Bulletin,* 1971, *75,* 379–398.

O'Leary, K. D., & Wilson, G. T. *Behavior therapy: Application and outcome.* New York: Prentice-Hall, 1975.

Phillips, E. L. Achievement place: Token reinforcement procedures in a home-style rehabilitation setting for "predelinquent boys." *Journal of Applied Behavior Analysis,* 1968, *12,* 213–223.

Premack, D. Reinforcement theory. In D. Levine (Ed.), *Nebraska symposium on motivation.* Lincoln: University of Nebraska Press, 1965.

Rachman, S. J. Clinical applications of observational learning, imitation, and modeling. *Behavior Therapy,* 1972, *3,* 379–397.

Rachman, S. J., & Philips, C. *Psychology and medicine.* Middlesex, England: Penguin, 1978.

Richards, C. S. Improving study behaviors through self-control techniques. In J. D. Krumboltz & C. E. Thoresen (Eds.), *Counseling methods.* New York: Holt, Rinehart & Winston, 1976.

Rimm, D. C., & Masters, J. C. *Behavior therapy techniques and empirical findings.* New York: Academic Press, 1974; 2nd ed., 1979.

Risley, T. R. The effects and side effects of punishing the autistic behavior of a deviant child. *Journal of Applied Behavior Analysis,* 1968, *1,* 21–34.

Ritter, B. The use of contact desensitization, demonstration plus participation and demonstration alone in the treatment of acrophobia. *Behaviour Research and Therapy,* 1969, *7,* 157–164.

Romancyzk, R. G. Self-monitoring in the treatment of obesity: Parameters of reactivity. *Behavior Therapy,* 1974, *5,* 531–540.

Sackett, D. L., Haynes, R. B., Gibson, E. S., Hackett, B. C., Taylor, D. W., Roberts, R. S., & Johnson, A. L. Randomized clinical trial of strategies for improving medication compliance in primary hypertension. *Lancet,* 1975, *1,* 1205–1207.

Safer, M. A., Tharp, Q., Jackson, T., & Leventhal, H. Determinants of three stages of delay in seeking care at a medical clinic. *Medical Care,* in press.

Sargent, J. D., Greene, E. E., & Walters, E. D. Preliminary report on the use of autogenic feedback training in the treatment of migraine and tension headaches. *Psychosomatic Medicine,* 1973, *35,* 129–135.

Shapiro, D., Tursky, B., & Schwartz, G. Control of blood pressure in man by operant conditioning. *Circulation Research,* 1970, *27,* 27–32.

Siecke, W. A., & McFall, R. M. Some determinants of self-monitoring effects. *Journal of Consulting and Clinical Psychology,* 1976, *44,* 958–965.

Sirota, A. D., & Mahoney, M. J. Relaxation on cue: The self-regulation of asthma. *Journal of Behavior Therapy and Experimental Psychiatry,* 1974, *5,* 65–66.

Skinner, B. F. *Science and human behavior.* New York: Macmillan, 1953.

Sobell, L. C., & Sobell, M. B. A self-feedback technique to monitor drinking behavior in alcoholics. *Behaviour Research and Therapy,* 1973, *11,* 237.

Stampfl, T. G., & Levis, D. J. Essentials of implosive therapy: A learning-theory-based psychodynamic behavioral therapy. *Journal of Abnormal Psychology,* 1967, *72,* 496–503.

Stuart, R. B. A three-dimensional program for the treatment of obesity. *Behaviour Research and Therapy,* 1971, *9,* 177–186.

Suinn, R. Behavior therapy for cardiac patients. *Behavior Therapy,* 1974, *5,* 569–571.

Thelen, M., Fry, R. A., Fehrenbach, P. A., & Frautschi, N. M. Therapeutic videotape and film modeling: A review. *Psychological Bulletin,* 1979, *86,* 701–720.

Thoresen, C. E., & Mahoney, M. J. *Behavioral self-control.* New York: Holt, Rinehart & Winston, 1974.

Twentyman, C. T., & Zimering, R. T. Behavioral training of social skills: A critical review. In M. Hersen, R. M. Eisler, & P. M. Miller (Eds.), *Progress in behavior modification,* Vol. 7. New York: Academic Press, 1979.

Watson, D. L., Tharp, R. G., & Krisberg, J. Case study in self-modification: Suppression of inflammatory scratching while awake and asleep. *Journal of Behavior Therapy and Experimental Psychiatry,* 1972, *3,* 312–315.

Watson, J. B., & Raynor, R. Conditioned emotional reactions. *Experimental Psychology,* 1920, *3,* 1–14.

Weathers, L., & Liberman, R. P. Contingency contracting with families of delinquent adolescents. *Behavior Therapy,* 1975, *6,* 356–366.

Wish, P. A., Hasazi, J. E., & Jurgela, A. R. Automated direct deconditioning of a childhood phobia. *Journal of Behavior Therapy and Experimental Psychiatry,* 1973, *4,* 279–283.

Wolpe, J. *Psychotherapy by reciprocal inhibition.* Stanford, Calif.: Stanford University Press, 1958.

Zlutnick, S., Mayville, W. J., & Moffat, S. Modification of seizure disorders: The interruption of behavioral chains. *Journal of Applied Behavior Analysis,* 1975, *8,* 1–12.

3

Designing, Implementing, and Evaluating a Behavioral Intervention Program

The behavioral approach to changing behavior is distinguished from other forms of intervention by its assessment process. This begins with the identification of the problem behavior and continues until the goals of the treatment program have been reached. This assessment process is called a *functional analysis of behavior* because it attempts to determine the relationships between the problem behavior that the patient exhibits and events in the environment that control the appearance and maintenance of the behavior. Once the relationships between the environmental events and the behavior problem have been determined, these events can be systematically altered to produce a desired change in the behavior. The focus is on what the patient does and on the context in which the behaviors occur. Table 3.1 outlines the steps necessary to explore these relations.

Table 3.1   Treatment Program Outline

I.   Selecting and defining target behavior(s)

        A. Behavioral excesses
        B. Behavioral deficits
        C. Inappropriate or defective stimulus control
        D. Behavioral assets

II.   Methods of collecting information

        A. Self-report measures
        B. Behavioral observations
        C. Patient self-monitoring
        D. Permanent product measures
        E. Physiological measures (instrumentation)

III. Functional analysis of behavior

        A. Antecedent events
        B. Consequences

IV.   Selecting and implementing an intervention program

        A. Motivation for change
           1. Patient (secondary gains)
           2. Significant others
        B. Assessment of available reinforcers
        C. Availability and cooperation of significant others and staff
        D. Factors maintaining the problem
           1. Skill deficit
           2. Lack of incentive (insufficient reinforcement)
           3. Excessive or insufficient arousal (anxiety, anger, depression)
        E. Treatment strategies

V.   Evaluation of the intervention program

        A. Continuous monitoring of progress during treatment (use of feedback to modify program as indicated)
        B. Programming for maintenance of behavior change (transfer to real life)
        C. Follow-up assessment (Is reinstatement of treatment program necessary?)

VI.   Termination of the intervention program (What was your treatment goal?)

Selecting a Target Behavior

The first step in establishing a behavioral program is to select or pinpoint the problem behavior that requires changing. This is referred to as the target behavior. Several factors should be considered in selecting a target behavior. First, it is important to consider whether the desired change in behavior is consistent with the goals and needs of the patient and others involved. If these individuals do not agree with the basic goals of the intervention program, it is unlikely that treatment will be successful. Second, in selecting a target behavior, it is important to consider whether the patient's life circumstances are capable of supporting and maintaining behavior change once formal treatment has been terminated.

Patients often exhibit more than one problem behavior. For the initial focus of treatment, it is best to choose one behavior that is likely to be readily altered by an intervention program. This initial target behavior may not be the main problem that concerns the patient. However, demonstrating the patient's ability to make use of a particular therapeutic strategy may facilitate the patient's motivation to handle more complex problems. Treatment procedures may then be applied to problems that are more resistant to change when the patient is more confident that compliance with the behavioral program will result in desired treatment effects.

It is not possible to give a single definition of problem behavior. The concerns that any one individual brings to a health care professional are varied, and must be considered within the context in which they occur. What is defined as a problem differs from individual to individual, and changes for the same person at different times. Nevertheless, it is possible to classify common target behaviors into categories. There are behavioral excesses, behavioral deficits, inappropriate or defective stimulus control, and behavioral assets (Kanfer & Saslow, 1969). Some target behaviors may fall into more than one category; however, a decision about primary classification helps the selection of an appropriate treatment strategy. A blank program outline for problem assessment is provided in the appendix.

Behavioral Excesses

Behaviors may be problems because they occur at a frequency, intensity, or duration that is judged to be too high for a particular environment or circumstance. For example, behavioral excess is exhibited by the overweight individual who eats too much and too often. A patient who suffers headaches of such an intensity that he or she cannot engage in other activities also has a behavioral excess.

Behavioral Deficits

For some patients, a behavior may present a problem because it occurs at an insufficient frequency, at an inadequate intensity, or in an inappropriate form. For example, an individual who lack social skills necessary to interact effectively with others manifests a behavioral deficit. A behavioral deficit is also evident in patients who fail to take their medication as prescribed.

Inappropriate or Inadequate Stimulus Control

In this category, a behavior is a problem because it occurs under inappropriate conditions or at inappropriate times. That is, the patient has adequate skills; however, they are not used in an adaptive manner, at a suitable time, or in the proper context. The behavior may also occur at an inappropriate rate. Here one finds problems such as enuresis, in which the individual makes the response at the wrong time and place. In addition to being a behavioral excess, obesity is also a problem of inappropriate stimulus control. Eating behavior may be associated with many environmental events or cues such as the sight of food, the time of day, and specific areas of the house. When these cues are present, eating behavior is likely to occur whether or not the person is, in fact, hungry.

Behavioral Assets

Before designing a treatment program, the therapist needs to identify a fourth category of behavior: the strengths of the patient. Unlike the previous three classes of behavior, this category does not represent any form of maladaptive behavior. Here, the therapist is concerned with the specific strengths and competencies or skills that the patient has acquired. It is important to identify these resources that the patient brings to the treatment setting because it is often necessary to build upon these strengths when implementing a treatment program to change the maladaptive behavior.

The need to consider the socially adaptive behaviors of the patient in developing a treatment plan can be illustrated in two ways. First, the frequency of an undesirable behavior is often maintained by well-intentioned but inappropriate attention to the patient by family members and friends. For instance, depressed patients are often reinforced with concern and sympathy that, rather than helping, only enhances their depression. Depressed patients clearly need the attention and support of family and friends. However, the family must learn to attend to and reinforce with attention and praise the positive strengths of the patient, for example, grooming habits or perseverence in the job situation. Thus, social support comes to enhance the healthy aspects of the personality, increasing their dominance in the behavior of the patient and reciprocally weakening the depressed elements. Second, the therapist is concerned with the patient's competencies as vehicles for teaching new adaptive behaviors. Treatment is more likely to be successful if the program builds on the patient's current talents and skills. For example, an elderly, socially isolated woman who spends most of her time knitting may be encouraged to use this activity as the basis for involvement with others who enjoy it as well.

Defining the Target Behavior

Once the target behavior has been agreed on, the next step is to define the behavior so that is can be clearly observed and measured. Initially, this definition may consist of a subjective description of the problem by the patient and others concerned. It is the task of the therapist to help specify the problem in an objective manner so that there is little doubt among the patient and staff as to whether or not the behavior has occurred. For example, a parent might describe the child as hyperactive. Such a term represents a subjective description of the problem since it has different meanings for different individuals and, therefore, leaves open to wide interpretation exactly what the parent means. This general label is not useful because it is too ambiguous and imprecise. Such ambiguities could result in the failure of the intervention procedures. A child who is labeled hyperactive may, however, display some of the following specific behaviors: sits quietly for only brief periods, interrupts other children by talking out of turn, hits siblings frequently, cries and throws objects when unable to complete a task, breaks toys, falls asleep two hours after going to bed, completes only three subtraction problems in twenty minutes. These behaviors represent objective descriptions of the problem because they can be observed and measured by the parents or other therapists. For example, they can count how many seconds the child remains seated during a given time period, or they can count how many times the child hits another child.

Measuring the Target Behavior

Establishing a Baseline

After the problem behavior has been defined in precise terms so that the change agents (hospital staff, parents, spouse, etc.) can agree on the specific behaviors that constitute the problem, the next step is to evaluate how often the behavior problem occurs prior to implementing an intervention program. This initial rate of the behavior, which is measured before treatment begins, is referred to as a *baseline level*. It is important to establish a baseline level for the target behavior for several reasons. First, general impressions of the frequency of the patient's behavior may not reflect an accurate picture of the extent to which the behavior actually occurs. For example, on a busy surgical ward where complaints of pain and discomfort are a common occurrence, a nurse may grossly misjudge how frequently a particular patient requested analgesic medication if she fails to keep a record and relies instead on her subjective impressions.

Baseline records also serve a second important function. They permit the therapist to evaluate the effectiveness of the intervention program. By comparing the baseline rate with the frequency of the behavior after treatment is initiated, the therapist can objectively determine whether the program is in fact changing the problem behavior. These records can also be used in treatment to reinforce the patients for progress toward therapy goals.

It is also important to assess the maladaptive behavior in each setting in which it occurs, as its frequency may vary with stimulus context. Baseline periods should be long enough to provide a stable picture of the behavior. If the target behavior occurs at least several times a day, a baseline period of approximately five to seven days is probably adequate. However, if the target behavior occurs only once or twice a week, the baseline period may have to extend for several weeks or more to yield a representative sample of the behavior problem. When the frequency of the observed behavior changes very little over several observation periods, an accurate sample of the behavior has probably been obtained.

Multiple Response Systems

The behavior problems that patients present may manifest themselves through one or more of three basic classes of responses: self-report, behavioral acts, and patterns of physiological arousal. Consider, for example, a patient who is anxious or fearful about getting out of bed several days following an operation. The patient's thoughts and feelings are expressed through self-report. The problem is defined in part by such statements as, "I am scared to stand on my feet or get out of bed because I become dizzy. I will faint, fall, and hurt myself even more." The patient's anxiety is also defined behaviorally by avoidance and noncompliance. Thus, when the physician tells the patient that it is important to begin exercising by walking around for several minutes a day, the patient hesitates and attempts to avoid the regimen. Physiological evidence of stress may also be observed. When asked to walk, the patient tenses his or her muscles, breathes irregularly, perspires excessively, and trembles or shakes for several minutes.

Since the behavior problem of interest may be reflected in several response systems, the health-care practitioner must be concerned with assessing the target behavior in each system that is practical or relevant. Furthermore, since the three response modalities do not always show change at the same rate or in a consistent manner across systems (Hodgson & Rachman, 1974), it is beneficial to assess as many dimensions of the target behavior as possible in order to insure maximum treatment effectiveness. In fact, predictions regarding the choice of the behavior change strategy can best be made by examining the discrepancies between these systems within the individual (Lang, 1977b). This issue is further addressed later in this chapter.

Methods of Collecting Information

Self-Report Measures

The patient's participation in the information-gathering process is critical. To assist the individual in describing his thoughts, feelings, and attitudes, one may use interviews (with the patient and significant others), questionnaires, and behavioral inventories. By giving the patient an opportunity to describe the problem in his or her own language, the patient-therapist relationship is also facilitated. Furthermore, self-report procedures are useful in that they provide some information about events that cannot be directly observed (e.g., thoughts) or which are not practical to observe in the clinic (e.g., frequency of urination, sexual behavior).

While the behavioral assessment literature has stressed the use of objective evaluation procedures, the interview continues to be the most extensive source of information about the patient and his or her problem behaviors. Behavioral interviews are focused on obtaining information directly relevant to treatment. This includes the nature of the target behavior and events in the patient's environment (including cognitions) that currently contribute to its instigation and maintenance (Mash & Terdal, 1976). Before devising a treatment program, it is important to evaluate the patient's perception of how the problem behavior interferes with his or her daily functioning. Furthermore, the interview explores information pertaining to the patients's behavioral assets such as skills, resources for coping with stress, and level of motivation for change. The patient's social and familial relationships, work, and educational experiences must be examined to determine whether they are related to the problem behavior.

Numerous questionnaires and inventories have been used for assessment purposes in behavioral treatment programs. Although many of these measures were initially developed as research instruments, they have proved useful to behavioral clinicians. They assist in assessing the degree of the problem and the specific situations and events associated with the problem, and they provide a baseline against which to compare treatment outcome. Used in conjunction with other assessment procedures, they can provide a comprehensive picture of the presenting problem. Typically, the patient is given a structured paper-and-pencil measure and is asked to rate his own behavior in various situations or settings. These instruments range from more global measures of functioning, such as the Life History Questionnaire (Lazarus, 1971), to measures of more specific and circumscribed problems such as fears: for example, Fear Survey Schedule (Wolpe & Lang, 1964); anxiety: for example, Taylor Manifest Anxiety Scale (Taylor, 1953); assertiveness: for example, Rathus Assertiveness Scale (Rathus, 1973); depression: for example, Beck Depression Inventory (Beck, 1967); marital satisfaction: for example, Marital Pre-Counseling Inventory (Stuart & Stuart, 1972); sexual behavior: for example, Sexual Interaction Inventory (LoPiccolo & Steger, 1974), and many others.

Behavioral Observations

Whenever practical, observations of the patient's behavior should be conducted in the setting in which the problem occurs. With most target behaviors, several observational techniques can be used effectively. Which strategy is used will depend to a large extent on the nature of the specific behavior and practical considerations, such as the schedules and availability of the health care personnel. In selecting a method for behavioral observation, it is important to remember that a goal of observation is to obtain a representative sample of the patient's behavior. Since behavior tends to vary over given time periods each day or throughout the week and in different settings, it is best to observe during as many of these periods as possible. For instance, an excessive smoker may find that he or she is smoking more in social situations or when being observed by others than when alone.

The recording of the target behavior does not have to be an unwieldy task. It is an important part of treatment, and must be carefully carried out. The observation procedure can be devised in such a way that it minimally interferes with the observer's usual routine. In addition, family members or even the patients themselves can be trained to note and record problem behaviors.

Event or Frequency Recording

In this procedure, the observer counts or tallies the number of times that the target behavior occurs during a given period of time. It is used with discrete responses that have clearly definable beginnings and ends. This observational procedure is particularly efficient with events that may occur at a low to moderate frequency throughout the day. For example, a nurse can keep a tally sheet of the number of times a patient presses the call button or asks for pain medication. Similarly, a parent may keep a record of the number of times a school-phobic child goes to school. Devices such as golf counters or grocery counters can be useful in recording very high frequencies of behavior.

Duration Recording

When the observer is interested in the length of time that a behavior occurs or the time between responses, duration recording should be used. The objective measure by use of a watch is superior to a subjective estimate of duration. For example, one can measure the length of time a patient practices exercises in physical therapy or the amount of time required by a patient in a sheltered workshop to complete an assembly task.

Interval Recording (Time Sampling)

With target behaviors that have moderate to high frequencies and that are not discrete (i.e., do not have clearly discernible beginnings and ends), the interval recording procedure is often used. This procedure is also referred to as time sampling because the behavior is sampled throughout a given time period rather than being recorded at each instance of the behavior. Each period of observation is divided into equal time intervals that typically range from five seconds to one minute. The observer then indicates whether or not the the target behavior occurred during each of the intervals. Interval recording permits the simultaneous observation of several behaviors or several patients. For very high-frequency behaviors, observational intervals should be small enough so that no more than one behavior is apt to occur during each interval. If the problem is more likely to be manifest at a particular time of day or in the presence of another individual, it might be more efficient to designate that situation under which its frequency is to be monitored. For instance, if a patient is much more likely to exhibit the problem when he or she is in an achievement situation, the work environment is a good place to record the instances of its occurrence. This procedure may be used, for example, to observe tics that occur very often throughout the day in patients with spasmodic torticollis and Gilles de la Tourette's syndrome. In this case, the receptionist might observe the patient while seated in the waiting room and record whether or not a tic occurs every fifteen seconds for a ten-minute period. Similarly, a nurse may check on a hospitalized asthmatic patient every hour during the day to record the presence or absence of wheezing.

Permanent Product Measures

An unobtrusive measure (Webb, Campbell, Schwartz, & Sechrest, 1966) that is simple to use, where appropriate, is a measure of permanent product. Some behaviors leave a lasting change in the environment. This procedure involves measuring physical evidence or enduring changes produced in the environment as a result of the target response. Instead of observing the target behavior directly, the staff would observe the presence of a particular product assumed to be the result of the behavior. For example, the presence of urine in the bedpan reflects the patient's fluid intake. Food left on the patient's tray indicates the quantity of food eaten. Similarly, the length of a nail biter's fingernails indicates the extent to which the patient has avoided the habit.

Patient Self-Monitoring

Frequently, you will be concerned with changing a behavior that does not occur in your presence. If a behavior cannot be directly observed by the treatment staff (e.g., thoughts, sexual behavior), you must teach the patient to observe his or her own behavior. This may include when, for how long, or in what situation the behavior occurred. As a first step, a patient may be given an index card on which to record the occurrence of the problem behavior and events associated with the behavior, such as who was present, the patient's mood, what activity was taking place, and what happened when the behavior occurred. This procedure is also useful in obtaining information about the patient's subjective feelings or reactions in specific situations. Thus, in assessing the experience of anxiety or pain, the patient can be asked to rate his or her feelings on a ten-point scale. This helps the patient to differentiate more accurately the intensity of these feelings in different situations. With this information, the therapist can select the most appropriate and easily measurable behavior. Thus, with a patient who suffers from headaches, it is not sufficient to ask the patient to merely keep a record of the number of headaches that occur. This would not provide the necessary information to construct a treatment program, and is not specific enough to permit the patient to comply with the task. Therefore, the patient is also instructed to record such things as the intensity of pain, whether an aura or forewarning was present, and whether pain medication was used.

In addition to providing information about the target behavior and progress throughout treatment, self-monitoring is a valuable procedure in that it facilitates the patient's active participation in the treatment program. However, it is important to recognize that self-monitoring may also be a reactive procedure—that the process of observing or monitoring one's own behavior can result in changes in the frequency of that behavior (Ciminero, Nelson, & Lipinski, 1977). That is, therapeutic improvements in the problem behavior may be noted as a result of the self-monitoring procedure. McFall (1970) noted reduced smoking frequency in patients required to record each cigarette. Since these reactive effects tend to be transitory, it is best to wait a week or so after the patient has started to self-monitor the target behavior (or until the frequency of the behavior has stabilized) before baseline information is collected.

Physiological Measures

In accordance with a multidimensional assessment strategy, a number of physiological measures (e.g., heart rate, blood pressure, muscle tension, respiration), have been used in behavioral treatment programs. Physiological measurement has received considerable application in the area of biofeedback since this treatment procedure directly attempts to modify a particular physiological response. Furthermore, physiological measures have been used as an index of various states of emotional arousal such as anxiety, fear, and sexual excitement. Frequently, several indices of physiological responses will be measured concurrently since there is evidence to suggest that responsivity in the various physiological channels may differ somewhat from one individual to another (Lacey, 1967).

Special equipment and instrumentation, such as the polygraph, are often used to provide accurate physiological measurement of the response indices of particular interest to the therapist. However, the high cost of such equipment may prohibit its availability for many health care practitioners. Fortunately, there are many physiological indices that can be readily measured with little time or cost involved. For example, one can easily measure the pulse and respiration rate of the patient. In addition, the palmar sweat index, a plastic impression method which enumerates sweat gland activity of the fingers, can be used as a simple index of physiological arousal. This measure has been shown to correlate highly with measures of electrodermal activity such as the galvanic skin response (Johnson & Dabbs, 1967).

Functional Analysis of Behavior

The primary goal of behavioral assessment is to identify the environmental events that have a functional or controlling relationship to the problem behavior. Behavioral approaches to assessment and treatment are based on the assumption that most behavior, whether adaptive or dysfunctional, is learned and maintained by environmental events. Consequently, the focus of a functional analysis is on the behavior problem and the current situations or conditions under which the behavior occurs. Past events or experiences are important to the assessment process only insofar as they shed light on the current behavior-environment relationships.

In order to identify the events that are presently maintaining the behavior problem, the therapist determines when and where the behavior occurs and what consequences result when the behavior occurs. Answers to these questions are obtained from a variety of sources, including interviews with the patient and significant others, patient self-monitoring, and observations of the patient in situations and settings where the maladaptive behavior occurs.

Of particular interest to the therapist in the assessment process is an elucidation of those events that occur immediately before or after the problem behavior. In one case of ulcerative colitis, for example, when a patient kept records of her stomach muscle spasms, it became clear that they were associated with such situations as social engagements and the avoidance of conflict with her husband. By identifying events that consistently precede and follow the maladaptive behavior, the therapist discovers potential events in the patient's environment that can be used to alter the problem behavior. From a repeated analysis of the sequence *Antecedent Events→Patient's Behavior→Consequences,* it becomes evident that the maladaptive behavior does not occur by chance, but is related to specific and identifiable environmental events.

Antecedent Events

Antecedent events and consequences have different controlling relationships to behavior. Events that precede the behavior tend to cue or set the occasion for the behavior's occurrence. For instance, a behavior may occur at certain times, in certain situations, or in the presence of specific settings or individuals. For example, some of the cues or setting events that may prompt the alcoholic to drink include being present in a stressful situation, seeing others drinking, and passing a liquor store.

Consequences

In most cases, the events of particular concern to the therapist are those that follow the problem behavior in a consistent and predictable pattern. The consequences of behavior are important to identify because such events may be responsible for maintaining the behavior in its present form.

There are basically two classes of consequences that may follow a behavior: reinforcing or positive consequences, and punishing or aversive consequences. The reinforcing consequences are the payoffs that result when the behavior occurs. If the payoffs continue, contingent on the appearance of the behavior, it is likely that the behavior will continue to occur in the future. For persons in a medical setting, there are many benefits that may accrue as a function of being a patient. As a result, a variety of sick role or other maladaptive behaviors may be maintained by the secondary gains or reinforcing consequences that occur as a function of the problem behavior. Thus, a patient may receive increased attention from family, friends, and medical personnel when he or she becomes ill; or, as a result of a particular medical problem, a patient may be removed from certain unpleasant life responsibilities. Finally, certain medical conditions can have secondary benefits in that they help the patient avoid possible anxiety-producing situations such as social interactions with members of the opposite sex. Therefore, during the assessment process, it is necessary to look for possible reinforcing consequences that may follow an undesirable behavior and contribute to its maintenance.

When aversive or unpleasant consequences consistently follow a behavior, it becomes less likely that the behavior will occur again in the future. Therefore, it is necessary to identify possible aversive events that may result as a consequence of adaptive or desirable behaviors and can decrease the frequency of occurrence of these positive behaviors. For instance, a patient may discontinue taking medication prescribed for a particular medical condition because of unpleasant side effects. Similarly, a patient may not follow an exercise program developed by a physical therapist because of the pain experienced in the attempt. Finally, a man may be unable to maintain an erection during sexual activity with a woman because his sexual performance has been criticized by previous partners. These aversive experiences need to be identified since a goal of treatment is to reduce or minimize the unpleasant events to permit the desirable behavior to occur.

On the other hand, aversive consequences can be used to decrease undesirable behavior as part of the treatment program. For example, response-cost programs are frequently employed to help an individual remain on a therapeutic regimen such as exercise or weight control. When patients do not comply with a prescribed treatment program, they may forfeit the opportunity to engage in pleasurable activities or may have to relinquish part of a security deposit.

Selecting and Implementing an Intervention Program

The most difficult task facing the behavioral clinician is selecting an appropriate treatment strategy for a particular patient. Included in the factors that must be considered in this process are the patient's motivation for change, the cognitive capacity of the patient, availability and cooperation of others, and a clear understanding of the factors maintaining the problem.

As part of the motivational analysis, the therapist attempts to determine what would be different for the patient and the family if the problem behavior did not exist. In discussing a patient's motivation, it is not necessary to view it as a factor that is within the patient and over which the therapist has no control. Instead, it is more useful to regard motivation as the external factors or incentives that occur contingent on a behavior and maintain the occurrence of that behavior. Many of the factors or events that motivate a patient's behavior are external to the patient. Once the therapist identifies these factors, it becomes possible to gain control over the incentives that will assist the therapist in the behavior change process.

Health care professionals are constantly faced with the task of insuring that their patients comply with specific activities and medical treatments, such as controlling their diets, taking medications, exercising, flossing their teeth. Despite the health benefits and avoidance of discomfort and suffering that would result when the patient follows the prescribed regimen, many patients do not comply with the instructions they have received. Reinforcement must be used to increase the probability that patients perform desired behaviors. The assessment procedure should include an exploration of potential reinforcers that are available in the health care settings, and that are appropriate for a particular patient.

What is reinforcing for one patient may not be reinforcing for another. Thus, reinforcers must be identified on an individual basis for each patient. Reinforcers can be selected for a patient using several procedures. A simple method is to ask the patient or significant others what he or she likes to do or wants or what the patient would miss if he or she did not have access to it. To assist the therapist in the assessment of reinforcers, Cautela and Kastenbaum (1967) have developed a self-report measure called the Reinforcement Survey Schedule. On this measure, the patient is asked to rate his degree of preference for a wide variety of activities, events, and items.

Another method for assessing potential reinforcers is to observe the activities or events in which the patient spends the most time when given the opportunity to do so. The Premack Principle (Premack, 1965) specifies that high-frequency behaviors can be used to reinforce or strengthen low-frequency behaviors. This principle can be used with the naturally occurring reinforcers in a given health care setting. Thus, for example, if a patient is observed to spend much of his or her free time resting in bed, watching TV, or socializing with other patients or hospital staff, these activities can be made contingent on the occurrence of low-frequency behaviors that the health care staff would like to increase, such as engaging in certain hygiene behaviors, attending occupational therapy, or eating a particular quantity of food.

A second set of factors that one must consider in designing a behavioral intervention program is the educational history and intellectual capacity of the patient. Although it is important to involve all patients in the planning and implementation of their own treatment program, the degree of involvement will depend to a large extent on these variables. For instance, a number of behavioral self-help manuals and books currently available are written for the layman and are directed at helping the reader to deal with a number of specific problems. This written material can often be used as an adjunct to a behavioral intervention program. However, the patient's ability to comprehend and utilize what he or she has read will obviously determine the use of such material.

The patient's intellectual ability and educational level should also be considered when presenting a conceptualization of the behavior problem within a behavioral framework. For some patients, a behavioral explanation of the problem may be too complex and difficult to understand. This may be illustrated in the case of a sixty-three-year-old man who was treated by the authors (Melamed & Siegel, 1975) for a debilitating obsessive compulsive checking ritual. We hypothesized that the patient's checking of safety features in the house (e.g., stove, electrical outlets, furnace) was maintained by a temporary reduction of his anxiety. The patient, however, attributed his inability to eliminate the checking behavior to a lack of "self-confidence," and he did not perceive the relationship between a buildup of anxiety and the onset of checking behavior. In this case, therefore, the treatment techniques were introduced to the patient as methods for helping to increase his self-control and, thereby, to regain his "self-confidence." Analyzing the problem in this way facilitated the patient's cooperation in the treatment program.

Furthermore, behavioral procedures have been successfully applied to persons with severe cognitive deficits (e.g., the mentally retarded, schizophrenic, autistic). These programs have succeeded without the patient's "understanding" of the treatment procedures as long as the consistent application of rewards and punishments was possible.

Who should be involved in the treatment program? The answer to this question, most simply stated, is anyone who will have direct contact with the patient while the treatment program is in effect. This includes members of the health care team, family, friends, and teachers. Because individuals in the patient's environment may not reinforce appropriate health-related behaviors or may, in fact, reinforce maladaptive behaviors, it is necessary to include these persons in various phases of treatment planning and implementation. If hospital staff, family, and friends do not support the treatment goals and do not cooperate in following the treatment strategy, it is likely that treatment will fail.

Consider, for example, the case of a young child who exhibited severe head banging. He was treated in the hospital with a time-out procedure in which he was removed to a quiet area on the ward immediately upon the occurrence of head banging. Despite a significant and continuous decrease in the frequency of the head-banging behavior, a single instance of failing to promptly remove the child to time-out resulted in a significant increase in head banging. The nurse, who instead held and comforted him because of his distress, felt that this solution was more appropriate. However, the end result was a considerable increase in the child's self-destructive behavior. This case clearly illustrates the importance of gaining the commitment of all persons who will be involved with the patient regardless of whether the procedures used are consistent with their own point of view.

An important consideration in enlisting the cooperation of others in the treatment process is that all those involved in the program need to be reinforced for their efforts. It should be noted at this point that we are all controlled by the consequences of our behavior. If we are not reinforced for what we do, it is unlikely that we will continue to behave in a similar manner. For health care professionals, there are a variety of reinforcers that can be used to maintain enthusiasm for the treatment programs. Such reinforcers include praise and approval from peers and supervisors, satisfaction from the patient's improvement, merit raises, professional advancement and promotions, letters of commendation from supervisors or administrators filed in the employee's personnel records, paid time off to attend professional conferences, and so on.

Determining Which Treatment Procedures to Use

Behavior therapy does not involve a cookbook approach to treating patients—simply applying a prepackaged treatment to standard problems. On the contrary, behavioral intervention programs are individually tailored to a patient's particular problem and the unique circumstances that contribute to its maintenance. The decision to select a given treatment strategy is based largely on the information obtained during the assessment process and on the goals that have been identified for each patient.

The individualized assessment of each maladaptive behavior provides specific guidelines for selecting one approach over another. Therapists should not use techniques simply because they are familiar or congruent with their particular theoretical bias or training. The patient's unique problem is the prime determinant of the treatment strategy.

In examining the antecedent events and consequences of problems within the context of a functional analysis, the therapist has identified the factors that contribute to and maintain the patient's maladaptive behaviors. With this strategy, one can evaluate whether social incompetence or sexual dysfunctions are due to a lack of specific skills or are based primarily on anxiety-mediated concerns. Patients with skill deficits would benefit more from a treatment approach that focuses on helping them acquire alternative responses or more appropriate use of the skills they already have. Such therapies as assertiveness training procedures, role playing, modeling, and operant techniques best fit this purpose. However, if anxiety is the primary debilitating factor, or the patient suffers excessive arousal associated with anger, or lack of arousal due to depression, methods that teach patients to modulate their visceral systems are appropriate. Thus, systematic desensitization and relaxation training would be most beneficial in helping patients control their stress reactions. Biofeedback and hypnotic procedures may be used where the visceral component can be directly shaped. Pharmacological agents may also be useful in lowering arousal.

Often, patients with psychophysiological disorders suffer from an inability to alter their major response tendency when stressed. For example, a patient with a cardiovascular disorder tends to overreact in this system with elevated blood pressure and heart rate acceleration. Hypnosis and biofeedback can help patients with Raynaud's disease, hypertension, asthma, cardiac arrythmias, and so on maintain a better homeostatic balance within their autonomic nervous system. Flooding can be useful in allowing patients to experience more arousal congruent with their fear or anger. Recent research on emotional imagery (Lang, 1977a; 1979) has shown that patients can be trained to have physiological responses that are more congruent with their self-report of arousal in stressful situations. Modeling of an individual confronting stress is another way in which patients can vicariously experience their emotions without negative consequences.

The need to apply cognitive strategies is more evident where the individual's problem is manifested or maintained by ideation, such as self-defeating statements, obsessive thoughts that trigger compulsive acts, and irrational beliefs. These can sometimes be altered by restructuring cognitions, covert rehearsal of new behaviors, and other self-instruction strategies that help patients control the anticipatory experience of stress.

It should be noted that it may be necessary to utilize several behavioral techniques concurrently in a treatment program in order to change most effectively the maladaptive behavior and insure persistence of these changes. It would be unusual to find the emotional states that the patient presents in a treatment context occurring in only one response system. On the other hand, when patients are confronted by emotional stimuli, they seldom show responses in all three systems (verbal, behavioral, and physiological) at comparable levels of intensity. Furthermore, a change in one aspect of the emotional response does not necessarily mean that other response components will also show progress (Lang, 1968; Hodgson & Rachman, 1974). Emotional responses are complex organizations of different behaviors. The laws that govern their interaction are still poorly understood.

Lang (1977b) proposes a vigorous multisystem program for the treatment of aversive emotional states. He further suggests that a pattern analysis of the three response systems could be helpful in guiding therapeutic intervention. Furthermore, he cautions against too narrow an intervention program, in which the assumption would be that change in one behavior will produce concurrent improvement in the other systems.

A careful analysis of the problem can help determine which of the response systems are primarily involved in the patient's stress response. Thus, it might be useful to develop a coding system such as that proposed by Lang (1977b) to provide a structure for treatment. He adapts a system similar to Sheldon's somatotypes, but in which verbal (V), motor (M), and physiological (P) responses in aversive emotional states are rated on a seven-point scale, therefore permitting assessment of these parallel systems. From this point of view, "it would be useful to know that an individual with social anxiety was a 7-1-1 (VMP) rather than a 1-1-7" (p. 183). That is, the person manifests high distress in the verbal system and low distress in the overt-motor and physiological systems. Lang further notes:

> The attention to response characteristics required by such a rating system would mitigate against the assumption that a patient's report of anxiety in the context of the problem situation is *ipse dixit* accompanied by sympathetic activation. Furthermore a cognitive restructuring technique is a more rational treatment choice than biofeedback, in those cases where verbal report is independent of visceral arousal. This orientation would also insure that we did not neglect real visceral distress, while attending exclusively to the modification of language behavior or social skills [p. 183].

The therapist approaching the problem may have some practical limitations that alter the order in which he can attempt to modify the presenting problem. For instance, although biofeedback might be useful, the necessary apparatus may not be available. Instead, the use of general relaxation instructions may need to be substituted with observable responses such as respiration rate being used to provide feedback regarding the patient's effective relaxation. Similarly, despite the need for a cognitive strategy, the patient may lack the intellectual awareness to benefit from this approach. Finally, Keefe, Kopel, and Gordon (1978) indicate that by selecting a treatment procedure that best fits into the patient's style of perceiving and solving problems, the effectiveness of the procedure is maximized. The obvious way to evaluate whether or not you have chosen the best treatment strategy is through the continuous monitoring of change in the problem behaviors.

Evaluating the Intervention Program

Is your treatment program working? Are you succeeding in changing the patient's behavior in the desired direction? A behavioral intervention approach permits you to answer these questions in an objective manner because evaluation of the patient's progress in treatment is an ongoing and systematic process that begins with baseline measurement and continues even after termination of treatment until a reasonable follow-up period has occurred. *Assessment and treatment are interrelated.* Since behavior tends to change in a gradual rather than rapid manner, continuous measurement of the target behavior provides feedback on the extent to which the behavior has changed since the last assessment period. If the evaluation procedures indicate that the patient is not progressing toward the treatment goals after a sufficient period of time, the therapist must reexamine various aspects of the treatment program. The functional analysis may have been incomplete, the behavior change techniques may have been applied inappropriately or inconsistently, or the treatment goals may no longer be appropriate for the patient.

A useful method for assisting the therapist in making treatment relevant decisions is to graph the data collected at each assessment period. Graphing provides clear, visual feedback regarding the effectiveness of the intervention strategies. Finally, a graph of the behavioral data serves as a reinforcer for the therapist, patient, and others in their attempt to follow the treatment procedures by enabling them to see the direct consequences of their efforts.

Recently, a systematic record-keeping procedure called problem-oriented recording has been adopted for use in many health care settings. Problem-oriented recording is compatible with a behavioral approach to assessment because it provides an objective method for continuously monitoring the patient's progress for each of the target behaviors (Katz & Woolley, 1975). A problem-oriented record clearly specifies the behaviors that require modification, how each problem is to be resolved, and how the behavior change is to be measured. Such records summarize the patient's progress and current level of functioning, and outline the intervention strategies to enable all those involved in primary patient care to follow the objectives of the treatment plan consistently. In summary, problem-oriented records are consistent with a behavioral assessment approach because both attempt to specify objective treatment goals and procedures to evaluate the patient's progress toward these goals.

Continuous monitoring of the target behavior provides the clinician with information about whether or not the behavior has, in fact, changed. It does not, however, permit the therapist to specify clearly what has *caused* the change in the behavior. Although the behavior may have changed coincident with the introduction of the treatment program, it is also possible that uncontrolled and extraneous events in the patient's environment may have effected the behavior change.

In order to demonstrate a causal relationship between the treatment program and a change in the target behavior, clinical investigators use several experimental designs. These designs permit the investigator to rule out the influence of factors other than the treatment procedures that may have produced the observed changes in behavior. Baer, Wolf, and Risley (1968), Hersen and Barlow (1976), Kazdin (1975), and Leitenberg (1973) provide a detailed discussion of the various research designs used in the evaluation of behavioral intervention programs.

Reversal Design

One method of demonstrating the efficacy of a particular treatment procedure is a *reversal* or *ABAB design*. This design involves the alternate presentation and withdrawal of the treatment program over time. The strategy followed in this experimental design involves:

1. measurement of the baseline level of the target behavior (also called the A phase),
2. introduction of the treatment program (B phase),
3. withdrawal of treatment and return to baseline conditions (A phase), and finally
4. reinstatement of the treatment program (B phase).

If the target behavior returns to near baseline levels when the treatment program is temporarily discontinued and changes in the predicted direction when the treatment program is reinstated, it is highly probable that the changes in behavior can be attributed to the treatment procedures.

The use of electromyograph (EMG) feedback procedures in the reduction of chronic tension headaches of 16 years duration in a thirty-nine-year-old man in whom extensive neurological examinations revealed no organic disturbance was evaluated by an ABAB withdrawal design (Epstein, Hersen, & Hemphill, 1974). (See Figure 3.1.) The A

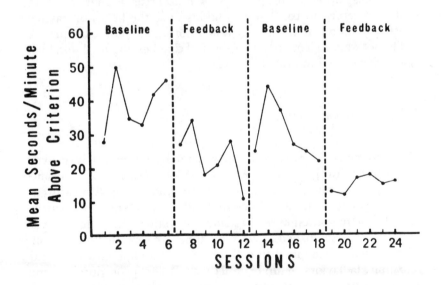

Figure 3.1   Mean seconds per minute that contained integrated responses above criterion microvolt level during baseline treatment.

From L. H. Epstein, M. Hersen, and D. Hemphill, Music feedback in the treatment of tension headache. *Journal of Behavior Therapy and Experimental Psychiatry*, 1975, *5*, 59–63. Copyright © 1974, Pergamon Press, Ltd. Reprinted by permission.

condition was a baseline of the mean number of seconds per minute
that the patient was able to maintain a low level of EMG activity (less
than 10 microvolts). During the B phase the patient received biofeedback, in the form of music, conditional on his ability to maintain a level
of EMG activity below 10 microvolts for each one-minute interval. He
was told to try to keep the music on. Each phase consisted of six
sessions in a three-day period. Return to baseline did result in an
increase in the EMG activity. The final feedback phase produced a
consistently low EMG level. In addition, the patient's self-report of
headache intensity dropped markedly during the feedback as compared to the no-feedback periods.

There are several factors that limit the use of the reversal design
in clinical research. This design assumes that the behavior will return
to baseline levels when the treatment program is withdrawn. However,
for some behaviors, this may not always be the case since once the
behavior has been altered by the treatment procedures, naturally occurring consequences in the environment may continue to maintain
the behavioral changes despite a discontinuation of the treatment program. More important, for practical or ethical reasons, it may be undesirable to return to baseline conditions once the behavior has been
effectively modified by the treatment program. For example, one
would not want to jeopardize the desired changes obtained with highly
aggressive or self-injurious behaviors.

Multiple-Baseline Design

A second method for demonstrating that behavior change is related to
the treatment program is the *multiple-baseline design.* In this experimental design, several different behaviors are simultaneously measured at
different points in time or in several individuals. The same behavior
may also be measured in several different settings. In essence, several
baselines are established at the same time. The treatment program is
then sequentially applied to each behavior. Baseline measures of the
remaining behaviors continue until the treatment procedure is eventually applied to all the baselines. If behavior change is observed only
when the treatment program is introduced sequentially across the
baselines, then it is highly likely that the changes are the result of the
treatment techniques rather than other factors.

The case of a nine-year-old diabetic girl who was taught to comply
with her medical regime in order to maintain her health illustrates how

a multiple-baseline design can be used to evaluate the most effective training procedure (Lowe & Lutzker, 1979). It can be seen in Figure 3.2 that written instructions from the physician (memo) had to be supplemented by a point system in which the patient received reinforcers for increased compliance to foot care and urine testing. However, the use of written instructions alone (memo) was sufficient in procuring excellent compliance with the dietary regime.

Because the multiple-baseline design does not require the withdrawal of treatment, it does not have the problems associated with the

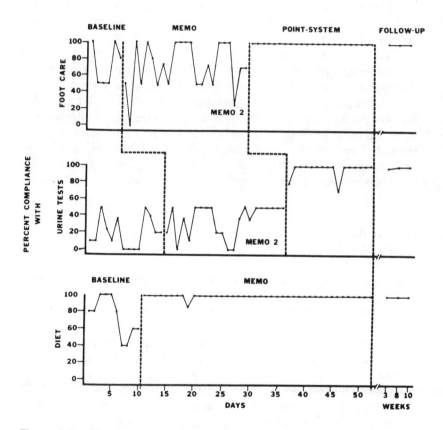

Figure 3.2   Percentage compliance to foot care, urine testing, and diet.

From K. Lowe and J. R. Lutzker, Increasing compliance to a medical regimen with a juvenile diabetic. *Behavior Therapy*, 1979, *10*, 57–64. Copyright © 1979 by the Association for the Advancement of Behavior Therapy. Reprinted by permission.

reversal design. However, one limitation of the multiple-baseline design is that the behaviors may not be completely independent of each other. Therefore, when the treatment program is applied to one baseline, changes may generalize to other baselines, simultaneously affecting the other behaviors.

Control-Group Design

The *control-group design* is another experimental method that has been used to demonstrate the efficacy of behavioral intervention procedures (see Campbell & Stanley, 1963, for a comprehensive review of this topic). In its most basic form, this research design consists of two groups. One group (referred to as the experimental group) receives the treatment program, while the other group (referred to as the control group) receives no treatment. To insure that the two groups differ only in the treatment they receive, subjects are randomly assigned to each group. In addition, control groups are often included for nonspecific factors that may contribute to treatment effects, such as attention, distraction, or expectancy. Changes in behavior are measured before and after treatment is introduced, and the differences between groups are statistically compared. Chapter 8 illustrates the use of the control group design in applied behavioral research.

Programming for the Maintenance of Treatment Effects

A treatment program is effective only if the desired behavior changes are maintained when the patient returns to the natural environment and systematic intervention has terminated. However, there is considerable evidence to indicate that treatment effects frequently do not persist when the treatment program is withdrawn if strategies for maintaining the newly acquired behaviors are not systematically included as part of the treatment program (cf., Marholin, Siegel, & Phillips, 1976; Stokes & Baer, 1977). Although procedures to enhance the durability and transfer of behavioral change beyond the treatment setting have only recently been the focus of systematic investigations, there are currently several promising strategies for the transfer and maintenance of treatment effects (Kazdin, 1975; Marholin & Siegel, 1978).

To insure that behavioral changes produced in treatment will transfer and be maintained in the patient's natural environment, the contingencies of reinforcement must be similar in both settings. If the patient leaves the health care facility, where reinforcement was provided contingent on desired behaviors, and returns to the community, where the contingencies of reinforcement are not consistent with those in the treatment program, it is likely that the newly acquired behaviors will eventually extinguish. It follows, therefore, that people significant for the patient—spouse, parents, teachers, siblings, peers—must be trained to follow the behavioral procedures and provide appropriate contingencies in the natural environment in order to facilitate the maintenance and transfer of treatment effects. Such training is particularly important when the assessment process has revealed that much of the patient's undesirable behavior is a function of the consequences provided in the real world. That is, the contingencies in the natural environment are often so incompatible with the treatment goals that maladaptive rather than desired behavior is reinforced. As a result, training individuals in the patient's community to provide contingencies that are compatible with the desired behavior is likely to facilitate maintenance of behavior change.

Ayllon and Azrin (1968) state in their "relevance of behavior rule" that one should teach behaviors only if they will continue to be reinforced following treatment. Implicit in this rule is the notion that the behaviors should eventually be maintained by naturally occurring reinforcers. However, consequences, such as token reinforcers or electric shock, that do not naturally occur in the patient's daily environment are frequently used to modify undesirable behaviors. Although such events are often necessary to initiate behavior change, consequences must eventually be substituted that are readily available in the natural environment if the resulting behavior changes are to be maintained following treatment. Social reinforcers, such as praise and attention, are important consequences to build into the treatment program because they are more readily available and easier to deliver contingently in the natural environment than most other reinforcers. Reinforcers may also follow naturally from the behavior itself—for example, mobility and independence achieved by a stroke patient who learns to walk again or the enjoyment and social attention obtained by a socially withdrawn child who learns to interact more frequently with his or her peers.

It is important to note that this shift from using planned consequences initially to modify the behaviors to using naturally occurring consequences prior to the termination of treatment must be a gradual process in order to maintain the desired behavior change. Furthermore, contingencies in the natural environment also tend to occur in an unsystematic manner; that is, they often fail to follow the desired behavior or occur long after the behavior has been performed. Therefore, in order to more closely approximate the real-life contingencies of the patient and, thereby, facilitate the transfer and maintenance of the newly acquired behaviors following treatment, reinforcement should be gradually faded to increasingly more intermittent schedules so that less reinforcement is provided, and the time period between the occurrence of the desired behavior and reinforcement should gradually be increased.

A final strategy for enhancing the generalization and maintenance of treatment effects is to teach the patient self-control techniques. Since the posttreatment environment does not always provide adequate reinforcement contingencies, it is advisable to teach the patient to control the consequences of his or her own behavior through self-reinforcement or self-punishment. The patient may also be taught to control the antecedent events of his or her behavior through self-instruction. As O'Leary and Wilson (1975) note, "while an external agent or influence is ultimately critical in maintaining behavior, the individual can learn to prompt and reinforce his own behavior when other people are not available" (p. 473). Self-reinforcement may involve self-administered consequences, such as going to the movies after losing a preselected goal of two pounds for the week, or it may take the form of verbal-symbolic self-reinforcement, such as self-praise for remembering to take medication at the appropriate times. Similarly, several authors have suggested that many behavioral techniques, such as systematic desensitization, teach the patient a general coping skill that can be used in the natural environment without the therapist's direction and control. For example, Goldfried (1971) regards desensitization as a procedure that teaches the patient to use relaxation as a self-control strategy and thus facilitates the patient's dealing with anxiety in a variety of settings and situations.

On occasion, the changes in behavior produced when the behavioral intervention strategies are in effect may not be maintained when the treatment program has ended. Because of the possibility that the therapeutic gains may not always endure after treatment, it is useful to conduct periodic follow-up evaluations with the patient. A follow-up assessment may indicate the need for "booster" sessions in which various aspects of the treatment program are temporarily reinstated until the target behavior occurs again at a desirable level.

Terminating Treatment

When is the treatment program discontinued? Formal termination of treatment is determined by the goals established for each patient. Once the evaluation procedures indicate that the patient is consistently performing the desired behaviors—that is, when the terminal goals of the treatment programs have been reached—contact with the patient may gradually be lessened until therapist-mediated intervention is completely terminated. Throughout treatment, the patient has been encouraged to practice newly acquired skills in the settings where the problematic behaviors occurred. In essence, the patient has been taught a general strategy for approaching new problems as they arise.

Summary

A functional analysis is the basic assessment tool of the behavior therapist. A behavioral program defines the behavioral excesses, deficits, and inappropriate stimulus controls, as well as the patient's assets. The treatment program outline is problem oriented, and proceeds in a stepwise fashion from the defining of behaviors to be changed to deciding how and when the treatment is to be terminated. Methods are described for objectively defining which behaviors constitute the problem in order to help the patient and therapist to establish therapy goals together.

In order to evaluate the effectiveness of the intervention program, it is necessary to have baseline records of the pertinent maladaptive behaviors prior to treatment. Since these behaviors may be reflected in the patient's verbal report of his or her experience and in somatic arousal responses as well as actual overt motor acts, an attempt to sample a broad range of responses is recommended. The indications of where the treatment efforts should be directed evolves from an analysis of these three response systems, their degree of independence, and their interaction. Self-report questionnaires, behavioral sampling techniques (event recording, duration recording, interval recording), permanent product measures, self-monitoring, and physiological measures are described. By identifying events that consistently precede and follow the maladaptive behavior, the therapist discovers potential events in the patient's life that can be used to change the problem behavior.

The decision to select a given treatment strategy is based on the functional analysis of the individual's behavior. Continuous monitoring of the problem behaviors, including the use of graphic or verbal feedback of progress, assists in problem-oriented decision making. Assessment and treatment are interrelated. The physical record summarizes the patient's progress and his current level of functioning, and it indicates whether the intervention is effective or needs to be modified.

Research procedures are discussed that permit assessment of the causal relationship between the treatment and the change in behavior. A reversal design involves the alternate presentation and withdrawal of the treatment program over time. The multiple-baseline design allows for the simultaneous assessment of several different behaviors or of the same behavior across several different settings. It does not require the withdrawal of treatment in order to assess its effectiveness. The control-group design compares the crucial treatment elements against other therapies designed to change the behavior, or a no-treatment sampling of the effects of time, or effects of repeated measurement.

Behavioral treatment is not terminated until the therapist can be assured that there has been a shift from the use of planned consequences for more adaptive behavior to those naturally occurring consequences in the real-life situation of the patient. In order to approximate real-life contingencies more closely and, thereby, facilitate transfer and maintenance of the newly acquired behaviors, the reinforcements should be gradually lessened. Patients should be taught self-control procedures, how to recognize potential problem situations, and to deliver rewards to themselves contingent upon appropriate independent behaviors.

References

Ayllon, T., & Azrin, N. H. *The token economy: A motivational system for therapy and rehabilitation.* Englewood Cliffs, N.J.: Prentice-Hall, 1968.

Baer, D. M., Wolf, M. M., & Risley, T. R. Some current dimensions of applied behavior analysis. *Journal of Applied Behavior Analysis,* 1968, *1,* 91–97.

Beck, A. T. *Depression: Clinical, experimental and theoretical aspects.* New York: Harper & Row, 1967.

Campbell, D. T., & Stanley, J. C. Experimental and quasi-experimental designs for research and teaching. In N. L. Gage (Ed.), *Handbook of research on teaching.* Chicago: Rand McNally, 1963.

Cautela, J. R., & Kastenbaum, R. A reinforcement survey schedule for use in therapy, training and research. *Psychological Reports,* 1967, *20,* 1115–1130.

Ciminero, A. R., Nelson, R. O., & Lipinski, D. Self-monitoring procedures. In A. R. Ciminero, K. S. Calhoun, & H. E. Adams (Eds.), *Handbook of behavioral assessment.* New York: John Wiley & Sons, 1977.

Epstein, L. H., Hersen, M., & Hemphill, D. Music feedback in the treatment of tension headache: An experimental case study. *Journal of Behavior Therapy and Experimental Psychiatry,* 1974, *5,* 59–63.

Goldfried, M. R. Systematic desensitization as training in self-control. *Journal of Consulting and Clinical Psychology,* 1971, *37,* 228–234.

Hersen, M., & Barlow, D. H. *Single case experimental designs: Strategies for studying behavior change.* New York: Pergamon Press, 1976.

Hodgson, R., & Rachman, S. Desynchrony in measures of fear. *Behaviour Research and Therapy,* 1974, *12,* 319–326.

Johnson, R., & Dabbs, J. M. Enumeration of active sweat glands: A simple physiological indicator of psychological changes. *Nursing Research,* 1967, *16,* 273–276.

Kanfer, F. H., & Saslow, G. Behavioral diagnosis. In C. M. Franks (Ed.), *Behavior therapy: Appraisal and status.* New York: McGraw-Hill, 1969.

Katz, R. C., & Woolley, F. R. Improving patients records through problem orientation. *Behavior Therapy,* 1975, *6,* 119–124.

Kazdin, A. E. *Behavior modification in applied settings.* Homewood, Ill.: Dorsey Press, 1975.

Keefe, F. J., Kopel, S. A., & Gordon, S. B. *A practical guide to behavioral assessment.* New York: Springer, 1978.

Lacey, J. I. Somatic response patterning and stress: Some revisions of activation theory. In M. H. Apple & R. Trumbull (Eds.), *Psychological stress.* New York: Appleton-Century-Crofts, 1967.

Lang, P. J. Fear reduction and fear behavior: Problems in treating a construct. In J. M. Schlien (Ed.), *Research in psychotherapy*, Vol. 3. Washington, D.C.: American Psychological Association, 1968.

———. Imagery in therapy: An information processing analysis of fear. *Behavior Therapy,* 1977, *8,* 862–886. (a).

———. Physiological assessment of anxiety and fear. In J. D. Cone & R. P. Hawkins (Eds.), *Behavioral assessment: New directions in clinical psychology.* New York: Brunner/Mazel, 1977 (b).

———. A bio-informational theory of emotional imagery. *Psychophysiology,* 1979, *16,* 495–512.

Lazarus, A. A. *Behavior therapy and beyond.* New York: McGraw-Hill, 1971.

Leitenberg, H. The use of single-case methodology in psychotherapy research. *Journal of Abnormal Psychology,* 1973, *82,* 87–101.

LoPiccolo, J., & Steger, J. C. The sexual interaction inventory: A new instrument of assessment of sexual dysfunction. *Archives of Sexual Behavior,* 1974, *3,* 585–595.

Lowe, K., & Lutzker, J. R. Increasing compliance to a medical regimen with a juvenile diabetic. *Behavior Therapy,* 1979, *10,* 57–64.

McFall, R. M. Effects of self-monitoring on normal smoking behavior. *Journal of Consulting and Clinical Psychology,* 1970, *35,* 135–142.

Marholin, D., & Siegel, L. J. Beyond the law of effect: Programming for the maintenance of behavioral change. In D. Marholin (Ed.), *Child behavior therapy.* New York: Gardner Press, 1978.

Marholin, D., Siegel, L. J., & Phillips, D. Treatment and transfer: A search for empirical procedures. In M. Hersen, R. M. Eisler, & P. M. Miller (Eds.), *Progress in behavior modification,* Vol. 3. New York: Academic Press, 1976.

Mash, E. J., & Terdal, L. G. (Eds.). *Behavior therapy assessment.* New York: Springer, 1976.

Melamed, B. G., & Siegel, L. J. Self-directed in vivo treatment of an obsessive-compulsive checking ritual. *Journal of Behavior Therapy and Experimental Psychiatry,* 1975, *6,* 31–36.

O'Leary, K. D., & Wilson, G. T. *Behavior therapy: Application and outcome.* Englewood Cliffs, N.J.: Prentice-Hall, 1975.

Premack, D. Reinforcement theory. In D. Levine (Ed.), *Nebraska symposium on motivation.* Lincoln: University of Nebraska Press, 1965.

Rathus, S. A. A thirty-item schedule for assessing assertive behavior. *Behavior Therapy,* 1973, *4,* 298–306.

Stokes, T. F., & Baer, D. M. An implicit technology of generalization. *Journal of Applied Behavior Analysis,* 1977, *10,* 349–367.

Stuart, R. B., & Stuart, F. *Marital precounseling inventory.* Champaign, Ill.: Research Press, 1972.

Taylor, J. A. A personality scale of manifest anxiety. *Journal of Abnormal and Social Psychology,* 1953, *48,* 285–290.

Webb, E. J., Campbell, D. T., Schwartz, R. D., & Sechrest, L. *Unobtrusive measures: Non-reactive research in the social sciences.* Chicago: Rand McNally, 1966.

Wolpe, J., & Lang, P. J. A fear survey schedule for use in behavior therapy. *Behaviour Research and Therapy,* 1964, *2,* 27–30.

Part II

APPLICATIONS OF BEHAVIOR THERAPY TO HEALTH CARE PROBLEMS

4

Patient Management

Recent advances in the behavioral treatment of specific physical disorders are widely recognized. Less well-known, but of equal importance, are the contributions of behavior therapy in the area of general patient management. The purpose of this chapter is to introduce a number of behavioral strategies in patient management that have been successfully applied by health care practitioners. Inadequate or inconsistent adherence to prescribed medical regimens is an especially vexing and pervasive problem for the primary care physician and other health professionals. This chapter will present techniques for dealing with patient behaviors that interfere with the effectiveness of treatment. We will also consider methods for enlisting the cooperation and enhancing the motivation of the patient to participate in both preventive and ameliorative aspects of health problems. Finally, behavioral techniques will be discussed for eliminating fears associated with medical procedures or equipment that result in avoidance and interfere with effective treatment.

Behavioral Model of Somatic Disorders

A consideration of health and illness from a social-behavioral perspective is a prerequisite for understanding factors that enhance or impede compliance with treatment programs. It is widely recognized that physical and constitutional factors interact with environmental, psychological, and social events in the development and maintenance of most illnesses (Kimball, 1970). Regardless of the specific etiology of bodily dysfunction, there is evidence that learning or conditioning mechanisms can be a significant factor in a variety of somatic disorders. Research has demonstrated, for example, that autonomic (visceral) responses can be affected and modified by both respondent (classical) or operant (instrumental) conditioning (Blanchard & Young, 1974; Miller, 1969; Schwartz, 1973). Until recently, it was assumed that autonomic responses were "involuntary" and, therefore, could be modified only through respondent conditioning. However, recent clinical and research evidence indicates that autonomic responses such as heart rate (Bleecker & Engle, 1973), blood pressure (Elder, Ruiz, Deabler, & Dillenkoffer, 1973), and others may be subject to voluntary control through operant conditioning mechanisms.

Davison and Neale (1974) have suggested that the primary role of operant and respondent conditioning in physical disorders "is probably best viewed as a factor that can exacerbate an already existing illness rather than cause it" (p. 157). In Chapter 2, the theoretical basis for operant and respondent conditioning was discussed. Through the process of respondent conditioning, involuntary or reflexive behaviors can be made to occur in the presence of a previously neutral stimulus (a stimulus that does not naturally elicit the physiological response). After repeated pairings of the neutral stimulus with the unconditioned or natural stimulus, the neutral stimulus itself acquires the ability to elicit the physiological response. This is illustrated in the case of an eight-year-old child who experienced abdominal pain for several days as a result of gastrointestinal symptoms developed during a viral infection. The child's drinking of milk during the illness appeared to worsen the stomachaches, and the pain became more intense. As a result of the learned association between the abdominal pain and the milk, the act of drinking milk alone was sufficient to elicit the stomach pains, even after the virus was no longer present. Thus, each time the child attempted to drink milk, the pains appeared for a short period of time.

In addition, stomach pains can be shaped and maintained by operant conditioning mechanisms. In the process of operant conditioning, a response occurs and is affected by its contingent consequences. The response is then more or less likely to occur in the future, depending on whether the consequences are reinforcing, punishing, or neutral. For example, a number of positive consequences, sometimes referred to as secondary gains, may follow in a contiguous manner the occurrence of stomachaches. The child may receive considerable adult attention and comfort for the reported pain. In addition, when the stomachache occurs, the child may stay home from school or avoid unpleasant activities such as completing household chores or doing homework. These consequences can function as reinforcers that maintain the symptomatic behavior, despite the fact that the illness, which may have initially precipitated the abdominal pain, no longer exists. Since the symptoms of many health problems are manifested as behaviors (in this case, complaints of stomach pains), the behaviors may subsequently be affected and modified by environmental factors.

With somatic disorders, knowledge of the behavioral etiology is not necessarily essential for developing a behavioral treatment program. Similarly, the efficacy of a particular treatment strategy does not necessarily provide information about the etiology of a given disorder treated by that approach (cf., Davison & Neale, 1974). Because events in the patient's environment may currently maintain the symptomatic behavior, regardless of the original cause, it is essential to assess the relationship between environmental factors and the illness or bodily dysfunction. This is accomplished by performing a functional analysis of behavior outlined in Chapter 3.

It is important to emphasize that many somatic disorders result in tissue damage or other physical changes in the body's organ systems. This is true regardless of whether the disorder is of an organic or nonorganic (e.g., environmental) origin. A similar issue involves the potential of a clear organic cause for a somatic disorder that typically has a nonorganic etiology. For example, enuresis can be caused by physical defects in the urinary tract, by neurological disorders, or by urinary-tract infections. Despite the fact that organic causes account for less than 10 percent of the cases of enuresis (Pierce, 1967), should any of these conditions exist, the effectiveness of behavioral interventions could be impeded; the disorder might even worsen if treatment is pursued in the context of inadequate medical evaluation. Therefore, where any physical or somatic complaints are presented as a problem, a thorough medical examination should always be completed prior to using behavioral treatment approaches. It is important to note that medical treatment does not preclude a coincident behavioral intervention. Behavioral techniques can serve a useful and highly effective adjunctive role in the direct treatment of physical disorders and indirectly through patient management. The simultaneous application of behavioral methods and medical procedures has been effective in preventing the exacerbation of symptomatic behaviors and in alleviating discomfort in a great variety of somatic disorders. In the treatment of asthma, for instance, behavioral techniques have been effective in providing symptomatic relief and in reducing abnormal responding of the respiratory tract during an asthmatic attack (e.g., Davis, Saunders, Creer, & Chai, 1973; Kahn, Staerk, & Bonk, 1973; Moore, 1965). In addition, behavioral approaches have been useful in modifying any dysfunctional behavior patterns that may have developed while the medical problem or illness was in existence. For example, patients who have been bedridden for extended periods of time may require an intervention program to increase their activity level.

Health and Illness Behavior

The Sick-Role Concept

The onset of illness and being sick is a social-psychological process as well as a physical process. Parsons (1951, 1958) has proposed a social-psychological conceptualization of the sick-role that suggests that there are both implicit and explicit rules in our society about being sick. Once an individual has become ill or develops a disability, the label of sick or ill can affect both the expectations that others have regarding the sick person's behavior and the expectations of the patient toward his or her own behavior. Twaddle and Hessler (1977) have noted that "an identity as sick is consequential. Not only is a sick person likely to behave differently from one defined as 'well,' but also this difference in behavior is permitted and expected" (p. 116). Thus the sick-role is associated with a particular set of privileges and obligations. The responses that the individual receives from others for being sick often reinforces the sick-role behavior, resulting in considerable dependency on the part of the patient.

The sick-role as outlined by Parsons (1951) is characterized by four basic features:

1.   Illness is involuntary and, therefore, the sick person is not responsible for his or her condition. Furthermore, the individual is unable to relieve his or her condition without professional assistance and therapeutic intervention. It follows from this that being labeled as sick places the individual in a position of dependence and helplessness since he or she must be cared for by others (Twaddle, 1972).

2.   Being labeled as sick by a member of the health care profession legitimizes role behavior that exempts the individual from performance of his or her typical social responsibilities and obligations.

Thus, the individual is permitted to relinquish his or her customary duties in the areas of employment, family, education, and so on.

3. The sick-role is legitimate only insofar as the individual engages in behaviors that indicate his or her desire to quickly return to a state of health.

4. Finally, the sick-role carries with it an obligation on the part of the individual to seek out and cooperate with competent health care providers and other treatment agents in order to improve his or her health-related behaviors.

Behavioral Expectations of the Sick-Role

From a behavioral perspective, the sick-role concept and its associated expectations and obligations guide the patient's behavior and the way in which others respond toward the patient (Berkanovic, 1972) by providing acceptable behavioral standards. Of particular importance are the consequences that are provided for the patient's sick-role or illness behavior. As Ullmann and Krasner (1976) have suggested, an individual "learns what is expected of him in terms of what behaviors are likely to be positively reinforced, and, just as important, what the probable consequences are of not emitting the behavior" (p. 89). Ullmann and Krasner (1976) further note that the role behavior that a patient assumes "may be viewed as a series of interrelated behaviors appropriate to a given situation and learned through past experience" (p. 89).

In summary, following the act of being labeled as sick, the individual responds differently, as do others toward him or her. This is beautifully illustrated in Rosenhan's (1973) pseudopatient research, which demonstrates that becoming a patient changes the perceptions of others. He had several graduate students and psychologists gain admission to mental hospitals by learning to verbalize delusional ideas to hospital admissions personnel. Not only were these "patients" accepted for inpatient treatment, but some of them had great difficulty convincing the staff that they were research participants and were capable of leaving the hospital. For instance, the staff interpreted the note-taking behavior of the pseudopatients as evidence of paranoid and delusional behavior; their pacing activity, which often occurred in response to boredom, was taken as an indication of "extreme agitation." Some of the pseudopatients spent as much as fifty-two days in the hospital. Only the true patients questioned their presence on the ward.

Secondary Benefits of the Sick-Role

Twaddle (1969) demonstrated that the more individuals accepted a notion of themselves as sick or disabled, the more likely their behavior was to change in the direction of the disability. Therefore, among persons reporting a medical condition, those who perceived themselves as sick (i.e., accepted the sick-role as appropriate) were more likely than those who did not conceive of themselves as sick or ill to seek opportunities to remove themselves from normal activities and responsibilities of daily life. In addition, there is evidence that individuals who receive preferential treatment from family members and friends as a result of an illness are apt to display considerable disability behavior, such as dependence, helplessness, and avoidance of ordinary social responsibilities.

Thus, while there may be a number of unpleasant aspects of having a particular disease or disability, there are also many potential benefits or *secondary gains* from an illness that can serve as reinforcers for the patient. These reinforcing consequences may, in turn, promote and maintain the patients' illness role and interfere with cooperation with treatment agents that would facilitate improvement of their health-related condition.

Creer and Christian (1976) have pointed out that significant others and health care personnel frequently get caught up in what they refer to as an "illness trap." They note that in dealing with persons with chronic illnesses and disabilities, family, friends, and treatment agents in health care settings typically give most of their attention to sick-role and maladaptive behaviors (e.g., dependence on others, health-related complaints, frequently calling for nursing assistance, noncompliance with treatment programs). As a result, the very patient behaviors that others find annoying and that interfere with the successful outcome of treatment may be reinforced and, thereby, become predominant in the patient's repertoire of behaviors. Although those who work in health care settings are aware of the need to encourage the patient's independence in performing behaviors that promote and maintain health, the manner in which they respond to patients does not always facilitate this goal of active patient participation in the treatment process. Instead, Mikulic (1971) notes that hospital staff typically conceive of their role as "doing for" the patient rather than prompting and reinforcing independence or self-care behaviors. The result is that patients learn that asking for assistance rather than trying to do things for themselves will elicit the attention of others. Thus, dependent behaviors are reinforced and maintained.

Mikulic (1971) observed whether nursing staff reinforced dependent or independent patient behaviors. Observations of patient-staff interactions were conducted over a six-week period in an extended health care facility. Independent behaviors were defined as performing activities of daily living without assistance or verbally indicating an ability to perform an activity (e.g., "I can dress myself"), rather than indicating disability-related behaviors (e.g., "I can't do my exercises because my back hurts"). The observations revealed that the nursing staff were providing considerably more positive reinforcement for dependent patient behaviors than for independent behaviors. Consistent with these consequences, there was a concomitant decrease in independent behaviors (due to extinction as a result of nonreinforcement) and an increase in dependent behaviors. The results of this study have important implications for health care providers. They clearly indicate the need to remain cognizant of the way in which treatment agents, family, and friends respond to the patient's behavior.

Learning Model of Chronic Illness

A comprehensive model of chronic illness behavior from a learning framework has been formulated by Wooley, Blackwell, and Winget (in press). According to these investigators, the behavior patterns characteristic of persons with chronic illnesses are acquired through three basic learning processes:

1. vicarious learning, particularly in childhood, by observing models display sick-role behavior in response to illness, or through observing other patients reinforced for illness behavior while in the hospital,
2. direct social reinforcement of illness behavior by significant others and health care practitioners, and
3. avoidance learning in which the individual is reinforced by a reduction in anxiety through exhibiting illness behaviors that enable the person to avoid or withdraw from unpleasant or unfavorable social relationships and occupational responsibilities.

Support for this model of illness behavior is presented by Wooley and her colleagues in a series of studies of over 300 patients treated for various somatic disorders in the hospital. Wooley, Blackwell, and Winget (in press), observed patients with chronic illnesses on a hospital ward and found that several maladaptive behaviors tended to be exhibited by these patients. Some of the most frequently occurring behaviors included:

1. demands for attention and care, such as asking for help with activities of daily living and frequent requests for personal care and medication,
2. helpless behaviors, such as inactivity, unresponsiveness to suggestions from the staff, and complaints of inability to do things without assistance from others, and finally,
3. excessive compliance behaviors such as expressions of appreciation for every action of the physician and other hospital staff.

These and other behaviors, it is suggested, elicit "care-taking" responses from others, which in turn reinforce and maintain the undesirable illness behaviors. Thus, a cycle is set in motion that perpetuates sick-role behaviors in the patient by maximizing the satisfactions or pay-offs for being ill.

In order to determine the manner in which patients promote and maintain care-taking behaviors in others, Wooley and Blackwell (1975) investigated the social contingencies that were present on a hospital ward for patients with a variety of illnesses. This was accomplished with ten "do-it-yourself tokens" that were given to each patient. The tokens consisted of blank forms on which the patients could specify changes in behavior that they wished to encourage in other patients or hospital staff or to reinforce an individual for behaviors that the patient wanted to see continued. Ward personnel were also presented with ten tokens, and they were asked to distribute them to other staff members with instructions similar to those given to the patients. After all the tokens had been distributed by the patients and staff, they were collected in order to analyze the content of the behaviors specified on the tokens. The tokens were analyzed using four possible categories:

1. care-taking behaviors (e.g., kindness, sympathy, support, favors),
2. sociability (e.g., taking part in social activities, being nice to others),
3. communication (e.g., clarifying, providing information, giving feedback), and
4. achievement (sharing interest in or achieving relevant goals, such as working toward improvement of the disorder that hospitalized the patient).

An analysis of the patterns of token distribution by the patients revealed that 70 percent of the tokens were given by the patients for care-taking behaviors and 22 percent for sociability. Only 5 percent of the tokens were for communication and 3 percent for achievement-related behaviors. The pattern of token exchange for the staff was nearly the exact opposite of that found for the patient group. The majority of the tokens (86 percent) were given to other staff members for behaviors dealing with achievement or communication. It is also interesting to note that only 6 percent of the tokens were used by the patients to request changes in behavior from others, while 24 percent of the tokens used by the staff were for this purpose. Furthermore, whereas the patients requested behavior change almost exclusively in the area of providing better care for themselves and others, most of the requests for change in the staff group were in the areas of task performance or communication.

These findings have particularly important implications for those individuals who work in health care settings. They indicate that many patients attempt to meet their needs and obtain reinforcement by teaching others to respond to them in a manner that can perpetuate maladaptive illness behaviors.

A comprehensive treatment program designed to reinforce independence in the patient and to intervene with patient behaviors that elicit care-taking responses from others has been developed by Wooley, Blackwell, and Winget (in press). Each facet of the program is designed to reduce any secondary gains that the patient may obtain from having an illness or a disability by reinforcing response patterns that are incompatible with illness behaviors. Thus, for example, environmental contingencies are arranged to occur when the patient displays independent rather than dependent behaviors. In addition, complaints of pain and verbalizations of helplessness are discouraged through nonreinforcement, or are restricted to specific occasions. To maximize opportunities for the acquisition of independent behaviors, patients are actively involved in setting their own behavioral goals, in designing a treatment program along with the hospital staff, and in keeping records of their progress in treatment. Family members also attend therapy sessions with the patient in which they are made aware of patterns of interaction in the family that reinforce illness behavior. They also learn how to support the patient's development of independent behaviors by providing appropriate reinforcement contingencies. Finally, to reduce the patient's anxiety and avoidance behaviors that result from skill deficits, especially social skill deficits, the patient is given training to enable him or her to cope more effectively in the problem area. Fordyce and his colleagues (Fordyce, 1971; Fordyce,

Fowler, Lehmann, DeLateur, Sand, & Trieschmann, 1973) also rearrange the environmental contingencies so that patients are rewarded for approximations toward adaptive behaviors. This treatment program with patients in rehabilitation settings is described in Chapter 7.

Following an illness or injury, many patients continue to present disability behavior that is disproportionate to any existing organic or physical problems. Invalidism resulting from anxiety and depression is often observed in patients following a serious illness, such as a cardiovascular disorder. In such individuals, disability behaviors may manifest themselves as a fear of returning to a premorbid level of work activity, despite assurances from a physician that a physical impairment no longer exists (Groden & Cheyne, 1972). There is eivdence, for example, that as many as 50 percent of the patients treated for cardiac diseases remain unemployed for excessive periods of time as a result of anxiety and depression related to their illness (Stoeckle, Zola, & Davidson, 1976).

Brown (1978) notes that patients may exhibit work-related fears because of their belief that work contributed to the onset of the illness and that a return to their previous employment will result in the recurrence of the illness with even more extensive physical impairment than resulted from the initial episode of the disorder. For example, Brown (1978) presents the case of a thirty-one-year-old man who developed a serious work phobia following open-heart surgery involving a valve repair. The patient, who was employed as a life insurance salesman, had not returned to work for fourteen months following surgery, despite medical clearance from both the cardiologist and surgeon. Fearing that the anxiety and stress from his competitive work situation would result in tearing of the sutures around the new valve and lead to a more serious physical problem, he remained at home and engaged in minimal physical activity. In addition, the patient was frequently severely depressed. He remained in bed until late in the day, and became increasingly isolated from social contacts. Finally, he ceased all sexual activity, which caused marital problems.

To reduce the patient's debilitating work-related fears, he was seen in therapy on an outpatient basis. Following training in progressive muscle relaxation, a hierarchy of twenty-five items related to his work fears was constructed for use in systematic desensitization. Some of the items on the hierarchy, for example, dealt with the anxiety associated with getting leads on a prospective client for insurance or closing a deal.

The patient's depression was treated by increasing the appropriate social reinforcement that he received from his environment. This was accomplished by involving the patient's family in the treatment program. Family members were instructed to ignore depressive behaviors such as crying, remaining at home all day, or self-deprecating statements such as "I am no good to anyone now" and to reinforce increasing attempts to return to premorbid levels of work activity and social behavior. Specific homework assignments, such as telephoning prospective clients, were carried out each week by the patient in an effort to increase both the frequency and duration of adaptive activities. In addition, the patient was instructed to keep records of various activities, such as the number of clients that the patient visited or the number of insurance forms he completed.

Behavioral records of the patient's progress in therapy and self-reports of levels of stress indicated that there were considerable reductions in complaints of anxiety and depression within six weeks after treatment began. These records also served to reinforce the patient's progress and sense of accomplishment. He reported feeling more relaxed, and there was a marked increase in his work activity. There was also a concomitant increase in social behaviors to earlier levels.

A six-month follow-up assessment, after treatment had terminated, revealed that the patient was maintaining levels of work behavior that were five times greater than his activity prior to treatment. He was more self-confident, and had made more appropriate adjustments to the physical limitations of his illness.

Increasing Compliance with Therapeutic Regimens

Patient noncompliance with prescribed medical regimens is a problem of major importance to primary care physicians and other health care providers. Failure to adhere to the treatment program (e.g., failing to take medication for hypertension) can considerably reduce the therapeutic benefits for the patient, can impede recovery from an illness or injury, or can seriously jeopardize the health of the patient, depending on the disorder for which he or she is being treated (Gillum & Barsky, 1974; Ludwig & Adams, 1968). Nonadherence to medical advice may be manifested as a failure to: "(a) enter into or continue a treatment program, (b) keep follow-up or referral appointments, (c) take prescribed medication, and (d) restrict or change one's activities, including smoking, diet, and exercise" (Kasl, 1975, p. 6).

The ultimate success of any treatment regimen depends on the patient's cooperation and compliance with all aspects of the program.

Noncompliance presents a particulary difficult problem when therapeutic intervention is conducted on an outpatient basis. Under such conditions, close supervision is impossible, and the patient or significant others (e.g., parents, in the case of young patients) must take the major responsibility for managing their own illness or disability. Addressing the specific problem of adherence to medication regimens, Stimson (1974) elaborates on this point:

> In general practice much of the treatment given to patients is in the form of drugs and medicines to be self-administered by the patient. Because the patient is responsible for using the medicine that has been prescribed he has the potential for considerable autonomy in the management of his treatment. The doctor may control which drugs the patient gets, and how much of them, but the doctor is not present to control how they are used [p. 97].

The literature on patient compliance with medical regimens demonstrates that many patients, even when the doctor's communication has been sufficient, substantially deviate from the prescribed treatment program or fail to follow any of the physician's recommendations (Davis, 1966; Marston, 1970). Studies on noncompliant behavior consistently reveal some degree of patient failure to follow the medical treatment regardless of the regimen prescribed or disorder being treated. Estimates of the rates of noncompliance range from 15 percent to 93 percent (Davis, 1966) and from 19 percent to 72 percent (Stimson, 1974). For example, using urine analysis as an estimate of compliance, Charney and his colleagues (1967) investigated the rates of correct medication taking in families who had been given a ten-day course of penicillin to treat otitis media and pharyngitis. On the fifth day of treatment 81 percent of the patients were taking the medication appropriately; on the ninth day, 56 percent, and by the end of the treatment period, only 13 percent were taking the medication as prescribed. Similarly, Johnson (1973) found that of patients prescribed medication for depression, 16 percent had ceased taking their medication during the first week of treatment (without their physician's knowledge), 41 percent had stopped within two weeks, and 68 percent had stopped within one month after treatment was initiated.

In view of the difficulties in establishing patient compliance with medication, diet, and exercise regimens, it might be useful to conceptualize illness in terms of the manner in which symptoms or the absence of these relate to the behavior of the patient. When people are ill, the presence of symptoms forms a focal event for reacting to medical advice (Kasl & Cobb, 1966). However, not all illnesses are equally reflected by the prominence of symptoms. The fact that adherence to a treatment program is more likely to occur where the medical relief of symptoms accompanies the complex behaviors associated with compliance (Haynes, 1976) argues for the usefulness of conceptualizing illnesses into three classes:

1. illness in which an exacerbation of physical symptoms accompanies the worsening of the disorder and is effectively reduced by compliance with the medical regimen (e.g., taking an antibiotic to relieve the temperature and discomfort of a viral infection),
2. illness that is chronic in nature and whose symptoms are fairly stable despite the regimen (e.g., mutiple sclerosis), and
3. illness in which the patient is asymptomatic, despite the continuing of chronic illness with serious future consequences (e.g., hypertension).

If one views the behavior of the individual within the framework of stimulus control properties of the symptoms, it becomes evident that in the above conception of disease processes, there is not equal reinforcement for maintaining health care behaviors. The delay of relief in symptoms may, in fact, encourage the patient to seek more immediate gratification, such as avoidance of unpleasant side effects of medication or increased satisfaction of high carbohydrates in a diabetic patient despite the long-term risk of offsetting the metabolic balance and precipitating ketoacidosis. The cue function of the symptom is affected, as are other maladaptive behaviors, by the consequences of the behavior that follows. Therefore, if the patient with hives is discomforted by the itching that results, scratching that may inadvertently worsen the illness temporarily achieves relief and is therefore reinforced. In the same way, it has been noted that mothers stop giving penicillin to children with acute infections when the symptoms subside, despite the doctor's instructions to complete a ten-day course of the antibiotic (Becker, Drachman, & Kirscht, 1972). Therefore, in the discussion of compliance, it is important to monitor the behavior that typically follows adherence to the regimen.

The patient's interpretation of symptoms is also important in understanding how it influences them to voluntarily act to ward off future health problems. Beliefs about the nature of illness may influence specific actions taken by the individual. Kirscht and Rosenstock (1979) reviewed literature that suggested that "an action was thought to be more likely where, in the presence of a threat, the action was seen as efficacious, and possible at a tolerable cost" (p. 203). Thus, patients will seek out preventive inoculations or tolerate horrendous debilitating effects of cancer chemotherapy and radiation if they define the illness as a real personal threat and feel that there is likely to be a benefit from the treatment.

Factors Influencing Compliance

Given the evidence for the low rates of compliance with therapeutic medical programs, a number of investigators have attempted to identify a variety of social, psychological, and physical factors that may contribute to (and also predict) noncompliance behaviors in patients (e.g., Becker, Drachman, & Kirscht, 1972; Davis, 1966, 1967; Levy, 1978; Vincent, 1971). In a comprehensive review of the research in this area, Haynes and Sackett (1974) note that the relationship of over 200 factors to patient noncompliance with medical regimens has been studied. Of these factors, only a limited number, such as complexity of the treatment regimen, duration of the treatment program, and the patient's belief in the efficacy of therapy, have been shown to have a positive correlation with adherence to the prescribed treatment strategy. Specific patient characteristics such as personality variables and a number of demographic factors such as socioeconomic status have not been shown to be consistently predictive of compliance with medical advice (Kasl, 1975; Marston, 1970; Puckett & Russell, 1977; Schmitt, 1977; Stimson, 1974). Thus, there appears to be no one pattern of differences between patients who follow their medical regimen and those who do not. Summarizing her review of the research on patient adherence to medical treatment, Marston (1970) notes that "no clear picture emerges concerning the determinants of compliance" (p. 321).

Complexity of the Program

Kasl (1975) suggests that a more reliable predictor of patient compliance with medical advice is the therapeutic regimen itself. For example, keeping appointments with the physician, reporting for diagnostic tests, or taking oral medication are likely to have higher rates of compliance than recommendations to restrict or change existing habit patterns and routines such as diet, physical activity, and so on (Davis, 1967; Gillum & Barsky, 1974). Thus, a course of treatment that necessitates considerable alterations in the patient's preexisting patterns of behavior is probably the most difficult to follow.

Complex therapeutic regimens that require the patient to adhere to multiple restrictions or recommendations for behavior change usually result in rates of compliance that are less than satisfactory (Kasl, 1975). Failure to take medications as prescribed (taking too little or too much medicine), for example, has a greater probability of occurring as the daily doses of a particular drug or the number of different drugs increases (Hulka, Kupper, Cassel, & Efira, 1975).

Aversive Side Effects

Medication regimens may not be followed if the drug produces aversive side effects. Van Putten (1974), for example, studied medication-taking behavior in chronic schizophrenic patients. As many as 46 percent of the patients failed to take their prescribed antipsychotic medication because of unpleasant extrapyramidal side effects.

Finally, Kasl (1975) indicates that "compliance is generally better if the medication provides some relief from symptoms and poor when it is taken for prophylactic reasons or when symptoms belie the need for medication" (p. 9). Thus, hypertensive patients often discontinue or fail to take their medication as prescribed because the disorder is typically asymptomatic (Caldwell, Cobb, Dowling, & de Jongh, 1970; Zeisat, 1978). Similarly, patients on a course of treatment with antibiotics will sometimes discontinue taking the medication sooner than their physician recommended, when the symptoms of the illness or infection have disappeared (Twaddle & Sweet, 1970).

Knowledge about the Illness

While health care practitioners expose patients to a wide variety of information regarding both prescriptive and proscriptive behaviors pertaining to their illness, knowledge about a disorder and its treatment does not insure compliance with a medical regimen (Kasl, 1975; Marston, 1970). For example, Becker et al. (1972) found that mothers who were well informed about the nature of their child's illness and the medications for its treatment did not necessarily give the medications in the proper manner.

Sackett et al. (1975) clearly demonstrated that educating patients about a disorder and its treatment does not increase compliance with a treatment program. They investigated the effects of an educational program on the rates of compliance to a regimen of antihypertensive medication. Men employed as steel workers were treated by either their own physician or in the factory where they worked. In each group, one-half of the patients were provided with an educational package that included facts about hypertension, the importance of following the medication regimen as prescribed by the doctor, and some ways of helping them to remember to take their medication. A six-month evaluation revealed similar findings in all groups regardless of the nature of the treatment provided. Rates of compliance ranged from 50 percent to 56 percent. Therefore, neither the convenience of the medical treatment available at their place of employment nor their learning about hypertension and its treatment resulted in satisfactory compliance with the medication regimens. The investigators conclude from these results that behavioral approaches that focus *directly* on changing medication-taking behaviors (rather than indirectly on them by providing information or encouraging attitude change, for example) may be a useful strategy for increasing rates of compliance.

Adherence to Medical Regimens

Following is a description of a six-point discussion of adherence to medical regimens:

1. selecting and defining a target behavior,
2. methods of collecting information,
3. functional analysis of behavior,
4. selecting and implementing an intervention program,
5. evaluation of intervention programs for improving compliance,
6. termination of the intervention program.

I. Selecting and Defining a Target Behavior

As noted earlier, the complexity, disruptiveness, or possible aversive aspects of a treatment regimen may contribute to lack of adherence to the therapeutic program. However, in order to achieve optimal treatment of the patient's disorder, a less-than-satisfactory treatment regimen from the patient's point of view may be required. To enhance patient compliance under these conditions, Zifferblatt (1975) proposes that noncompliance with medical regimens be regarded as a behavioral problem and "subject to principles and procedures based in behavioral science" (p. 173). Through a functional analysis of compliance behavior, he suggests that adherence to medical regimens may be best understood "in terms of what people should actually do and the conditions under which it must occur" (p. 174).

Chapter 3 presents a detailed description of the rationale and procedure for performing a functional analysis of behavior. As noted in this discussion, the primary goal of a functional analysis is to identify the relationship between environmental events and the target behavior of concern, in this case compliance with therapeutic programs. Using medication-taking behavior as an example of an important activity for the maintenance of the patient's general health, Zifferblatt (1975) illustrates a functional analysis of compliance behavior with medication regimens.

II. Methods of Collecting Information

Based on a functional analysis of compliance, medication taking may be seen as a function of events that immediately precede (antecedents) and follow (consequences) the behavior. To assist the health care practitioner in identifying events that facilitate or impede patient compliance behavior, Zifferblatt advocates the use of a behavioral diary or log. The patient is asked to keep a written record of both environmental events and thoughts that precede and follow the taking of medication. Since these factors may affect the occurrence of the desired behavior, their identification permits the therapist to alter the events that contribute to noncompliance with the treatment program. Table 4.1 represents a segment from a behavioral diary for a patient on a regimen of cholestyramine taken twice each day. Such a record helps to specify problem areas where the therapist may intervene to increase compliance behavior.

Unfortunately, the patient's self-report is not always a reliable measure. Self-reports may yield overestimates of adherence to recommendations (Gordis, Markowitz, & Lilienfeld, 1969). Even carefully kept diaries of eating behavior, physical exercise, alcohol consumption, and smoking behavior may reflect the patients' attempt to over-report "good" behavior. The reactivity of self-monitoring often results in temporary reductions and, therefore, misleading impressions of the incidence of problem behaviors (Ciminero, Nelson, & Lipinski, 1977).

It is possible to obtain indirect behavioral evidence of compliance by recording the patients' tendency to keep appointments, obtain immunizations, fill prescriptions, and telephone the physician's office about daily symptoms.

Table 4.1 Excerpts from a Functional Analysis Diary

Date	Time	Antecedents (cues and people)	Consequences	Relevant thoughts
5/16	9:00 a.m.	Take vitamins, pocket book, orange juice.	Lump in throat and stomach, nausea. Ate breakfast.	A bit grainy, easy to mix.
	12:00 p.m.	Pocket book, orange juice.	Sipped slowly, lump disappeared, slight nausea.	Glad I remembered. Hope it decreases my appetite!
5/17	2:00 p.m.	Forgot last evening's medication! Pocket book, orange juice.	Put packets on kitchen counter where I can see them.	
5/18	9:00 a.m.	Take vitamins, see packets on counter, orange juice	Slight nausea, put glass and spoon on counter, late breakfast.	Maybe I can make this easier. Ate out. Did not want to take medication along. Too much to explain. Not going to do it!

Date	Time	Situation	Action	Comments
5/19	9:00 a.m.	Take vitamins, see packets on counter, orange juice, glass, spoon.	Replace packets, glass and spoon, ate breakfast.	Oops! Went out and forgot to take medication. Too sleepy when I came home! That medication is staring at me!
	1:00 a.m.	Relaxed and nothing to do, reading, alone.	Replace packets, glass and spoon, ate a sandwich.	
5/20	9:00 a.m.	Take vitamins reminded by Charlie, packets on counter, orange juice, glass, spoon.	Replace packets, glass and spoon, ate breakfast.	
	1:00 a.m.	Reading, relaxed, alone and hungry.	Replaced packets, glass and spoon, ate a sandwich.	This medication is increasing my appetite!
5/21	9:00 a.m.	Take vitamins, packets on counter, orange juice, glass, spoon.	Replace packets, glass and spoon, ate breakfast.	Going smoothly! Charlie didn't need to remind me!
	12:30 a.m.	TV, relaxed, alone and hungry.	Replace packets, glass and spoon, ate some yogurt, went to sleep.	Am I taking the medication to get something to eat? This has got to stop! Evening medication is chaos!

From S. M. Zifferblat, Increasing compliance through the applied analysis of behavior. *Preventative Medicine*, 1975, *4*, 173–182. Copyright © 1975 by Academic Press, Inc. Reprinted by permission.

Permanent product measures also provide indirect evidence about adherence to medical regimens and may include: amount of medication and quantity of food left over; body-weight records; urine output; and Clinistix. Unfortunately, pill counts are not easy to do and pose a series of problems as medications are not always kept in their original containers, supplies are divided up, and containers are not always returned on request. Patients are not likely to admit failures to take pills. Daily weight may fluctuate because of factors other than compliance, such as increased intake of salt and period into the menstrual cycle. Also, if weight is recorded only as pounds lost or gained, the record fails to account for the influence of other factors, such as body fat, age, and activity level. The use of Clinistix by diabetics to record the amount of acetone and sugar present in the urine has been useful in adjusting the need for insulin. It has been used as feedback in teaching juvenile diabetics to maintain diet restrictions (Lowe & Lutzker, 1979). By having the patient save a small sample of the urine specimens, the reliability of their use of this procedure in addition to a measure of compliance is obtained.

Medical interest focuses on health outcomes of medication regimens. Therefore, the course of the illness can be monitored by periodic checks of physiological indices, such as blood pressure, heart rate during stress tests, control of metabolic processes, or a reversal of a disease process. It is also possible to measure patients' compliance with a drug regimen by blood and urine analyses. For instance, when 125 children were followed during a ten-day course of penicillin for acute infections, a check of urine samples midway revealed that over 50 percent were no longer receiving the medication, despite physicians' instructions and free medication provided to the mothers (Becker, Drachman, & Kirscht, 1972). Physiological assessments have advantages, but may be costly and may alter the behavior of patients only when they know they are going to be tested. In addition, the presence of a drug in the body is dependent on its pattern of uptake and the physical characteristics of the individual, so that variation occurs in blood level of a drug even under conditions of perfect compliance (Kirscht & Rosenstock, 1979).

The modification of life-style behaviors, such as diet, smoking, and exercise, must be assessed over a long time. Therefore, researchers must take measurements repeatedly, rather than assuming behavioral consistency. It is also necessary to evaluate and plan for the generalization of the results of compliance outside of the hospital. If family members are included as supportive agents in data collection, this may enhance adherence. In a study of 200 hypertensive patients attending an outpatient clinic, it was found that patients who were highly motivated to comply had a high degree of support from physicians and their own spouses (Caplan, Robinson, French, Caldwell, & Shinn, 1976).

III. Functional Analysis of Behavior

Events that precede health-related behaviors (antecedents) serve as cues that trigger or set the occasion for the behavior to occur. An effective cue, for example, tells the patient that "this is the time or place to take my medication." Compliance behavior is more likely to result if the cues are highly specific and readily detectable by the patient than if the cues are ambiguous and not easily detectable. A functional analysis of several medication-taking behaviors is presented in Table 4.2, illustrating that compliance with the prescribed regimen is more or less likely to occur depending on the characteristics of the events that precede and follow the desired behavior.

Consequences that immediately follow the desired behavior also affect the probable occurrence of that behavior. If the consequences are pleasant or reinforcing, the health-related behavior is more likely to occur, whereas compliance with the therapeutic regimen is less likely to occur if the compliance behavior results in either no reinforcing consequences or aversive events. For example, natural consequences may follow shortly after the ingestion or injection of medication. The quick relief from the pain of a headache or arthritis is a reinforcing experience that increases the likelihood that the patient will take the medication as recommended by the physician. On the other hand, a low probability of adherence to the prescribed medication regimen is likely to occur if the medication results in unpleasant side effects, such as dizziness or nausea. However, as Zifferblatt aptly notes, many medical regimens are prescribed for preventive reasons (e.g., antihypertensive drugs, dietary restrictions), and, therefore, there are few if any immediate positive consequences. As a result, the probability of occurrence of health-related behaviors aimed at preventing illness is generally quite low. A solution to this problem, Zifferblatt (1975) suggests, is to arrange the patient's environment in such a way that positive consequences are made to follow the patient's health-related behavior. For example, an individual might eat dinner or watch television only after taking the prescribed medication.

Since failure to comply with a prescribed medical regimen may be a function of inadequate antecedent events and/or consequences in

Table 4.2 Comparison of a Number of Similar Medication-Taking Behaviors through a Functional Analysis

	Antecedents		Behavior	Consequences		
	Cue specificity	Event		Event	Latency	Probability of reoccurrences
			1. Open packet for bottle			
			2. Mix powder with liquid or take tablet			
			3. Drink mixture			
(1)	Easily detected and specific to response	Upset stomach	Antacid	Relief of discomfort	5-10 min.	High
(2)	Easily detected and specific to response	Headache	Headache powder	Relief of headache	10-15 min.	High
(3)	Ambiguous cues-discernable	None	Aspirin	Avoidance of arthritic pain	Preventive	Low
(4)	Ambiguous	None	Gelatin (brittle nails)	None	Preventive	Low
(5)	Ambiguous	None	Vitamins	None	Preventive	Low
(6)	Ambiguous	None	Diuretic (hypertension)	None	Preventive nausea	Low
(7)						
(a)	Ambiguous	None	Cholestyramine	None	Preventive	Low
(b)	Explicit time or occasion	Buzzer breakfast spouse cue, table	Cholestyramine	Access to breakfast	1 min.	High
(c)	Ambiguous	None	Cholestyramine	$20 bill per ingestion	5 sec.	High

From S. M. Zifferblat, Increasing compliance through the applied analysis of behavior. Preventive Medicine, 1975, 4, 173-182. Copyright © 1975 by Academic Press, Inc. Reprinted by permission.

the patient's environment, the systematic programming of these factors is essential to insure that the patient will follow the therapeutic programs as recommended by the health care practitioner. Zifferblatt (1975) outlines four basic attributes that enhance the effectiveness of situational cues and reinforcing consequences. Cues in the environment and positive reinforcers should:

1. be highly salient (i.e., be meaningful or have significances for each patient),
2. be highly compatible with the patient's everyday routine and general life-style,
3. have a short latency of occurrences in relation to the health care behavior, and
4. be highly explicit (i.e., be clearly related and appropriate to the health care behavior).

By identifying specific cues and consequences that have these attributes and integrating them into the patient's environment, it is possible to increase the patient's compliance to the medical regimen.

IV. Selecting and Implementing an Intervention Program

A behavioral treatment program utilizing this strategy was developed by Zeisat (1978) to increase adherence to a medical regimen with patients having essential hypertension. The primary goal of treatment was to reduce the patients' blood pressure by establishing patterns of behavior that facilitated the use of antihypertensive medication four times a day. In general, the default rate is high for patients placed on a regimen of antihypertensive medication. This low rate of compliance is attributed to the asymptomatic nature of the disorder and the possible side effects of the medication (Caldwell et al., 1970).

Ten male outpatients (mean age fifty-two years) were seen for four weekly group sessions at the hospital. During each session, the patients' blood pressure was measured and recorded, and social reinforcement such as praise from the group was provided for weekly decreases in blood pressure. Patients whose blood pressure had increased from the previous week were asked to suggest reasons why they were not making progress and to discuss ways to improve their medication-taking behavior. Each patient was also trained to monitor his own blood pressure at home with a manual-style sphygmomanometer and to keep a graph of his daily records.

The major treatment strategy used by Zeisat (1978) was to modify the context in which the patients took their antihypertensive medication. This was accomplished by helping the patients to select environmental cues conducive to compliance with their medication regimen. Patients chose one prominent object in their environment or an event that consistently occurred in their daily routine. For example, some patients associated medication taking with meal-times; others placed their medication on the dining room table as a conspicuous cue.

Family members and friends were also incorporated into the treatment program as "social allies." A social ally is an individual with whom the patient has frequent contacts and who can provide the patient with both reminders to follow the treatment regimen and social reinforcement for desired health-related changes (Stuart & Davis, 1972). For example, the wife of one patient helped remind him to keep his medication on the dining room table.

V. Evaluation of Intervention Programs for Improving Compliance

This treatment program resulted in significant reductions in blood pressure, despite the short intervention period. These results are particularly impressive, considering the potent reinforcement for remaining sick that all patients received in the form of disability compensation (secondary gain).

Similar strategies are suggested by Suinn (1977) to increase compliance to therapeutic programs for modifying health-related behaviors that contribute to the risk of developing cardiovascular disease. There appears to be a strong causal link to cardiovascular disease of such behavioral characteristics as obesity, hypertension, physical inactivity, and strategies for coping with the stresses and demands of daily life—also referred to as the Type A behavior pattern (Henderson & Enelow, 1976). To increase compliance to antihypertensive medication regimens, for example, Suinn (1977) suggests that the times for taking the medication should be made to coincide with events in the patient's daily schedule that occur on a regular basis such as eating breakfast at 8 A.M. and lunch at 12 noon. Patients might, then, incorporate effective cues into their environment by highlighting these times on a watch or clock with a marking pen or by attaching a reminder note to their lunch bag. The frequent association between the medication-taking behavior and consistent environmental events should help to establish the desired behavior as a habit pattern.

VI. Termination of the Intervention Program

Prior to terminating a program, procedures that assure that these new behaviors will be maintained can be enhanced by incorporating them into the patient's basic life-style. Suinn (1977) notes that patients are more likely to adopt health-related activities into their repertoire if the activity fits into their daily routine. For example, to encourage a patient to engage in physical activity, a formal exercise program such as jogging may be too difficult to implement because it necessitates considerable disruptions in the patient's daily schedule. However, a patient is more likely to engage in physical exercise such as skipping every other stair at home or using stairs instead of an elevator because these activities are more readily included in the patient's daily routine.

The use of written contracts between the physician and the patient has been effective with hypertensive patients (Stekel & Swain, 1977). A key point of this procedure was to encourage the patients to write the contract and to assist them in analyzing the process into manageable steps. All patients in this study complied with the contracts that they shared in preparing.

Bigelow, Strickler, Liebson, and Griffiths (1976) investigated the effects of a security-deposit *contingency contract* on the maintenance of Antabuse intake with 25 male alcoholics. The patients were volunteers with a history of chronic drinking problems. A contract was signed by each patient in which he agreed to take the medication at an outpatient clinic every day for the first two weeks and every other day for the remainder of the treatment program, which lasted three months. Patients also deposited approximately $70 with the researchers, of which they forfeited $5 to $10 each time they failed to take the Antabuse as scheduled. The remaining balance was returned to the patient after the contract period. Following this intervention strategy, 80 percent of the patients achieved a longer duration of abstinence compared to the three years prior to treatment. Furthermore, the results showed that the patients remained abstinent for over 95 percent of the days when the treatment program was in effect, indicating a high rate of compliance with the medication regimen.

The therapeutic benefits of many medications are obtained only if the patient maintains a prescribed dosage schedule. Therefore, the medication must be taken by the patient at regular time intervals. An apparatus small enough to place in a pocket or purse was developed by Azrin and Powell (1969) to increase appropriate medication-taking behavior utilizing the principle of *negative reinforcement*. This device sounded a tone each time the medication was to be taken. When the patient terminated the tone, by turning a lever, the apparatus automatically delivered a pill. The results from this study demonstrated that such a device can serve as a highly effective cue for initiating medication-taking behavior. Patients who used this procedure missed fewer pills and took the medication at the prescribed schedule more often than did patients who had access only to a portable alarm or a wristwatch.

Epstein and Masek (1978) compared the efficacy of several strategies for increasing the intake of Vitamin C, advanced by Nobel prizewinner Linus Pauling as a method to prevent colds. The preventive use of Vitamin C is similar to medications prescribed for disorders such as hypertension in that the compliance rate is typically low.

In order to measure medication compliance accurately, two types of tablets the same size, shape, and color were used. One type of tablet contained only ascorbic acid. The other tablets were composed of the same dosage of ascorbic acid and, in addition, contained a chemical agent that produces a discoloration of the urine. This chemical served as a tracer technique to permit a reliable estimate of compliance. Finally, some tablets were also flavored with quinine or orange flavor to give them a distinctive taste.

Subjects were given a weekly supply of tablets, and were instructed to take them four times daily at specific time periods. The tablets were arranged in a random sequence, and contained a predetermined number of Vitamin C and tracer tablets. Each week, subjects were instructed to keep a record of the times that urine discolorations were observed. Compliance rates were determined by comparing the time when the subjects first observed the discoloration with the time when discoloration was expected to occur based on the appropriate use of the tracer tablets. During the first three weeks of the study, subjects were given Vitamin C tablets and were informed that some of the tablets contained the tracer chemical. The subjects also deposited $9 with the investigators that was forfeited if their record sheets were not turned in at the end of each week. Based on these records, the 40 most noncompliant subjects were identified. These subjects were randomly assigned to four groups in the Treatment I phase of the study. The groups included the following conditions:

1. self-monitoring only—subjects recorded the time when the medication was taken;
2. taste only—subjects were given flavored tablets to assess the effects of increasing the salience of the medication on compliance behavior;

3. taste- and self-monitoring—subjects recorded the flavor of the tablet instead of the time when the medication was taken, and

4. no treatment control.

In the Treatment II phase of this study, half of the subjects continued to follow the procedures in Treatment I. The other half of the subjects, in addition to following Treatment I conditions, also participated in a *response-cost* procedure. Subjects agreed to forfeit $1 of their deposit each week that they failed to comply satisfactorily with the medication-taking regimen.

The results from this study indicated that in the Treatment I condition both the self-monitoring-only group and the taste- and self-monitoring group produced significant increases in medication compliance compared to the taste-only and control groups. Significant increases in compliance rates were observed in all the treatment groups when the response-cost procedure was introduced in the Treatment II condition. The considerable improvements in appropriate medication-taking achieved with the response-cost procedure suggests that this strategy be further investigated with other therapeutic regimens that have poor compliance rates.

Diabetes is a disorder that requires patients to make considerable changes in their daily patterns of living and to adhere to specific medical regimens in order to control the disease. Knapp (1977) has noted in this regard that:

> To the patient diabetes is a way of living. It is learning to self-administer insulin of the appropriate type and amount, and within a specified time period each day. It is maintaining a rigid diet, eating exact amounts of food at regular intervals, whether prompted by hunger or not. It is staying on a routine exercise schedule, making adjustments in insulin and meals as exertion varies. It is recording several times each day the level of sugar in one's urine. It is being ever watchful for the alerting signs of insulin shock. It is all this and more, but it is essentially a problem in *behavior management* rather than medical treatment [p. 1].

Once the disorder has been diagnosed, the medical practitioner is faced with the task of helping the patient to adopt new health care behaviors and change preexisting daily routines. Lowe and Lutzker (1979) describe a treatment program for increasing compliance to a medical regimen with a nine-year-old diabetic girl. The goal of treatment was to increase the frequency with which the patient engaged in activities necessary to prevent physical complications that often occur

Table 4.3   Average Compliance Rates of a Juvenile Diabetic to a Medical
Regimen

Target Behavior	Pretreatment	Posttreatment
Foot care	72%	100%
Urine testing	19%	97%
Diet control	72%	99%

with diabetes. She and her mother had been seriously neglecting these activities to the extent that hospitalization for complications associated with the diabetes was necessitated on several occasions over a short period of time. These health-related activities included dietary management, urine testing, and foot care. A *contingency management* procedure based on a point system was implemented as the primary treatment strategy. Points were earned for engaging in the desired behaviors and could be exchanged for a variety of pleasurable events and activities. As can be seen from Table 4.3, the treatment program resulted in substantial increases in the target behaviors to near maximum levels. These improvements in the medically prescribed behaviors were maintained at a ten-week follow-up evaluation. A *token reinforcement* program was also effective in significantly increasing compliance to a complex medical regimen in an elderly patient with serious heart problems (Dapcich-Miura & Hovell, 1979). (See Table 4.4.)

Promoting Life-Style Changes

It is now widely recognized that maladaptive health habits and a number of life-style behavior patterns increase the risk of illness, disease, and death (Bass & Grantham, 1978; Meyer & Henderson, 1974). Health care providers are, therefore, concerned with modifying and preventing habits and styles of living that represent a potential risk to the patient's health. In this regard, Berkanovic (1976) has aptly noted:

> Central to modern concepts of prevention is the notion that the personal behaviors of individuals as they conduct their day-to-day lives must somehow be changed if the health of the citizenry is to be improved. Indeed, there is evidence that such personal behaviors as alcohol consumption, poor eating habits, cigarette smoking, lack of adequate rest and exercise,

as well as the failure to recognize potentially dangerous symptoms and act promptly on them, all contribute to an incidence of disease that is much higher than it need be [p. 93].

Behavioral treatment approaches provide practitioners in the various health professions with a number of strategies for promoting changes in these conditions (Bass & Grantham, 1978; Pomerleau, 1976; Pomerleau, Bass, & Crown, 1975; Pomerleau & Brady, 1975). Since these behavior patterns are associated with a higher mortality rate and such disorders as cardiovascular disease, renal disease, pulmonary disease, and lung cancer among others, the development of effective behavior-change strategies for these life-style factors has significant implications for the prevention of serious health problems.

Reducing Health Risk Factors Associated with Cardiovascular Disease

Within the past several years there have been a number of reports suggesting exciting prospects for the behavioral intervention with a variety of health risk factors. For example, Meyer and Henderson (1974) report the behavioral treatment of multiple risk factors to prevent cardiovascular disease. Patients considered by their physicians to be at high risk for heart disease were instructed in behavioral techniques to effect change in weight, diet, smoking, and physical activity. The treatment program was conducted over twelve sessions. Patients who received behavioral treatment, individually or in groups, showed significantly greater change in the above-mentioned variables, including improvements in their cholesterol and triglyceride levels, compared to patients who received only physician consultation. Furthermore, these changes were maintained at a three-month follow-up assessment. Similar positive changes in plasma cholesterol and triglyceride levels were found with behavioral intervention programs for modifying eating and nutrition habits and/or for reducing response to stress (Foreyt, Scott, Mitchell & Gotto, 1979; Suinn, 1974).

Essential Hypertension

The treatment of essential hypertension is important because it has been identified as a major risk factor for a number of illnesses, including cardiovascular disorders. As many as 30 percent of the adult population is estimated to have essential hypertension (Stamler, Stamler, Riedlinger, Algera, & Roberts, 1976). While pharmacological

Table 4.4   Treatment Program to Promote Adherence to a Medical Regimen

I.   Target behavior _noncompliance_   defined as:

   A. (too much) _refusal to take pills, failure to take pills consistently,_
      overmedicates

   B. (too little) _compliance, exercise, diet control_

   C. (cued by or in reaction to) _laziness, aversive side-effects of drug,_
      lack of symptoms, lack of symptom relief

   D. (strengths and skills) _good health habits in other.areas, likes activity_

II. Methods of collecting information

   A. (interviews, questionnaires, test results) _self-report, behavioral_
      diary

   B. (overt manifestations of patient's behavior) _pill-taking, refill_
      prescriptions

   C. (what patient self-monitors and records) _pill-taking, pain intensity, body_
      weight, number of prescription refills, antecedent, consequences, condition

   D. (lasting changes in the environment--e.g., food left over, work output)
      empty pill containers, urine test results, blood test

   E. (physiological indices--e.g., GSR, pulse rate) _blood pressure,_
      heart rate during stress test, blood-level test of drug

III. Functional analysis of behavior

   A. (events preceding target behavior) _lack of easily detected and specific_
      cues, upset stomach, headache

   B. (events following target behavior) _no relief from pain, nausea or_
      unpleasant side effects, medication increases appetite

(continued)

IV. Selecting and implementing an intervention program

    A. Motivation for change

        1.(benefits of "sick-role"--e.g., attention, avoidance or responsibility)

          preventive, reduction of pain

        2. (What would be different for patient/significant others if problem did not exist?) *control of chronic illness (e.g., hypertension), patient able to be more active*

    B. Meaningful environmental consequences

        1. Likes *activities, meals*

        2. Dislikes *gaining weight*

    C. Significant others (spouse, siblings, parent, teacher) *spouse, physician*

    D. Factors maintaining the problem *lack of symptoms, no specific cues to pill-taking*

    E. Treatment strategies *(1) Specify cues: explicit time or occasion; (2) fit regimen into ongoing activities; (3) reward medication taking explicitly (4) written contract (e.g., response cost for failure to comply)*

V. Evaluation of intervention program

    A. Monitoring of treatment progress *behavioral diary, self-monitoring, number of refills*

    B. Programming for maintenance of behavior change *wife cues, pills taken at specific time of day or meal, pleasurable activities contingent on pill-taking*

    C. Follow-up assessment *telephone report of symptom changes, periodic physical examination*

VI. Termination (What was your treatment goal?) *to increase patient's probability of taking the appropriate amount and type of medications and at correct time intervals* intervention remains the primary treatment approach for this disorder, there are several drawbacks to the use of medication, including potential undesirable side effects and the finding that it does not adequately control blood pressure levels in all patients (LoGerfo, 1975).

Recently, several behavioral treatment strategies have been investigated as alternative or adjunctive approaches to the pharmacological treatment of essential hypertension. Progressive muscle relaxation, relaxation-like techniques (e.g., yoga, meditation), and biofeedback are the most frequently investigated procedures for directly or indirectly controlling essential hypertension. In a thorough review of the research in this area, Seer (1979) concludes that "psychological approaches have had only limited success in controlling essential hypertension" (p. 1039) primarily because the magnitude of reduction in blood pressure has been too small to be clinically meaningful. Furthermore, the research evidence for the comparative efficacy of biofeedback and relaxation-like procedures is inconclusive. In this regard, Seer (1979) suggests that relaxation training may be a more promising treatment for hypertension than biofeedback because it does not require complex instrumentation and because relaxation training has been shown to be effective in teaching the patient a general coping response to stress-related situations.

There is some evidence that behavioral treatment procedures may be selectively effective with specific patient populations. For example, in their view of relaxation therapy for hypertension, Jacob, Kraemer, and Agras (1977) conclude that this treatment strategy results in the most significant reductions in blood pressure for patients having higher pretreatment levels. Thus, these authors suggest that, for patients whose blood pressure remains high despite the use of medications, relaxation procedures might serve as an effective adjunct to pharmacological intervention.

Personality Types of Coronary-Prone Patients

Suinn (1974; 1977) developed a comprehensive treatment program to teach patients with a Type A behavior pattern strategies for coping with stress. The Type A person has been found to exhibit such behavioral characteristics as achievement orientation, self-imposed deadlines, desire for recognition, impatience, physical and mental alertness, competitiveness, and a strong drive toward self-selected but poorly defined goals (Suinn, 1977). This behavior pattern has consistently been found to be associated with a high risk for cardiovascular disease (Brand, Rosenman, Sholts, & Friedman, 1976; Rosenman, Brand, Jenkins, Friedman, Straus, & Wurm, 1975).

Men with a Type A pattern were treated with stress management techniques in a program referred to as Cardiac Stress Management Training. Treatment was conducted in six to eight sessions over a two- to three-week period. First, the patients were taught deep muscle relaxation as a strategy for coping with stress. Next, they were taught to identify muscular and other physiological cues that were associated with anxiety arousal. Finally, visual imagery was used to rehearse alternative responses to Type A behaviors that they were to practice in real-life stress situations. This treatment package produced significant reductions in a variety of Type A behaviors, considerably reduced systolic and diastolic blood pressure, and lowered anxiety levels as assessed by state and trait measures.

Obesity

One health risk factor that has received considerable attention in the literature is obesity. Because it is a prevalent and serious health-related problem, this section presents a detailed description of the behavioral approach to the treatment of obesity. While this discussion deals with only one behavior problem, many of the issues and behavioral intervention strategies are applicable to a number of the other health risk factors (e.g., smoking and alcoholism). For example, many of these life-style patterns can be regarded as learned maladaptive habits that have been acquired over time (Bass & Grantham, 1978). In addition, these problems are similar in that they represent a deficit in self-control skills (Pomerleau, Bass, & Crown, 1975). Therefore, as Berkanovic (1976) points out, motivation to change such behaviors is a necessary but not sufficient condition. In the case of smoking, for example, he notes: "many people who are motivated to quit smoking lack the behavioral skills required to realize their motivation. . . . They need to learn the specific skills that will allow them to bring their smoking behavior under control" (p. 98).

With an estimated 40 million to 80 million persons in the United States being considerably overweight, obesity is a national health problem (U.S. Department of Health, Education and Welfare, 1967). Obesity is associated with a number of physical problems, including cardiovascular and renal disease, diabetes, and hypertension (Meyer & Henderson, 1974; Stuart & Davis, 1972). In addition to having a higher risk for complications during surgery, the mortality rate for obese persons is approximately 50 percent greater than for normal-weight individuals (Kennedy & Foreyt, 1968; Mann, 1974). Obesity may also have adverse effects on a patient's social and sexual functioning.

Only a small percentage of the cases of obesity are attributable to organic factors (Stunkard & Mahoney, 1976). Accordingly, obesity may be defined as a behavior disorder. Behavior therapists regard obesity as the result of a set of learned behaviors that terminate in the final act of overeating. The obese individual exhibits inappropriate patterns of both eating and activity. These behavior patterns, in turn, result in increased body weight as a result of excessive caloric (energy) intake in relation to the enery that is expended (Jeffrey, 1976). Excessive overeating is maintained by its immediate reinforcing consequences (e.g., satisfying taste and reduction of hunger) (Bellack, 1975).

Traditional medical and dietary approaches to the treatment of obesity have not been effective in producing weight loss. Although obese patients may reduce their weight, with these methods they quickly regain it (Stunkard, 1958). Furthermore, the dropout rate from medical weight-reduction programs has been reported to be as high as 80 percent. In sharp contrast to these findings, behavioral programs have considerably lower dropout rates, and result in significantly greater weight loss (Stunkard, 1972; Stunkard & Rush, 1974).

Behavioral Management of Obesity

There is a considerable body of research evidence demonstrating the superiority of behavioral techniques for the treatment of obesity when compared to other approaches (reviews of this area include Abramson, 1973; Hall & Hall, 1974; Leon, 1976; Stunkard & Mahoney, 1976; Williams, Martin, & Foreyt, 1976). While more problematic, behavioral approaches have shown promise in the area of maintenance of the weight loss (Leon, 1976).

Because a basic component of many behavioral treatment programs for obesity is based on the pioneering work of Schachter, a brief review of his research is in order. In a series of studies, Schachter and his colleagues (Schachter, 1968, 1971: Schachter, Goldman, & Gordon, 1968) studied the eating behavior of obese and nonobese persons in various real-life situations and under controlled laboratory conditions. Taken together, these studies consistently demonstrate that food intake in obese individuals is influenced more by external events or cues than it is in normal-weight persons, whose eating behavior is regulated more by internal or physiological cues. Specifically, the eating patterns of obese persons tend to be affected by events such as time of day; taste, smell, and sight of food; and availability of food. On the other hand, nonobese persons are more sensitive to hunger cues in regulating their eating patterns.

Because excessive food intake in obese persons is under the control of environmental events (external antecedent stimuli), it follows that reduced food consumption can be achieved by modifying the environment in which the patient's eating occurs. Therefore, the primary focus of behavioral treatment programs for obesity is not on weight loss, per se, but on altering the patient's maladaptive eating behaviors.

A number of different behavioral techniques have been used to produce weight loss (Bellack, 1975). These techniques have been used individually and in combination as a treatment package. One of the most effective procedures for the control of obesity is the strategy of *stimulus control* (Stunkard & Mahoney, 1976). This procedure has often been an important component of comprehensive behavioral treatment programs for obesity that have resulted in significant weight losses in overweight patients (Levitz & Stunkard, 1974; McReynolds, Lutz, Paulsen, & Kohrs, 1976; Penick, Filion, Fox, & Stunkard, 1971; Stuart, 1967; Wollersheim, 1970).

It has been suggested that for the obese person eating typically occurs in many situations and has been associated with many reinforcing events in the environment. With repeated associations, these environmental stimuli come to cue or initiate the eating behavior (Ferster, Nurnberger, & Levitt, 1962). Thus, to modify maladaptive eating patterns, the patient must learn to identify the cues that elicit the eating behavior and then to separate the behavior from the cues. This disassociation of the behavior from environmental events in order to permit the patient to regain control over eating cues is accomplished by stimulus control procedures. Stimulus control strategies are concerned with eliminating or restricting the cues that prompt maladaptive eating behaviors. Eating cues can be eliminated directly by avoiding situations in which the cues are present and engaging in alternative behaviors (e.g., staying away from the food table at a party or not walking past a bakery), or the range of cues can be narrowed (e.g., eating only at specific times and only in one place in the house).

Another important fact about eating is that the act itself is immediately reinforced by its pleasurable consequences, such as the taste of the food and a decrease in hunger. On the other hand, the potential negative consequences of excessive eating, such as weight gain, not fitting into clothes, or physical illness, are considerably delayed and long-term in their effects. This conflict between immediate and delayed consequences makes eating a prepotent response and, therefore, reduces the probability of weight loss. In addition, weight loss in most treatment programs is typically a slow process, with noticeable beneficial effects occurring many weeks after the start of the weight loss program.

In order to deal with these problems, a second main component of most behavioral programs for obesity is the direct manipulation of contingencies associated with maladaptive and appropriate eating behaviors (Stuart, 1971). Short-term, immediate consequences must be used to develop and maintain appropriate eating behaviors. This is accomplished primarily by reinforcing eating patterns that are incompatible with obesity. The patient is instructed in the use of self-reward techniques to reinforce contingently appropriate eating. For example, when patients successfully maintain appropriate eating during the holidays, they might use self-praise (e.g., "I really did a great job of sticking to my diet"), or they might permit themselves a special privilege, such as buying a new dress or visiting a friend.

Patients are also trained to use self-punishment procedures contingent on inappropriate eating. This might include refraining from watching a favorite television show or engaging in an unpleasant activity, such as cleaning the garage. To make the long-term consequences of obesity more immediate, patients can also think about the "ultimate aversive consequences" of excessive eating. In this procedure, the patient thinks of some of the possible consequences of engaging in inappropriate eating behavior; for example, "If I eat too much I will look fat in my bathing suit this summer." In addition, patients might carry a picture of themselves that clearly shows their excessive weight and that they can look at when they are tempted to eat inappropriately. The picture might also be attached to the refrigerator to serve as a reminder not to overeat.

As noted earlier in this chapter, patient compliance with treatment programs to modify life-style patterns is often poor. Patient compliance with the behavioral treatment of obesity may be enhanced by involving family members or friends in the program. These individuals can serve as a source of support, encouragement, and reinforcement for the patient's progress, and can learn ways to help restrict cues that elicit eating behavior in the patient. In this regard, Brownell et al. (in press) found that obese patients whose spouses attended treatment sessions in a behavioral program had lost significantly more weight by a three- and six-month follow-up than had patients whose spouses were not involved in the training program.

Many behavioral treatment programs for obesity are conducted in groups. In addition to being more efficient, this treatment format can also provide another important source of encouragement and can facilitate patient compliance with the program. Modeling and peer pressure to engage in appropriate eating patterns and praise and recognition for progress and success are some of the advantages of a group treatment approach.

Motivation to lose weight is essential if treatment is to be effective. One strategy is to require the patient to make a private and public commitment to lose weight by informing family members or friends of his or her intention (McReynolds & Paulsen, 1976).

Another technique for enhancing commitment and increasing compliance with the treatment program is to use a contract. Contingency contracts specify in writing the exact behaviors required of the patient and therapist, and indicate the consequences for compliance with the contract. Table 4.5 illustrates a sample contract for use in a behavioral management program for weight reduction. Similar contracts were an important component of a treatment program that resulted in significant weight losses in obese patients (Mann, 1972).

A Comprehensive Behavioral Treatment Program. This section describes the basic components of a comprehensive behavioral treatment program for weight control. The procedures described below follow directly from the treatment program developed and evaluated by McReynolds, Lutz, Paulsen, and Kohrs (1976). This program has been selected as an illustration for several reasons. First, a treatment manual is available that outlines the intervention strategies in detail (McReynolds, Paulsen, Lutz, & Kohrs, 1975). Second, and more important, research has demonstrated the efficacy of this program in producing sizable and highly significant weight loss in patients who were 15 percent to 60 percent overweight. Furthermore, a second study by Beneke et al. (1978) using patients from the McReynolds et al. (1976) investigation found the patients had maintained 80 percent of their weight loss at an eighteen-month follow-up assessment. These results are indeed impressive when compared to weight-loss maintenance data typically reported in other studies (O'Leary & Wilson, 1975; Leon, 1976).

Patients are treated in groups of five to eight persons and attend fourteen weekly sessions. Throughout the program, patients keep a daily food record, on which they indicate all foods eaten, including the amount, the time of day, and the place where the food is eaten. A completed food record for a patient is presented in Figure 4.1. These records help to identify inappropriate foods and environmental circumstances associated with the eating behavior. This information helps the patient to become aware of previously automatic behaviors

Table 4.5 Sample Contract for Weight Management Program

I, __(Name of Patient)__ , agree to participate in the Family Practice
Weight Management Program, to reach my goal of __(Target Weight)__ lbs.
by __(Target Date)__.
I understand that this goal will help me accomplish the following
for losing weight) eg:

    a. To improve the state of my health and reduce the chances
       of diabetes.
    b. To fit into a smaller dress suit.
    c. To save money on food.
    d. To gain mastery over a bad habit.
    e. To please my husband/wife and make myself more attractive
       to him/her.
    f. To gain approval from my friends.

1. I agree to the following: (use individual rules developed
   by and with patient)

    a. I will eat three meals each day in the dining room at
       approximately 7:30 a.m. 12:00 noon, and 6:00 p.m.
    b. I will not eat at any other times.
    c. I will put down my fork after each bite.
    d. I will not watch television or read while eating.
    e. I will record all of the food and amount I plan to eat
       before each meal.
    f. I will weigh myself daily.
    g. I will consume six glasses of water daily.
    h. When I feel hungry I will call a friend and chat for ten
       minutes.
    i. I will carry with me a list of reasons for not eating to
       look at when I feel the urge to eat.

2. For doing these activities I will reward myself by the
   following methods: (the patient's rewards)

    a. I will save 50 cents each day in a glass jar. This money
       will be used for the purchase of new clothes.
    b. When I reach my weekly rate I will plan a visit with a
       friend for one hour.
    c. For suppressing an urge to eat, I will congratuate
       myself by looking in a mirror and saying, "Congratulations,
       you did it again!"
    d. For eating only one small plate of food at each meal I
       will receive congratulations from my family.
    e. For each pound lost my husband/wife will give me $1
       for my bank.

3. I will provide my physician with the following records:

    a. Daily food and water intake on the recording forms
       provided by my doctor.
    b. My daily weights for the periods between visits.
    c. Monthly reports on the amount of money saved.
    d. Monthly letters summarizing my feelings about the
       program.

(continued)

4. My physician agrees to provide the following services:

   a. To collect and record weekly weight on the weight chart.
   b. To plot weekly calories as provided by the patient onto a graph.
   c. To discuss with the patient changes in health status.
   d. To reward the patient for reduction in weight by providing a "Certificate of Completion" when the target weight is reached.
   e. To provide one free office visit for a family member for each 20 pounds lost.

5. I assert that I have discussed the above-named objectives for the change of my behavior and I consent to work toward the achievement of these objectives.

6. I further assert that I have discussed the above-named intervention techniques with my physician and that I consent to apply these techniques.

7. I further assert that I shall provide the above-named data in order to determine the effectiveness of the use of the intervention techniques.

8. I further assert that I have freely entered into this contract knowing the therapeutic objectives and both the positive and negative potential effects of the intervention techniques.

9. I further assert that I shall provide my physician with the following compensation for his/her efforts on my behalf:

   _____

10. I further assert that I have been assured on my right to terminate my participation in treatment at any time, for any reason, without the need to offer explanation, and without penalty.

11. I further specifically agree that the information provided can be used for research reports which will not in any way identify me to others unless I have offered my specific, written permission.

12. I further agree that I shall keep all scheduled appointments and shall give at least 48 hours notice of my intention to cancel any appointment.

13. Other agreements:

   _____

   _____

Date _____   Patient _____

Witness _____   Physician _____

From J. T. Tapp, R. S. Krull, M. Tapp, and R. H. Seller, The application of behavior modification to behavior management: Guidelines for the family physician. *The Journal of Family Practice,* 1978, *6,* 293–299. Copyright © 1978 by Appleton-Century-Crofts. Reprinted by permission.

Name *Mary C.*

Date *March 17, 1977*   Day of Week *Tuesday*

Time and Place	Kind of Food & Description	Amount
6:45 am kitchen table at home	soft boiled eggs	2
	orange juice	4 oz.
	white bread	1 slice
	margarine	1 tsp.
	coffee (black)	1 cup
10:15 am employees lounge at work	large orange	1
	diet cola	12 oz.
12:30 pm restaurant	tuna fish	3 oz.
	mayonnaise	2 tsp.
	whole wheat bread	2 slices
	lettuce	1 leaf
	potato chips	12
	diet cola	12 oz.
6:00 pm kitchen table at home	tomato juice	1 cup
	hamburger (broiled)	4 oz.
	broccoli	1 cup
	lettuce and tomato salad	2 cups
	vinegar and oil dressing	2 tbsp.
	vanilla pudding	½ cup
	skim milk	10 oz.
9:00 pm in the den watching TV	graham cracker	1
	coffee (black)	1 cup

Figure 4.1   A completed daily food record for a patient, including time of day, place, description of food, and amount.

and enables the therapist to intervene in problem areas. For example, the food records may indicate that a patient is eating excessively in the evening or while watching television.

The patient's progress is monitored on a weight-loss graph (Figure 4.2). On a weekly basis, the patient's weight is charted on the graph. The upper and lower diagonal lines indicate a weight-loss rate of one and three pounds respectively. During the treatment program the patient's weight loss should remain between the two lines. If the patients comply with the program, they should lose at least one pound each week; a weight loss of more than three pounds is not considered healthy, and indicates excessive food deprivation that can eventually lead to further overeating (McReynolds et al., 1975). As McReynolds

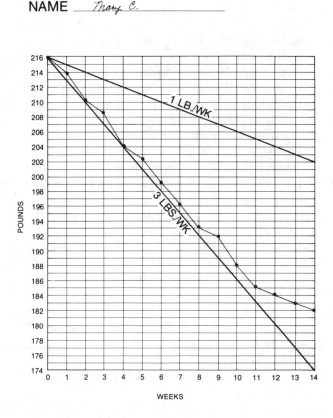

Figure 4.2   A graph illustrating a patient's weekly weight loss within therapist-established boundaries for rate of loss.

and Paulsen (1976) indicate: "Much of the problem with maintenance of weight loss seems to be related to the types of changes made during dieting. Many weight loss programs involve dramatic changes in diet that cannot be continued on a permanent basis because they are not compatible with the dieter's life-style or food preferences" (p. 160). Similarly, Bass and Grantham (1978) point out: "People who tend to be unsuccessful in managing life-style changes also tend to set unreasonably high goals for themselves" (p. 118).

In addition to a concern with nutrition and eating behaviors, a comprehensive behavioral program for obesity also focuses on increasing the patient's physical activity to facilitate energy expenditure. Often, patients attempt to engage in daily exercise programs that they discontinue after a short period of time because the exercises are unrealistically difficult and do not fit into the patient's daily routine. As we previously suggested, consistent performance of physical activity is maintained by selecting activities that can become part of the patient's regular schedule. For example, jogging for many persons may be difficult to arrange on a frequent basis or not consistent with a patient's preferences. However, a patient can be encouraged to walk or ride a bicycle rather than drive, or to use stairs instead of taking an elevator. In addition, a patient can participate in enjoyable activities with others, such as playing tennis.

Following from the research evidence of Schachter and his colleagues discussed earlier, a specific goal of the McReynolds et al. (1975) treatment program is to help the patient acquire self-control skills through stimulus control procedures so as to reduce the influence of environmental events on eating. These investigators conceptualize eating as a chain of behaviors with each step in the chain serving as a stimulus for the next step. The eating chain begins with the purchase of food, followed by storing the food, cooking or preparing it, serving the food, eating it, and finally cleaning up leftovers. Because each step in the chain can influence eating, the intervention program focuses on each of these steps in order to modify inappropriate food consumption. At each group session, patients receive information pertaining to techniques in the form of specific dos and don'ts for controlling each stage in the eating chain.

Food Buying. The first step in the eating chain is the purchase of food. Eating is determined by the availability of food in the house since as McReynolds et al. (1975) note, "You don't eat what you don't buy." Food buying suggestions include: *Do* buy groceries from a shopping list. *Do* go grocery shopping after a meal. *Do* buy for specific meals and try to buy just enough food to minimize leftovers. *Do* buy food that requires at least some preparation.

Food Storage. Once food is bought, it should be stored in such a way as to reduce its accessibility. This is important since the sight of food can affect eating. Strategies for food storage include: *Do* store problem foods (e.g., candies, potato chips) in inaccessible as well as out-of-sight places (e.g., back of bottom cupboard). *Do* store all refrigerator foods in non-see-through containers to take them out of clear sight. *Don't* remove the natural wrapping or cover from food before you are ready to cook or eat it.

Food Preparation. The manner in which food is prepared can influence eating. Suggestions for food preparation to reduce inappropriate eating include: *Do* prepare the exact amount of food that you need to avoid excesses or leftovers unless use of them is in your menu plan for the week. *Do* prepare family favorites (but not your own favorites). *Don't* cook before meals when you are hungry—have a light snack before starting to cook to cut down on tasting. *Don't* hover over cooking food that you will be tempted to taste or eat.

Serving Food. Patients are provided with a plate and bowl that are slightly smaller than usual, and are instructed to eat only from these dishes. In addition, they are instructed to take only one helping of food. This procedure helps reduce food consumption by controlling the amount of food available. Another method to control the quantity of food is the monitoring of serving size by using measuring utensils or a food scale. Some of the serving suggestions that the patients receive include: *Do* put on the table only what is needed for the meal. *Do* serve yourself last. *Do* eat only off of your plate. *Don't* let serving dishes gather around your eating place to tempt you.

How to Eat. Another point of intervention is the eating response itself. Overweight persons often eat a small amount of food during the day and excessive amounts in the evening. Since most individuals are most active during the day, this eating pattern contributes to increased weight. Therefore, patients are encouraged to distribute their eating throughout the day to prevent long periods of food deprivation that tend to lead to binge eating. Distributed eating typically involves three meals a day; however, where more than three meals are eaten, smaller amounts of food are consumed at each meal. How-to-eat suggestions include: *Do* shorten eating time to minimize exposure to table food temptation (without gulping). *Do* leave the table as soon as you are finished or remove your plate and utensils where you are sitting. *Do* get into the habit of leaving a small amount of food on your plate—

just for effect. *Don't* eat just because it's time. *Don't* save favored foods until the last so that you eat them no matter how satisfied you feel.

What to Eat. Throughout the program, patients receive nutritional information. Specific diets are not prescribed, but patients are encouraged to eat nutritionally sound meals. Instead of counting calories, which can be a tedious procedure, patients are taught to use a *food exchange system* in which foods are grouped in six categories according to similar caloric values. Dietary planning is more convenient with this procedure. Specific suggestions in this area include: *Do* eat small portions of all nutritious foods. *Don't* eat high-calorie food when low-calorie food can be substituted.

Clean-Up. The final step in the eating chain that may contribute to inappropriate eating is the method for cleaning up leftover food. Many individuals find it difficult to throw away food, and as a result, will eat whatever food remains on the table. Strategies for managing this problem include: *Do* have someone else scrape the dishes and handle the leftovers. *Don't* eat anything that isn't on your own plate. *Don't* even lick the service utensils before washing them.

At the last session of the McReynolds et al. (1975) treatment program, the patients are presented with several strategies to help them maintain their weight loss once they have achieved their desired weight. Patients are instructed to continue monitoring and graphing their weight on a weekly basis. They are also encouraged to alter their clothing to fit their new smaller size so that there are fewer excuses to regain weight. If patients are maintaining appropriate eating habits, their weight should fluctuate no more than five pounds. However, should they begin to exceed this weight gain, they are instructed to return to the techniques they have learned in the program, including the use of the special dishes. This will help to reestablish appropriate eating and activity patterns. Periodic follow-up visits to catch any substantial relapses also may be beneficial. If relapses do occur, booster treatment sessions may be necessary to get the patients back on the right track.

Treatment of Medical Phobias

Few individuals actually relish the experience of receiving an injection or having their blood drawn. Nevertheless, to permit the physician and other health care staff to diagnose, prevent, or treat an illness, most patients are cooperative and readily submit to these procedures. However, there is a small, but troublesome, group of patients who exhibit such an extreme fear of even minor medical procedures that their problematic behavior may clearly be considered a phobia. Such individuals, as a result of their phobia, attempt to avoid the necessary treatment, and make the job of the medical practitioner all the more difficult.

Chapter 2 discusses a number of behavioral techniques for eliminating anxiety states and avoidance behaviors. These techniques are similar to the extent that they expose the patient to events that elicit the anxiety in a controlled manner and under conditions where the feared consequences do not occur. The patient is exposed to these events through imagination, real life, or the observation of others interacting with the feared situation in a competent and effective manner. Several of these strategies have been successfully applied to the treatment of persistent medical phobias. These behavioral procedures have enabled the patient to encounter the feared situation, and as a result, have increased the patient's cooperation with the medical treatment. Furthermore, the behavioral techniques have produced rapid treatment effects.

Injection Phobias

A multifaceted program for the treatment of injection phobias is presented by Nimmer and Kapp (1974). The patients had a longstanding history of extreme fear of receiving an injection, which was manifested by fainting when faced with this situation.

One aspect of the treatment program was the in vivo presentation of events related to receiving an injection arranged in a hierarchy from the least to most anxiety-producing. The items in the hierarchy are listed in Table 4.6. In addition to real-life exposure to the feared events in the therapy session, the patients took the materials home and were instructed to practice the items that they had successfully completed during the preceding session. Patients were considered to have successfully completed an item when they no longer reported experiencing anxiety with that item. A final component of the treatment program was a modeling procedure in which the patients observed other individuals who received injections and who did not respond adversely to the situation.

The patients required an average of five treatment sessions. At the end of this period, they were all able to receive an injection without fainting or reporting any feelings of discomfort. These results were maintained at a six-month follow-up assessment.

Table 4.6   Standard Hierarchy Used for All Three Subjects (Items are ranked in descending order of their anticipated anxiety-arousing potential)

18. Receiving injection by physician.

17. Syringe, shield off, held by therapist and darted quickly to subject's arm.

16. Syringe, shield on, held by therapist and darted quickly to subject's arm.

15. Syringe, shield off, held by subject and darted quickly to therapist's arm.

14. Syringe, shield on, held by subject and darted quickly to therapist's arm.

13. Syringe, shield off, held by therapist and touched to subject's arm.

11. Syringe, shield off, held by subject and touched to her own arm.

10. Syringe, shield on, held by subject and touched to her own arm.

 9. Syringe, shield off, held by subject and touched to therapist's arm.

 8. Syringe, shield on, held by subject and touched to therapist's arm.

 7. Syringe is placed leaning against subject's arm, shield off.

 6. Syringe is placed leaning against subject's arm, shield on.

 5. Being prepared for an injection (sleeve up, rubbed with swab).

 4. Handling syringe with shield off.

 3. Handling syringe with shield on.

 2. Viewing syringe on table with shield off the needle.

 1. Viewing hypodermic syringe on table with shield on the needle.

From W. H. Kimmer and R. A. Kapp, A multiple impact program for the treatment of an injection phobia. *Journal of Behavior Therapy and Experimental Psychiatry*, 1974, *5*, 257–258. Copyright © 1974 by Pergamon Press, Ltd. Reprinted by permission.

A similar treatment program was used by Turnage and Logan (1974) to treat a severe case of a hypodermic needle phobia. The patient was a twenty-seven-year-old woman who had exhibited an extreme fear of pain from a hypodermic needle since early childhood. At the time that she sought treatment for this phobia, the patient required physical restraint by several adults in order to have her blood drawn or receive an injection.

Following training in progressive muscle relaxation, a hierarchy of fear events was constructed for use in an in vivo systematic desensitization procedure. The actual stimuli used for the treatment program were four hypodermic syringes of various sizes. Items in the hierarchy were varied across three dimensions: size of syringe, duration of exposure to the stimulus, and proximity of the stimulus to the patient. The hierarchy was constructed so that each item gradually increased along these dimensions. For example, one item from the hierarchy involved a 5 cc syringe that was held 3 feet from the patient for a period of three seconds. A needle was included in the hierarchy when the patient was able to observe the syringes without experiencing any anxiety.

The patient was able to comfortably tolerate a 20 cc syringe and needle from a distance of 6 inches for thirty seconds by the ninth treatment session. At this point, a participant modeling procedure was introduced, using the tactile components of the stimuli. First, the patient observed the therapist touch the syringe and needle to his arm. The patient then imitated the therapist, performing the behavior on herself. Finally, she imitated the therapist, who used the syringe to withdraw water from a cup and then injected the water back into the cup. During a two-week period that preceded the tenth session, the patient's husband practiced drawing blood from her arm stopping just short of actually sticking her with the needle. In the tenth session, she remained relaxed while she permitted her husband to draw blood from her. Moreover, she reported no pain or discomfort from the experience.

Hemodialysis

Katz (1974) describes the rapid treatment of a hemodialysis phobia in an adolescent patient with renal failure. The patient required three dialysis treatments each week. However, since his first dialysis, he continued to have panic attacks when he came to the hospital for treatment, and experienced considerable pain and anxiety during the procedure.

The patient's intense fear of dialysis was eliminated in only one treatment session using systematic desensitization. Table 4.7 presents the hierarchy of anxiety-producing events used in the treatment program. The patient was instructed to imagine each of these scenes while remaining relaxed. Within a ninety-minute session, he successfully completed the hierarchy without reporting any distress. Following systematic desensitization, the patient was able to be dialyzed by the technician without experiencing any anxiety attacks.

In order to maintain this reduction in the patient's level of anxiety, he was initially dialyzed only by technicians with whom he was familiar. Later new technicians were gradually introduced into the dialysis treatment by assuming increasingly greater involvement with the patient. In addition, the patient received considerable social reinforcement for cooperating with the technicians and for responding in a relaxed man-

Table 4.7   Hierarchy Used in the Treatment of a Hemodialysis Phobia

---

1. Waking upon the morning of a scheduled dialysis treatment.

2. At the hospital being weighed in and having blood pressure and temperature taken.

3. In bed being prepared for Xylocaine injection.

4. Visualizing the dialysis catheter.

5. Having the catheter inserted by a trusted technician.

6. Having the catheter inserted by a new technician.

7. Having the catheter withdrawn immediately after it was inserted.

8. Having the catheter reinserted.

From R. C. Katz, Single session recovery from a hemodialysis phobia: A case study. *Journal of Behavior Therapy and Experimental Psychiatry,* 1974, *5,* 205–206. Copyright © 1974 by Pergamon Press, Ltd. Reprinted by permission.

ner. A six-month follow-up assessment revealed no recurrences of the panic episodes.

Finally, the treatment of several patients with severe needle phobias through participant modeling is presented by Taylor, Ferguson, and Wermuth (1977). The patients were hospitalized for diagnostic tests or surgery that necessitated multiple insertion of needles or intravenous catheters for the withdrawal of blood samples or injection of medication. However, because of their intense fear of needles, they fainted or refused to cooperate with the medical procedures. A participant modeling procedure adopted from Bandura was employed.

Bandura (1976) has argued that a combination of modeling and guided reinforced practice, what Bandura calls participant modeling, is the most powerful modeling treatment for eliminating phobias. It involves the guided practice of the target behavior during or following observation of the model's performance. Participant modeling is a carefully structured and graduated process in which modeled performances by the therapist are immediately imitated and practiced by the patient under gradually more difficult and real-life conditions, with the therapist initially providing extensive encouragement, physical or verbal prompts, and positive reinforcemnt for the patient's practice attempts.

Bandura and his associates have also found that behavior change can be accelerated and that patients can be assisted through difficult and stressful situations by the use of adjunctive procedures or "response-induction aids" (e.g., prompts, joint performance with the therapist, gradually increasing time of exposure to the feared object or event) and "self-directed performance" (e.g., additional self-directed practice with a variety of situations, following the initial participant modeling treatment) (Bandura, Jeffrey, & Gajdos, 1975; Bandura, Jeffrey, & Wright, 1974).

This basic procedure was followed by Taylor et al. (1977) in the treatment of needle-phobic patients. After an explanation of the procedure, the patients were given an instrument tray containing intravenous equipment: syringes, covered needles, alcohol swabs, etc. When the patient was able to tolerate having the tray in the room, the therapist identified and handled each item and gave it to the patient. The patient was then instructed to handle the equipment until he or she felt comfortable in doing so. In addition, the patient was asked to handle increasingly larger covered needles. This was continued until the patient no longer reported feeling anxious, at which time the covers were removed from the needles. When the patient was able to hold the syringe and open needle in a comfortable manner, the therapist demonstrated touching the needle to his own skin, moving the needle up and down his arm. The patient was then asked to imitate this behavior. A syringe was then filled with medication, and the patient was asked to copy the therapist's behavior of injecting the medication into an orange. The patient continued to practice this until anxiety was no longer experienced. Finally, the therapist stuck the needle into his own arm to demonstrate that there were no adverse consequences. The treatment session culminated in the therapist drawing the patient's blood. This procedure, which lasted approximately one hour, considerably reduced the patients' anxiety and distress, and enabled them to engage in the previously feared situation. After treatment the patients were able to tolerate the repeated drawing of blood samples and the use of intravenous catheters postoperatively.

Summary

The simultaneous application of behavioral methods and medical procedures have been shown to be effective in reducing or eliminating factors that exacerbate the symptomatic behaviors and in alleviating the discomfort that often results from bodily illness. This chapter describes techniques for dealing with patient behaviors that interfere with the effective treatment of their health-related problems: sick-role behavior; failure to comply with medical regimens; difficulties in modifying health risk factors; and fears of medical procedures.

The responses that an individual receives from others for being sick often reinforce sick-role behavior, resulting in considerable dependency of the patient on health care personnel. The more the individual accepts a self-concept of being sick or disabled, the more likely his or her behavior is to change in the direction of disability. Among persons reporting a medical condition, those who perceived themselves as sick were more likely to seek opportunities to remove themselves from normal activities and responsibilities of daily life. Following an illness or injury, many patients continue to present disability behaviors that are disproportionate to any existing organic or physical problems. Invalidism may be maintained by the anxiety and depression that result from a serious illness or accident. Patients may resist returning to their premorbid level of activity or exhibit work-related fears because of their belief that those activities contributed to the onset of the illness.

The literature on patient compliance with medical regimens demonstrates that many patients, even when the doctor's communication has been clear, substantially deviate from prescribed treatment programs or fail to follow any of the physician's recommendations. The characteristics of the therapeutic regimen, such as complexity and duration of the treatment program, as well as the patient's belief in the efficacy of the therapy are more important than any personality or demographic factors in determining adherence to medical treatment. Compliance with drug regimens is generally better if the medication provides some immediate relief from symptoms and poor when it is taken for prophylactic reasons or where symptomatic discomfort is minimal. Studies show that information about the illness and treatment does not insure compliance with the medical regimen. In this chapter, noncompliance with medical regimens is regarded as a behavioral problem. Examples of how noncompliance may be modified by behavioral principles and procedures are presented. A functional analysis is used to identify the relationship between the environmental events and the target behavior (e.g., not taking medication as described by the physician). Patients are more likely to adopt health-related activities (e.g., medication taking, exercise programs, smoking or eating reductions) when these activities fit into the daily routine. A comprehensive program for weight control is detailed.

The application of behavioral principles to modify behaviors that manifest themselves as fears (e.g., receiving injections, having blood drawn) is illustrated through case examples. People with extreme fear of injections or medical examinations may avoid getting the necessary treatment and increase their potential health problems. The use of systematic desensitization, participant modeling, and gradual exposure has produced rapid treatment effects in many cases.

References

Abramson, E. E. A review of behavioral approaches to weight control. *Behaviour Research and Therapy*, 1973, *11*, 547–556.

Azrin, N. H., & Powell, J. Behavioral engineering: The use of response priming to improve prescribed self-medication. *Journal of Applied Behavior Analysis*, 1969, *2*, 39–42.

Bandura, A. Effecting change through participant modeling. In J. D. Krumboltz & C. E. Thoresen (Eds.), *Counseling methods*. New York: Holt, Rinehart & Winston, 1976.

Bandura, A., Jeffrey, R. W., & Gajdos, E. Generalizing change through self-directed performance. *Behaviour Research and Therapy*, 1975, *13*, 141–152.

Bandura, A., Jeffrey, R. W., & Wright, C. L. Efficacy of participant modeling as a function of response induction aids. *Journal of Abnormal Psychology*, 1974, *83*, 56–64.

Bass, F., & Grantham, R. P. Preventative medicine. In R. E. Rakel & H. F. Conn (Eds.), *Family practice* (2nd ed.). Philadelphia: W. B. Saunders, 1978.

Becker, M. H., Drachman, R. H., & Kirscht, D. P. Predicting mothers' compliance with pediatric medical regimens. *Journal of Pediatrics*, 1972, *81*, 843–854.

Bellack, A. S. Behavior therapy for weight reduction. *Addictive Behaviors*, 1975, *1*, 73–82.

Beneke, W. M., Paulsen, B., McReynolds, W. T., & Lutz, R. N. Long-term results of two behavior modification weight loss programs using nutritionists as therapists. *Behavior Therapy*, 1978, *9*, 501–507.

Berkanovic, E. Lay conceptions of the sick role. *Social Forces*, 1972, *51*, 53–64.

————. Behavioral science and prevention. *Preventative Medicine*, 1976, *5*, 92–105.

Bigelow, G., Strickler, D., Liebson, I., & Griffiths, R. Maintaining disulfiram ingestion among outpatients alcoholics: A security-deposit contingency contracting procedure. *Behaviour Research and Therapy*, 1976, *14*, 378–381.

Blanchard, E. B., & Young, L. D. Clinical applications of biofeedback training: A review of evidence. *Archives of General Psychiatry*, 1974, *30*, 573–589.

Bleecker, E. R., & Engle, B. T. Learned control of cardiac rate and cardiac conduction in Wolff-Parkinson-White syndrome. *Seminars in Psychiatry*, 1973, *5*, 475–479.

Brand, R. J., Rosenman, R. H., Sholts, R. I., & Friedman, M. Multivariate prediction of coronary heart disease in the Western Collaborative Group

Study compared to the finding of the Framingham Study. *Circulation,* 1976, *53,* 348–355.

Brown, M. A. A behavioral approach to post-catastrophic illness work phobia. *International Journal of Psychiatry in Medicine,* 1978, *8,* 235–241.

Brownell, K. D., Heckerman, C. L., Westlake, R. J., Hayes, S. C., & Monti, P. M. The effects of couples training and partner cooperation in the behavioral treatment of obesity. *Behaviour Research and Therapy,* in press.

Caldwell, J. R., Cobb, S., Dowling, M. D., & de Jongh, D. The dropout problem in antihypertensive therapy. *Journal of Chronic Disease,* 1970, *22,* 579–592.

Caplan, R., Robinson, E., French, J., Caldwell, J. R., & Shinn, M. *Adhering to medical regimens.* Ann Arbor: Institute for Social Research, University of Michigan, 1976.

Charney, E., Bynum, R., Eldredge, D., Frank, D., McWhinney, J. B., McNabb, N., Scheiner, A., Sumpter, E. A., & Iker, H. How well do patients take oral penicillin? A collaborative study in private practice. *Pediatrics,* 1967, *40,* 188–195.

Ciminero, A. R., Nelson, R. O., & Lipinski, D. Self-monitoring procedures. In A. R. Ciminero, K. S. Calhoun, & H. E. Adams (Eds.), *Handbook of behavioral assessment.* New York: Wiley, 1977.

Creer, T. L., & Christian, W. P. *Chronically ill and handicapped children: Their management and rehabilitation.* Champaign, Ill.: Research Press, 1976.

Dapcich-Miura, E., & Hovell, M. F. Contingency management of adherence to a complex medical regimen in an elderly patient. *Behavior Therapy,* 1979, *10,* 193–201.

Davis, M. H., Saunders, D., Creer, T., & Chai, H. Relaxation training facilitated by biofeedback apparatus as a supplemental treatment in bronchial asthma. *Journal of Psychosomatic Research,* 1973, *17,* 121–128.

Davis, M. S. Variations in patient's compliance with doctor's orders: Analysis of congruence between survey responses and results of empirical investigations. *Journal of Medical Education,* 1966, *41,* 1037–1048.

———. Predicting non-compliant behavior. *Journal of Health and Social Behavior,* 1967, *8,* 265–271.

Davison, G. C., & Neale, J. M. *Abnormal psychology: An experimental clinical approach.* New York: Wiley, 1974.

Elder, S. T., Ruiz, Z. R., Deabler, H. L., & Dillenkoffer, R. L. Instrumental conditioning of diastolic blood pressure in essential hypertensive patients. *Journal of Applied Behavior Analysis,* 1973, *6,* 377–382.

Epstein, L. H., & Masek, N. J. Behavioral control of medicine compliance. *Journal of Applied Behavior Analysis,* 1978, *11,* 1–9.

Ferster, C. B., Nurnberger, J. I., & Levitt, E. B. The control of eating. *Journal of Mathetics,* 1962, *1,* 87–109.

Fordyce, W. E. Behavioral methods in rehabilitation. In W. S. Neff (Ed.), *Rehabilitation psychology.* Washington, D.C.: American Psychological Association, 1971.

Fordyce, W. E., Fowler, R. S., Lehmann, J. F., DeLateur, B., Sand, P. L., & Trieschmann, R. B. Operant conditioning in the treatment of chronic pain. *Archives of Physical Medicine and Rehabilitation,* 1973, *54,* 399–408.

Foreyt, J. P., Scott, L. W., Mitchell, R. E., & Gotto, A. M. Plasma lipid changes in the normal population following behavioral treatment. *Journal of Consulting and Clinical Psychology,* 1979, *47,* 440–452.

Gillum, R. F., & Barsky, A. J. Diagnosis and management of patient noncompliance. *Journal of the American Medical Association,* 1974, *228,* 1563–1567.

Gordis, L., Markowitz, M., & Lilienfeld, A. The inaccuracy of using interviews to estimate patient reliability in taking medications at home. *Medical Care,* 1969, *7,* 49–54.

Groden, B., & Cheyne, A. Rehabilitation after cardiac illness. *British Medical Journal,* 1972, *2,* 700–703.

Hall, S. M., & Hall, R. G. Outcome and methodological consideration in behavioral treatment of obesity. *Behavior Therapy,* 1974, *5,* 352–364.

Haynes, R. B. A critical review of the "determinants" of patient compliance with therapeutic regimens. In D. L. Sackett and R. B. Haynes (Eds.), *Compliance with therapeutic regimens.* Baltimore: John Hopkins University Press, 1976.

Haynes, R. B., & Sackett, D. L. *An annotated bibliography on the compliance of patients with therapeutic regimens.* Paper presented at Compliance with Therapeutic Regimens Conference, McMaster University, Ontario, Canada, May, 1974.

Henderson, J. B., & Enelow, A. J. The coronary risk factor problem: A behavioral perspective. *Preventative Medicine,* 1976, *5,* 128–148.

Hulka, B. S., Kupper, L. L., Cassel, J. C., & Efira, R. L. Medication use and misuse: Physician-patient discrepancies. *Journal of Chronic Diseases,* 1975, *28,* 7–21.

Hyman, M. D. Disability and patient's perceptions of preferential treatment: Some preliminary findings. *Journal of Chronic Diseases,* 1971, *24,* 329–342.

Jacob, R. G., Kraemer, H. C., & Agras, W. S. Relaxation training in the treatment of hypertension. *Archives of General Psychiatry,* 1977, *34,* 1417–1427.

Jeffrey, D. B. Behavioral management of obesity. In W. E. Craighead, A. E. Kazdin, & M. J. Mahoney (Eds.), *Behavior modification: Principles, issues, and applications.* Boston: Houghton Mifflin, 1976.

Johnson, D. A. Treatment of depression in general practice. *British Medical Journal,* 1973, *2,* 18.

Kahn, A. V., Staerk, M., & Bonk, C. Role of counterconditioning in the treatment of asthma. *Journal of Psychosomatic Research,* 1973, *17,* 389–392.

Kasl, S. V. Issues in patient adherence to health care regimens. *Journal of Human Stress,* 1975, *1,* 5–17.

Kasl, S. V., & Cobb, S. Health behavior, illness behavior, and sick role behavior. *Archives of Environmental Health,* 1966, *12,* 246–266, 531–541.

Katz, R. C. Single session recovery from a hemodialysis phobia: A case study. *Journal of Behavior Therapy and Experimental Psychiatry,* 1974, *5,* 205–206.

Kennedy, W. A., & Foreyt, J. P. Control of eating behavior in an obese patient by avoidance conditioning. *Psychological Reports,* 1968, *22,* 571–576.

Kimball, C. P. Conceptual developments in psychosomatic medicine: 1939–1969. *Annals of Internal Medicine,* 1970, *73,* 307–316.

Kirscht, J. P., & Rosenstock, I. M. Patient adherence to antihypertensive medical regimes. *Journal of Community Health*, 1977, *3*, 115–124.

————. Patients' problems in following recommendations of health experts. In G. C. Stone, F. Cohen, & N. E. Adler (Eds.), *Health psychology.* San Francisco: Jossey-Bass, 1979.

Knapp, T. J. *Behavior management procedures for diabetic persons.* Paper presented at the meeting of the Midwestern Association of Behavior Analysis, Chicago, May, 1977.

Leon, G. R. Current dimensions in the treatment of obesity. *Psychological Bulletin*, 1976, *33*, 557–578.

Levitz, L. S., & Stunkard, A. J. A therapeutic coalition for obesity: Behavior modification and patient self-help. *American Journal of Psychiatry*, 1974, *131*, 423–427.

Levy, S. M. *Correlates of compliance in hospitalized cardiac patients.* Paper presented at the meeting of the Midwestern Psychological Association, Chicago, May, 1978.

LoGerfo, J. P. Hypertension. Management in a prepaid health care project. *Journal of the American Medical Association*, 1975, *223*, 245–248.

Lowe, K., & Lutzker, J. R. Increasing compliance to a medical regimen with a juvenile diabetic. *Behavior Therapy*, 1979, *10*, 57–64.

Ludwig, E. G., & Adams, S. D. Patient cooperation in a rehabilitation center: Assumption of the client role. *Journal of Health and Social Behavior*, 1968, *9*, 328–336.

McReynolds, W. T., Lutz, R. N., Paulsen, B. K., & Kohrs, M. B. Weight loss resulting from two behavior modification procedures with nutritionists as therapists. *Behavior Therapy*, 1976, *7*, 238–291.

McReynolds, W. T., & Paulsen, B. K. Stimulus control as the behavioral basis of weight loss procedures. In B. J. Williams, S. Martin, & J. P. Foreyt (Eds.), *Obesity: Behavioral approaches to dietary management.* New York: Brunner/Mazel, 1976.

McReynolds, W. T., Paulsen, B. K., Lutz, R. N., & Kohrs, M. B. Treatment manuals for two successful behavior therapeutic approaches to weight control. *JSAS Catalogue of Selected Documents in Psychology*, 1975, *5*, 286.

Mann, G. V. The influence of obesity on health, Parts 1 and 2. *New England Journal of Medicine*, 1974, *289*, 178–186 and 226–232.

Mann, R. A. The behavior-therapeutic use of contingency contracting to control an adult behavior problem: Weight control. *Journal of Applied Behavior Analysis*, 1972, *5*, 99–109.

Marston, M. V. Compliance with medical regimens: A review of the literature. *Nursing Research*, 1970, *19*, 312–323.

Meyer, A. J., & Henderson, J. B. Multiple risk factor reduction in the prevention of cardiovascular disease. *Preventative Medicine*, 1974, *3*, 225–236.

Mikulic, M. A. Reinforcement of independent and dependent behavior by nursing personnel: An exploratory study. *Nursing Research*, 1971, *20*, 162–165.

Miller, N. E. Learning of visceral and glandular responses. *Science,* 1969, *163,* 434–445.

Moore, N. Behavior therapy in bronchial asthma: A controlled study. *Journal of Psychosomatic Research,* 1965, *9,* 257–276.

Nimmer, W. H., & Kapp, R. A. A multiple impact program for the treatment of an injection phobia. *Journal of Behavior Therapy and Experimental Psychiatry,* 1974, *5,* 257–258.

O'Leary, K. D., & Wilson, G. T. *Behavior therapy: Application and outcome.* Englewood Cliffs, N.J.: Prentice-Hall, 1975.

Parsons, T. *The social system.* Glencoe, Ill.: Free Press, 1951.

———. Definitions of health and illness in light of American values and social structure. In R. Jaco (Ed.), *Patients, physicians, and illness.* New York: Free Press, 1958.

Penick, S. G., Filion, R., Fox, S., & Stunkard, A. J. Behavior modification in the treatment of obesity. *Psychosomatic Medicine,* 1971, *33,* 49–55.

Pierce, C. M. Enuresis. In A. M. Freedman & H. I. Kaplan (Eds.), *Comprehensive textbook of psychiatry.* Baltimore: Williams and Wilkins, 1967.

Pomerleau, O. You can get patients to change their habits. *Medical Times,* 1976, *104,* 149–158.

Pomerleau, O., Bass, F., & Crown, V. Role of behavior modification in preventative medicine. *New England Journal of Medicine,* 1975, *292,* 1277–1282.

Pomerleau, O., & Brady, J. P. Behavior modification in medical practice. *Pennsylvania Medicine,* 1975, *78,* 49–59.

Puckett, M. J., & Russell, M. L. *Behavior therapy and adherence to medical regimens.* Paper presented at the meeting of the Association for Advancement of Behavior Therapy, Atlanta, Dec., 1977.

Rosenhan, D. L. On being sane in insane places. *Science,* 1973, *179,* 250–258.

Rosenman, R. H., Brand, R. J., Jenkins, C. D., Friedman, M., Straus, R., & Wurm, M. Coronary heart disease in the Western Collaborative Group Study: Final follow-up experience of 8½ years. *Journal of the American Medical Association,* 1975, *233,* 872–877.

Sackett, D. L., Haynes, R. B., Gibson, E. S., Hackett, B. C., Taylor, D. W., Roberts, R. S., & Johnson, A. L. Randomized clinical trial of strategies for improving medication compliance in primary hypertension. *Lancet,* 1975, *1,* 1205–1207.

Schachter, S. Obesity and eating. *Science,* 1968, *161,* 751–756.

———. Some extraordinary facts about obese humans and rats. *American Psychologist,* 1971, *26,* 129–144.

Schachter, S., Goldman, R., & Gordon, A. Effects of fear, food deprivation, and obesity on eating. *Journal of Personality and Social Psychology,* 1968, *19,* 91–97.

Schmitt, D. P. Patient compliance: The effect of the doctor as a therapeutic agent. *Journal of Family Practice,* 1977, *4,* 853–856.

Schwartz, G. E. Biofeedback as therapy: Some theoretical and practical issues. *American Psychologist,* 1973, *28,* 666–673.

Seer, P. Psychological control of essential hypertension: Review of the literature and methodological critique. *Psychological Bulletin,* 1979, *86,* 1015–1043.

Stamler, J., Stamler, R., Riedlinger, W. F., Algera, G., & Roberts, R. H. Hypertension screening of 1 million Americans. *Journal of the American Medical Association,* 1976, *235,* 2299–2306.

Stekel, S., & Swain, M. The use of written contracts to increase adherence. *Hospitals,* 1977, *51,* 81–84.

Stimson, G. V. Obeying doctor's orders: A view from the other side. *Social Science and Medicine,* 1974, *8,* 97–104.

Stoeckle, J., Zola, I., & Davidson, G. The quantity and significance of psychological distress in medical patients. *Journal of Chronic Disease,* 1976, *17,* 959–970.

Stuart, R. B. Behavioral control of eating. *Behaviour Research and Therapy,* 1967, *5,* 357–365.

———. A three-dimensional program for the treatment of obesity. *Behaviour Research and Therapy,* 1971, *9,* 177–186.

Stuart, R. B., & Davis, B. *Slim chance in a fat world: Behavioral control of obesity.* Champaign, Ill.: Research Press, 1972.

Stunkard, A. J. The management of obesity. *New York State Journal of Medicine,* 1958, *58,* 79–87.

———. New therapy for the eating disorders: Behavior modification of obesity and anorexia nervosa. *Archives of General Psychiatry,* 1972, *26,* 391–398.

Stunkard, A. J., & Mahoney, M. J. Behavioral treatment of the eating disorders. In H. Leitenberg (Ed.), *Handbook of behavior modification.* Englewood Cliffs, N.J.: Prentice-Hall, 1976.

Stunkard, A. J., & Rush, J. A critical review of reports of untoward responses during weight reduction for obesity. *Annals of Internal Medicine,* 1974, *81,* 526–533.

Suinn, R. M. Behavior therapy for cardiac patients. *Behavior Therapy,* 1974, *5,* 569–571.

———. Type A behavior pattern. In R. B. Williams & W. D. Gentry (Eds.), *Behavioral approaches to medical treatment.* Cambridge, Mass.: Ballinger, 1977.

Taylor, C. B., Ferguson, J. M., & Wermuth, B. M. Simple techniques to treat medical phobias. *Postgraduate Medical Journal,* 1977, *53,* 28–32.

Turnage, J. R., & Logan, D. L. Treatment of a hypodermic needle phobia by in vivo systematic desensitization. *Journal of Behavior Therapy and Experimental Psychiatry,* 1974, *5,* 67–69.

Twaddle, A. C. Health decisions and sick role variations: An exploration. *Journal of Health and Social Behavior,* 1969, *10,* 105–115.

———. The concepts of the sick role and illness behavior. In Lipowski (Ed.), *Advances in psychosomatic medicine,* Vol. 8. Basel: Karger, 1972.

Twaddle, A. C., & Hessler, R. M. *A sociology of health.* St. Louis: C. V. Mosby, 1977.

Twaddle, A. C., & Sweet, R. Factors leading to preventable hospital admissions. *Medical Care*, 1970, *8*, 200–208.

Ullmann, L. P., & Krasner, L. *A psychological approach to abnormal behavior* (2nd ed.). Englewood Cliffs, N.J.: Prentice-Hall, 1976.

United States Department of Health, Education, and Welfare. *Obesity and health: A source book of current information for professional health personnel.* Arlington, Va.: U. S. Public Health Service, 1967.

Van Putten, T. Why do schizophrenics refuse to take their drugs? *Archives of General Psychiatry*, 1974, *31*, 67–72.

Vincent, P. Factors influencing patient noncompliance: A theoretical approach. *Nursing Research*, 1971, *20*, 509–515.

Williams, B. J., Martin, S., & Foreyt, J. B. (Eds.), *Obesity: Behavioral approaches to dietary management.* New York: Brunner/Mazel, 1976.

Wollersheim, J. P. The effectiveness of group therapy based upon learning principles in the treatment of overweight women. *Journal of Abnormal Psychology*, 1970, *76*, 462–474.

Wooley, S. C., & Blackwell, B. A behavioral probe into social contingencies on a psychosomatic ward. *Journal of Applied Behavior Analysis*, 1975, *8*, 337–339.

Wooley, S. C., Blackwell, B., & Winget, C. A learning theory model of chronic illness behavior: Theory, treatment, and research. *Psychosomatic Medicine*, in press.

Wooley, S. C., Epps, B., & Blackwell, B. Pain tolerance in chronic illness behavior. *Psychosomatic Medicine*, 1975, *37*, 98.

Zeisat, H. A. Behavior modification in the treatment of hypertension. *International Journal of Psychiatry in Medicine*, 1978, *8*, 257–265.

Zifferblatt, S. M. Increasing patient compliance through the applied analysis of behavior. *Preventative Medicine*, 1975, *4*, 173–182.

5

Management of Childhood Disorders

This chapter addresses many of the questions that parents bring to health care professionals concerning their children. Some merely need reassurance about normal child development trends. Others need to learn how to manage problems such as those of eating, bowel training, hyperactivity, excessive crying, fear of school, or fighting with others.

Others have children who are chronically ill. Asthma can be life threatening, as can ruminative vomiting, anorexia, and juvenile diabetes (Creer & Christian, 1976: Melamed & Johnson, in press). Wright (1975) correctly points out that almost all children with medically involved conditions have unmet psychological needs. The physician must not only meet the medical needs of the child, but also understand and treat the entire family constellation. Stedman (1970) has discussed the use of learning principles in pediatric practice. It has been found that many behavioral techniques are successful adjuncts in the management of enuresis, encopresis, seizures, anorexia, hives, and hyperkinesis, even when the physician must prescribe medication and evaluate possible organic involvement.

Preparing children for special medical and dental procedures is also part of the health care professional's job. (Chapter 8 deals with preparing individuals for surgery, and is particularly recommended for all general practitioners, pediatricians, and their staffs. Chapter 9 focuses on the treatment of dental fears and problems such as bruxism.)

This chapter has been organized by type of problem. In most cases, the child was treated through a parent. Thus, health care providers must know how to instruct the patient and family to carry out these procedures. Illustrations chosen are based on what parents can actually be helped to implement. Follow-up is extremely important in behavioral treatment. It is suggested that a receptionist can help maintain these programs by taking information about progress and referring questions to the physician if the data indicate a need for a change in procedures. Although this practice may initially take additional time, it will yield long-term benefits in that the parents will learn strategies they will be able to apply to other problem behaviors with little extra help.

Management of the Patient in the Office

Evidence shows that the longer the child patient is in the waiting room, the more anticipation anxiety builds up (Opton, 1969). It is important to arrange a progression of steps that lead to the actual contact. Booklets on health care can be handed to the entering mother. Some doctors have made use of audiovisual materials to introduce the patient to the doctor and his or her office procedures. Filmed preparation of children for medical procedures has been developed; it has proven valuable in decreasing fear and improving cooperative patient behavior (Melamed & Siegel, 1975; Melamed, Meyer, Gee, & Soule, 1976; Vernon & Baily, 1974). Figure 5.1 represents a typical scene. A film (Geidel & Gulbrandsen, 1974) has been prepared to show preschool children what to expect during a physical examination, including blood test and inoculations. There are a number of books that do, in fact, prepare the child by taking some of the uncertainty out of the visit. A doctor and/or nurse kit and dolls is available to acquaint the child with the personnel; some of the equipment can be helpful in giving the child an opportunity to voice his or her concerns.

The ill child and his or her parents need information about what to expect, encouragement to express fears and concerns, and a trusting relationship with physicians and staff. A gradual introduction of the child to medical personnel and procedures allows handling of concerns at every step. The waiting room should be friendly in appearance, with toys and books to amuse the not-so-sick child. Children should initially visit the doctor's office when they are well, so that anxiety and pain do not become associated with the office. Much parental concern about the child's contracting even worse diseases at the doctor's office can be alleviated if the receptionist screens seriously ill children from those who are there for checkups, inoculations, and

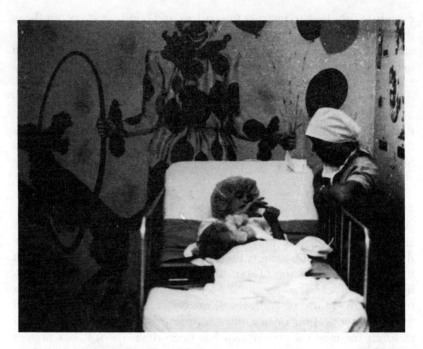

Figure 5.1   A child is waiting for his turn in the operating room. He has seen
a film about what to anticipate during his hospitalization.

Reproduced from *Ethan Has an Operation,* produced by Case Western
Reserve University Health Sciences Center; Melamed & Siegel, 1975.

camp physicals. Thus, if space allows, a well room and a sick room
should be allocated.

The assistant can often do much to allay a child's anxiety by
establishing easy rapport (e.g., by knowing the name by which each
child likes to be called). Research indicates that a friendly interaction
with the assistant can reduce fear before a dental visit (Sawtell, Simon,
& Simeonsson, 1974). Often, if the initial weighing and measuring are
done in the examining room in the presence of two friendly adults—
mother or father and the assistant—it becomes less frightening. The
child observes the instruments and objects in the room, and becomes
desensitized when allowed to view them in the presence of familiar and
comforting persons. Therefore, hypodermic needles and other frightening instruments that trigger anxiety should be kept out of sight. If
the patients are undressed in preparation for the examination, they
may feel self-conscious. It doesn't hurt at this rather embarassing time
to share a few tidbits of mutual interest with the patient before the

examination begins. Some doctors also avoid white laboratory coats, which may seem sterile and forbidding, in order to relax their patients.

If the child clings to his or her mother and refuses to cooperate with the examination, it may be necessary to control the child by sending the mother outside the door until the child is calmed. When given the contingency, "Mother can come back in when you are quiet," the child will often regain composure. The worried and ill child needs to know what behavior is expected. A tell-show-do technique (Addelston, 1959) spells out some of the requisite behaviors. The strangeness of the instruments is explained. The uncertainty of what will happen is reduced. It helps for the doctor to demonstrate expected behavior on himself or herself or on an assistant and to model that behavior. The physician may also describe the sensations that will occur: "When I put this (stethoscope) on your chest it will feel cold; I'll want you to take a deep breath just like this." Johnson and her colleagues (1971; 1974) cite data that indicate that preparation for the sensations that will be experienced during a particular procedure improves cooperation. It has been shown that if the child is invited to participate in the procedures, the sense of control evokes adequate coping responses. Thus, the doctor can invite the patient to listen to his or her own heartbeat, hold the throat swab, or engage in other activities to assist in the examination. Honesty is important. No child likes to be tricked into believing that the doctor's procedure will not hurt a bit. The child would rather be informed as to what it will feel like and how soon it will be over. If there have been unpleasant experiences, no general "treat" for visiting the doctor is going to undo the child's feeling. It is also more efficient from a learning point of view to reward the child for specific behaviors rather than for just being present. Thus, at each stage of cooperation, praise, attention, a smile, or a light pat should be used to reward the child for "sitting still," "keeping your mouth open nice and wide," etc. In the case of crying youngsters, if they are told that they can cry but only briefly (as, for example, during the shot), this permission often becomes calming. But the idea of crying should not be introduced if it has not come up. If a child is told too far in advance that a shot will be coming, he or she may become increasingly anxious and disruptive.

Once the doctor has determined the child's problem, the information is shared with the parents and the child. The need for a particular treatment regimen is clearly described, and a chance to ask questions is provided. To insure that prescriptions are followed, the physician should write down instructions very carefully. Gentry (1977) made the point that to increase compliance, instructions should be given step by step, and should be nondisruptive of the patient's normal daily living activities. Instructions should detail the circumstances under which the parent is to check back with the doctor. Other methods for increasing patient compliance with medical regimens are discussed in Chapter 4.

Parents as Therapists

The parents' potential for aiding in the treatment of their child's problem should not be underestimated, since they have a vested interest in their child's well-being. There has been an increasing number of reports of successful programs for training parents to change their children's behaviors by altering reinforcement contingencies related to those behaviors (Berkowitz & Graziano, 1972; O'Dell, 1974; Patterson, 1971a). The training of parents has also been conducted in groups (Mira, 1970; Patterson, Cobb, & Ray, 1970; Wahler, Winkel, Peterson, & Morrison, 1965). In most cases, a motivated parent with at least an eighth-grade education can read a pamphlet and grasp the basic learning principles (Andrasak, Klare, & Murphy, 1976). Becker's *Parents Are Teachers* (1970), Patterson and Gullion's *Living with Children* (1968), and Patterson's *Families* (1971b) are useful materials that can be lent to parents to engage their cooperation and evaluate their motivation for participating in treatment. Almost all the illustrative cases to be presented in this chapter involve the parent at some level of intervention and suggest some ways in which parents can be integrated into the treatment program. The chance of maintaining success beyond the doctor's office is much greater if the physician has taken the trouble to involve the parent. It is also often the only economical and efficient way to provide care for the patient.

Early Developmental Problems

Many parents, particularly first timers, have concerns about how their child's growth is progressing. The physician's sharing of actual concerns about the child's well-being is sometimes the first step in engaging the parents as therapeutic agents. The doctor can reassure them that problems will be called to their attention during regularly scheduled appointments. It is appropriate to discourage parental tendencies to compare one child with another and to reassure them that each child develops both physically and emotionally at his or her own rate. Since the parents represent the primary source of information regarding their child's medical condition, they must be taught to be good observers. Behavioral approaches are consistent with the way most physicians deal with problems. The treatment program guide in Chapter 3 should prove useful in helping to clarify the treatment goals and communicating these to the parent and child.

Behavioral strategies are often used adjunctively with a number of medical treatment programs. It would be injudicious, if not unethical, for a behavior therapist to undertake to treat a child with a bed-wetting or soiling problem without first insisting that a physician determine that no urinary-genital tract or sphincter problem exists or without simultaneous medical treatment. In the treatment of eating disorders, especially anorexia nervosa, an internist or physician with necessary specialties must consult constantly on the case. Sometimes, as in the case of school phobia, physical symptoms such as vomiting and nausea may accompany the behavior problem. In these cases, a mild tranquilizer may be useful along with the behavioral management of the case. In children suffering seizures, it has been found that even with organic involvement (e.g., epilepsy), behavioral approaches are a useful adjunct to antiseizure medications in reducing the frequency of seizure activity (Mostofsky & Balaschack, 1977; Zlutnick, Mayville, & Moffat, 1975).

In planning a program, there frequently are alternative approaches to reaching the same goal. Often, a combination of treatment approaches is most effective. How does one select a treatment plan? The intervention program selected should fit into the daily life activities of the family. The therapist must assess the willingness and ability of the parents and siblings or teachers to participate in the therapy program. A careful functional analysis of the precipitating events must be undertaken. The natural reinforcers in the environment for maintaining more adaptive behaviors must be considered in choosing a program.

Psychophysiological Disorders

Rationale for Behavioral Treatment of Somatic Disorders

There is a growing interest in the treatment of psychophysiological disorders by both medical and psychological intervention (Katz & Zlutnick, 1975; Knapp & Peterson, 1976; Price, 1974). It has become evident that the interaction of many complex factors (physical, consti-tutional, environmental, and social) contributes to the development and maintenance of most physical disorders (Kimball, 1970; Lipton, Sternschneider, & Richmond, 1966; Schwab, McGinnis, Morris, & Schwab, 1970). The emotional state of the patient is now recognized as playing an important role in the precipitation or exacerbation of many illnesses, including multiple sclerosis, pneumonia, cancer, tuber-culosis, and the common cold (Davison & Neale, 1974). Evidence of the interaction between environmental and psychological factors on the one hand and the physiological state of the body on the other suggests that, at least for some illnesses, methods of intervention beyond traditional medical approaches may be appropriate (Siegel & Richards, 1978). Therefore, a collaborative treatment approach be-tween medical and behavioral practitioners is indicated.

Although conditioning may not play a causative role in psycho-physiological disorders, it probably can best be viewed as a factor potentially exacerbating an already-existing illness. Chapter 4 de-scribes the process in more detail.

An understanding of the etiology of the somatic disorder may not be essential to the development of a behavioral treatment program. Disorders of both an organic and nonorganic origin have been success-fully treated with behavioral techniques. Even when medical interven-tions are called for, behavioral techniques can serve a useful collaborative or adjunctive role in treatment involving chemotherapy or surgery. In addition, behavioral approaches have been useful in changing dysfunctional behavior patterns that may have developed while the medical problem was in existence. For example, two eight-month-old infants learned to become dependent upon a tracheostomy cannula, and had to be gradually weaned by a shaping procedure before they could breathe normally or accept food. The behavioral treatment allowed them to return home (Wright, Nunnery, Eichel, & Scott, 1968). Or, more generally, children who have been physically ill may become whiny and demanding of attention. When their exces-sive dependency is not met, they may throw tantrums. These negative behaviors can be further prolonged when they are reinforced by oth-ers' attending responses. Behavioral methods of handling these types of problems include the use of time-out procedures (Allen, Hart, Buell, Harris, & Wolf, 1964; R. Patterson, 1972; Williams, 1959). An-other approach involves the use of positive reinforcement through contingent attention for more age-appropriate behaviors.

Nocturnal Enuresis

Bed-wetting can be caused by physical defects in the urinary-genital tract, by neurological disorders, or by urinary-tract infections. While less than 10 percent of enuresis in children can be attributed to these organic factors, such factors need to be ruled out or, if indicated, medicated (Siegel & Richards, 1978). Otherwise, behavioral treatment will not be effective. For treatment to be deemed appropriate, two criteria must be met:

1. involuntary discharge of urine during sleep must be seen beyond the normal age of three to four years, when children usually gain bladder control, and
2. organic causes for this behavior must not be present, or should be under medical control.

Then, it must be determined whether the case is one of primary enuresis, in which the child has never had bladder control. If this is true, the treatment approach suggested might rely more on the assumption of a skill deficit and involve the use of positively oriented approaches, perhaps with the aid of a commercially available bell-and-pad device (Mowrer & Mowrer, 1938). The parents of the enuretic child play a crucial role in the treatment process. The enuretic child may not have learned to exercise adequate control of the bladder's sphincter muscles, and therefore, may fail to inhibit the bladder reflex controlling urination under conditions of bladder extension. Sometimes this occurs because the child is a heavy sleeper. In the bell-and-pad method, the child sleeps on a specially constructed pad. As soon as he or she begins to urinate, the circuit activates a bell (or buzzer). This serves to inhibit further urination by causing the bladder muscles to contract reflexly. This is where the physician's consultation with the mother or father becomes crucial. The parent can assist by accompanying the child to the bathroom immediately, as he or she still likely has a full bladder. The parent should encourage the drinking of fluids before bedtime to insure that sufficient pairing of the bell and the act of urination occur. This differs considerably from advice typically given to parents, which is to limit the child's fluid intake and wake the child up to urinate at the parents' bedtime.

The child usually will learn in a few short trials to wake up to the cues for bladder fullness and the need to urinate. The older child can be taught to shut off the bell immediately and go to urinate. The device should be reset and a dry sheet placed on the bed. The parents can usually handle the treatment with the doctor's encouragement and the instructions that come with the device. To evaluate the program's effectiveness and maintain parental cooperation, the physician should arrange for them to keep a daily record of clean sheets (or call their data in to the receptionist). The child also should be praised and reinforced for each dry night. The use of the device is discontinued after fourteen consecutive dry nights. Any relapses in excess of two wet nights a week will call for reinstatement of the device. Many children require four to eight weeks before the bed-wetting is completely controlled. This respondent conditioning procedure has been found superior to traditional psychotherapy (De Leon & Mandell, 1966; Werry & Cohressen, 1965) and drug therapy (Forrester, Stein, & Susser, 1964; Young & Turner, 1965). In fact, Doleys (1977) cites greater relapse in children for whom drugs were used as an adjunct. More detailed descriptions of this procedure are presented in Lovibond and Coote (1970) and Werry (1967). The success rate is over 80 percent, and the 20 percent relapse rate following termination of treatment (O'Leary & Wilson, 1975) is probably due to lack of reintroducing the bell and pad when warranted. A recent review (Doleys, 1977) reported a relapse rate of 41 percent. He notes that studies that employed an intermittent schedule of alarm presentation and overlearning reduced the relapse rate. If there are other behavioral problems coexistent with bed-wetting, a referral to a psychologist should be made.

Enuretic children tend to urinate a smaller volume at more frequent intervals than do children with bladder control (Muellner, 1960). Therefore, a treatment program focused on shaping bladder control can be used. The child is encouraged to drink frequently. When the child feels the need to urinate, he or she is asked to "hold it in" for five minutes and then to use the bathroom. This withholding period is gradually increased several minutes each day until the child can delay thirty to forty minutes (Kimmel & Kimmel, 1970). The child is reinforced with praise and tokens (later exchangeable for TV shows, favorite food, and toys). While this procedure may seem painstaking, if records are kept of the frequency of daytime urinations, volumes of urine, and the number of dry nights, three weeks' efforts may save two more years of wet sheets, scoldings, and embarrassment. Adolescents (J. M. Stedman, 1972) can usually follow this program without parental assistance. However, Doleys (1977) warns about a lack of appropriate studies with substantial follow-up data.

A combination of bell-and-pad and retention-control training procedures is described in Table 5.1 adapted from Azrin, Sneed, and

Table 5.1   Dry-Bed Procedure in the Treatment of Enuresis

I. *Intensive training (one night)*
   (A) *One hour before bedtime*
      1. Child informed of all phases of training procedure
      2. Alarm placed on bed
      3. Positive practice in toileting (20 practice trials)
         (a) child lies down in bed
         (b) child counts to 50
         (c) child arises and attempts to urinate in toilet
         (d) child returns to bed
         (e) steps (a), (b), (c) and (d) repeated 20 times
   (B) *At bedtime*
      1. Child drinks fluids
      2. Child repeats training instructions to trainer
      3. Child retires for the night
   (C) *Hourly awakenings*
      1. Minimal prompt used to awaken child
      2. Child walks to bathroom
      3. At bathroom door (*before* urination), child is asked to
         inhibit urination for one hour (omit for children under 6)
         (a) if child could not inhibit urination
            (i) child urinates in toilet
           (ii) trainer praises child for correct toileting
          (iii) child returns to bed
         (b) if child indicated that he could inhibit
           urination for one hour
            (i) trainer praises child for his urinary control
           (ii) child returns to bed
      4. At bedside, the child feels the bed sheets and comments
         on their dryness
      5. Trainer praises child for having a dry bed
      6. Child is given fluids to drink
      7. Child returns to sleep
   (D) *When an accident occurred*
      1. Trainer disconnects alarm
      2. Trainer awakens child and reprimands him for wetting
      3. Trainer directs child to bathroom to finish urinating
      4. Child is given Cleanliness Training
         (a) child is required to change night clothes
         (b) child is required to remove wet bed sheet
            and place it with dirty laundry
         (c) trainer reactivates alarm
         (d) child obtains clean sheets and remakes bed
      5. Positive Practice in correct toileting (20 practice
         trials) performed immediately after the
         Cleanliness Training
      6. Positive Practice in correct toileting (20 practice
         trials) performed the following evening
         before bedtime

II. *Post training supervision (begins the night after training)*
   (A) *Before bedtime*
      1. Alarm is placed on bed
      2. Positive Practice given (*if* an accident occurred
         the previous night)
      3. Child is reminded of need to remain dry and of
         the need for Cleanliness Training and Positive
         Practice if wetting occurred
      4. Child is asked to repeat the parent's instructions
   (B) *Night-time toileting*
      1. At parents' bedtime, they awaken child and send
         him to toilet
      2. After each dry night, parent awakens child
         30 minutes earlier than on previous night
      3. Awakening discontinued when they are scheduled
         to occur within one hour of child's bedtime

(continued)

162 *Applications of Behavior Therapy to Health Care Problems*

(C) *When accidents occurred, child receives Cleanliness Training
and Positive Practice immediately upon wetting and at bedtime
the next day*
(D) *After a dry night*
1. Both parents praise child for not wetting his bed
2. Parents praise child at least 5 times during the day
3. Child's favorite relatives are encouraged to
praise him

III. *Normal routine--initiated after 7 consecutive dry nights*
(A) *Urine-Alarm is no longer placed on bed*
(B) *Parents inspect child's bed each morning*
1. If bed is wet, child receives Cleanliness Training
immediately and Positive Practice the following evening
2. If bed is dry, child receives praise for keeping
his bed dry
(C) *If two accidents occur within a week, the Post-Training
Supervision is reinstated*

From N. H. Azrin, T. J. Sneed, and R. M. Foxx, Dry-bed training: Rapid elimination of childhood enuresis. *Behaviour Research and Therapy,* 1974, *12,* 147–156. Copyright © 1974 by Pergamon Press, Ltd. Reprinted by permission.

Foxx (1974). This involves operant procedures, such as hourly wakenings, positive practice in going to the toilet, punishment (child changes sheet), and positive reinforcement for going to the bathroom at night. Dry-bed training, in a child of sufficient age to ensure the capability for bladder control, has been found to work in as short a time as one intensive evening of training. It requires more active participation of the parents, but the improvement is much quicker. This is the treatment of choice with highly motivated parents and a child who is old enough to understand the procedures. There has been no substantial relapse reported during six months' follow-up evaluations of this procedure. Clear communication from the doctor or behavioral specialist about how to follow the procedures accurately is needed. Encouragement, by use of the telephone for obtaining reports of daily progress, serves to reward success and allows for clarification or modification of the treatment program. The parents gain a sense of achievement and are more ready to heed future advice. The child feels grown up and remains dry.

The same retention-control procedures work for the child who has previously been trained and has a relapse. Miller (1973) was able to eliminate bed-wetting completely in two adolescents who had become enuretic several years prior to treatment. The program involved only the children. They kept weekly records of the number of times they wet their beds and the frequency of daytime urinations.

They delayed urination an additional ten minutes each week. At the end of treatment, they had achieved three consecutive weeks of dry nights, and no relapse was reported after seven months.

Encopresis

Encopresis is defined as any voluntary or involuntary passage of feces that results in soiled clothing (Wright, 1973). It is usually accompanied by chronic constipation. The stool retention for prolonged periods can result in relaxed sphincter muscles and a distended colon. As a result, periodic involuntary passage of fecal matter may occur. A thorough physical examination to evaluate organic problems must be carried out prior to any behavioral procedure. Often, mineral oil or suppositories can alleviate the discomfort involved in defecation after severe constipation. Wright and Walker (1978) routinely used suppositories or enemas to promote regular defecation in the toilet. However, a careful functional analysis should be obtained to understand each individual case, so that appropriate treatment can be determined. Operant techniques (positive reinforcement strategies and changing the focus of parental attention) work best, and sometimes necessitate adjunctive medical procedures (enemas to clear the colon, a suppository before meals if a spontaneous bowel movement does not occur, or a stool softener).

CASE ILLUSTRATION

Tommy was a six-and-one-half-year-old child with a soiling problem. His mother brought him for treatment after all efforts at praise, punishment, and reasoning had failed. She was at her wit's end. Her older son had never had this problem, and she did not know what the source of Tommy's problem was. She did feel that the father's absence from home for business purposes was exacerbating the problem. Marital disharmony was increasing.

The treatment outline (Table 5.2) illustrates how this problem was resolved. Here, again, it is useful to determine whether the child has ever been bowel trained. It is more difficult, but still possible as in this case, to treat regressive soiling. One must pay careful attention to the secondary gains that may accrue to the

Table 5.2 Treatment Program for a Six-Year-Old with Regressive Soiling

I. Target behavior *encopresis (soiling)* defined as:

    A. (too much) *2-3 soiling incidents/day; tantrums, noncompliance, hits brother*

    B. (too little) *few self-care behaviors; lack of responsibility for pet and toys; finicky eating habits*

    C. (cued by or in reaction to) *toilet not used for defecation; fear of being flushed; not sensitive to soiled pants*

    D. (strengths and skills) *solitary play*

II. Methods of collecting information

    A. (interviews, questionnaires, test results) *parents interviewed, read Patterson's "Families"*

    B. (overt manifestations of patient's behavior) *number of soiling incidents, frequency of tantrums, appropriate behaviors (e.g., feed dog, pick up toys)*

    C. (what patient self-monitors and records) *clean pants, appropriate toilet use*

    D. (lasting changes in the environment—e.g., food left over, work output) *number of clean pants in dresser drawer*

    E. (physiological indices—e.g., GSR, pulse rate) *none*

III. Functional analysis of behavior

    A. (events preceding target behavior) *presence of mother or father, demand made for compliance, father away on business trip*

    B. (events following target behavior) *inconsistent maternal attention (made him shower, change clothes, wiped his behind, ignored, loved him)*

IV. Selecting and implementing an intervention program

    A. Motivation for change

        1. (benefits of "sick-role"—e.g., attention, avoidance or responsibility) *lots of attention, keeps friends away, sent home from camp*

        2. (What would be different for patient/significant others if problem did not exist?) *buttock sores would disappear, mother wouldn't have to clean after him, mother and father would not need to fight about his problem*

(continued)

B. Meaningful environmental consequences

   1. Likes *candy, games with mother, iron-on patches, money*

   2. Dislikes *time-out from TV or social contact with family*

C. Significant others (spouse, siblings, parent, teacher)
brother, father, and mother

D. Factors maintaining the problem *mother's attention, fear of the toilet, and painful buttocks*

E. Treatment strategies *token economy program for shaping self-care behaviors including toileting, ignore soiling, time-out for tantrums*

V. Evaluation of intervention program

A. Monitoring of treatment progress *daily changes in incidence of soiling and tantrums, using the toilet for defecation*

B. Programming for maintenance of behavior change *gradual elimination of token program*

C. Follow-up assessment *two and one-half years with only one incident of soiling, despite parents' separation*

VI. Termination (What was your treatment goal?) *toileting for defecation, reduction of tantrums, increase self-care behaviors*

---

child. Even scolding the child reinforces the undesirable behavior. If left untreated, encopresis develops serious secondary pathological problems, such as rejection by the peer group, emotional immaturity, and more serious psychological disturbance. This problem should command the doctor's immediate attention, or the family should be referred to a behavior specialist.

The mother and father were both requested to come in without their child to clarify whether they viewed the problem the same way and if, in fact, marital therapy was indicated.

I. Selecting a Target Behavior(s)

A. BEHAVIORAL EXCESSES. When asked what Tommy was doing wrong, they described his daily soiling. Often, two to three incidents occurred each day. In addition, he was throwing tantrums, hitting his brother, and in general being noncompliant and negativistic.

B. BEHAVIORAL DEFICITS. In terms of deficits, he did not show age-appropriate behaviors, for example, dressing himself, taking responsibility for the dog, and cleaning his toys. His eating behavior had also deteriorated.

C. DEFECTIVE STIMULUS CONTROL. Tommy used the toilet for urinating, but would not use it for defecation. He complained of sore buttocks and painful stools. He also feared that he would be flushed down the toilet. He did not respond with discomfort to his soiled pants.

D. BEHAVIORAL ASSETS. The parents were asked, "What do you like about Tommy?" They could not think of anything likable about this child, and compared him unfavorably with his older brother. They jointly agreed that Tommy spent a lot of time in his room drawing, and saw this as creativity. It was clear that the parents were not focusing on reinforcing any of his strengths.

II. Methods of Collecting Information

The interview with the parents revealed that normal bladder control was achieved by three years of age. The bowel training was inconsistent and delayed because of job relocations. Soiling continued to be a problem, although the parents believed he did have fecal control for about a four-month period when he was five. At the age of three, Tommy developed a rash. It was diagnosed as a rare blood disease thought to be fatal. Thus, he was smothered with affection, and inconsistent demands were placed on him. The diagnosis turned out to be incorrect, and the symptoms disappeared.

At the age of three and one-half, Tommy saw his maternal grandfather have a nonfatal heart attack. This is when his mother first noticed the soiling. Pediatricians ruled out any organic problems, prescribed mineral oil, and reassured the mother that nobody ever died from soiling. However, it was almost time for first grade, and this youngster was beginning to have peer problems. His friends did not like the way he smelled, and he was frequently left out of activities with other children. Much sibling rivalry existed. The mother was concerned that her returning to school to earn her college degree was exacerbating the soiling problem. The father knew his wife was upset, but tried to absolve himself of any responsibility by bringing the boys nice gifts. He justified the business trips by saying that they were critical at this point in his career. Their marriage, he felt, was far better than their friends', and he refused marital counseling recommendations made by the therapist. The couple rarely socialized together. At this time, the mother was in counseling with the minister.

Who is the most appropriate therapeutic agent? The mother was available and motivated. The father was reluctant. The child was already commanding a great deal of attention, albeit negative. The parents were given Patterson's *Families* to read, and were told to make behavioral observations by recording incidents of soiling for the following week. They were to check his pants one-half hour after each meal and once before bedtime to determine if he had soiled. This time-sampling-recording technique led to decreased arguing with the child over "had he or hadn't he?" They also used a frequency method of recording the number of tantrums he threw each day (a tantrum was defined as over sixty seconds of crying or screaming). The need for an objective definition of the problem was clear from the extreme discrepancy between the parents in their first attempt at measuring the tantrums. An additional goal of the program was to focus the parents' attention on the child's appropriate behavior. Therefore, they were instructed to keep count on a daily basis of whether he picked up his toys, fed the dog, helped the mother, and played with friends. A sample of their recording sheet is provided in Table 5.3, a chart that they constructed, with the help of the therapist, that can be easily filled out and displayed for the child. Note that although they were

Table 5.3 Chart for Increasing Self-Care Behaviors in an Encopretic Child

Independent Behavior	Mon.	Tues.	Wed.	Thurs.	Fri.	Sat.	Sun.
Makes bed							
Feeds dog							
Finishes meal							
Picks up toys							
Socializes							
Helps Mom							
Uses toilet							
Clean pants							

recording soiling incidents, the chart, which is displayed for the child, describes the desired toileting categories, rather than presenting the problem in a negative manner.

In some cases of encopresis, the child can be instructed to put his soiled pants in a special container, thus yielding a concrete, permanent product measure of number of soiled pants. Tommy did not spontaneously change his clothes.

No physiological instrumentation was used. There is a case described in the literature (Schuster, 1974) in which a special balloon was inserted into a six-year-old with life-long soiling and chronic constipation to record internal and external pressure of sphincter muscles. Then, arousal biofeedback and verbal praise were used, and sphincter control was refined in four sessions. However, spincter control was not a problem with the present patient. In fact, Tommy did not soil in nursery school or with baby sitters. It seemed to occur in the presence of the mother, father, and grandmother. His sphincter control was *too* good.

III. Functional Analysis of Behavior

Part of a functional analysis entails determining what precipitates the problem behavior and what consequences follow. The mother had already volunteered that it always happened more frequently when the father was out of town. She stated that she had tried everything—spanking, making him shower and change clothes, loving him more, wiping his buttocks with lotions, and even ignoring (and this is not an easy behavior to ignore). She reported that he had good control at school and never soiled when left with a sitter.

In terms of reinforcing consequences, the child was remaining the center of attention by manipulating his parents. He was being yelled at, scolded, and pleaded with at a higher rate than his older brother. Secondary gain was clearly evident.

Punishing consequences occurred because it hurt to go to the bathroom. The sores on his buttocks that resulted from not cleaning himself after the soiling were painful. More serious problems involving poor interpersonal relationships were already evidenced by his lack of friends.

Motivation for the mother was quite apparent. She would be relieved not to have to clean up after him. The marital conflicts were being intensified by the parents' disagreement over management of the child's behavior.

After examination of the baseline data and interview information, a program could be formulated.

IV. Selecting and Implementing a Treatment Program

Figure 5.2 illustrates the baseline data gathered by the parents for two weeks. There were eleven instances of soiling (about one a day) and two appropriate defecations in the toilet. Tommy had eleven tantrums.

Because of the parents' frustration and feeling that they lacked control over this six-year-old, it was recommended that they start by focusing not on the soiling, but on the tantrums. A time-out procedure was employed in which Tommy was put in his father's study at the onset of a tantrum. The study was selected because it was an unattractive setting for the child, and did not provide any opportunity for reinforcement. The child remained in time-out until three minutes passed in which there was no crying or kicking.

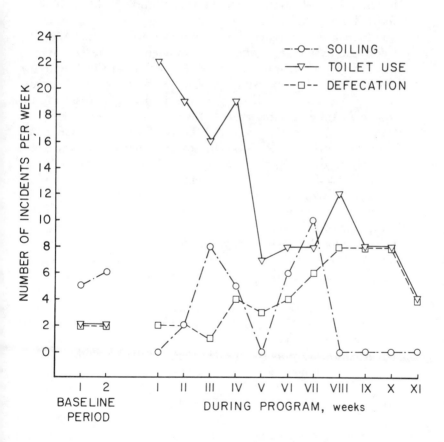

Figure 5.2   Frequency of soiling and toileting behaviors per week during the pretreatment baseline period and each week of the program.

This worked well; only one tantrum occurred the following week. This convinced the mother that consistent consequences do in fact alter behavior. The program to reduce soiling and increase social behaviors (self-care skills and play with others) is briefly summarized in Table 5.4 to indicate week-by-week changes. At first, the child was reinforced for successive approximations to actual toilet use: for using the toilet for sitting, wiping, and flushing, regardless of whether the child defecated. These behaviors were already within the child's repertoire. An immediate tangible reward (candy treat) was given if he had a bowel movement at any time on the toilet. The requirement for reward for toilet use was successively shaped so that by week five he had to defecate in the toilet to receive the reward. This shaping program was instituted because the evaluation revealed that the child was afraid of being flushed down the toilet. The parents were told to ignore soiling and to make clean underpants readily available for him. Week by week, the exchange periods were thinned out. He was at first allowed to exchange his tokens each evening, at which time the mother and father praised him for specific increase in socially appropriate behaviors. During the third week an increase in soiling is illustrated on the figure. This may have resulted from too long a delay before he received the reinforcers. The child had been permitted to exchange his tokens only every other day. Therefore, the program reverted to a more gradual exchange rate. This led to marked improvement. The increase in soiling during the sixth week may reflect the mother's having put the youngster on mineral oil without consulting the therapist—an indication that deviations from the program must be continuously monitored if an effective program is not to be prematurely terminated. Also, a reasonable time period of continued control should be required before the program is considered successful.

V. Evaluation of the Intervention Program

It is clear from Figure 5.2 that achievement of success was not smooth; the parents needed much encouragement for continued participation. Parents should be reminded that the behavior that one is attempting to alter did not develop in a day, and it would be naïve to expect overnight change. However, it took only seven weeks for control over bowel function to be restored.

VI. Termination of the Intervention Program

Once the change in the boy was achieved, he was slowly phased off the program, and received a diploma for feeding the dog,

Table 5.4 Week-by-Week Changes in the Token Reinforcement Program for an Encopretic Child

Week	Contingency	Result	Circumstances for Revising
I	Institute token reward system. Immediate exchange for prizes each night, with praise for appropriate behaviors.	No soiling 2 appropriate defecations, "toilet use" each day.	More required for toilet use. He must sit, wipe and flush. Make it easy to earn prizes.
II	Continue program, rewarding as above	2 soiling episodes.	
III	Every other day exchange of tokens	8 soiling incidents. 4 tantrums.	Mother lost data for one day. Father out of town. Inconsistent time-out for tantrums. Perhaps delay for exchange too great
IV	Exchange 2 days accumulate 1 day Child could earn privileges and time with parents	5 soiling incidents	Keep same reinforcement schedule
V	Same exchange program in effect	No incident of soiling	Try again to wean off exchange ratio
VI	Every other day exchange	6 incidents of soiling 4 defecations in toilet	Mother was using mineral oil under Drs.' advice
VII	Every other day change. 5¢ bonus for each day with total "clean pants."	10 soiling incidents 6 appropriate defecations.	Child concerned about death, Gov. Wallace shot. Mother sprained ankle and rushed to hospital. Child has stomachache and diarrhea. Brother placed on a reward program, without therapist advice.
VIII	Every other day exchange. Mineral oil would stop if he went to bathroom regularly (every other day). Bonus: if no soiling he takes family to McDonald's Restaurant	No soiling	
IX	Limit to only 2 exchanges/week. (3 days apart) 5¢ for 2 consecutive soil free days	No soiling	
X	Exchange every 4th day	No soiling	Remove clean pants category from chart Refocus on positive achievements
XI	All toileting categories removed		

dressing himself, etc. He felt he was a big boy now, and no longer even wanted the tokens. He began to play better with his brother and other children. After termination of the program, the mother was told to keep the therapist informed of any recurrences of more than a single incident of soiling. At the six-month follow-up, the child had been able to attend camp, and had entered the first grade without any difficulties. One instance of soiling was reported on the first day of camp. As noted earlier, the onset of the problem was associated with the grandfather's illness. After the treatment program, the grandfather died, but the problem did not return. Two years later, the parents have been through a separation of seven months, and are now reunited. During this time the child remained in control of his bowel function.

Eating Disturbances

Evidence suggests that eating difficulties in children are a significant clinical problem, with the incidence in young children reportedly as high as 45 percent (Bentovim, 1970). Most eating problems can be treated with little professional assistance. It is the most serious form of food refusal known as anorexia nervosa, however, that usually requires intensive medical and psychological involvement. Reviews of the literature on anorexia nervosa (Bemis, 1978; Bhanji & Thompson, 1974) revealed that studies that employed operant conditioning programs led to increased weight during hospitalization. The failure to produce enduring effects after discharge from the hospital underlines the need for planning for transfer to reinforcers existing in the natural environment.

The problems the physician is likely to confront are those in which children have very limited food preferences and in which childhood obesity is recognized by the parent to be a potential problem.

Both operant and respondent behavioral treatment programs have modified eating patterns of food refusal in children. Typically, the treatment consists of gradually shaping the range of foods a child will accept by using preferred foods to reinforce the eating of foods that the child dislikes. Social reinforcement, such as praise and attention, and TV viewing were also used contingent upon eating small amounts of table food (Bernal, 1972). Siegel and Richards (1978) reviewed treatment programs that have been used to reinstate normal eating patterns in children who may have developed eating disorders as a result of temporary illness or faulty dietary patterns.

Obesity

Obesity in children is an important concern of the pediatric practitioner, not only because of its effects on the physical health of the child, but also because of the psychosocial problems that often result. In addition, data indicate that over 85 percent of overweight children are likely to become overweight adults (Abraham & Nordsieck, 1960). The problems of eating have become so well established by adulthood that the patient may be more resistant to treatment. Hirsch (1975) also has data that the number of fat cells is established at a relatively early age, and may contribute to subsequent obesity.

In viewing childhood obesity as primarily a disorder in the regulation of body weight, whereby the intake of food is greater than the expenditure of energy (once metabolic factors have been explored), the behavioral program focuses on establishing better eating habits and greater exercise involvement. The child's eating patterns are developed within the context of the family and are controlled to a large extent by parental attitudes toward food consumption and nutrition. The program most likely to produce permanent change in the development of eating habits conducive to appropriate body weight is one that involves the parents.

The efficacy of behavioral treatment for producing short-term weight loss has been demonstrated in several investigations. Argona, Cassady, and Drabman (1975) studied parent training groups: the parents were taught to keep daily records of the child's caloric intake, weight, and kind of food eaten, and were then instructed in reinforcing the child for exercising and for following self-control procedures. The researchers found such treatment to result in weight loss that was maintained at a seven-month follow-up. The use of response cost—having the parent forfeit a deposit that could be earned back through compliance with the program and weight loss—served as additional motivation.

Wheeler and Hess (1976) reported on the results of individualized treatment programs that involved joint participation of the parent and the child. The program emphasized changing the conditions in the environment that maintained overeating (e.g., free access to high-caloric snacks) and altering the parent's reinforcement of overeating behaviors. The results of this program are encouraging. Kingsley and Shapiro (1977) also provide evidence that mothers' involvement in treatment led to significantly better weight-loss maintenance. It appears that improvement was due to better eating habits rather than to dieting. It should be remembered, in guiding a weight reduction program over a period of time, that the children are continually developing. Some weight increases are expected. Also, as a standard of treatment progress, the parent can be provided with a measure more objective than number of pounds: one that takes into account the child's height, weight, and skin-fold thickness. In addition, the therapist's reinforcement of changes in eating and exercising patterns, which may occur more rapidly than actual weight loss, may be very effective in maintaining the family's active participation. A school-based technique improved eating and exercise behavior, but wasn't maintained after the school year ended, underlining the need for generalization (Epstein, Masek, & Marshall, 1978).

Seizures

Behavioral procedures have been used successfully to supplement drugs and reduce the frequency and severity of epileptic seizure disorders (Mostofsky & Balaschack, 1977). It is estimated that 7 out of every 100,000 school-aged children have seizures (Bakwin & Bakwin, 1972). Despite the significant reduction in seizures often produced by anticonvulsant drugs, as many as 50 percent of the children who take this medication continue to have occasional seizures. In addition, nearly 20 percent of the children who have a seizure disorder have been completely refractory to drug treatment (Carter & Gold, 1968). The child's daily activities can be seriously disrupted, and physical injury is always a possibility if seizures cannot be adequately controlled.

A behavioral treatment approach makes use of the fact that preseizure behaviors can usually be identified reliably prior to the actual seizure. Children sometimes report an aura, or a parent or teacher may notice behaviors, such as stereotyped motor activities or a vacant stare. In self-induced seizures, precipitating factors can be identified, such as flashing colors, grid patterns, or arm waving (Wright, 1973). If the seizure is viewed as the terminal link in a chain of behaviors, prevention of their occurrence through interference with the preseizure behaviors is possible. Both positive reinforcement for nonseizure activities and punishment of preseizure behaviors have reportedly reduced the frequency and severity of seizures (Siegel & Richards, 1978).

Zlutnick, Mayville, and Moffat (1975) described a series of treatment programs using these two operant procedures (contingent punishment and the reinforcement of behavior incompatible with seizures). These cases illustrate the use of parents and teachers as agents of change in the home and school environments. Each child in these studies had a formal diagnosis of epilepsy based on electroencephalogram (EEG) records or on an evaluation by a neurologist. The seizure activity occurred at least once a day. The punishment contingency involved recognizing preseizure activity, shouting "No!" loudly and sharply, and grasping the patient by the shoulders with both hands and vigorously shaking him or her once. Figure 5.3 is representative of data presented by Zlutnick et al. (1975).

Figure 5.3 illustrates the record of treatment progress of a fourteen-year-old girl with a seizure history dating to the age of eighteen months. EEG results were abnormal, confirming a diagnosis of minor motor and facial epilepsy. Even with anticonvulsant medication, sei-

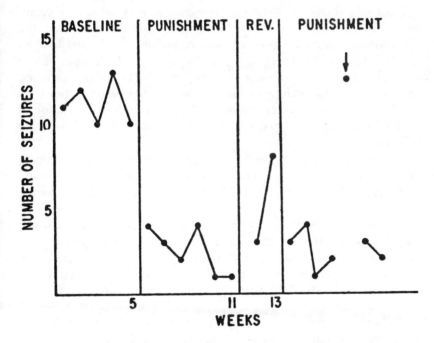

Figure 5.3   The number of minor motor seizures per week for Subject 4.

From S. Zlutnick, W. J. Mayville, and S. Moffat, Modification of seizure disorders: The interruption of behavioral chains. *Journal of Applied Behavior Analysis*, 1975, *8*, 1–12. Copyright © 1975 by the Society for the Experimental Analysis of Behavior, Inc. Reprinted by permission.

zure activity remained relatively high, averaging slightly less than twice a day. Seizures were reliably preceded by arm raising. The girl was treated at home, since the severity and regularity of her seizures prohibited her from attending school. The girl's mother was used as the therapist, and other siblings were frequently employed as data collectors. During baseline recording, seizure occurrences were not found to be dependent upon people, location, time, or activity. Yet, with the introduction of the punishment contingency, the frequency was quickly reduced and eventually stabilized at an average of one every two days. To substantiate the fact that it was punishment alone that brought about the reduction, the procedure was discontinued during weeks twelve and thirteen, and a recurrence of seizures was noted. The arrow on the figure indicates another recurrence of seizures coincident with the girl's start of her mentrual cycle, indicating the possible influence of hormonal activity on the behavior. At the six-month follow-up, the level of seizures remained far below the initial baseline.

Systematic desensitization of preseizure activity has also been employed successfully (Ince, 1976; Parrino, 1971). In this procedure, the self-control of the patient is stressed. A twelve-year-old boy learned how to interrupt the onset of a seizure by calling up the feelings he had learned to associate with the cue word "relax." He had been trained to relax while imagining himself in anxiety-provoking situations related to having a seizure at school. There was a complete cessation of both grand mal and petit mal seizures; it persisted at the nine-month follow-up.

Biofeedback procedures have also been successful in producing changes in EEG patterns so that seizures are inhibited (Finley, Smith, & Etheron, 1975; Sterman, 1973; Sterman, MacDonald, & Stone, 1974).

Seizure activity evoked by sensory input, mentioned earlier, which may be precipitated by flashing lights, certain visual patterns, or noises, has been treated by stimulus fading techniques (Forster, 1967). This involves gradually but repeatedly exposing the child to increasingly noxious levels of the patterns until he or she can tolerate them without a seizure.

These studies reveal that environmental conditions can be manipulated to control the frequency of some organically based and nonorganic seizures, even when chemotherapy has not been totally successful.

Phobias and Excessive Dependency

Fear is an emotion stimulated by present or impending danger. Children experience many fears in the normal course of development. Most of these fears are adaptive and prevent harmful consequences, for example, fear of hot objects, deep crevices, strangers, falling. Marks (1969) described developmental trends in the acquisition and extinction of fears. The common fears change in children with increasing age. Fears can come and go in children between the ages of two and four years. By the age of four to six, fears of dark and imaginary creatures begin to predominate. After age six, children become resistant to acquiring new animal fears unless a traumatic incident occurs. The older child fears bodily injury and interpersonal awkwardness (Jersild & Holmes, 1935). Fears and rituals may appear and disappear for no apparent reason. Children may regress during illness, and forgotten fears may reappear, disappearing when the child recovers from the illness. Therefore the therapist is faced with the question of when fearful behavior should become of concern. A phobia is a special form of fear that:

1. is out of proportion to the demands of the situation,
2. cannot be explained or reasoned away,
3. is beyond voluntary control, and
4. leads to avoidance of the feared situation.

Therefore, a debilitating fear interferes with daily functioning or social development. Actually, only a small percentage of all referrals of children to psychiatric clinics involve phobic disorders. Agras, Chapin, and Oliveau (1972) reported that 100 percent of untreated phobic children improved over a five-year period; this did not occur for phobic adults. They also noted that the more specific and focused the fear, the better the prognosis for behavior change.

An additional problem is that of defining excessive fear in a child. Girls and younger children of both sexes may be more than willing to admit their fears because of a variety of social and cultural factors. Fears may be expressed in a variety of ways, including what the child says, how he or she behaves in a fear situation, and what autonomic indices might be present. No one response system necessarily connotes fear. Often, there is inconsistency between what one says and what one does.

Thus, in assessing children's fears, one must consider age and whether the fears are typical at that developmental level. Fears that have lasted beyond the age at which they normally disappear are appropriate for treatment, particularly if they interfere with the child's normal social development or are associated with somatic complaints, sleeping difficulties, nightmares, or obsessive ruminations (Johnson & Melamed, 1979). School phobias, which often present such problem behaviors, will be discussed below.

Often, it is the parents or teachers of the child who call the maladaptive behavior to the attention of the therapist. It is important to focus on how these individuals in the child's environment may also in some way help maintain his or her fears. The treatment program must seek to change their behavior as well. Some children's fears are modeled after those of their parents. There are high correlations between the number of similar fears reported by mothers and by their children. The mother who communicates her fears of medical and dental procedures may have a child who is reluctant to go for routine visits.

It is premature to focus on changing only behavior or only verbal expressions of fear in providing treatment. Anxiety is a construct defined by many behaviors that represent subjective distress, behavioral disruption, and/or visceral overreactivity. Any intervention plan must specify which component is the most important to change. It is unclear whether or not treating only one component is as efficient as treating all three response systems (verbal, motor, or somatic). Modifying the entire constellation of fearful behavior may lead to a better long-term maintenance of treatment gains. Behavioral approaches to childhood fears are reviewed by Graziano et al. (1979) and Hatzenbuehlen and Schroeder (1978).

School Phobia

School phobia remains a prevalent problem that necessitates immediate intervention to reinstate consistent school attendance. Each school year, 17 out of 1,000 children are estimated to stay out of school because of excessive fears (Kennedy, 1965). Any treatment program that puts the child back in the classroom before failure to attend becomes a chronic pattern is likely to lead to improvement.

The treatment programs focusing on early intervention typically emphasize forced school attendance, parental praise for attendance, and systematic extinction of the child's somatic complaints and expressions of fear or anxiety. Medical examinations for complaints of abdominal pains or headaches are scheduled before or after school hours, and do not serve as a means for the child to avoid going to school. In several cases, the parents were found to be inadvertently reinforcing the child's absence from school. In treatment, they were instructed not to attend to the child's complaints and to reward going to school (Tahmasian & McReynolds, 1971).

A central issue to choosing a treatment for facilitating school attendance is that of identifying which factors are responsible for the child's avoidance behavior. Occasionally, the child's anxiety over separation from the mother must be treated concurrently with that centered on the school situation. However, the longer the child stays home, the more isolated he or she becomes from peers and the more difficult it is to catch up on schoolwork missed. The reinforcing consequences children sometimes receive from adults and peers for being school phobic must be identified and eliminated. The child's school phobia can then be treated according to whether anxiety mediates the problem. In this case, systematic desensitization, social skills training, or gradual reexposure would be the treatment of choice. If, however, the child has been reinforced for school avoidance behavior in the absence of emotional responses, an operant approach to treatment is appropriate. In this case, one alters reinforcers so that school attendance becomes a prerequisite to gaining the attention and approval of individuals important to the child.

Shyness or Excessive Dependency

As in the case of childhood fears, a fairly large proportion of individuals who considered themselves to be shy in childhood are able to overcome these problems with increasing age (Zimbardo, Pilkonis, & Norwood, 1974; 1975). The appropriate treatment approach depends on a careful functional analysis of what relationship anxiety or skill deficit may have to the absence of appropriate interpersonal performance. It is important to consider whether inability to make friends, to express opinions, or to enjoy social occasions is a result of a skill deficit. Many anxious and withdrawn children do not possess the social skills necessary to deal effectively with their problems. They must be given the opportunity to observe others behaving assertively and to try out other responses that are comfortable for them. Socially awkward children are likely to have equally socially inept parents (Sherman & Farina, 1974). Therefore, treatment usually requires more than just offering advice to the parents. Teaching the parent to reinforce assertive responses directly led to a lessening of dependency behaviors in a child whose frequent crying and lack of appropriate play was maintained by his inability to stand up for his own rights (R. Patterson, 1972). Interventions that focus on teaching social skills have a better chance of success. Film modeling proved effective (O'Conner, 1969; 1972) in modifying the socially withdrawn behavior of preschool children, but not of older children (Walker & Hops, 1973). A current trend is to treat socially isolated children in groups with normally assertive peers (Clement, Roberts, & Lantz, 1970). Once the new behaviors are learned through behavioral rehearsal, they must be reinforced in the natural setting in order to be maintained. Teacher attention has been found to act as a powerful reinforcing stimulus for preschool children (Buell, Stoddard, Harris, & Baer, 1968). Older children may require tangible as well as social reinforcers (Clement, 1968). If a child is so inhibited that he or she cannot speak in the classroom, stimulus fading procedures may be used (Jackson & Wallace, 1974) in order to increase social participation in a gradual manner. A five-year-old boy's interaction with his classmates was improved simply by having him pass out candy (Kirby & Toler, 1970).

Aggressive Behavior Problems

The whining, crying child is reinforced by his or her tantrums. These aversive responses on the part of the child bring rewards. The child gets what he or she wants, or avoids an unpleasant situation. The parent receives short-term relief for yielding. The screaming child temporarily stops, thereby reinforcing the parents' use of nagging, leaving the scene, or giving in to the child's demands.

It is necessary to demonstrate to the parents how their reaction influences the child's behavior. A classic illustration of the degree of control the parents really have was demonstrated in a treatment program involving a time-out procedure to reduce tantrums in a two-year-old child (Williams, 1959). Figure 5.4 illustrates the immediate success the parents had in extinguishing their son's tyrannical tantrum behavior merely by staying out of his bedroom once he had been put to bed. It is of interest to note that the child had been seriously ill during the first eighteen months of life and had received much special care and attention from his parents and aunt. In the course of treatment, it was noted that spontaneous recurrence of the tantrums occurred after a week and that this was reinforced by the aunt's attention. A second extinction period was necessary to eliminate the tantrum behavior completely.

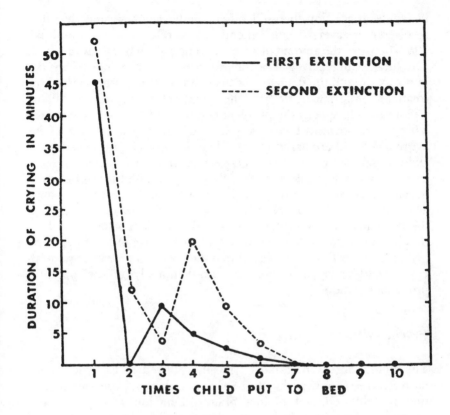

Figure 5.4 Length of crying in two extinction series as a function of successive occasions of being put to bed.

From C. Williams, The elimination of tantrum behavior by extinction procedures. *Journal of Abnormal and Social Psychology,* 1959, *59,* 269. Copyright © 1959 by the American Psychological Association. Reprinted by permission.

A child who appears to be hyperaggressive may have learned through cumulative experiences to get his or her way by exhibiting high-intensity negative behaviors. Patterson, Cobb, & Ray (1970) regard attempts to modify these patterns through treatment of the child by a professional therapist as unlikely to produce lasting effects. Instead, they recommend retraining parents and teachers to alter the reinforcement schedules they inadvertently provide. In studies of families with aggressive, out of control boys, Patterson and Reid (1970) found that the deviant child tended to obtain more positive reinforcers in family interaction than did other family members and that they received more aversive consequences. A correlation was found (Reid, 1967) between the amount of aversive stimuli given by family members and the amount received. Teaching parents to track their own behavior in responding to the demands of the child is an important part of the treatment program. A programmed textbook (Patterson & Gullion, 1968) can help specify the problem behaviors. This book reduces the parents' tendency to focus on guilt and blame. The parents of the aggressive child are asked to provide more appropriate ways for the child to gain attention. The therapists's role in maintaining the parents' efforts is to make sure that they have defined the problem in observable terms and have made the recording task as easy as possible. They can be taught to strengthen adaptive behavior in their child at the same time as they are extinguishing the problem behaviors. Often, they learn how to modify their own tendency to nag or lecture. Therapeutic efforts will be rewarded in that the parents are learning a strategy of child management that they can then apply to other potential problem situations.

Hyperactivity

The childhood disorder most typically referred to as hyperactivity (also referred to as hyperkinetic behavior syndrome, hyperkinetic reaction of childhood, and minimal brain dysfunction) represents a frequent complaint brought by parents and teachers to the attention of pediatricians and mental health professionals who work with children. Some estimates indicate that as many as 20 percent of elementary school children are effected by this disorder (Minskoff, 1973). Thirty to forty percent of all children seen at child guidance centers have been referred because of hyperactive behaviors; the majority of them are boys (Cantwell, 1975). While there is considerable lack of agreement as to the nature of this disorder (Werry & Sprague, 1970), hyperactive children are usually characterized by the following problem behaviors: short attention span, distractibility, excessive and purposeless motor activity, impulsivity, overexcitability, and aggressiveness (Millichap, 1968; Safer & Allen, 1976). In addition, these children often have learning problems or specific learning disabilities that may result from attentional deficits (Ross, 1976).

The most frequently used treatment strategy for children diagnosed as hyperactive is pharmacological intervention, primarily with stimulant drugs (Safer & Allen, 1976). Between 60 percent and 90 percent of hyperactive children have been shown to exhibit some behavioral improvement with stimulant medications (Whalen & Henker, 1976). However, a number of investigators have discussed potential drawbacks in the use of drugs as the treatment of choice with hyperactive children. For example, there is some evidence that in as many as 30 percent to 50 percent of the cases in which stimulant drugs are used, they are not effective in managing many of the problematic behaviors associated with this disorder (Wender, 1971). A number of troublesome side effects, such as appetite loss, insomnia, and delayed growth, have been reported with the use of stimulants with children (Freedman, 1971). Furthermore, although these drugs have been shown to improve hyperactive children's performance on various measures of activity level and tasks requiring sustained attention, Sroufe (1975) has noted that there is little evidence that stimulant medication alone improves academic performance or problem-solving abilities. Finally, recent concern has been expressed about the long-term consequences of using drugs to manage the behavior problems of hyperactive children, not only because of potential physical side effects of the medication, but also in terms of the child's perceived ability to control his or her own behavior and to affect personally the outcomes of various events (Whalen & Henker, 1976). The research findings of Bugental, Whalen, and Henker (1977) led them to conclude that "many children taking medication are learning to attribute behavioral *improvement* to causes beyond personal control and to devalue their own personal contributions to problem solutions" (p. 882). In this regard, Ross (1976) suggests that:

> Drug treatment of hyperactive children should, when used, be combined with behavior therapy so that the child can come to view his increased ability to sit still and to attend as something *he* is learning to master. It might be that with such a combination of approaches (chemical and psychological), the improvement could be maintained when the drug is withdrawn after a relatively short time [p. 103].

Several behavioral strategies have been successfully applied to the management of problem behaviors exhibited by children diagnosed as hyperactive. These behavioral techniques have been used alone and in combination with medication. Behavioral approaches have focused primarily on two aspects of the hyperactive disorder: modifying distractability and attentional deficits by training the child to use more appropriate cognitive strategies, and reducing excessive gross motor activity and disruptive behaviors through contingency management procedures.

Possibly the most frequent complaint from a parent or teacher about a hyperactive child is that "he or she never sits still, and is always disrupting others or destroying things." Safer and Allen (1976) pointed out that training parents of hyperactive children in behavior management strategies is particularly important since physicians usually recommend that a child take medication only during school hours to reduce the risks of potential side effects. As a result, the therapeutic effects of the medication are not operating while the child is at home.

Stableford et al. (1976) described a home-based treatment program for an eleven-year-old boy who had been diagnosed as hyperactive at an early age. He was on a very high dosage level of stimulant medication, and both his parents and physician felt that the medication should be discontinued since he had been taking it for a long period of time. However, his parents continued to complain about high levels of activity and disruptive behavior at home. The child was reinforced with one point for each desirable behavior, such as picking up his clothes, going to bed on time, and any positive behavior that indicated that he was "relaxed" or "calm." For each undesirable behavior, such as yelling, stealing, or running around the house after he was asked to stop, one point was subtracted. At the end of each day, he could exchange the points he had earned for money (six points=25¢). During the first twenty-five days of the program, the child continued to take his usual medication; then the dosage level was gradually reduced until he was eventually taking a placebo.

This program resulted in a considerable reduction in the child's activity level and negative behaviors at home. The gradual reduction in medication did not increase the undesirable behaviors. While no intervention program was introduced at school, the child's teacher never reported any behavioral or academic problems despite the fact that the medication had been withdrawn.

A treatment program for hyperactive children in the classroom, one that necessitated parent-teacher cooperation, is described by O'Leary et al. (1976). Treatment involved teacher praise for appropriate classroom behavior and home rewards contingent on daily report cards that were individually tailored to specific target behaviors for each child. At the end of each school day, the teacher noted on the report card whether the child had successfully performed the desired behaviors, such as completing assignments, bringing in homework, and cooperating with others. The focus of treatment was, therefore, not on the hyperactive behaviors per se, but on academic performance and desirable behaviors (i.e., behaviors that were incompatible with hyperactive and disruptive ones were reinforced).

The children took their report cards home each day, and if they had successfully met their daily goals, they were reinforced with various desired activities or events. Parents were assisted in selecting meaningful reinforcers for their children, including special desserts, time with a parent to play a game, money, and additional TV time. Moreover, special rewards, such as eating dinner at a restaurant with the family or a fishing trip, were provided at the end of the week if the child earned four out of five report cards indicating acceptable classroom behavior. Teacher reports and behavioral observations indicated that this treatment program resulted in much-improved classroom performance and considerable reduction in such hyperactive behaviors as excessive motor activity (e.g., fidgeting in the chair, walking around the room, and not attending to appropriate tasks).

Ayllon, Layman, and Kandel (1975) were able to decrease disruptive classroom behaviors in three chronically hyperactive children by means of behavioral procedures. The problem behaviors, including excessive gross motor movement, disruptive noise, and disrupting others, were decreased to a level similar to that achieved by the stimulant drugs that the children had previously taken. The intervention strategy involved a token reinforcement program in which each child was reinforced for satisfacory performance on math and reading assignments. Tokens were exchangeable for a variety of special activities at school. This treatment program improved academic performance over the level obtained when the children were on the medication, for although the drug had reduced undesirable behaviors, it had failed to improve the children's deficient academic performance. Their academic achievement improved only when it was directly reinforced.

Douglass (1974) has noted that in addition to the problems of high levels of activity and disruptive behavior, hyperactive children also have difficulty in sustaining attention for extended periods of time and in approaching tasks in an organized, planning manner. As a result, these children are often diagnosed as having problems in impulse control. From a behavioral perspective, these children lack self-control, and therefore, tend to respond quickly without evaluating or monitoring their responses. Because of this deficit in self-control, they are apt to make many errors when they do respond.

Several training programs have been developed to help the hyperactive child improve his or her performance on tasks that require careful planning prior to responding. These training programs have focused on teaching the child self-instructional or self-guidance skills in which the child learns to use self-directed verbal commands when approaching a task. It is assumed that internalized verbal commands mediate the child's control over reflective responding (Kendall, 1977).

Meichenbaum and Goodman (1971) used a self-instructional program to help seven- to nine-year-old "impulsive" children gain control over their responding through self-verbalizations. The training program was conducted over a two-week period and consisted of four half-hour individual sessions. Each child learned the self-instructional procedures while performing tasks such as copying various patterns or designs. The training program involved the following steps:

1. the therapist performed the task while verbalizing aloud as the child observed,
2. the child performed the same task as the therapist instructed aloud,
3. the child performed the task while verbalizing the instructions aloud,
4. the child performed the task while whispering the instructions, and finally
5. the child performed the task while covertly verbalizing the instructions.

An example follows of the instructions that the child was taught to verbalize overtly and then covertly during a particular task.

> Okay, what is it that I have to do? You want me to copy the picture with the different lines. I have to go slow and be careful. Okay, draw the line down, down, good; then to the right, that's it; now down some more and to the left. Good, I'm doing fine so far. Now back up again, No, I was supposed to go down. That's okay. Just erase the line carefully . . . Good. Even if I make an error I can go slowly and carefully. Okay, I have to go down now. Finished. I did it [p. 117].

This brief training program resulted in considerable improvement in the children's performance on a number of tasks. Furthermore, these improvements were maintained at a four-week follow-up assessment.

Ross (1976) aptly notes that given the heterogeneous group of children subsumed under the diagnostic label of hyperactivity, it is unlikely that any one treatment strategy will be effective with all the problematic behaviors that they present. Behavioral procedures provide an alternative approach with hyperactive children or a useful adjunctive strategy where medication is necessary. Furthermore, when behavioral approaches are used concurrently with pharmacological intervention, a reduction in dosage levels of the medication is often

possible (Sroufe & Stewart, 1973; Wender, 1971). An excellent overview of issues in the treatment of hyperactive children may be found
in Safer and Allen (1976).

Summary

This chapter discussed general management problems with pediatric
patients. Preparation of children for medical examinations has been
shown to reduce anxiety and increase cooperation. The need to involve parents in the actual treatment programs was illustrated. The
problems cited represent those which frequently occur as children
develop physically and emotionally, or those such as bed-wetting, soiling, and eating problems which accompany physical illness or severe
emotional distress. A rationale is given for the use of behavioral intervention in somatic disorders where behavioral concomitants are reliably observed, such as seizure disorders and hyperkinesis. The
importance of determining when fear and excessive shyness should be
considered problems in need of intervention is considered. The use of
a functional analysis to decide whether treatment procedures should
focus on reducing anxiety, teaching more adaptive social skills, or both
was illustrated through examples involving school phobia and severe
social withdrawal. The development and modification of hyperaggressive behaviors in children was discussed. An evaluation of the effectiveness of behavioral intervention in treating children with hyperkinesis
or minimal brain dysfunction presents a strong argument for use of
cognitive and operant approaches to control distractibility and to teach
impulse control. It is necessary simultaneously to reward skills required for academic achievement. When behavioral approaches are
used adjunctively with pharmacological intervention, a reduction in
medication dosage levels is often possible.

References

Abraham, S., & Nordsieck, M. Relationships of excess weight in children and
    adults. *Public Health Reports,* 1960, *75,* 263–273.
Addelston, H. Child patient training. *Fortnightly Review of the Chicago Dental
    Society,* 1959, *38,* 17.
Agras, W. S., Chapin, H., & Oliveau, D. C. The natural history of phobia.
    Archives of General Psychiatry, 1972, *26,* 315–317.

Allen, K., Hart, B., Buell, S., Harris, R., & Wolf, M. Effects of social reinforcement on isolate behavior of a nursery school child. *Child Development,* 1964, *35*, 511–518.

Andrasak, F., Klare, G. R., & Murphy, W. D. Readability and behavior modification texts: Cross-comparisons and comments. *Behavior Therapy,* 1976, 539–543.

Argona, J., Cassady, J., & Drabman, R. S. Treating overweight children through parental training and contingency contracting. *Journal of Applied Behavior Analysis,* 1975, *8,* 269–278.

Ayllon, T., Layman, D., & Kandel, H. S. A behavioral educational alternative to drug control of hyperkinetic children. *Journal of Applied Behavior Analysis,* 1975, *8,* 137–146.

Azrin, N. H., Sneed, T. J., & Foxx, R. M. Dry-bed: Rapid elimination of childhood enuresis. *Behaviour Research and Therapy,* 1974, *12,* 147–156.

Bakwin, H., & Bakwin, R. M. *Behavior disorders in children.* Philadelphia: W. B. Saunders, 1972.

Becker, W. *Parents are teachers: A child management program.* Champaign, Ill.: Research Press, 1970.

Bemis, K. Current approaches to the etiology and treatment of anorexia nervosa. *Psychological Bulletin,* 1978, *85,* 593–618.

Bentovim, A. The clinical approach to feeding disorders of childhood. *Journal of Psychosomatic Research,* 1970, *14,* 267–276.

Berkowitz, B. P., & Graziano, A. M. Training parents as behavior therapists: A review. *Behaviour Research and Therapy,* 1972, *10,* 297–317.

Bernal, M. E. Behavioral treatment of a child's eating problem. *Journal of Behavior Therapy and Experimental Psychiatry,* 1972, *3,* 43–50.

Bhanji, S., & Thompson, J. Operant conditioning in the treatment of anorexia nervosa: A review and retrospective study of 11 cases. *British Journal of Psychiatry,* 1974, *124,* 166–172.

Buell, J., Stoddard, P., Harris, F. R., & Baer, D. M. Collateral social development accompanying reinforcement of outdoor play in a preschool child. *Journal of Applied Analysis of Behavior,* 1968, *1,* 167–173.

Bugental, D. B., Whalen, C. K., & Henker, B. Causal attributions of hyperactive children and motivational assumptions of two behavior-change approaches: Evidence for an interactionist position. *Child Development,* 1977, *48,* 874–884.

Cantwell, D. P. *The hyperactive child.* New York: Spectrum, 1975.

Carter, S., & Gold, A. Convulsions in children. *New England Journal of Medicine,* 1968, *278,* 315–317.

Clement, P. W. Operant conditioning in group psychotherapy with children. *Journal of School Health,* 1968, *38,* 271–278.

Clement, P. W., Roberts, P. V., & Lantz, C. Social models and token reinforcement in the treatment of shy, withdrawn boys. *Proceedings of the 78th Annual Convention of the American Psychological Association,* Washington, D.C.: APA, 1970.

Creer, T. L., & Christian, W. P. *Chronically ill and handicapped children: Their management and rehabilitation.* Champaign, Ill.: Research Press, 1976.

Davison, G. C., & Neale, J. M. *Abnormal psychology: An experimental clinical approach.* New York: Wiley, 1974.

DeLeon, G., & Mandell, W. A comparison of conditioning and psychotherapy in the treatment of functional enuresis. *Journal of Clinical Psychology,* 1966, *22,* 326–330.

Doleys, D. Behavioral treatments for nocturnal enuresis in children: A review of recent literature. *Psychological Bulletin,* 1977, *84,* 30–54.

Douglass, V. I. Differences between normal and hyperkinetic children. In C. K. Conners (Ed.), *Clinical use of stimulant drugs in children.* Amsterdam: Excerpta Medica, 1974.

Epstein, L. H., Masek, B. J., & Marshall, W. R. A nutritionally based program for control of eating in obese children. *Behavior Therapy,* 1978, *9,* 766–778.

Finley, W. W., Smith, H. A., & Etherton, M. D. Reduction of seizures and normalization of the EEG in a severe epileptic following sensorimotor biofeedback training: A preliminary study. *Biological Psychology,* 1975, *2,* 189–203.

Forrester, R., Stein, Z., & Susser, M. A. A trial of conditioning therapy in nocturnal enuresis. *Developmental Medicine and Child Neurology,* 1964, *6,* 158–166.

Forster, F. M. Conditioning of cerebral dysrhythmia induced by pattern presentation and eye closure. *Conditioned Reflex,* 1967, *2,* 236–244.

Freedman, D. Report of the Conference on the use of stimulant drugs in the treatment of behaviorally disturbed young school children. *Psychopharmacological Bulletin,* 1971, *7,* 23–29.

Geidel, S., & Gulbrandsen, M. *Use of videotape as a modeling tool for reducing stress in preschool children having a physical examination.* Unpublished Master of Science thesis. Madison: University of Wisconsin, 1974.

Gentry, D. Compliance with medical regimes. In R. Williams and D. Gentry (Eds.), *Behavioral approaches to medical treatment.* Cambridge, Mass.: Ballinger, 1977.

Graziano, A. M., DeGiovanni, I. S., & Garcia, K. A. Behavioral treatment of children's fears: A review. *Psychological Bulletin,* 1979, *86,* 804–830.

Hatzenbuehlen, L. C., & Schroeder, H. E. Desensitization procedures in the treatment of childhood disorders. *Psychological Bulletin,* 1978, *85,* 831–844.

Hirsch, J. Cell number and size as determinant of subsequent obesity. In M. Winnick (Ed.), *Childhood obesity.* New York: Wiley, 1975.

Ince, L. P. The use of relaxation and a conditioned stimulus in the elimination of epileptic seizures in a child: A case study. *Journal of Behavior Therapy and Experimental Psychiatry,* 1976, *7,* 39–42.

Jackson, D. A., & Wallace, R. F. The modification and generalization of voice loudness in a fifteen-year-old retarded girl. *Journal of Applied Behavior Analysis,* 1974, *7,* 461–471.

Jersild, A. T., & Holmes, F. B. Children's fears. *Child Development Monographs,* 1935, *20.*

Johnson, J., & Leventhal, H. Effects of accurate expectations and behavioral instructions on reactions during a noxious medical examination. *Journal of Personality and Social Psychology,* 1974, *29,* 710–718.

Johnson, J., Leventhal, H., & Dabbs, Jr., J. Contributions of emotional and instrumental response processes in adaptation to surgery. *Journal of Personality and Social Psychology,* 1971, *20,* 55–64.

Johnson, S., & Melamed, B. G. The assessment and treatment of children's fears. In B. Lahey and A. Kazdin (Eds.), *Advances in clinical child psychology,* Vol. 2. New York: Plenum, 1979.

Katz, R. C., & Zlutnick, S. (Eds.), *Behavior therapy and health care: Principles and applications.* New York: Pergamon, 1975.

Kendall, P. C. On the efficacious use of *verbal* self-instructional procedures of children. *Cognitive Therapy and Research,* 1977, *1,* 331–341.

Kennedy, W. A., School phobia: Rapid treatment of fifty cases. *Journal of Abnormal Psychology,* 1965, *70,* 285–289.

Kimball, C. P. Conceptual developments in psychosomatic medicine: 1939–1969. *Annals of Internal Medicine,* 1970, *73,* 307–316.

Kimmel, H. D., & Kimmel, E. An instrumental conditioning method for the treatment of enuresis. *Journal of Behavior Therapy and Experimental Psychiatry,* 1970, *1,* 121–123.

Kingsley, R. G., & Shapiro, J. A comparison of three behavioral programs for the control of obesity in children. *Behavior Therapy,* 1977, *8,* 30–36.

Kirby, F. D., & Toler, H. C., Jr. Modification of preschool isolate behavior: A case study. *Journal of Applied Behavior Analysis,* 1970, *3,* 309–314.

Knapp, T. J., & Peterson, L. W. Behavior management in medical and nursing practice. In W. E. Craighead, A. E. Kazdin, & M. J. Mahoney (Eds.), *Behavior modification: Principles, issues, and applications.* Boston: Houghton Mifflin, 1976.

Lipton, E. L., Sternschneider, A., & Richmond, J. B. Psychophysiological disorders in children. In L. W. Hoffman & M. L. Hoffman (Eds.), *Review of child development research,* Vol. 2. New York: Russell Sage, 1966.

Lovibond, S. H., & Coote, M. A. Enuresis. In C. G. Costello (Ed.), *Symptoms of psychopathology.* New York: Wiley, 1970.

Marks, I. M. *Fears and phobias.* New York: Academic Press, 1969.

Meichenbaum, D., & Goodman, J. The nature and modification of impulsive children: Training impulsive children to talk to themselves. Paper presented at the Society for Research in Child Development, Minneapolis, Minn.: April 1971.

————. Training impulsive children to talk to themselves: A means of developing self-control. *Journal of Abnormal Psychology,* 1971, *77,* 115–126.

Melamed, B. G., & Johnson, S. B. Treatment and assessment of chronic illness: Asthma and juvenile diabetes. In E. Mash and L. Terdal (Eds.), *Behavioral assessment of childhood disorders,* New York: Guilford Press, in press.

Melamed, B., Meyer, R., Gee, C., & Soule, L. The influence of time and type of preparation on children's adjustment to hospitalization. *Journal of Pediatric Psychology*, 1976, *1*, 31–37.

Melamed, B. G., & Siegel, L. J. Reduction of anxiety in children facing hospitalization and surgery by use of filmed modeling. *Journal of Consulting and Clinical Psychology*, 1975, *43*, 511–521.

Miller, P. M. An experimental analysis of retention control training in the treatment of noctural enuresis in two institutionalized adolescents. *Behavior Therapy*, 1973, *4*, 288–294.

Millichap, J. G. Drugs in management of hyperkinetic and perceptually-handicapped children. *Journal of the American Medical Association*, 1968, *206*, 1527–1530.

Minskoff, J. G. Differential approaches to prevalence estimates of learning disabilities. *Annals of New York Academy of Sciences*, 1973, *205*, 139–145.

Mira, M. Results of a behavior modification training program for parents and teachers. *Behavior Research and Therapy*, 1970, *8*, 309–311.

Mostofsky, D. I., & Balaschack, B. A. Psychobiological control of seizures. *Psychological Bulletin*, 1977, *84*, 723–750.

Mowrer, O. H., & Mowrer, W. M. Enuresis: A method for its study and treatment. *American Journal of Orthopsychiatry*, 1938, *8*, 436–459.

Muellner, S. R. The development of urinary control in children: A new concept in cause, prevention, and treatment of primary enuresis. *Journal of Urology*, 1960, *84*, 714–716.

O'Conner, R. D. Modification of social withdrawal through symbolic modeling. *Journal of Applied Behavior Analysis*, 1969, *2*, 15–22.

———. Relative efficacy of modeling, shaping, and the combined procedures for modification of social withdrawal. *Journal of Abnormal Psychology*, 1972, *79*, 327–334.

O'Dell, S. Training parents in behavior modification: A review. *Psychological Bulletin*, 1974, *81*, 418–433.

O'Leary, K. D., Pelham, W. F., Rosenbaum, A., & Price, G. H. Behavioral treatment of hyperkinetic children: An experimental evaluation and its usefulness. *Clinical Pediatrics*, 1976, *15*, 510–515.

O'Leary, K. D. & Wilson, G. T. *Behavior therapy: Application and outcome.* Englewood Cliffs, N.J.: Prentice-Hall, 1975.

Opton, E., Jr. Psychological stress and coping processes in the practice of dentistry. *International Dental Journal*, 1969, *19*, 415–429.

Parrino, J. Reduction of seizures by desensitization. *Journal of Behavior Therapy and Experimental Psychiatry*, 1971, *2*, 215–218.

Patterson, G. R. Behavioral intervention procedures in the classroom and in the home. In A. E. Bergin & S. L. Garfield (Eds.), *Handbook of psychotherapy and behavior change.* New York, Wiley, 1971a.

———. *Families: Applications of social learning to family life.* Champaign, Ill.: Research Press, 1971b.

Patterson, G. R., Cobb, J., & Ray, R. A social engineering technology for retraining aggressive boys. In H. Adams & J. Unikel (Eds.), *Georgia Symposium in Experimental Clinical Psychology*, Vol. 2. New York: Pergamon, 1970.

Patterson, G. R., & Guillion, M. E. *Living with children.* Champaign, Ill.: Research Press, 1968.

Patterson, G. R., & Reid, J. B. Reciprocity and coercion: Two facets of social systems. In C. Neuringer & J. Michael (Eds.), *Behavior modification in clinical psychology,* New York: Appleton-Century-Crofts, 1970.

Patterson, R. Time-out and assertive training for a dependent child. *Behavior Therapy,* 1972, *3,* 466–468.

Price, K. The application of behavior therapy to the treatment of psychosomatic disorders: Retrospect and prospect. *Psychotherapy: Theory, Research, and Practice,* 1974, *11,* 138–155.

Reid, J. B. Reciprocity and family interaction. Unpublished doctoral dissertation, University of Oregon, 1967.

Ross, A. O. *Psychological aspects of learning disabilities and reading disorders.* New York: McGraw-Hill, 1976.

Safer, D. J., & Allen, R. P. *Hyperactive children: Diagnosis and management.* Baltimore: University Park Press, 1976.

Sawtell, R., Simon, J., & Simeonsson, R. The effects of five preparatory methods upon child behavior during the first dental visit. *Journal of Dentistry for Children,* 1974, *41,* 37–45.

Schuster, M. M. Operant conditioning in gastrointestinal dysfunction. *Hospital Practice,* 1974, *9,* 135–143.

Schwab, J. J., McGinnis, N. H., Morris, L. B., & Schwab, R. B. Psychosomatic medicine and the contemporary social scene. *American Journal of Psychiatry,* 1970, *126,* 1632–1642.

Sherman, H., & Farina, A. Social inadequacy of parents and children. *Journal of Abnormal Psychology,* 1974, *83,* 327–330.

Siegel, L. J., & Richards, C. S. Behavioral intervention with somatic disorders in children. In D. Marholin II (Ed.), *Child behavior therapy.* New York: Gardner Press, 1978.

Sroufe, L. A. Drug treatment of children with behavior problems. In F. Horowitz (Ed.), *Review of child development research,* Vol. 4. Chicago: University of Chicago Press, 1975.

Sroufe, L. A., & Stewart, M. A. Treating problem children with stimulant drugs. *New England Journal of Medicine,* 1973, *289,* 407–413.

Stableford, W., Butz, R., Hasazi, J., Leitenberg, H., & Peyser, J. Sequential withdrawal of stimulant drugs and use of behavior therapy with two hyperkinetic boys. *American Journal of Orthopsychiatry,* 1976, *46,* 302–312.

Stedman, D. The applications of learning principles in pediatric practice. *Pediatric Clinics of North America,* 1970, *17,* 427–436.

Stedman, J. M. An extension of the Kimmel treatment method for enuresis to an adolescent: A case report. *Journal of Behavior Therapy and Experimental Psychiatry,* 1972, *3,* 253–256.

Sterman, M. B. Neurophysiological and clinical studies of sensorimotor EEG biofeedback training: Some effects on epilepsy. *Seminars in Psychiatry,* 1973, *5,* 507–525.

Sterman, M. B., MacDonald, L. R., & Stone, R. K. Biofeedback training of the sensorimotor electroencephalogram rhythm in man: Effects on epilepsy. *Epilepsia,* 1974, *15,* 395–416.

Tahmasian, J., & McReynolds, W. Use of parents as behavioral engineers in the treatment of a school phobic girl. *Journal of Counseling Psychology,* 1971, *18,* 225–228.

Vernon, D., & Bailey, W. The use of motion pictures in the psychological preparation of children for induction of anesthesia. *Anesthesiology,* 1974, *40,* 68–72.

Wahler, R. G., Winkel, G. H., Peterson, R. F., & Morrison, D. C. Mothers as behavior therapists for their own children. *Behaviour Research and Therapy,* 1965, *3,* 113–124.

Walker, H. M., & Hops, H. Group and individual reinforcement contingencies in modification of social withdrawal. In L. A. Hamerlynck, L. C. Hardy, & E. J. Mash (Eds.), *Behavior change: Methodology concept and practice.* Champaign, Ill.: Research Press, 1973.

Wender, P. H. Minimal brain dysfunction in children. New York: Wiley, 1971.

Werry, J. S. Enuresis nocturna. *Medical Times,* 1967, *95,* 985–991.

Werry, J. S., & Cohressen, J. Enuresis—An etiologic and therapeutic study. *Journal of Pediatrics,* 1965, *67,* 423–431.

Werry, J. S., & Sprague, R. L. Hyperactivity. In C. Costello (Ed.), *Symptoms of psychopathology.* New York: Wiley, 1970.

Whalen, C., & Henker, B. Psychostimulants and children. A review and analysis. *Psychological Bulletin,* 1976, *83,* 1113–1130.

Wheeler, M. E., & Hess, K. W. Treatment of juvenile obesity by successive approximation control of eating. *Journal of Behavior Therapy and Experimental Psychiatry,* 1976, *7,* 235–241.

Williams, C. The elimination of tantrum behavior by extinction procedures. *Journal of Abnormal Social Psychology,* 1959, *59,* 269.

Williams, R., & Gentry, D. *Behavioral approaches to medical treatment.* Cambridge: Ballinger, 1977.

Wright, L. Psychology as a health profession. *The Clinical Psychologist,* 1972, *29,* 16–19.

———. Handling the encopretic child. *Professional Psychology,* 1973, *4,* 137–144.

———. Outcome of a standardized program for treating psychogenic encopresis. *Professional Psychology,* 1975, *6,* 453–456.

Wright, L., Nunnery, A., Eichel, B., & Scott, R. P. Application of operant conditioning principles to problems of tracheostomy addiction in children. *Journal of Consulting and Clinical Psychology,* 1968, *32,* 603–606.

Wright, L., & Walker, C. E. A simple behavioral treatment program for psychogenic encopresis. *Behaviour Research and Therapy,* 1978, *16,* 209–212.

Young, G. V., & Turner, R. CNS stimulant drugs and conditioning of nocturnal enuresis. *Behaviour Research and Therapy,* 1965, *3,* 93–101.

Zimbardo, P., Pilkonis, P., & Norwood, R. The silent prison of shyness. Unpublished manuscript. Department of Psychology, Stanford University, Stanford, Calif., 1974.

————. The social disease called shyness. *Psychology Today,* 1975, *8,* 69–72.

Zlutnik, S., Mayville, W. J., & Moffat, S. Modification of siezure disorders: The interruption of behavioral chains. *Journal of Applied Behavior Analysis,* 1975, *8,* 1–12.

6

Management of Psychiatric Disorders Associated with Medical Problems

From the inception of behavior therapy, its techniques have been applied primarily to the treatment of psychiatric disorders (cf., Eysenck, 1959; Lindsley, Skinner, & Solomon, 1953; Wolpe, 1958). In fact, Eysenck chose to define behavior therapy as the application of "modern learning theory" to the treatment of psychiatric disorders (O'Leary & Wilson, 1975). Many of the intervention strategies currently used to modify the diverse array of behavior problems presented throughout this book were developed, refined, and evaluated with psychiatric patients. As a result, the first decade of the systematic application of behavioral principles to clinical problems was dominated by a literature that focuses on the treatment of disorders specified by the *Diagnostic and Statistical Manual of Mental Disorders* (American Psychiatric Association, 1968). The reader interested in a more extensive coverage of this topic is referred to the following sources: Bellack and Hersen (1977), Kazdin (1977), Leitenberg (1976), O'Leary and Wilson (1975), Paul and Lentz (1977), Rimm and Masters (1974, 1978), and Walen, Hauserman, and Lavin (1977).

This chapter is organized into three basic categories, which reflect the many complex interactions between physical and psychological factors. These are:

1. psychosomatic disorders,
2. psychological problems associated with acute physical or chronic illness, and
3. psychiatric disorders with primarily somatic concerns.

First, the traditional concept of psychophysiological disorders is presented, in which disease is held to result from an interaction of psychological and physical (organic) factors.

> There is a significant interaction between somatic and psychological components, with varying degrees of weighting in each component. Psychophysiological disorders may be precipitated and perpetuated by psychological and social stimuli of a stressful nature. Such disorders ordinarily involve those organ systems that are innervated by the autonomic or involuntary portion of the central nervous system. . . . Structural change occurs . . . , continuing to a point that may be irreversible and that may threaten life in some cases [Group for the Advancement of Psychiatry, 1966, p. 258].

However, the concept "psychosomatic" is of limited usefulness because it may lead the practitioner to look for the etiology of the disorder as being entirely psychological (emotional) or entirely physical. This dichotomy is highly artificial since both factors must be simultaneously attended to during treatment. For example, with a patient who presents a problem of ulcers, an intervention program must not only focus on treating the tissue damage to the gastrointestinal system, but must also help the patient to acquire more adaptive strategies for controlling and modulating his or her reactions to potentially stressful situations. A case of anorexia nervosa is presented here to illustrate how an interdisciplinary approach to medical and behavioral intervention leads to an effective treatment strategy for this psychophysiological disorder.

Second, the patient's response to an acute physical disorder or a chronic illness is often compounded by disruptions in a number of common life functions that were previously taken for granted. For example, the patient may develop an altered sleep pattern as a result of hospitalization and medical treatments or in reaction to the stress from the illness itself or from disordered family functioning. Fatigue from lack of sleep may, in turn, enhance the patient's feelings of inadequacy or lack of control over his or her life's circumstances. Problems related to eating may also develop since appetite is often affected by medication and changes in activity level. Physical exercise, although frequently prescribed during the period of recovery from the illness, can be difficult for patients to implement as they may not have the strength or motivation to resume prior activities of daily living. Fears of reinstating circumstances that might have precipitated the illness can lead to further avoidance of strenuous or physically demanding experiences. Sexual activity, for example, may be affected by such concerns. A case is presented illustrating the postcoronary patient who is reluctant to resume a normal sexually active life, and a general approach is outlined for dealing with sexual dysfunctions where psychological factors are thought to be of primary importance. Behavioral treatment has also been used to successfully increase sexual satisfaction of couples, when sexual problems are the result of the illness (such as diabetes) or are due to side effects of the prescribed medication.

Most patients receive medication for their illness. A psychological dependence on drugs may develop through the association between the taking of the medication and the lack of occurrence of physical symptoms. As a result, the patient feels the need to continue taking the medication even in the absence of the recurrence of the symptomatic behavior. In some patients this persists long after the physician has recommended discontinuing the drug.

Furthermore, patients with medical illnesses may develop excessive concerns with bodily functions. They may become so preoccupied with self-diagnosis and minor variations of bowel functions or cardiovascular responses that this precludes their participation in former pleasurable interests. Disability benefits may further serve to keep patients focused on dysfunctional behavior and to interfere with their return to work.

Third, there are those patients who seek medical care who present only verbal complaints of bodily illness. These individuals need careful evaluation and treatment so that they do not receive inappropriate or unnecessary medical services or become reinforced for assuming a sick-role. Their sickness is not simply "in their heads," and dismissing them as hypochondriacs merely makes them look elsewhere for medical assistance. They do, in fact, require behavioral treatment. Their preoccupation with physical symptoms is often further reflected in additional maladaptive behaviors. Obsessional patients may become preoccupied with contamination or infection. This can lead to ritualistic behaviors, such as hand washing or checking (Is the door closed?

Is the gas tap turned off?), that interferes with normal life activities and restricts other family members. Two case illustrations are provided. These cases deal with a similar problem, obsessive concerns about safety, bodily injury, and illness. However, functional analyses of the antecedents and consequences have led to two different treatment approaches: in one case, response prevention and systematic desensitization; in the other, in vivo flooding. The details shed light on how the functional analysis helps in decisions regarding the most effective treatment.

There are some patients, usually referred to as agoraphobics, whose concern with physical symptoms leads to avoidance of public places. These patients confine themselves to the immediate home environment so as not to put themselves in any situation that could lead to a loss of control. The panic of the anxiety symptoms (dizziness, heart palpitations, nausea) serves to maintain the illness. For example, one patient with this problem married a nurse, and would only leave home when his route could be planned so that he was at all times within a three-block radius of a hospital emergency room. He carried ammonia salts, and loaded up on Valium in preparation for any venture from home. These patients attend to subtle bodily cues, responding with anxiety and increased autonomic arousal, which enhance their own discomfort. A vicious cycle is promoted in which psychological events influence physiological events. Symptoms are repeatedly regenerated by the patient's concern and attention to them.

Psychosomatic Disorders

Behavior therapy has been applied to psychophysiological disturbances as diverse as urinary retention (Lamontagne & Marks, 1973), spasmodic dysmenorrhea (Chesney & Tasto, 1975), asthma (Knapp & Wells, 1978), hypertension (Benson, Rosner, Marzetta, & Klemchuk, 1974a, b; Brady, Luborsky, & Kron, 1974; Deabler, Fidel, Dillenkoffer, & Elder, 1973; Patel, 1976), and anorexia nervosa (Bachrach, Erwin, & Mohr, 1965; Bemis, 1978; Leitenberg, Agras, & Thomson, 1968; Agras, Barlow, Chapin, Abel, & Leitenberg, 1974). Uncertainty about the specific etiology of these disorders has not limited the sucessful use of systematic desensitization, cognitive modification, biofeedback, and operant procedures in reducing the amount of discomfort associated with these bodily disturbances. In fact, many behavioral problems, such as vomiting, seizure activity, spasmodic tics, and headache episodes, have been brought under the patient's control, not eliminating, but reducing, their occurrence.

The task facing the clinician is to analyze functionally the specific problem behaviors associated with the illness to decide whether a behavioral intervention would be a useful adjunct to the medical intervention. This decision involves the consideration of somatic, behavioral, and subjective factors associated with the disease. The patient's own resources for coping and the cooperation of other significant individuals must also be considered in the formulation of a treatment program. This section illustrates assessment and treatment through case examples of anorexia nervosa, tension and vascular headaches, and spasmodic torticollis. Each of these disorders has complex origins. A brief description of each disorder is followed by a review of behavioral approaches used. An examination of the antecedents and consequences associated with the behavioral manifestation in a particular patient illustrates how the health care professional determines the treatment of choice.

Anorexia Nervosa

Description of the Disorder

The treatment of anorexia nervosa provides an excellent sample of the necessary collaboration between medical and behavioral specialists. The disorder occurs primarily in females between the ages of fourteen and twenty-five. It poses a grave danger to the patient, with estimates of mortality as high as 15 percent (Dally & Sargent, 1966). Typically, it is defined by the patient's refusal to eat. This results in profound weight loss, amenorrhea, and serious electrolyte imbalances. The patient usually requires hospitalization and intensive care. Once medical examination has ruled out other known medical syndromes associated with severe weight loss, the behavioral analysis begins with a definition of the nature of the symptoms in a particular individual. Anorectic patients characteristically have a distorted perception of body image, preoccupation with food preparation, unrealistic fears of growing fat, and a lack of sensitivity to internal cues of hunger and fatigue. The anorectic should be differentiated from patients whose refusal to eat is part of a more general oppositional pattern. In the latter case, the food has not lost its reinforcing properties, and the secondary gain in the manipulation of others must be explored. The anorectic patient's refusal to eat, on the other hand, is associated with aversive thoughts and feelings. The anorectic may engage in compulsive overeating followed by self-induced vomiting or intensive overactivity in an attempt to reduce the fear of becoming obese. Figure 6.1 shows the physical appearance of one of these patients as it changed during the course of her illness.

The etiology of anorexia is not well established. Anorectics tend to be described as model children. However, parental—particularly maternal—conflicts are often noted in the background history. Psychodynamic theories emphasize sexual concerns of the patient. Hormonal imbalance has been suggested by others (Nemiah, 1958). The behavioral approaches make no assumption regarding the historical origins of the disorder, but seek to control factors that are associated with the maladaptive eating patterns.

Behavioral Treatment Approaches

In the past, traditional treatment approaches have included high-calorie diets, tube feedings, hormone therapy, and even psychosurgery (Walen, Hauserman, & Lavin, 1977). These procedures have not yielded long-term success. Chemotherapy, including chlorpromazine, has had good results, particularly when used in conjunction with behavioral contingencies (Brady & Rieger, 1972).

Behavioral principles in operant conditioning and systematic desensitization have been very effective in modifying the behaviors associated with anorexia nervosa. The behavioral framework leads to different procedures based on whether the symptoms are maintained primarily because of phobic concerns (such as fear of gaining weight and not being able to stop, fear of being watched eating, fear of specific foods) or because of the symptoms' consequences for the patients' continued sick-role behaviors. A brief review of treatment programs precedes a case illustration in which a combined treatment approach proved most effective in alleviating the problem.

Contingency Management. Patients in the hospital can be treated for weight gain by controlling the environment so as to reward appropriate eating patterns. It is necessary to establish what is reinforcing for a particular patient. It has been found that high levels of activity are rewarding to patients; this has been used as a reinforcer in several operant programs (Blinder, Freeman, & Stunkard, 1970). For other patients, the privilege of socializing has been used as the reinforcer (Bachrach, Erwin, & Mohr, 1965; Browning & Miller, 1968). Favorite foods and cigarettes have also been employed (Bianco, 1972). Once

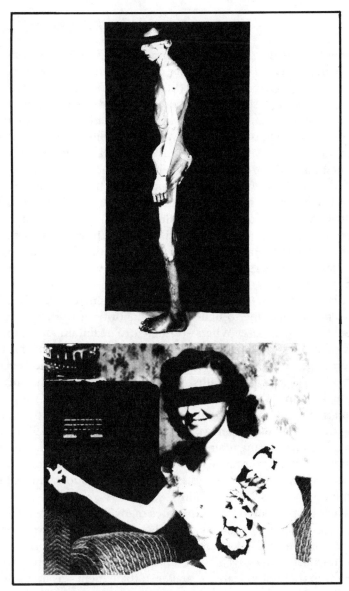

Figure 6.1 An anorectic patient (at top) prior to behavioral intervention. As shown at bottom, she weighed 120 lbs. at age eighteen. At the time of hospital admission, she was 5 feet, 4 inches tall and weighed 47 lbs. She could stand only with assistance.

From A. J. Bachrach, W. Erwin, and J. P. Mohr, The control of eating behavior in an anorexic by operant conditioning techniques. In L. P. Ullmann and L. Krasner (Eds.), *Case studies in behavior modification.* New York: Holt, Rinehart & Winston, 1965, pp. 153–163. Copyright © 1965 by L. P. Ullmann and L. Krasner. Reprinted by permission.

the reinforcer is determined, clear contingencies must be communicated to the patient. The importance of daily feedback about treatment progress has been emphasized (Elkin, Hersen, Eisler, & Williams, 1973). Leitenberg, Agras, and Thomson (1968) demonstrated a decrease in physical complaints by having the staff consistently ignore statements of dizziness, headaches, and eating difficulties. At the same time, praise for increases in mouthfuls of food eaten led to progressive increments in caloric intake followed by weight gain.

Systematic Desensitization. Other approaches have focused primarily on the fear components of the disorder using systematic desensitization to reduce fears of obesity, criticism, and rejection (Lang, 1965; Wolpe, 1971). In the case presented below, both fear and anger were prominent components, and had to be dealt with in order to improve the patient's interpersonal skills. Therefore, use was made of systematic desensitization and behavioral rehearsal.

It is not as easy to treat this disorder as a cursory review of case studies might lead one to believe. The majority of studies were conducted with inpatients. When strategies to maintain the improved behavior outside the hospital are not directly instituted in the home environment, there is often a return of the symptomatic behavior. Bruch (1974) cautioned against the use of a narrow behavioral approach (focusing only on weight gain) that fails to deal with family dynamics. In one instance, where an attempt was made to treat the family in a behavioral framework (Hauserman & Lavin, 1975), many repeated failures in maintaining weight gains were noted. The posthospital treatment program used an extended behavioral contract with the patient and her relatives, systematic desensitization, rational emotive therapy, and assertion training.

The case presented here illustrates many of the features that have been noted in the treatment of anorectic patients. Intervention was instituted in the hospital where the patient was under the primary care of an internist and a psychiatrist, and the behavior therapist worked closely with these physicians. Transfer of the patient was first achieved from the hospital to supervised apartment living under the care of a nurse. Subsequently, a return home was accomplished by careful contracting with family members. In many cases of anorexia, family members focus unduly on the patient's eating problem. It is often necessary to broaden their basis of interaction with the patient to activities and topics other than behavior at the dinner table.

CASE ILLUSTRATION 6.1

The patient, Judy, was a twenty-three-year-old woman referred for behavioral evaluation by her internist and psychiatrist after an eight-month hospitalization for the physical deterioration associated with anorectic behavior. She was transferred from the psychiatric unit to the general medical unit and was receiving forced feedings and potassium in an attempt to maintain her electrolyte balance. She was allowed to work off the hospital grounds at a part-time job in a grocery store. She received Librium for her complaints of nervousness whenever she felt she needed it. At the time of the consult, the patient was 5 feet 8 inches tall, and weighed 64 pounds. This was a 50 percent reduction over her previous average weight of 120 pounds. The patient was also amenorrheic and appeared severely malnourished.

Judy had been hospitalized for a short period two years previously in a psychiatric facility and had received intensive dynamically oriented psychotherapy without any alleviation of her symptoms. Although the background history was rich in potential contributing events, including an alcoholic mother, a seductive father, a traumatic sexual experience, and extreme pressures for social achievement, only the current problem behaviors were evaluated in initially developing a behavioral program. The onset of the primary symptom of regurgitation was associated with forced oral intercourse with a casual acquaintance, which led to her suicide attempt and withdrawal from college. Table 6.1 outlines the treatment formulation.

I. Defining the Target Behavior
A. BEHAVIORAL EXCESSES. The clarification of the problem revealed behavioral excesses related to eating behavior and emotional affect. She was engaging in compulsive eating and gorging behavior throughout the day. She reported that these were triggered by feelings that certain foods did not mix well, a feeling of bloatedness, a need to cleanse herself, and a fear of obesity. Despite this latter fear, she gorged on high-calorie foods, giving herself the excuse that she would shortly vomit it up.

A Fear Survey Schedule questionnaire (Wolpe & Lang, 1964) revealed a great many phobic concerns: fear of bodily injury,

Table 6.1 Treatment Program for an Anorectic Patient

I.   Target behavior ___anorexia nervosa___ defined as:

    A. (too much) _self-induced vomiting, gorging on high-calorie food, frequent snacking, anger outbursts, muscle tremors_

    B. (too little) _weight gain, self-control, interpersonal skill_

    C. (cued by or in reaction to) _feelings of bloatedness, fear of obesity, feeling angry, need to cleanse, bad food combinations, high-calorie snacks_

    D. (strengths and skills) _articulate, high activity level, previous and current work skills_

II. Methods of collecting information

    A. (interviews, questionnaires, test results) _Fear Survey Schedule, interview of patient and father_

    B. (overt manifestations of patient's behavior) _vomiting, weight loss, food refusal, picking at food on plate, gorging_

    C. (what patient self-monitors and records) _number of vomiting episodes, number of meals kept down_

    D. (lasting changes in the environment--e.g., food left over, work output) _food left over, weight record_

    E. (physiological indices--e.g., GSR, pulse rate) _electromyographic recordings from frontalis, neck, and shoulders_

III. Functional analysis of behavior

    A. (events preceding target behavior) _feelings of bloatedness, snacking on high-calorie foods, bad food combinations, anger situations_

    B. (events following target behavior) _reduced feelings of bloatedness, attention from others, weight loss, nausea, and disgust_

IV. Selecting and implementing an intervention program

    A. Motivation for change

        1.(benefits of "sick-role"--e.g., attention, avoidance or responsibility) _attention from family and hospital personnel, avoidance of full-time job or school experience_

        2. (What would be different for patient/significant others if problem did not exist?) _could live alone or return home, pursue modeling career, return to sexual functioning, reduced nausea_

(continued)

```
    B. Meaningful environmental consequences
       1. Likes activity, magazines, radio, people, travel, sweets, painting
       2. Dislikes forced I.V. or tube feedings, being criticized
    C. Significant others (spouse, siblings, parent, teacher) internist,
       father, psychiatrist, psychologist, hospital staff, visiting nurse
    D. Factors maintaining the problem poor interpersonal skills, free access
       to food, money, and attention of father, easy arousal of anger
    E. Treatment strategies operant reinforcement for meals kept down; systematic de-
       desensitization of fears of obesity, criticism; behavioral rehearsal of
       interpersonal and dating skills
V. Evaluation of intervention program
    A. Monitoring of treatment progress weight records, vomiting frequency,
       number of meals kept down
    B. Programming for maintenance of behavior change transition out of hospital
       with live-in nurse, patient self-monitoring of weight, outpatient therapy
    C. Follow-up assessment (two years) patient employed as bank clerk,
       no hospital readmission for weight problems
VI. Termination (What was your treatment goal?) stabilize weight at 105 pounds
    or better, stabilize eating patterns, improve social skills and handling of anger
```

witnessing or anticipating surgical operations, becoming nauseous, losing control of her emotions, looking foolish, being teased, feeling disapproved of, making mistakes, feeling different from others, and thoughts of being mentally ill. In addition, she was anxious about her own angry and sexual feelings, people in authority, angry people, and parting from friends. Consistent with this self-report, the patient verbalized that she would become upset and anxious if excessive demands and expectations were placed on her. She could not tolerate being criticized or being told what to do. Judy often remarked, "When I get mad, I throw up." The hostility was reflected behaviorally in anger outbursts directed at the hospital staff, physician, and psychotherapist.

Her high activity level—which is typical of anorectics—often resulted in her falling. Muscle spasms and sweaty palms frequently accompanied the vomiting episodes, as did subjective feelings of disgust.

B. BEHAVIORAL DEFICITS. Although the patient verbalized a desire to become an airline stewardess or model, she possessed neither the physical appearance nor the interpersonal skills that would allow her to achieve these goals. Her interactions with people were marred by angry outbursts and a lack of social grace. She alienated fellow patients and co-workers by not being able to verbalize her needs to others appropriately. At work, she got into conflict with the boss because she was unable to ask for clarification of a job demand, request a lunch break, or deal with noncompliant patrons. She had excessive concern about being criticized. She also avoided men.

C. INAPPROPRIATE OR DEFECTIVE STIMULUS CONTROL. The patient's eating habits were not typical of normal individuals. She ate at all hours of the day, regardless of any feelings of hunger. She also avoided eating in public places. Her ability to regurgitate her food had become a persistent and well-developed habit, averaging ten times per day. This vomiting was usually in response to distorted feelings of being fat or was due to poor food-mixtures.

D. BEHAVIORAL ASSETS. Despite her problems, Judy was a verbally facile, intelligent woman. She had a very high level of energy, and was always eager to get involved in activities. She had been able to maintain a part-time job, which involved her traveling away from the hospital, keeping to a schedule, and moderately strenuous physical activity.

II. Methods of Collecting Information

The assessment procedure consisted of her self-report of fears through a traditional interview and in response to the Fear Survey Schedule questionnaire. An attempt was made to have the patient self-monitor her frequency of vomiting in order to acquire baseline information of the behavior. This was difficult because of the patient's reluctance to admit regurgitating, her refusal to be observed, and the problem in defining a discrete vomiting sequence. The patient's records revealed that the maladaptive behavior occurred throughout the day, since she had free access to the cafeteria, with an average occurrence of ten times per day. The records also indicated that the patient lacked any stable eating pattern. She often left food on her plate, but would gorge desserts and other high-calorie foods. Therefore, the patient was instructed instead to keep track of the number of meals that she was able to keep down. This served to focus attention on the adaptive behavior. The behavioral data regarding actual daily weight fluctuations was obtained from nurses' records until later in the program, when Judy became responsible for providing this information.

Since thoughts of anger or fear preceded vomiting episodes, physiological recordings of muscle tension associated with this imagery was used to evaluate and to order a hierarchy of distressing situations that were later used for systematic desensitization therapy. In addition, electromyographic recordings from the frontalis, neck, and shoulder sites were used to monitor the effectiveness of relaxation training.

III. Functional Analysis of Behavior

The decisions regarding selection of a treatment program required a further analysis of the reinforcing consequences of this maladaptive behavior. The immediate precipitants of the gorging were cognitions about bloatedness, bad food combinations, or weight gain. Therefore, a naturally reinforcing consequence of vomiting was the reduction of these feelings. Another consequence of the behavior was increased concern for her well-being from medical personnel and family members. In addition, her continued hospitalization allowed her to avoid returning to college or a full-time job. Judy also was anxious about heterosexual relations, and her deteriorated appearance gave her a further excuse to avoid socializing with others. All these factors contributed to maintaining the problem.

There were also negative consequences for the patient's continued maladaptive behavior. Her physical disability made it difficult for her to be as active as she desired. Periods of loss of equilibrium led to several serious falls. The patient had continuous feelings of nausea. The pressures were mounting from hospital personnel to discharge the patient because of her belligerence and demands. She had been transferred from the psychiatry division because she refused to participate in any of their structured-milieu therapy programs. She was also being threatened with forced tube feedings, which she regarded as aversive, if her weight loss did not decrease. It is interesting to note that immediately following a fall on this unit, which led to a minor concussion, the patient forgot her habit and resumed normal eating, until her memory was restored.

IV. Selecting and Implementing a Treatment Program

Motivation for change was a complex issue. Did Judy have more to lose by overcoming her problem? She had a certain position in her family typical of one who assumes the sick-role (described in detail in Chapter 4). There was unlimited financial support as a result of her family's upper-class socioeconomic position. In addition, her father was willing to shower her with attention and luxuries that were not contingent upon her getting well. Returning home, in the psychoanalyst's opinion, might threaten the mother because of the father's overinvolvement with Judy. Nevertheless, there was sufficient motivation to attempt a treatment program. She did enjoy working and wanted to get an apartment of her own in the city in order to explore job possibilities in modeling. Individuals cooperating in her treatment included her psychiatrist, her internist, her father, and a nurse he hired to help during outpatient adjustment.

Decisions regarding different treatment strategies followed directly from the information obtained. In order to help her with her social skill deficit, a systematic desensitization hierarchy to reduce tension regarding interpersonal situations was used first. Then, through guided participation, the patient was encouraged to express her feelings verbally with the behavior therapist, who joined her at one meal a day. Behavioral rehearsal was used to help her learn to recognize and use response alternatives when anger was evoked and in preparing her for job interviews. In establishing more normal eating patterns, the number of meals kept down was selected as the primary target of change. Judy developed a contingency management program (Table 6.2) in which she would earn certain rewards as she progressed toward her behavioral goals. Both Judy and her father agreed to withhold free access to these reinforcers until the desired behaviors (increased number of meals kept down, weight gain) had been achieved.

V. Evaluation of the Intervention Program

The initial baseline records had failed to indicate a consistent relationship between time of day and vomiting. The need to limit the patient's food intake to regular mealtimes was necessary since she ate frequently and used food to gorge. Within two months, the patient was able to keep down two consecutive meals per day and to limit her snacking to two times per day. The weight gains further reflected treatment progress. By the end of the first month, the patient had regained 10 pounds. Long-term rewards such as new clothes were added to assure weight maintenance. A repeated follow-up sampling of vomiting frequency showed a substantial reduction in vomiting to two or three episodes a week.

Table 6.2 Contingency Management for Appropriate Eating Behavior and Weight Gain in an Anorectic Patient

Goal	Contract	Reward
1	2 consecutive days - 2 meals	American Home Magazine
2	2 consecutive days - 3 meals	House Beautiful Magazine
3	3 consecutive days - 1 main meal	Sketch pad
4	1 day - 2 main meals	Colored paper
5	2 consecutive days - 2 main meals	Decorator book
		Gordon Lightfoot Cassette
6	1 day - only 2 snacks	1 tube polymer paint
7	1 day - one legal snack (evening)	2 tubes polymer paint
8	Weight - 75 lbs.	Surprise package (clothes)
9	Weight - 77.8 lbs.	Retrieval of radio

These goals DO NOT have to be achieved in order.

Note: Items 6 and 7 are repeatable.

Remember to: Keep weight record (minimum 2 times per week)

Chart frequency of vomiting

Record successful meals (meals kept down)

VI. Termination of the Intervention Program
   In attempting to transfer her gains to the real-life situation, discharge was set a month in advance. Judy practiced living in an apartment with a live-in nurse's aide during that period. She was still employed part-time, and returned to the hospital overnight. Her therapy sessions were reduced from daily to weekly sessions. Her psychiatrist terminated treatment with her as he was relocating; this did not produce any relapse. At discharge, Judy had increased her weight to 105 pounds. She was now wearing a brassiere, and menses had resumed. She was dating one of the orderlies she had met while in the hospital, but avoided any sexual relationship. Her family maintained an interest in her progress, but her father was no longer playing such a closely protective role.

She received employment in her local community and maintained an apartment close by. Frequent visits home were encouraged in a progressive manner from brief to longer periods of time. The patient was initially encouraged to visit without eating at home. Through a gradual shaping program, she progressed from being able to have dessert to joining the family at Thanksgiving dinner. Treatment effectiveness depended on support of the family and physician, and at follow-up, their monitoring of her progress was still necessary. However, the patient had acquired new skills for dealing with stress, maladaptive vomiting had been reduced, personal independence had increased, and some social and occupational successes had been achieved.

Headaches

Description of the Disorder

A common complaint in general medical practice is the occurrence of headache pain. It is estimated that as much as 90 percent of the population experiences headaches, with women generally reporting a higher frequency of headaches and greater pain intensity than men (Philips, 1977; Turner & Stone, 1979).

The two most frequently diagnosed headaches are the muscle contraction or tension headache and the vascular or migraine headache (Ad Hoc Committee on Classification of Headache, 1962). As the names suggest, each type of headache is presumed to originate from a different pathophysiological source. Muscle contraction headaches are assumed to result from sustained contraction of muscles of the face, scalp, and neck (Bakal, 1975; Martin, 1972; Ostfeld, 1962). Migraine headaches, on the other hand, are thought to result from excessive responding (vasoconstriction and vasodilation) of cranial and cerebral arteries (Bakal, 1975; Wolff, 1963).

Recent evidence from psychophysiological investigations of headache patients suggests that there is little data to support this distinction between tension and migraine headaches. More specifically, the literature indicates that high levels of tension in the muscles of the head and neck and vasoconstriction of scalp arteries have been observed in both types of headaches. Interestingly, a wide range of muscle tension in the head and neck has been found in some patients suffering from tension headaches, whereas others show normal levels of muscle activity (Cohen, 1978; Philips, 1978). Further research is clearly needed to determine what, if any, differences exist between tension and migraine headaches. The etiology of both types of headaches appears to be varied and often difficult to specify. However, headaches without an established organic basis are widely held to be responses to stressful stimulation (Bakal, 1975; Ostfeld, 1962).

Behavioral Approaches to Tension Headaches

Behavioral approaches to the treatment of headaches have involved two basic strategies. In one procedure, the patient is taught a physiological response that is incompatible with the pathophysiological response presumed to underlie the headache. This has typically been accomplished through biofeedback techniques. The other strategy consists of helping patients to identify reliably those environmental events which precipitate headache episodes and teaching patients specific skills to cope with these stressful events. Throughout the treatment program, the patient is instructed to monitor the daily frequency, duration, and intensity of headache pain and the quantity and type of medication used. These measures are used to evaluate the effectiveness of the treatment program.

In a critical review of literature, Philips (1978) proposed that it is necessary to observe the separate relationship between headache symptoms as they are associated with somatic arousal, pill-taking, and self-reports of headache activity. It is, therefore, important in reviewing the studies presented below that the procedures be evaluated with regard to the type of behavior change that is facilitated. It is quite possible that, for some patients, reduction in tension levels through biofeedback would not lead to corresponding reductions in medication use or report of headache complaints. Biofeedback procedures should not be used in patients whose normal levels of muscle activity do not justify its application. The following review illustrates the similarity of effective treatments. Although discussed here in two sections, the distinction between migraine and tension headaches is not always made by researchers, and could be questioned in view of the overlap in symptoms and treatments.

Biofeedback. Given the widely held assumption that sustained muscle contraction of the head and neck is a major component of tension headaches, a primary goal of treatment is to reduce muscle activity through relaxation and, thereby, to reduce headache pain. Electromyographic (EMG) biofeedback to assist the patient to achieve deep levels of muscle relaxation has been one of the most frequently investigated behavioral treatment approaches for tension headaches. Typically, the patient receives feedback from muscle activity of the forehead area (frontalis muscle) and is trained to reduce the frontalis EMG to increasingly low levels voluntarily. The frontalis muscle is used most often as the site of EMG feedback in treating tension headaches because it has been suggested that a reduced frontalis tension generalizes to other muscles, producing a total body relaxation (Budzynski & Stoyva, 1969). However, as Surwit and Keefe (1978) point out in their review of this area, there is currently little empirical support for using the frontalis muscle as a general indicator of muscle tension in other areas of the body. Moreover, there appears to be no consistent relationship between frontalis EMG levels and self-reports of frequency and intensity of headache pain (Epstein, Abel, Collins, Parker, & Cinciripini, 1978; Harper & Steger, 1978). These findings suggest that for some headache patients, factors other than muscle tension may account for subjective reports of pain. (See Chapter 7 for a discussion of the effects of environmental and social factors on pain behavior.) It has also been suggested that the treatment procedures may differentially affect the physiological, subjective, and behavioral components of headache pain, resulting in different rates of change in these three response systems (Epstein & Abel, 1977; Philips, 1978). Therefore, a comprehensive treatment program may be necessary in order to modify each of the response systems directly.

Budzynski et al. (1973) reported the first systematic investigation of frontalis EMG feedback in the treatment of patients suffering from frequent tension headaches. Patients in one group were trained over sixteen sessions to lower frontalis EMG activity using biofeedback equipment in the laboratory. They were also instructed to practice relaxation at home at least once each day without the assistance of the biofeedback equipment. The data indicated that, throughout the treatment period and at a three-month follow-up, patients receiving EMG feedback training reported significantly less headache activity and use of medication than did the patients in the control groups. These treatment effects were maintained at an eighteen-month follow-up for a subsample of the patients still available. Wickramasekera (1973a) also found that EMG feedback combined with relaxation training was effective in reducing the frequency and intensity of tension headache pain.

Relaxation Training. Instruction in relaxation alone has also been shown to be effective in the treatment of tension headaches. Tasto and Hinkle (1973) trained six patients in deep muscle relaxation during four sessions over a three-week period. The patients were instructed to practice relaxation each day, and were told to engage in relaxation at the earliest indication of a headache. More than two months following treatment, all patients' records indicated a considerable decrease in the frequency of headaches.

Several studies have directly compared the effectiveness of EMG biofeedback and relaxation training in the treatment of tension headaches (Cox, Freundlich, & Meyer, 1975; Haynes, Griffin, Mooney, & Parise, 1975). Patients with chronic tension headaches were randomly assigned either to a group that received EMG feedback, a group that was instructed in progressive muscle relaxation, a no-treatment group, or an attention-placebo control group. These studies found that both EMG biofeedback and relaxation instructions produced significant reductions in headache activity as compared to the control groups. The two treatment groups did not differ from each other. These results were maintained at four- to seven-month follow-up assessments.

Cognitive Strategies. Holroyd and his colleagues (Holroyd & Andrasik, 1978; Holroyd, Andrasik, & Westbrook, 1977) have developed a treatment program for patients with tension headaches based on the rationale that headaches are a result of the patient's cognitive response to stressful experiences. The treatment program attempts to modify directly the patient's maladaptive cognitions presumed to underlie the occurrence of the headaches. The patient is taught to monitor maladaptive thoughts and to use cognitive coping skills to manage potentially stressful situations previously associated with the occurrence of headaches. (See Chapter 2 for a further discussion of cognitive intervention strategies.)

In several studies, Holroyd and his colleagues compared this cognitive coping strategy with other behavioral procedures, including frontalis EMG biofeedback and instructions in relaxation training that focused on head and neck muscles. These investigators found that although biofeedback training resulted in greater reduction in EMG activity, only the cognitive coping skills group demonstrated considerable improvements in self-reports of headache activity. Furthermore, it was shown that cognitive self-control procedures and relaxation training were equally effective in reducing the frequency and intensity of headaches.

The clinician who views this diversity of treatment approaches can certainly feel overwhelmed in selecting a particular method. Since a number of factors other than EMG activity may account for pain reports in patients with chronic tension headaches (Epstein & Abel, 1978; Epstein, Abel, Collins, Parker, & Cinciripini, 1978), it is important to conduct a functional analysis of the pain behavior to identify the specific variables influencing a particular patient's headaches. The treatment procedures used should follow directly from the variables that affect the reports of headache pain. For example, where EMG levels for a particular patient are within the normal range, Philips (1978) suggests that it would be inappropriate, and probably ineffective, to use biofeedback techniques to reduce muscle tension. She further proposes that although biofeedback or relaxation procedures may be appropriate for patients demonstrating a high correspondence between physiological and self-report systems, cognitive and contingency management procedures may be appropriate for patients reporting pain as a function of psychological factors.

In summary, despite earlier assumptions that tension headaches are a result of sustained muscle contraction, it would appear that tension headaches are a heterogeneous class of headaches that can be affected by multiple factors. It remains for the relationship between EMG activity and headache pain to be clarified by further research. At the present time, one cannot assume a direct relationship between physiological and self-report measures of headache activity (Cohen, 1978; Surwit & Keefe, 1978).

Behavioral Approaches to Migraine Headaches

While the specific pathophysiology of migraine headaches is unknown, a disturbance of the circulation in cranial arteries is most often implicated as the cause of the debilitating pain accompanying this type of headache (Bakal, 1975; Sacks, 1970). To modify this presumed abnormal response of the cranial arteries, a thermal biofeedback procedure has frequently been used in the treatment of migraine headaches. In this procedure, the patient is trained to control voluntarily the bloodflow in a specific area of the periphery of the body (usually the hands), producing a concomitant increase in the skin temperature of that area. It is thought that since migraine headaches are a result of excessive dilation of cranial arteries, temperature biofeedback functions to increase bloodflow away from the forehead, thereby decreasing arterial dilation (Budzynski, 1973). By teaching patients to increase the temperature of their hands, migraine attacks might then be reduced or prevented.

The first clinical application of peripheral temperature training was reported by Sargent, Walters, and Green (1973). Their treatment procedure grew out of an incidental finding with a woman who was participating in a study investigating the effects of temperature feedback on hand-warming. Coincidentally, the woman had a history of migraine headaches, and was able to prevent an impending attack during the experiment by engaging in the hand-warming response. As a result of this finding, a treatment program was developed for patients with migraine headaches in which patients were provided with differential temperature feedback and trained to raise the temperature of their hands relative to the temperature of their forehead. In addition to biofeedback, a form of relaxation was induced through autogenic training based on the procedures described by Schultz and Luthe (1969). This latter technique involves the patient subvocally repeating phrases such as "I feel warm and relaxed" while engaged in the temperature biofeedback training.

This treatment program was administered, at weekly intervals, to patients suffering from migraine headaches. Training continued until the patients were able reliably to raise their hand temperature relative to their forehead temperature. They were instructed to practice this procedure at home without the assistance of the biofeedback equipment.

The investigators report that 81 percent of the patients improved considerably and achieved some symptomatic relief, and 60 percent learned to terminate an impending headache. A follow-up study of these patients, however, indicated that many of the treatment gains were not maintained following termination of the program (Solbach & Sargent, 1977). Because of the research design used in this study, it is difficult to evaluate the efficacy of thermal biofeedback apart from the use of the autogenic training procedure.

Wickramasekera (1973b) used the same differential temperature feedback procedure described by Sargent et al. (1973), without the autogenic training component, to treat two patients with chronic migraine headaches. Both patients had previously been unsuccessfully treated with medication, psychotherapy, and frontalis EMG biofeedback. Following a three-week baseline period, during which the patients monitored the frequency and intensity of headache pain, the treatment program was implemented. Using temperature feedback from the forehead and hand, the patients were instructed to concentrate on increasing their hand temperature while remaining relaxed. They were also encouraged to practice the hand-warming procedure at home without the assistance of the feedback unit. Within several weeks, the patients had acquired the hand-warming skill. As this skill improved, there was a concomitant decrease in the frequency and intensity of the headaches. At a three-month follow-up, headache activity was significantly reduced in both patients, and medication use was virtually eliminated. Similar results are reported by Turin and Johnson (1976) using thermal biofeedback with seven patients. Instead of differential temperature training between the forehead and hand, however, temperature feedback was provided only from the hand. The treatment program lasted for fourteen weeks.

The comparative efficacy of several treatment strategies in the management of migraine headaches was investigated by Lake, Rainey, and Papsdorf (1979). Twenty-four patients suffering from migraine headaches were randomly assigned to one of four conditions:

1. frontalis EMG biofeedback,
2. finger temperature biofeedback (both hand-warming and cooling),
3. finger temperature biofeedback plus rational-emotive therapy (see Chapter 2 for a description of this latter procedure), and
4. self-monitoring of headache activity, which served as a waiting-list control group.

The results indicated that temperature feedback, both alone and in combination with rational-emotive therapy, was no more effective in reducing headache activity than was self-monitoring. Furthermore, while patients in the EMG-feedback group demonstrated considerable reductions in headache activity at a three-month follow-up assessment, the hand-warming response was not maintained and failed to differentiate patients who achieved symptom relief from those who did not improve.

Bakal and Kaganov (1977) used frontalis EMG training as a treatment strategy for patients with tension or migraine headaches. The investigators found that this treatment procedure was equally effective in reducing headache frequency and intensity in both groups of patients.

Multistrategy Treatment. Assertion training, relaxation training, and systematic desensitization were combined by Mitchell and Mitchell (1971) as a treatment program for chronic migraine headache patients. The investigators state that the goal of this program was to provide patients with more effective strategies for responding to a variety of stressful situations thought to contribute to migraine episodes. An anxiety hierarchy for systematic desensitization was constructed for each patient based on distressing events revealed during assessment interviews. Significantly, greater symptom relief was obtained by this group with the combined treatment package than by a group that received only training in progressive muscle relaxation or systematic desensitization. In addition, the groups receiving a single treatment procedure did not differ from a no-treatment control group in headache activity.

In a second, more complex investigation, Mitchell and White (1977) used a behavioral self-management paradigm that was designed to teach patients to identify antecedent stressors (both environmental and cognitive) thought to precipitate a migraine attack, and to help them acquire a wide array of coping skills to respond more effectively to stressful and demanding aspects of their environment. Self-recording, in which the patient kept a record of the frequency of headaches, and self-monitoring, in which the patient observed and recorded stressful events, were ineffective in reducing headache activity. Training patients in skills for relaxation and self-desensitization, however, resulted in a 45 percent reduction in headache frequency, and training patients in an additional thirteen behavioral skills such as thought stopping, assertion training, imaginal modeling, and cognitive restructuring, produced a 73 percent reduction in the number of headaches reported by the patients.

At the present time, the mechanism for the clinical effectiveness of thermal biofeedback in the treatment of migraine headaches remains highly speculative (Shapiro & Surwit, 1976). Evidence for the efficacy of the hand-warming procedure is equivocal and should be cautiously regarded until more adequately controlled research is conducted. The role of temperature control in the management of migraine headaches is further clouded the research evidence which suggests that this type of headache may be treated equally effectively with a diverse number of procedures. It is particularly interesting that several investigations report that EMG-feedback training and other relaxation procedures, which have been demonstrated to be effective in reducing tension headache activity, also appear to be effective in the treatment of at least some patients with migraine headaches. However, as Cohen (1978) notes, this latter finding is not unexpected, given data that indicate that high levels of muscle tension are present in patients with either type of headache. Finally, it would appear that a number of complex variables may contribute to the occurrence of migraine headaches; therefore, as Mitchell and White (1977) have suggested, no single treatment strategy is apt to be effective in the management of this disorder. A careful functional analysis is the best guide for the selection of a particular focus of treatment with each patient.

Reducing the Use of Pain Medication for Headaches

The case illustration that follows provides an example of the ease of decreasing a patient's overuse of medication for headaches, when the behavioral goal is clearly defined as "a reduction in the number of pills taken." It depicts how a program based on the patient's resources and successful coping skills can lead to straightforward alteration of a maladaptive habit.

CASE ILLUSTRATION 6.2

The following case illustrates the treatment approach taken with a thirty-one-year-old divorced woman who complained of addiction to Fiurinal, a drug prescribed for earlier episodes of migraine headaches. The patient also reported a family history of these headaches. It is interesting that the patient, a master's level psychologist, indicated that she had not had any recent migraine episodes, but she was reluctant to give up the medication for fear that they might return. Susan described herself as rather unhappy in her current job situation and reported that mild headaches and tension occurred during the day at work, but not on the weekends. Although she had contemplated a job change, she had not actively pursued new employment. Her headaches were not keeping her from engaging in other activities. Her boyfriend took very little notice of their occurrence and was supportive of her desire to give up the pills.

Susan routinely took headache pills at regular time intervals: when she first awoke in the morning, at lunch, dinner, and before going to bed at night. Her self-monitoring records revealed that she was taking the medication the same time each day irrespective of any headache pain. Susan indicated that she feared decreasing the drug dosage because a headache might overwhelm her; she also felt that the Fiurinal gave her energy. Despite these concerns, she expressed a desire to change her behavior because the current prescription for medication was running out, and the physician felt that a refill of the prescription was unwarranted. Susan also prided herself on considerable self-control. She had successfully given up smoking by going cold-turkey. She had also used meditation techniques to relax herself. Therefore, she was annoyed with herself for this excessive dependence on drugs. She was concerned about biological addiction and the cost of medication. The motivation for change was good. Biofeedback temperature training was found to be ineffective because she never experienced headaches during the training sessions. Electromyographic recordings revealed normal levels of muscle tension even when she was instructed to imagine stressful events. Given the availability of her boyfriend as a primary reinforcing agent and her previous self-reported success in giving up smoking, an operant treatment program was designed. Susan initially contracted not to take a pill at one of the usual medication times during one day. In the first week of treatment, she was able to skip her lunch pills on two consecutive days. Given a long holiday weekend (Thanksgiving), she agreed to use only five pills over the four-day period, as she felt job-related headaches would not occur over the vacation. During the next two weeks, she continued to decrease her pill taking, and was encouraged to vary the time of day that she took any remaining pills in order to eliminate what had become a conditioned cue for medication-taking. She used self-reinforcement techniques, such as buying a new cookbook, going to a movie, or eating favorite foods to reward herself for not taking the medication. During the fourth week, she announced that she had flushed the remaining pills down the toilet. A six-month follow-up revealed one period during which she again used the medication prescribed by her doctor after a car accident. However, on her own initiative, she reinstituted the self-monitoring program, and was able to completely discontinue pill-taking after two days. It should be noted that the patient continued to take Valium, and on occasion she reported that food binges distressed her. She was, however, more self-confident about controlling the circumstances of her life. At the last contact (one-year follow-up), the patient had changed jobs, and remained free from Fiurinal addiction.

Nervous Habits—Spasmodic Torticollis

Description of the Disorder

There are several disorders of the musculoskeletal system that manifest themselves as dysfunctional motor responses such as tics or spasmodic muscular contractions. These disorders usually are not associated with any organic conditions and are assumed to be beyond the voluntary control of the patient. The physical symptoms are often so disruptive and disabling to the individual that many daily activities must be curtailed. In addition, the symptomatic behaviors result in considerable embarrassment to the patient and often severely restrict social interactions.

The etiology of these disorders is not known. Within a behavioral framework, it has been suggested that the nervous habits or tics are learned in response to a traumatic or stressful event. The dysfunctional motor behaviors then persist even after the stressful experience, and are strengthened through habitual or automatic performance. Social reinforcement through attention from others may also maintain the behavior (Azrin & Nunn, 1973).

Behavioral Treatment Approaches

There are a number of reports of the successful treatment of spasmodic disorders with behavioral techniques. Many of these problems are intractable to such traditional intervention as chemotherapy, psychotherapy, and even surgery.

One such disorder is spasmodic torticollis. Also referred to as "wry neck," this disorder affects the cervical and sternocleidomastoid muscles. Spasms in these muscles result in an abnormal positioning of the head and neck to the right or left (Brierly, 1967).

Negative Practice. Agras and Marshall (1965) successfully reduced the abnormal head positioning in a thirty-eight-year-old woman with spasmodic torticollis using negative practice. Negative practice is a procedure in which the patient is instructed to voluntarily engage in the problematic head and neck movements in a repeated manner. It is assumed that this procedure is effective because it is aversive to the patient, resulting in muscular fatigue (Hersen & Eisler, 1973).

During the therapy sessions, the patient was instructed to perform the dysfunctional head movements 200 times. She was also assigned the task of practicing these movements 400 times each day at home. A considerable reduction in the problem behavior was observed one month following the start of treatment. A two-month follow-up indicated that the patient was symptom free.

In a second case of spasmodic torticollis reported by Agras and Marshall (1965), there was no improvement in the behavior using negative practice. The authors suggest that this procedure was not effective with this patient because she was unable to return her head to a normal position, and thus, the tic-like behavior could not be accurately performed.

Shaping Procedure. Ericksen and Huber (1975) used a metronome in an operant conditioning paradigm to treat spasmodic torticollis in a twenty-nine-year-old patient diagnosed as schizophrenic. The patient was unable to move his head from a tonic position toward the left without considerable pain. Medication was ineffective in providing symptom relief.

The procedure consisted of the patient's making small head movements that were synchronized to the beat of a metronome. It was felt that the metronome would serve as a rhythmic external cue to help the patient regain voluntary control over the head and neck muscles. The patient was seated so that a target point on the wall was in his visual field when his neck was in the tonic (left) position. He was instructed to turn his head from the visual stimulus to the target stimulus and back again with each beat of the metronome (forty beats per minute). The patient practiced this procedure for ten minutes each day. Every two days, the stimulus was moved one foot further to the right. This strategy required the patient gradually to increase his head turning until he was able to hold his head 180 degrees from his original tonic position. Within eight sessions, the patient was able to regain voluntary control of his neck muscles. A nine-month follow-up indicated that he was continuing to hold his head in an appropriate manner with no recurrence of the symptomatic behavior. This is an example of shaping or successive approximation, discussed in Chapter 2.

Biofeedback. Nine patients with spasmodic torticollis were treated by Brudney, Grynbaum, and Korein (1974) using EMG biofeedback. The problems were of longstanding duration, some as long as fifteen years, and failed to respond to other treatment approaches. Auditory and visual feedback were used to enhance muscle relaxation and to increase contractions and muscle strength to facilitate appropriate head and neck positions. The average treatment program lasted ten weeks, with biofeedback sessions conducted three to five times each week. This procedure resulted in a significant or total reduction in the symptomatic behavior. There were concomitant improvements in the patient's social relationships and a decrease in depression.

Habit Reversal. Finally, Azrin and Nunn (1973) describe a detailed treatment program for a number of nervous habits and tics using procedures they refer to as habit reversal exercises. In this procedure, an incompatible motor act is substituted for the maladaptive habit pattern. The goal of this intervention strategy is to establish a physically competing response to interfere with the habit and to strengthen the antagonistic muscle groups that have atrophied from disuse. In addition, the components of the treatment program are designed to enhance the patient's awareness of the maladaptive motor movements that have become an automatic response. The basic components include:

1. a "response description procedure," in which the patient describes in detail the physical movements of the habit (a mirror is used to facilitate this process),
2. a "response detection procedure," in which the patient is taught to detect and monitor each instance of the maladaptive movement,
3. an "early warning procedure," in which the patient learns to detect the initial response in the motor movement chain, and
4. a "competing response practice," in which the patient is taught to tense briefly muscles that are incompatible with the maladaptive motor acts and thus prevent their performance.

These competing responses were selected to be inconspicuous so that they could be performed in social situations and so would not interfere with ongoing activities. Figure 6.2 illustrates the various habit problems treated with this program and their corresponding competing motor response.

Azrin and Nunn (1973) used this program to reduce a number of nervous habits in twelve patients ranging in age from five to sixty-four. These maladaptive behaviors had hampered the patients for from three to seven years. When the patients felt the urge to engage in the habit pattern, they were instructed to perform the competing motor response for about three minutes. Family and friends were involved in treatment to enhance patient compliance and to provide a source of social reinforcement for the patient's efforts. The results indicated that the problem behaviors were eliminated in ten of the twelve patients by the third week of treatment. In the remaining two patients, there was a 90 percent reduction in the symptomatic behaviors. A seven-month follow-up revealed a 99 percent reduction in the maladaptive habits from the baseline levels.

These studies indicate that tics and other disorders involving spasmodic muscular contractions can be brought under the patient's voluntary control through a diverse number of behavioral techniques. Factors that determine which treatment strategy is selected for a particular patient include whether the affected muscles can return to their normal position and whether there are natural competing motoric responses available.

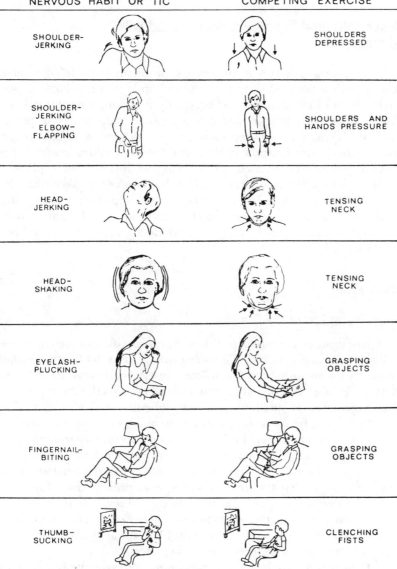

NERVOUS HABIT OR TIC	COMPETING EXERCISE
SHOULDER-JERKING	SHOULDERS DEPRESSED
SHOULDER-JERKING ELBOW-FLAPPING	SHOULDERS AND HANDS PRESSURE
HEAD-JERKING	TENSING NECK
HEAD-SHAKING	TENSING NECK
EYELASH-PLUCKING	GRASPING OBJECTS
FINGERNAIL-BITING	GRASPING OBJECTS
THUMB-SUCKING	CLENCHING FISTS

Figure 6.2 *Left:* Pictorial representation of the various types of nervous tics or habits. *Right:* Type of competing exercise used for corresponding tic or habit. The arrows show the direction of isometric muscle contraction being exerted by the client.

From N. H. Azrin and R. G. Nunn, Habit reversal: A method of eliminating nervous habits and tics. *Behaviour Research and Therapy,* 1973, *11,* 619–628. Copyright © 1973 by Pergamon Press, Ltd. Reprinted by permission.

Psychological Problems Associated with Illness

The following behavior disorders are problems that are often associated with a physical illness. Sleep and appetite disturbances, inactivity, bowel irregularities, and sexual dysfunction, if not attended to by the health care practitioner, can contribute to more serious psychiatric problems in which depression and anxiety may become prominent features (see Chapter 7). The problems of treating insomnia and sexual dysfunction are used in this section to illustrate the application of behavioral approaches in disorders that often occur secondary to a physical illness. A brief review of behavioral approaches to insomnia and sexual dysfunction is provided. A detailed case illustration using a program with a couple facing sexual difficulties after coronary illness is presented.

Insomnia

Description of the Disorder

Insomnia is a complex problem, not a specific disease entity with a well-established etiology. Chronic insomnia is a debilitating malady suffered by an estimated 30 million Americans (Karacan, Williams, Littell, & Salis, 1973). Individuals with sleep disturbance comprise a heterogeneous population reporting difficulty in sleep onset, sleep dissatisfaction, frequency of awakenings, nightmares, or early awakenings. The complaint may indicate problems secondary to medical illness, physiological arousal, sleep apnea, nocturnal myoclonus, or a variety of problems associated with chronic stress, depression, or major life change events. Given the widespread prescription of hypnotic drugs to people complaining of sleep difficulties, it is important for behaviorally oriented therapists to undertake a careful functional analysis to determine the nature of the problem for any particular patient and to determine what drugs are being used.

One major problem for determining effective treatment is the individual differences in perception of how much sleep one needs. There is no systematic research that provides a basis for how much sleep is physically necessary for a given individual. In fact, many people who complain of insomnia do not in fact sleep for shorter periods than do satisfied sleepers. A person's judgment of how long and how well he or she sleeps often affects other behaviors, such as irritability, fatigue, and inability to concentrate. Rachman and Philips (1978) question the continued tendency of physicians to rely on the patient's self-description of sleep satisfaction when prescribing drugs. Studies are cited in which poor sleepers misperceive the length of time of falling asleep as compared to good sleepers when EEG criteria of sleep are used. Therefore, treatment studies must be evaluated with respect to the nature of the population being studied.

Behavioral Treatment Approaches

A large proportion of insomnia sufferers have psychiatric disorders including depression and anxiety. They should be evaluated carefully before treatment. Since anxiety has been shown to affect both the speed of onset of sleep and the number of awakenings during the night, anxiety-reducing methods such as progressive relaxation have been appropriately employed. Borkovec and his colleagues (Borkovec & Fowles, 1973; Borkovec & Weerts, 1976; Steinmark & Borkovec, 1974) demonstrated the effectiveness of progressive relaxation with or without systematic desensitization in college students with sleep problems. In cases of severe insomnia, it may be necessary to combine psychological methods of treatment with tranquilizing or hypnotic drugs. Until recently, the treatment of insomnia has been primarily pharmacological. Unfortunately, the drugs generally lose their effectiveness within a brief period of time and may have addictive or harmful side effects (Kales, Allen, Scharf, & Kales, 1970). The drugs can suppress the rapid eye movements associated with the dreaming state of sleep. Drug withdrawal often produces a rebound effect, which inadvertently enhances sleep problems by producing excessive nightmares or inability to fall asleep.

Behavioral treatments of insomnia have included progressive relaxation, autogenic training (Traub, Jencks, & Bliss, 1973), biofeedback (Freedman & Papsdorf, 1976; Hauri & Good, 1975; Hauri & Cohen, 1977), and cognitive restructuring (Thoresen, Coates, Zarcone, Kirmil-Gray, & Rosekind, in press). The evaluation of these treatments are hampered by the unreliability of an individual's estimates of the trouble he or she has falling asleep, the lack of all-night monitoring of sleep activity, and the lack of follow-up information. The laboratory studies that have monitored physiological arousal throughout the night have yielded contradictory results. Freedman and Papsdorf (1976) failed to provide support for the notion that poor sleepers have unusually high physiological arousal levels. Although electromyographic biofeedback reduced onset of sleep time (EEG criterion), patients receiving progressive relaxation instructions were as successful. The data suggest that the use of repetitive, meditation-like techniques might also be useful in treating insomnia (Benson, Beary, & Carol, 1974).

At the present time, despite the lack of agreement about the classification of patients as insomniacs, effective clinical procedures involve teaching the patients to limit before bedtime activities that heighten arousal level, such as concentrated study or intense physical exercise. Procedures that involve repetitive, boring stimulation can lead to sleep (Bohlin, 1974; Oswald, 1960). Methods of stimulus control, in which the environment is structured so that the patient is told to use the bed for nothing but sleep, to go to bed only when sleepy, and to avoid associating other activities such as eating, reading, or watching TV with bedtime have also been successful (Bootzin, 1972; Borkovec & Boudewyns, 1976).

It is felt that a thorough understanding of the nature of the individual's sleep problem can best determine the direction of treatment. If overarousal seems to be the precipitating factor, relaxation and biofeedback techniques or drugs would be most effective. When excessive concern over illness is the source of the problem, reassuring the patient about the medical aspects of treatment would be appropriate. If an individual suffers from nightmares, exploration of these fears and possible application of systematic desensitization might be attempted. Finally, self-management techniques, particularly stimulus control, should be the treatment of choice when the patient has irregular bedtime patterns.

Sexual Dysfunction

Description of the Disorder

The sexual adjustment of patients with physical illnesses or disabilities is one area of functioning that has frequently been ignored by health care providers. There are a number of illnesses or physical disorders that are often associated with sexual dysfunction. Among these conditions are diabetes (Renshaw, 1978), chronic renal failure (Abram, Hester, Sheridan, & Epstein, 1978), multiple sclerosis (Kaplan, 1974), and spinal cord injuries (Higgins, 1978). Often, drugs used to control these illnesses impair sexual functioning (Kaplan, 1974). Patients and their sexual partners must be informed about these potential problems.

Although the physiological effects of an illness may contribute to problems in sexual functioning, psychosocial factors account for the majority of sexual dysfunctions in men and women, even when a disease or illness is present (Scalzi, Loya, & Golden, 1977). This is often observed in patients with a diagnosis of cardiovascular disease, particularly following a myocardial infarction or heart attack. Friedman (1978), in a review of the literature, concludes that:

> ... many cardiac patients do have sexual difficulties, ranging from reduced activity to total impotence. Furthermore, these problems are not necessarily related to age, severity of infarct, and capacity for nonsexual activity, and they may not be evident from studies that use such criteria as return to work or degree of physical impairment as measures of successful rehabilitation. Yet sexual difficulties can be one of the most important problems a heart attack victim has to face [p. 374].

Most postcoronary patients regain the physical capacity to resume sexual intercourse within four to eight weeks after the infarction (Puksta, 1977). A patient who is able to tolerate an exercise stress test (during which heart and respiratory rate and blood pressure are monitored) has the physical capacity to engage in normal sexual activity (Kavanagh & Shepard, 1977). However, despite physiological and symptomatic recovery, many coronary patients unnecessarily reduce their sexual activity, some failing to return to any sexual activity at all.

In a study of postmyocardial infarction patients, Block, Maeder, and Haissly (1975) found that fear of death or another heart attack was a primary concern of the patient and spouse, and this fear was frequently associated with a number of sexual problems. Similar findings are reported by Hackett and Cossem (1973). Friedman (1978) points out that sexual dysfunction in postcoronary patients often can be prevented by alleviating the fear and depression that may result from insufficient or inaccurate information regarding the effects of the illness on their sexual functioning.

Behavioral Treatment Approaches

Sexual dysfunction, when it does occur, has been effectively treated with techniques based on behavioral principles. The classic research of Masters and Johnson (1970), which led to the development of an intervention program for sexual problems, is consistent with a behavioral approach. Within this framework, sexual dysfunction is seen as the result of incorrect or insufficient information, performance anxieties, skill deficits, and/or faulty attitudes.

A careful assessment of physical, environmental, and cognitive factors that may contribute to the patient's sexual problem is essential for the development of an effective treatment program. A detailed description of assessment strategies for sexual dysfunction, including the format for a sexual history interview, is presented in Keefe, Kopel, and Gordon (1978), Lobitz and Lobitz (1978), and LoPiccolo and Heiman (1978).

Annon (1974) has proposed an intervention program in which the actual strategy (or strategies) selected by the therapist is determined by a sequential assessment of both the patient's problem and progress in treatment. Using this model of intervention, Annon (1974) suggests the following steps:

1. giving permission to the couple to engage in certain sexual behaviors or thoughts to reassure them that they are normal functioning individuals,
2. giving factual information about human sexuality that is relevant to the couple's sexual problem,
3. giving specific suggestions regarding sexual techniques (brief intervention), and
4. if warranted, intensive intervention, which may necessitate treatment of more complex factors such as physical or marital problems in addition to the sexual difficulties.

The direct treatment of sexual dysfunction in men and women is described in detail in several texts on the subject (e.g., Annon, 1974; 1975; Kaplan, 1974; Masters & Johnson, 1970). LoPiccolo (1978) has outlined the basic components of one such behavioral treatment program. These components include:

1. *Mutual Responsibility.* Both partners are seen in therapy and encouraged to accept responsibility for changing their behavior, regardless of which member is experiencing the sexual problem.

2. *Information and Education.* Lack of accurate information about sexual functioning can result in skill deficits and anxiety, which lead to sexual dysfunction. Information is, therefore, provided through various sources, such as lectures, written material, and films.

3. *Attitude Change.* Many patients with sexual problems have negative or faulty attitudes regarding sexual behavior. As a result of these negative attitudes, the individual may respond to sexual experiences with negative emotional reactions (anxiety, guilt, displeasure), which may, in turn, inhibit adequate sexual functioning. Attitude change is accomplished by exposing the patient to experiences or materials (written materials, lectures, therapist self-disclosure) that convey a positive orientation toward human sexuality. Where negative attitudes are based on religious attitudes, discussions with clergy who are supportive of the treatment goals is useful.

4. *Eliminating Performance Anxiety.* Patients with sexual dysfunctions often have unrealistic expectations about their own sexual behavior with their partner. Self-imposed pressure for sexual performance can lead to inhibiting anxiety. The couple is instructed to provide each other sexual pleasure other than through intercourse, thereby reducing performance anxiety. Permission is given to be "selfish" and to focus on the pleasure they derive from the experience rather than whether they succeed in having an erection or orgasm. As LoPiccolo (1978) points out, "the therapeutic procedure for forbidding intercourse in the treatment of erectile failure makes it possible for the patients to enjoy mutual kissing, hugging, body massage, and manual or oral stimulation of the genitals without anxiety about whether erection sufficient for intercourse will occur" (p. 5).

5. *Increasing Communication and Effectiveness of Sexual Techniques.* Couples experiencing a sexual dysfunction are frequently unable to discuss such sexual matters as their likes and dislikes with each other. In therapy sessions, both are encouraged to share with each other such information as their sexual fantasies. It is further suggested that they try new sexual techniques other than the ones they typically practice and that they engage in such activities as reading erotic literature together. Finally, they are instructed to communicate with each other during their sexual interaction.

6. *Changing Destructive Life-Styles and Sex Roles.* With sexually dysfunctional couples, sex is often relegated to a lower priority compared to other activities. LoPiccolo (1978) suggests that sex must become a "leisure" activity for the couple and that they must schedule their day to facilitate their sexual experiences (e.g., by sending the children to a babysitter or having a romantic dinner). The couple is also encouraged to develop a more satisfying relationship by engaging in more shared activities. One strategy is to help the couple develop more flexible sex-role behaviors that permit them to assist each other on a more equal basis in childcare, housework, and so on.

7. *Prescribing Changes in Behavior.* To reduce performance anxiety and to enhance sexual arousal, the therapist assigns the couple specific activities that they are instructed to engage in over the course of treatment. Graded sexual assignments are provided that reduce evaluation aspects of the patient's sexual performance and increase the pleasurable aspects of the couple's sexual interaction. Initially, the couple is instructed to engage in various pleasuring activities referred to as "sensate focus" (kissing, body massage), but are told to refrain from all other sexual activity. As the couple is able to engage in each assignment without reporting any discomfort or anxiety, the therapist proceeds to each succeeding step, involving increasing genital contact and, eventually, intercourse. This is an illustration of in vivo systematic desensitization.

CASE ILLUSTRATION 6.3

Scalzi, Loya, and Golden (1977) illustrate the various components of a brief intervention program for sexual dysfunction in a couple with serious cardiovascular disease. George, fifty-five years old, and Mary, sixty years old, had been married for twenty-two years. Mary had had two severe myocardial infarctions eleven years earlier and again eight years later. The second attack occurred in her husband's presence. Her physician advised Mary to retire from her job and to refrain from any sexual activity. Two years after the second infarction, Mary had a coronary bypass operation. At this time, she became preoccupied and fearful about her own physical condition and that of her husband. Scalzi et al. (1977) note, "Significantly, Mary neither asked about reinstating any type of sexual activity nor did any of her physicians advise or educate her in this regard. In her own estimation, sex was within the domain of 'normal activities.' As a direct result, she did not permit herself any sexual activity until her physician said she could resume 'normal activities' " (p. 238).

One year following Mary's operation, George had a myocardial infarction; however, because of extensive coronary artery disease a bypass operation was not possible. He was also prohibited from returning to work. During a physical examination, approximately a year after the infarction, George revealed that he was having consistent erectile failure, and was referred for treatment for this problem.

Assessment interviews indicated that there had been no sexual problems prior to Mary's first myocardial infarction. Both reported satisfaction with their sexual and marital relationship. It was revealed that shortly after Mary's first infarction, George was aware of a slight change in his desire for sexual activity. This may have involved his concern about precipitating another attack.

Sometime prior to her second heart attack, the frequency of intercourse decreased from three to two times weekly.

When Mary had her second myocardial infarction, changes in their sexual relationship became more evident. During the nine-month period of Mary's recovery, there was no sexual activity. It resumed at a rate of once or twice each week. More important, George reported that at this time, his attitude toward intercourse had changed. He was feeling guilty that he continued to desire intercourse despite his wife's physical condition. George also feared that he would physically hurt Mary while engaged in sexual intercourse because of the weight of his body on hers.

Following Mary's open-heart surgery, following her second attack, there was another extended period with no sexual activity. When intercourse was attempted eight months later, Mary found it painful, contributing further to George's negative attitudes and fears. "The therapists' assessment of the painful intercourse suggested that George's fears may have manifested in the form of attempting to 'get it over' as quickly as possible. Therefore, Mary may not have been stimulated to the point that adequate lubrication occurred" (p. 239).

At this point, George was experiencing erectile dysfunction approximately 50 percent of the time that intercourse was attempted. However, after George had his myocardial infarction, he was unable to maintain an erection at all. Despite George's participation in a physical exercise program as part of his postcoronary treatment, he continued to fear a heart attack during intercourse. Mary reported similar fears because of her enlarged heart, and was concerned that the pressure of George's body would cause her "chest stitches to burst." None of these fears was discussed with each other prior to treatment. This underlines the need to improve communication between the couple, as recommended by the behavioral therapists.

The couple entered sex therapy four months after George's myocardial infarction. George's erectile failure was the primary focus of intervention. However, both partners actively participated in therapy. Treatment was conducted over a fourteen-week period by a male-female cotherapy team. Medical evaluations indicated that both George and Mary were capable of tolerating the physical activity necessary to engage in sexual intercourse.

The first four sessions of therapy were devoted to discussing the sensate focus exercises that the couple were to perform at home.

The exercises are designed to reduce performance anxiety by prohibiting all sexual activity except that assigned during treatment. The couple was encouraged to experiment with various ways to give and receive pleasurable sensations through touching and caressing each other. "Emphasis is directed toward 'new' pleasurable body sensations rather than the more familiar sensations of sexual arousal associated with intercourse and orgasm" (Scalzi et al., 1977, p. 240). In the final step of this procedure, mutual body massages excluding the breasts and genitals were assigned. They were also instructed to communicate to each other what they liked and did not like while receiving a massage. George reported that he enjoyed the experience and that the sensations made him feel "real sexy." However, Mary indicated that she was uncomfortable being nude because she feared that George no longer found her sexually appealing. These concerns were allayed when George reassured her that he still found her attractive.

Sessions five and six were spent discussing their fears regarding an impending cardiac catheterization that George was to receive to assess his need for surgery. Both George and Mary expressed concerns about the effects of surgery on his physical health and about possible death. During this time, assignments dealing with sexual activities were temporarily discontinued, and instead they were instructed to discuss their feelings about the possible surgery. This discussion served to reduce their fears, permitting them to refocus on the sexual problem.

The next three sessions were devoted to body massage involving nongenital and genital caressing. As in previous sessions, the couple was instructed to concentrate on the pleasurable sensations they derived from the experience, instead of on concerns to achieve an erection or orgasm. Initially, George was anxious and reported experiencing discomfort from a hematoma on his leg caused by the catheterization. George and Mary were reassured by a physician that this was a common problem associated with this procedure, and that the hematoma was healing. They were also informed that the sexual activities were not harmful and would not cause the hematoma to burst. When these misconcepts were clarified and their fears reduced by providing factual information about the hematoma, George reported feeling aroused and able to achieve a full erection.

In session eleven, the therapist gave the couple the assignment of producing orgasm through full body-genital massage and manual stimulation. The purpose of this task was to help George to achieve a consistent and reliable erection to enhance his sense of self-confidence in having the capacity to obtain an erection during sexual activity. Using this strategy, George's erectile response was reliably reestablished.

Because George had experienced control over his erections, the suggestion to attempt sexual intercourse was presented during the next session. It was presented as an optional assignment to reduce the pressure to resume sexual activity that in the past had resulted in dysfunctional behavior. The couple chose to proceed with this assignment, and "were delighted with their ability to achieve orgasm in coitus as they had before" (p. 243).

The authors note that had this assignment not succeeded, the couple would have been instructed to use an intermediate step involving vaginal containment of the penis without orgasm. In this procedure, the man inserts his penis into his partner's vagina without any movement except his own.

The final two sessions were concerned primarily with a discussion of ways to insure that the couple would maintain their sexual behavior. As one procedure, the couple was asked to list desirable sexual and nonsexual behaviors that they wanted to see their partner continue. In addition, they discussed the things that they could do on their own to maintain the desired behaviors. Finally, a joint meeting with the couple and their physician was held to facilitate the continued monitoring of their sexual adjustment as part of their health care program with the physician.

Phobias and Obsessions Concerned with Illness or Bodily Injury

Illness Phobias

A substantial proportion of outpatients in a general hospital require reassurance that they do not have a physical basis for their bodily complaint. Many people with fears of illness are so preoccupied with seeking medical advice from numerous physicians that a psychiatric evaluation is often overlooked. Specific illness fears, such as fears of cancer or heart disease, may be transient and promoted by news stories. Some represent temporary concerns following the death of a relative or associated with a depressive illness. It is when the fear is constant and distracts the patient from his everyday activities that it should be considered out of proportion to reality and, therefore, a problem in need of professional treatment. In fact, these patients often misinterpret normal physiological sensations: a headache signals a brain tumor; a chest pain is interpreted as an impending coronary attack. This anxiety itself may produce new symptoms, such as abdominal pain and discomfort due to pylorospasm or hyperventilation with accompanying dizziness, that reinforce the patient's belief that he or she is ill.

Description of the Disorder

Illness phobia is not a clearly defined syndrome. Fears and concerns about health accompany many diffuse anxiety states. Agoraphobia, in which the patient may fear leaving the safety of home, is often maintained by panic anxiety about symptoms similar to those occurring from a physical illness. For example, palpitations, weakness, breathlessness, and giddiness may provoke panic in these patients severe enough to lead to avoidance of any life activities outside the home. A generally nervous person recovering from true physical illness may have a further setback when experiencing these symptoms, which are similar to those of the nervous disorder.

Marks (1969; 1978) differentiates the illness-phobic person from the hypochondriac. Where the fears are about several bodily symptoms and a variety of illnesses, the patient is said to have hypochondriasis. When the fear is persistently localized around a single symptom or illness in the absence of another psychiatric disorder, one talks of an illness phobia. Since hypochondriasis may be a feature of many different conditions, this syndrome may not be useful to clinical decisions about treatment.

Behavioral Treatment Approaches

Agoraphobia is treated primarily through gradual reexposure of the patient to the avoided situations. Weekes (1977) described a program that employs strategies similar to flooding techniques, in which the patients are encouraged to remain in the anxiety-provoking situations even in the face of their fear. In this way, the second fear—fear of panic itself—can be extinguished. The treatment of illness phobias involves graduated approaches using imagery, relaxation, and repeated practice in situations that are feared. (Since these are similar to systematic desensitization of other fears discussed in Chapter 2 and Chapter 4, the reader is referred to those sections for details on constructing anxiety hierarchies and relaxation training.)

Obsessive-Compulsive Disorders

Description of the Disorder

While obsessive-compulsive disorders afflict only one to two percent of the psychiatric population, they are a treatment problem in that they are disruptive to the individual's daily activities and quite distressing to the patient (Marks, 1975). Obsessive-compulsive disorders consist of obsessive thoughts—including repetitive and distressing urges, ideas, and beliefs, such as fear of death or contamination from dirt or germs—and compulsive behaviors or repetitive acts or rituals, such as persistent hand-washing or checking behaviors.

Obsessive-compulsive disorders have generally been highly resistant to treatment by traditional intervention approaches (e.g., electroconvulsive therapy, chemotherapy, leucotomy, and psychotherapy) (Kringler, 1965). A number of behavioral techniques have been used in the treatment of these disorders with varying degrees of success. At the present time, the most encouraging results have been obtained with a strategy that includes exposure to the anxiety-provoking thoughts, objects, or situations that trigger the compulsion (in vivo flooding), following which the patient refrains, or is restrained, from engaging in the ritualistic behavior (response prevention) (Marks, 1975). Using this procedure, chronic obsessive-compulsive behaviors have been considerably reduced in frequency or eliminated completely (Hodgson, Rachman, & Marks, 1972; Levy & Meyer, 1971; Mills, Agras, Barlow, & Mills, 1973). Furthermore, follow-up assessments from one to six years after treatment indicate that these behavioral changes have been maintained.

Behavioral Treatment Approaches

Most behavioral treatment programs of obsessive-compulsive disorders have been carried out in a hospital setting under the close supervision of trained personnel. Inpatient treatment permits the patient's environment to be more consistently controlled and monitored, and facilitates prevention of the ritualistic behaviors. Although outpatient treatment has been less frequent, obsessive-compulsive disorders have been successfully treated on that basis as well (Alban & Nay, 1976; Melamed & Siegel, 1975). Regardless of the treatment setting, Marks (1975) has noted that a high level of patient motivation for change is a critical factor to insure the intervention program's effectiveness. Since the patient typically experiences considerable anxiety when prevented from engaging in the compulsive ritual, the patient must be willing to cooperate with this aspect of the program. Family members often need to be involved in treatment to learn strategies to encourage the patient to resist the rituals and to avoid reinforcing the undesirable behavior with their attention.

It has been suggested that obsessive patients engage in ritual behavior to relieve anticipating anxiety that results from the patient's belief that some adverse consequences will occur if the ritual is not performed (Marks, 1975; Meyer & Levy, 1973). Furthermore, the compulsive ritual is maintained by the temporary anxiety reduction that follows completion of the ritual. The findings of Roper, Rachman, and Hodgson (1973) support this anxiety relief theory. Within this framework, the therapeutic effects of in vivo exposure and response prevention may be attributed to extinction of anxiety, in which the patient experiences the anxiety-provoking stimuli without the occurrence of the anticipated aversive consequences.

To illustrate the selection of a particular behavioral treatment of obsessive-compulsive disorders, two cases describe in detail the treatment of obsessive-compulsive checking rituals using different intervention strategies, prompted by the individual functional analyses.

CASE ILLUSTRATION 6.4

Melamed and Siegel (1975) used a multifaceted treatment program to successfully eliminate a checking ritual in a sixty-three-year-old man. The treatment program was carried out in the home by the patient, Mr. R., and his wife during a fifteen-week period. Components of the intervention strategy included operant reinforcement, disruption of the chain of ritualistic behaviors through gradual time restriction, systematic desensitization of related fears, and response prevention.

Mr. R. had developed an extensive checking ritual approximately nine months before entering therapy. The problem had become extremely time-consuming and frustrating, and created much conflict between him and his wife.

The compulsive checking began when a minor malfunction in the gas line caused Mr. R. to worry that a possible fire or explosion might occur. Despite reassurance from a repairman that an automatic shutoff valve would prevent any accidents, he began to engage in a ritualistic trip to the basement to check that the pilot light in the furnace was still on before he could go to sleep. Within the next several weeks, the checking behavior had generalized to the entire house. Each evening before going to bed, he was spending more than three hours checking such things as electrical appliances to make sure they were turned off, wall sockets and wires to see if they were touching anything, windows and doors to make sure they were locked, and ashtrays to clean them of any cigarette ashes (this is termed behavioral excess).

At approximately the same time each evening, Mrs. R. would go to her bedroom and Mr. R. would begin his checking, examining each room in the house in the same order every night. Mrs. R. had to be in her bedroom before the checking could begin, because Mr. R. was afraid that she might disturb something after he had checked it or leave her cigarettes burning in an ashtray that he had already checked. This behavior was very annoying to Mrs. R., and she refused his repeated requests to assist him in his checking.

It is interesting to note that Mr. R.'s daytime job involved detailed checking behavior. Since he was responsible for checking airbrakes on railroad cars, it was important that the treatment program eliminate only checking behavior that was inappropriate.

A second problem that required intervention was Mr. R.'s fear of having a hernia operation. The hernia was causing him considerable pain and discomfort, but he had canceled surgery on several occasions because of his fear that he would not awaken from the anesthetic after the operation. These medical fears were noted on several items on the Fear Survey Schedule (Wolpe & Lang, 1964).

During the baseline assessment period, Mr. R. was given a stopwatch and instructed to keep a record of the time that he spent checking in each room of the house. Baseline records indicated that the patient was spending an average of sixty-seven minutes checking each evening. Because Mr. R. and his wife had suggested that he typically spent at least three hours each evening engaged in checking activities, it was felt that the procedure of monitoring his own behavior contributed to a reduction in the amount of time he regularly spent checking. Weekly changes in the total time that the patient spent checking throughout the intervention program are illustrated in Figure 6.3.

Mr. R. was instructed to refrain from checking the living room during the first week of treatment because baseline records indicated that he was spending the least amount of time in this

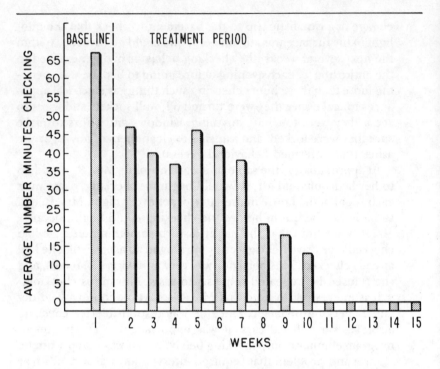

Figure 6.3   Average number of minutes spent daily in ritualistic checking during baseline and treatment.

From B. G. Melamed and L. J. Siegel, Self-directed in-vivo treatment of an obsessive-compulsive checking ritual. *Journal of Behavior Therapy and Experimental Psychiatry,* 1975, *6,* 31–36. Copyright © 1975 by Pergamon Press, Ltd. Reprinted by permission.

room, and thus, would most easily be able to comply with this restriction. He was also asked to complete his checking in less than sixty minutes, a time that he agreed was a reasonable goal. As reinforcement for successfully carrying out this assignment, he received a hug and a kiss from his wife, and could work a crossword puzzle, one of the few reinforcers that had been identified for Mr. R. This strategy produced a considerable decrease in average checking time—to forty-seven minutes each evening. In addition, he was able to completely eliminate the living room from his checking ritual.

Although Mr. R. reported substantial anxiety relief following completion of his checking, he continued to experience some tension, which made it difficult for him to fall asleep. Progressive muscle relaxation training was initiated, therefore, and he was instructed to practice relaxing for fifteen minutes each evening before bedtime throughout the treatment program.

During the following week, Mr. R. was told to discontinue checking the bedroom. He was to reinforce himself with a cross-word puzzle for each evening that he spent less than fifty minutes checking. An additional incentive of a dollar reduction in the clinic fee was included for each day he successfully completed this assignment.

The data indicated that he was able to eliminate both the living room and bedroom from his checking activities, and managed to decrease his average checking time to forty minutes each night. Furthermore, he earned a five dollar reduction in the clinic fee.

For the fourth through seventh week of the program, Mr. R. was given a list of the remaining rooms of the house (arranged in a random order) that he was asked to follow each evening during his checking. It was felt that this procedure would disrupt the checking ritual, which was conceptualized as a chain of behaviors, with each component of the chain maintained by the terminal reinforcer of relief from anxiety. The strategy of instructing Mr. R. to check the rooms in a different order each evening did not result in the expected decrease in his checking time.

Mr. R. reported during this period that he had seen a physician and had scheduled a date for surgical repair of his hernia the following month. Because of his fear of surgery, a hierarchy of nine fear-related items was prepared with his assistance for use in systematic desensitization during the next three sessions.

When asked to eliminate another room from his checking ritual, Mr. R. chose the basement because it had a door that he could close as a reminder not to check. He was also instructed to practice muscle relaxation for fifteen minutes before he began checking in order to reduce his reported anticipatory anxiety. Because he was able to eliminate the basement from his ritual (the room in which he was spending the most time), he was able to reduce his average checking time to eighteen minutes during this period.

A response prevention program was discussed with Mr. R. and his wife during the ninth treatment session. It was explained that his hospitalization for surgery would be an important aspect of the response prevention since it would be the first time that he would be away from home and unable to check. The therapist also suggested that when he returned home, he would no longer feel the urge to check since no adverse consequences would have occurred in his absence. He was encouraged to resist checking completely at least one evening during the week prior to hospitalization. Mrs. R. was instructed to escort him to his bedroom and to close the door. He was to remain there for the reminder of the evening and practice muscle relaxation for at least fifteen minutes. He was informed that he could call the therapist if he felt the need to check, but was told not to leave his bedroom once the door was closed. Mr. R. was able to remain in his bedroom without checking for two evenings. His average checking time during this week was only thirteen minutes.

The following week, Mr. R. was admitted to the hospital for surgery. It is significant that he did not experience any distress about not having the opportunity to engage in checking behavior. He reported that desensitization had helped him to cope with the hospital experience. Prior to discharge, the therapist visited the hospital, where Mr. R. and his wife were reminded of the response prevention program to be reinstituted for a week following his return home.

The final session was held with Mr. R. and his wife during the fifteenth week of the program. Mr. R. reported that he no longer had the urge to check, nor did he experience the extreme anxiety that had previously necessitated relief through performing the checking ritual.

A one-month follow-up assessment revealed that Mr. R. remained symptom free. He was feeling more relaxed than he had in a long time, and his social contacts had increased considerably. Mrs. R. also reported greater satisfaction with their marital relationship. At four months, the patient recontacted the therapist to report a return of the urge to check, although the actual checking behavior did not recur. He was instructed to reinstate the response prevention program for one week. Two years following treatment, Mr. R. remained free of the maladaptive behavior, and he no longer reported an urge to check.

Although some reduction in the frequency of the checking ritual can be attributed to the operant reinforcement strategy, the problem behavior was not completely eliminated until the response prevention program was introduced. Deep muscle relaxation facilitated the patient's ability to refrain from checking by producing a significant decrease in anticipatory anxiety. This procedure may account for the ease with which he was able to eliminate the most anxiety-provoking room (the basement) from his checking ritual. Indeed both Mr. and Mrs. R. expressed amazement at this particular achievement.

An important component of this treatment program was the self-directed and graduated reduction of the checking behavior. This permitted the patient to regain a sense of self-control and mastery over his own behavior and resulted in an improvement in his self-concept.

Although the checking rituals had begun prior to the need for Mr. R's operation, it is possible that desensitization to the hospital fears would have led to a reduction in these rituals. However, Mr. R. would not even consider the idea of hospitalization prior to his moderate success during the operant program. The issue of self-control was particularly important in this case because the patient perceived the problem as a "loss of his self-confidence." Finally, systematic desensitization enabled the patient to enter the hospital and to achieve success in this previously avoided area, further enhancing his sense of self-mastery.

In another patient, although similar rituals involving checking were present, the functional analysis focused more on increasing the exposure to potentially dangerous events by a flooding technique.

CASE ILLUSTRATION 6.5

A patient who repeatedly consulted physicians with somatic concerns received the label hypochondriac. This offered no solution for the sufferer, however, and he continued to seek out a reassuring physician at the cost of lengthy, repetitive, and expensive medical diagnostic procedures. A behavioral evaluation disclosed a circumscribed pattern of ritualistic behaviors and obsessive concerns, particularly regarding bodily functions, which accompanied the patient's physical complaints. This patient also had a checking ritual that involved a series of repetitive acts that was assumed to forestall potentially catastrophic events he felt would have led to bodily harm to himself or others in his environment. Although the patient was embarrassed by his own behavior, he was impelled, as if by an external force, to perform the ritualistic behavior. A different therapeutic approach was used in this case.

Don, a twenty-six-year-old man with a graduate degree, was unable since college graduation to retain employment because of his increasing need to perform checking rituals on the job and in his apartment. Don spent several days each week consulting with various physicians about potential medical conditions, ranging from minor eye problems to fear of a heart attack. The rest of his days were spent in worrying about his health and safety.

At the time of the behavioral consultation, Don was unable to live alone due to his fears and financial problems. Since traditional psychotherapy had not diminished the checking rituals, his brother, with whom he shared an apartment, had delivered an ultimatum regarding this behavior. The brother could no longer tolerate the patient's restrictions on his sleeping and eating habits, such as not using the kitchen after dinner in order to avoid possible risks to their safety, and asked him to find another apartment.

Where does the behavioral therapist start? Attempting to talk such a patient out of his fears has been shown not to be productive. Dealing with underlying feelings of guilt and unworthiness had not altered the patient's excessive checking rituals in two years of psychoanalytic treatment. The behavior itself becomes the target of concern. The patient was instructed to self-monitor his ritualistic checking, including the frequency, place, time of the checking, and his mood. This itself served to limit the amount of time spent in checking from the estimated five hours per evening to approximately two hours. Thus, some self-control over the chain of behaviors was demonstrated.

The evaluation also revealed an excessive somatic component. When Don discussed the thoughts that triggered the behavior, he sweated profusely, became flushed, and experienced extreme tenseness in the muscles of his arms and shoulders. Relaxation training was attempted without success because of his inability to inhibit distressing thoughts about fire, explosion, and disaster. In addition, the patient was unable to relax in his home setting as the mere sight of the stoves, faucets, and electrical outlets elicited the urge to check.

Since this somatic overreaction motivated doctor-seeking behaviors and seemed to reinforce the chain of events that initiated ritualistic avoidance of presumed danger, a flooding procedure to extinguish this somatic arousal was chosen. Secondary gain resulted from the attention of physicians; thus, the therapist contracted with the patient that only emergency room visits would be permitted during the course of behavioral treatment. In addition, the brother was instructed not to check the stove or report back to the patient regarding the safe condition of the apartment.

A flooding procedure was initiated in the therapist's office (see Chapter 2 for a description of this procedure). The patient was instructed to imagine the consequences of his failure to check the stove, faucet, and thermostat. This imagery experience was monitored with electromyograph recordings until the patient reported increasing discomfort consistent with the physiological response and subsequent reduction for both. He was instructed to continue the exposure treatment at home by eliminating one step from his compulsive checking routine each week. During subsequent treatment sessions, guided imagery was enhanced with slides of mutilated, drowned, and burned victims that were imagined to result from his failure to check.

Despite the intense focus on the specific events that he feared, his self-monitoring data indicated that progressive flooding was accompanied by decreased time spent checking at home. Figure 6.4 illustrates the course of treatment. The week following an absence of flooding in therapy, due to a conjoint session with brother at which other topics were discussed, the checking behavior was once again increased. This provided a demonstration of a reversal procedure (discussed in Chapter 2), which indicates that the flooding procedure was, in fact, producing the desired behavior change. His brother was also instructed to play no further role in the checking and to engage in any behavior without regard to whether it enhanced the patient's concerns, including late snacks in the kitchen, if he so desired.

The flooding procedure continued for a total of five sessions and resulted in a constant decrease in the time that he spent checking. With the decrease of ritualistic behavior, the patient turned his attention toward pursuing employment and obtaining an apartment of his own. Role rehearsal was implemented to improve his interview skills. Shortly thereafter, he was hired for a job in his area of expertise.

Although he reported a recurrence of the urge to check, he was able to suppress further maladaptive behavior both at work and at home. The need to consult physicians for numerous physical complaints likewise diminished considerably over the next few months. Weekly telephone contacts for six months following termination of treatment confirmed the maintenance of therapeutic

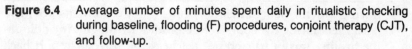

Figure 6.4   Average number of minutes spent daily in ritualistic checking
during baseline, flooding (F) procedures, conjoint therapy (CJT),
and follow-up.

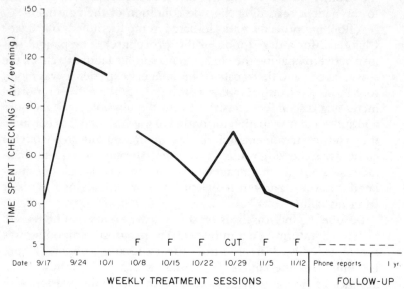

gains. At a one-year follow-up, the patient was still employed and
no longer reported checking rituals.

Summary

The multiple and complex interactions between physical and emotional problems were illustrated by cases ranging from disorders of a
primarily organic nature, as in anorexia nervosa, to disturbances
affected by psychological attitudes and behaviors secondary to medical
illness. In addition, cases of a primarily psychiatric nature, such as
obsessive-compulsive disorders, phobias, and hypochondriacal concern with bodily harm or illness, were interpreted in this chapter from
the viewpoint of the medical preoccupations that are reflected in the
thought disorder.
    Despite the diverse nature of these problems, the behavioral ap-
proaches used in their treatment were often similar. Contingency man-

agement procedures were effectively employed in the case of an anorectic female patient with severe malnutrition caused by self-induced vomiting, in the self-control program of a migraine headache sufferer to reduce her drug dependence, and in the treatment of a severe checking ritual in a sixty-three-year-old man with obsessive concerns about his safety. The use of a combination of biofeedback and relaxation procedures were demonstrated to be effective in the control of headaches, spasmodic torticollis, and insomnia. Variants on systematic desensitization were used in the treatment of postcoronary sexual difficulties, in an anorectic's fears of obesity, anger, and criticism, and in the preparation of a patient for a hernia operation.

In each of these cases, the role of the physician in communicating with the patients and their immediate families was a major facilitative factor in insuring the maintenance of the treatment success. The application of a systematic functional analysis provided the behavioral therapists with information regarding the selection of the treatment procedure most clearly related to the patients' primary complaint. This process provided important guidance with respect to the appropriateness of a particular behavioral technique in promoting behavior change in the most expedient manner.

References

Abram, H. S., Hester, L. R., Sheridan, W. F., & Epstein, G. M. In J. LoPiccolo & L. LoPiccolo (Eds.), *Handbook of sex therapy.* New York: Plenum, 1978.

Ad Hoc Committee on Classification of Headache. Classification of headache. *Journal of the American Medical Association,* 1962, *179,* 717–718.

Agras, S., Barlow, D., Chapin, H., Abel, G., & Leitenberg, H. Behavior modification of anorexia nervosa. *Archives of General Psychiatry,* 1974, *30,* 279–286.

Agras, S., & Marshall, C. The application of negative practice to spasmodic torticollis. *American Journal of Psychiatry,* 1965, *122,* 579–582.

Alban, L. S., & Nay, W. R. Reduction of ritual checking by a relaxation-delay treatment. *Journal of Behavior Therapy and Experimental Psychiatry,* 1976, *7,* 151–154.

American Psychiatric Association. *Diagnostic and statistical manual of mental disorders* (2nd ed. –DSM–II), 1968.

Annon, J. S. *The behavioral treatment of sexual problems. Vol. 1. Brief therapy.* Honolulu: Enabling Systems, 1974.

———. *The behavioral treatment of sexual problems. Vol. 2. Intensive therapy.* Honolulu: Enabling Systems, 1975.

Azrin, N. H., & Nunn, R. G. Habit reversal: A method of eliminating nervous habits and tics. *Behaviour Research and Therapy,* 1973, *11,* 619–628.

Bachrach, A. J., Erwin, W. J., & Mohr, J. P. The control of eating behavior in an anorexic by operant conditioning techniques. In L. P. Ullman & L. Krasner (Eds.), *Case studies in behavior modification.* New York: Holt, Rinehart & Winston, 1965, pp. 153–163.

Bakal, D. A. Headache: A biopsychological perspective. *Psychological Bulletin,* 1975, *82,* 369–382.

Bakal, D. A., & Kaganov, J. A. Muscle contraction and migraine headache: Psychophysiological comparison. *Headache,* 1977, *17,* 208–215.

Bemis, K. M. Current approaches to the etiology and treatment of anorexia nervosa. *Psychological Bulletin,* 1978, *85,* 593–617.

Bellack, A. S., & Hersen, M. *Behavior modification: An introductory textbook.* Baltimore: Williams & Wilkins, 1977.

Benson, H., Beary, J., & Carol, M. The relaxation response. *Psychiatry,* 1974, *37,* 37–45.

Benson, H., Rosner, B. A., Marzetta, B. R., & Klemchuk, H. M. Decreased blood pressure in borderline hypertensive subjects who practice meditation. *Journal of Chronic Diseases,* 1974, *27,* 163–169 (a).

Benson, H., Rosner, B. A., Marzetta, B. R., & Klemchuk, H. M. Decreased blood pressure in pharmacologically treated patients who regularly elicited the relaxation response. *Lancet,* 1974 *1,* 289–290 (b).

Bianco, F. Rapid treatment of two cases of anorexia nervosa. *Journal of Behavior Therapy and Experimental Psychiatry,* 1972, *3,* 223–224.

Blanchard, E. B., & Young, L. D. Clinical application of biofeedback training: A review of evidence. *Archives of General Psychiatry,* 1974, *30,* 573–589.

Blinder, B. J., Freeman, D. M., & Stunkard, A. J. Behavior therapy of anorexia nervosa: Effectiveness of activity as a reinforcer of weight gain. *American Journal of Psychiatry,* 1970, *126,* 1093–1098.

Block, A., Maeder, J., & Haissly, J. Sexual problems after myocardial infarction. *American Heart Journal,* 1975, *90,* 536–537.

Bohlin, G. Monotonous stimulation, sleep onset and habituations of the orienting reaction. *Electroencephalography and Clinical Neurophysiology,* 1974, *31,* 593–601.

Bootzin, R. Stimulus control treatment of insomnia. *Proceedings, 80th Annual Convention.* APA, 1972, 395–396.

Borkovec, T. D., & Boudewyns, P. A. Treatment of insomnia with stimulus control and progressive relaxation procedures. In J. D. Krumboltz and C. E. Thoresen (Eds.), *Counseling methods.* New York: Holt, Rinehart & Winston, 1976.

Borkovec, T. D., & Fowles, D. Controlled investigation of the effects of progressive and hypnotic relaxation on insomnia. *Journal of Abnormal Psychology,* 1973, *82,* 153–158.

Borkovec, T. D., & Weerts, T. E. Effects of progressive relaxation on sleep disturbance: An electroencephalographic evaluation. *Psychosomatic Medicine,* 1976, *38,* 173–180.

Brady, J. P., Luborsky, L., & Kron, R. E. Blood reduction in patients with essential hypertension through metronome conditional relaxation: A preliminary report. *Behavior Therapy,* 1974, *5,* 203–209.

Brady, J. P., & Rieger, W. Behavioral treatment of anorexia nervosa. *Proceedings of the International Symposium on Behavior Modification* (Minneapolis, Minn., Oct. 4–6, 1972). New York: Academic Press, 1972.

Brierly, H. The treatment of hysterical spasmodic torticollis by behavior therapy. *Behaviour Research and Therapy,* 1967, *5,* 139–142.

Browning, C. H., & Miller, S. I. Anorexia nervosa: A study in prognosis and management. *American Journal of Psychiatry,* 1968, *124,* 1128–1132.

Bruch, H. Perils of behavior modification in treatment of anorexia nervosa. *Journal of the American Medical Association,* 1974, *230,* 1414–1422.

Brudney, J., Grynbaum, B., & Korein, J. Spasmodic torticollis: Treatment by feedback display of EMG. *Archives of Physical Medicine and Rehabilitation,* 1974, *55,* 403–408.

Budzynski, T. H. Biofeedback procedures in the clinic. *Seminars in Psychiatry,* 1973, *4,* 537–547.

Budzynski, T. H., & Stoyva, J. An instrument for producing deep muscle relaxation by means of analogue information feedback. *Journal of Applied Behavior Analysis,* 1969, *2,* 231–237.

Budzynski, T. H., Stoyva, J. M., Adler, C. S., & Mullaney, D. EMG biofeedback and tension headache: A controlled outcome study. *Psychosomatic Medicine,* 1973, *35,* 484–496.

Chesney, M. A., & Tasto, D. L. The effectiveness of behavior modification with spasmodic and congestive dysmenorrhea. *Behaviour Research and Therapy,* 1975, *13,* 245–253.

Cohen, M. J. Psychophysiological studies of headache: Is there similarity between migraine and muscle contraction headache? *Headache,* 1978, *18,* 189–196.

Cox, D. J., Freundlich, A., & Meyer, R. G. Differential effectiveness of electromyographic feedback, verbal relaxation instructions, and medication placebo with tension headaches. *Journal of Consulting and Clinical Psychology,* 1975, *43,* 892–899.

Dally, R., & Sargent, W. Treatment and outcome of anorexia. *British Medical Journal,* 1966, *2,* 793–795.

Deabler, H. L., Fidel, E., Dillenkoffer, R. L., & Elder, S. T. The use of relaxation and hypnosis in lowering high blood pressure. *American Journal of Clinical Hypnosis,* 1973, *16,* 75–83.

Elkin, T., Hersen, M., Eisler, R., & Williams, J. Modification of caloric intake in anorexia nervosa: An experimental analysis. *Psychological Reports,* 1973, *32,* 75–78.

Epstein, L. H., & Abel, G. C. An analysis of biofeedback training effects for tension headache patients. *Behavior Therapy,* 1977, *8,* 37–47.

Epstein, L. H., Abel, G. C., Collins, F., Parker, L., & Cinciripini, P. M. The relationship between frontalis muscle activity and self-reports of headache pain. *Behaviour Research and Therapy,* 1978, *16,* 153–160.

Ericksen, R. A., & Huber, H. Elimination of hysterical torticollis through use of a metronome in an operant conditioning paradigm. *Behavior Therapy,* 1975, *6,* 405–406.

Eysenck, H. J. Learning theory and behaviour therapy. *Journal of Mental Science,* 1959, *105,* 61–75.

Freedman, R., & Papsdorf, J. D. Biofeedback and progressive relaxation treatment of sleep-onset insomnia: A controlled, all-night investigation. *Biofeedback and Self-Regulation,* 1976, *1,* 253–270.

Friedman, J. M. Sexual adjustment of the postcoronary male. In J. LoPiccolo & L. LoPiccolo (Eds.), *Handbook of sex therapy.* New York: Plenum, 1978.

Group for the Advancement of Psychiatry. *Psychopathological disorders in childhood: Theoretical considerations and a proposed classification* (Report No. 62), 1966, *6.*

Hackett, T. P., & Cossem, N. H. Psychological adaptation in myocardial infarction patients. In J. P. Naughton & H. K. Hellerstein (Eds.), *Exercise testing and exercise in coronary heart disease.* New York: Academic Press, 1973.

Harper, R. G., & Steger, J. C. Psychological correlates of frontalis EMG and pain in tension headache. *Headache,* 1978, *18,* 215–218.

Hauri, P., & Cohen, S. The treatment of insomnia with biofeedback: Final report of Study I. *Sleep Research,* 1977, *6,* 136.

Hauri, P., & Good, R. Frontalis muscle tension and sleep onset. *Sleep Research,* 1975, *4,* 222.

Hauserman, N., & Lavin, P. A broad spectrum behavioral therapy in the post-hospitalization treatment of anorexia nervosa. Unpublished manuscript. Townson State University, 1975.

Haynes, S. N., Griffin, P., Mooney, O., & Parise, M. Electromyographic biofeedback and relaxation instructions in the treatment of muscle contraction headache. *Behavior Therapy,* 1975, *6,* 672–678.

Hersen, M., & Eisler, R. M. Behavioral approaches to study and treatment of psychogenic tics. *Genetic Psychology Monographs,* 1973, *87,* 289–312.

Higgins, G. E. Aspects of sexual response in adults with spinal cord injury: A review of the literature. In J. LoPiccolo & L. LoPiccolo (Eds.), *Handbook of sex therapy.* New York: Plenum, 1978.

Hodgson, R., Rachman, S., & Marks, I. M. The treatment of chronic obsessive-compulsive neurosis: Follow-up and further findings. *Behaviour Research and Therapy,* 1972, *10,* 181–189.

Holroyd, K. A., & Andrasik, F. Coping and the self-control of chronic tension headache. *Journal of Consulting and Clinical Psychology,* 1978, *46,* 1036–1045.

Holroyd, K. A., Andrasik, F., & Westbrook, T. Cognitive control of tension headache. *Cognitive Therapy and Research,* 1977, *1,* 121–133.

Kales, A., Allen, C., Scharf, M., & Kales, J. Hypnotic drugs and their effectiveness. *Archives of General Psychiatry,* 1970, *23,* 226–232.

Kaplan, H. S. *The new sex therapy: Active treatment of sexual dysfunctions.* New York: Brunner/Mazel, 1974.

Karacan, I., Williams, R. L., Littell, R. C., & Salis, P. J. Insomniacs: Unpredictable and idiosyncratic sleepers. In W. Koella, & P. Levin (Eds.), *Sleep: Physiology, biochemistry, psychology, pharmacology, clinical implications.* Basel: Karger, 1973.

Kavanagh, T., & Shepard, R. J. Sexual activity after myocardial infarction. *Canadian Medical Association Journal,* 1977, *116,* 1250–1253.

Kazdin, A. E. *The token economy: A review and evaluation.* New York: Plenum, 1977.

Keefe, F., Kopel, S., & Gordon, S. *A practical guide to behavioral assessment.* New York: Springer, 1978.

Knapp, T. J., & Wells, L. A. Behavior therapy for asthma: A review. *Behavior Research and Therapy,* 1978, *16,* 103–115.

Kringler, E. Obsessional neurotics. *British Journal of Psychiatry,* 1965, *3,* 709–722.

Lake, A., Rainey, J., & Papsdorf, J. D. Biofeedback and rational-emotive therapy in the management of migraine headache. *Journal of Applied Behavior Analysis,* 1979, *12,* 127–140.

Lamontagne, Y., & Marks, I. M. Psychogenic urinary retention: Treatment by prolonged exposure. *Behavior Therapy,* 1973, *4,* 581–585.

Lang, P. J. Behavior therapy with a case of nervous anorexia. In L. P. Ullman & L. Krasner (Eds.), *Case studies in behavior modification.* New York: Holt, Rinehart & Winston, 1965.

Leitenberg, H. (Ed.). *Handbook of behavior modification and behavior therapy.* Englewood Cliffs, N.J.: Prentice-Hall, 1976.

Leitenberg, H., Agras, W. S., & Thomson, L. A sequential analysis of the effect of selective positive reinforcement in modifying anorexia nervosa. *Behaviour Research and Therapy,* 1968, *6,* 211–218.

Levy, R., & Meyer, V. Ritual prevention in obsessional patients. *Proceedings Royal Society of Medicine,* 1971, *64,* 1115–1118.

Lindsley, O. R., Skinner, B. F., & Solomon, H. C. *Studies in behavior therapy. Status Report 1.* Waltham, Mass.: Metropolitan State Hospital, 1953.

Lobitz, W. C., & Lobitz, G. K. Clinical assessment in the treatment of sexual dysfunctions. In J. LoPiccolo & L. LoPiccolo (Eds.), *Handbook of sex therapy.* New York: Plenum, 1978.

LoPiccolo, J. Direct treatment of sexual dysfunctions. In J. LoPiccolo & L. LoPiccolo (Eds.), *Handbook of sex therapy.* New York: Plenum, 1978.

LoPiccolo, L., & Heiman, J. R. Sexual assessment and history interview. In J. LoPiccolo & L. LoPiccolo (Eds.), *Handbook of sex therapy.* New York: Plenum, 1978.

Marks, I. M. *Fears and phobias.* New York: Academic Press, 1969.

Marks, I. M. Behavioral treatments of phobic and obsessive-compulsive disorders: A critical appraisal. In M. Hersen, R. M. Eisler, & P. M. Miller (Eds.), *Progress in behavior modification,* Vol. 1. New York: Academic Press, 1975.

Martin, M. J. Muscle-contraction headache. *Psychosomatics,* 1972, *13,* 16–19.
Masters, W. H., & Johnson, V. E. *Human sexual inadequacy.* Boston: Little, Brown, 1970.
Melamed, B. G., & Siegel, L. J. Self-directed in vivo treatment of an obsessive-compulsive checking ritual. *Journal of Behavior Therapy and Experimental Psychiatry,* 1975, *6,* 31–35.
Meyer, R., & Levy, R. Modification of behavior in obsessive-compulsive disorders. In M. Adams & I. Umikel (Eds.), *Issues and trends in behavior therapy.* Springfield, Ill.: Charles C. Thomas, 1973.
Mills, H. L., Agras, W. S., Barlow, D. H., & Mills, R. J. Compulsive rituals treated by response prevention. *Archives of General Psychiatry,* 1973, *28,* 524–529.
Mitchell, K. R., & Mitchell, D. M. Migraine: An exploratory treatment application of programmed behavior therapy techniques. *Journal of Psychosomatic Research,* 1971, *15,* 137–157.
Mitchell, K. R., & White, R. G. Behavioral self-management: An application to the problem of migraine headache. *Behavior Therapy,* 1977, *8,* 213–221.
Nemiah, J. C. Anorexia nervosa, fact and theory. *American Journal of Digestive Diseases,* 1958, *3,* 249–274.
O'Leary, K. D., & Wilson, G. T. *Behavior therapy: Application and outcome.* Englewood Cliffs, N.J.: Prentice-Hall, 1975.
Ostfeld, A. M. *The common headache syndromes: Biochemistry, pathophysiology, therapy.* Springfield, Ill.: Charles C. Thomas, 1962.
Oswald, I. Falling asleep open-eyed during intense rhythmic stimulation. *British Medical Journal,* 1960, *1,* 1450–1455.
Patel, C. Reduction of serum cholesterol and blood pressure in hypertensive patients by behavior modification. *Journal of the Royal College of General Practitioners,* 1976, *26,* 211–215.
Paul, G. L., & Lentz, R. J. *Psychosocial treatment of chronic mental patients: Milieu vs. social-learning approaches.* Cambridge, Mass.: Harvard University Press, 1977.
Philips, C. Headache in general practice. *Headache,* 1977, *16,* 322–329.
———. Tension headache: Theoretical problems. *Behaviour Research and Therapy,* 1978, *16,* 249–261.
Puksta, N. S. All about sex . . . After a coronary. *American Journal of Nursing,* 1977, *77,* 602–605.
Rachman, S. J., & Philips, C. *Psychology and medicine.* Middlesex, England: Penguin, 1978.
Renshaw, D. C. Impotence in diabetes. In J. LoPiccolo, & L. LoPiccolo (Eds.), *Handbook of sex therapy.* New York: Plenum, 1978.
Rimm, D. C., & Masters, J. C. *Behavior therapy: Techniques and empirical findings.* New York: Academic Press, 1974, 1978 (revised).
Roper, G., Rachman, S., & Hodgson, R. An experiment on obsessional checking. *Behaviour Research and Therapy,* 1973, *11,* 271–277.
Sacks, O. *Migraine.* Berkeley: University of California Press, 1970.

Sargent, J. D., Walters, E. D., & Green, E. E. Psychosomatic self-regulation of migraine headache. *Seminars in Psychiatry*, 1973, *5*, 415–428.

Scalzi, C. C., Loya, F., & Golden, J. S. Sexual therapy of patients with cardiovascular disease. *Western Journal of Medicine*, 1977, *126*, 237–244.

Schultz, J. H., & Luthe, W. *Autogenic therapy*. New York: Grune & Stratton, 1969.

Shapiro, D., & Surwit, R. S. Learned control of physiological function and disease. In H. Leitenberg (Ed.), *Handbook of behavior modification and behavior therapy*. Englewood Cliffs, N.J.: Prentice-Hall, 1976.

Solbach, P., & Sargent, J. D. A follow-up of the Menninger pilot migraine study using thermal training. *Headaches*, 1977, *17*, 198–202.

Steinmark, S., & Borkovec, T. Active and placebo treatment effects on moderate insomnia under counterdemand and positive demand instructions. *Journal of Abnormal Psychology*, 1974, *83*, 157–163.

Surwit, R. S., & Keefe, F. J. Frontalis EMG feedback training: An electronic panacea? *Behavior Therapy*, 1978, *9*, 779–792.

Tasto, D. L., & Hinkle, J. E. Muscle relaxation treatment for tension headaches. *Behaviour Research and Therapy*, 1973, *11*, 347–349.

Thoresen, C., Coates, T., Zarcone, V., Kirmil-Gray, K., & Rosekind, M. Treating the complaint of insomnia: Self-management perspectives. In J. M. Ferguson and C. B. Taylor (Eds.), *A comprehensive handbook of behavioral medicine*. Jamaica, N.Y.: Spectrum Publications, in press.

Traub, A. C., Jencks, B., & Bliss, E. L. Effects of relaxation training on chronic insomnia. *Sleep Research*, 1973, *3*, 164.

Turin, A., & Johnson, W. G. Biofeedback therapy for migraine headaches. *Archives of General Psychiatry*, 1976, *33*, 517–519.

Turner, D. B., & Stone, A. J. Headache and its treatment: A random sample survey. *Headache*, 1979, *19*, 74–77.

Walen, S., Hauserman, N. M., & Lavin, P. *Clinical guide to behavior therapy*. Baltimore: Williams & Wilkins, 1977.

Weekes, C. *Simple effective treatment of agoraphobia*. New York: Hawthorn Books, 1977.

Wickramasekera, I. The application of verbal instructions and EMG feedback training to the management of tension headache: Preliminary observations. *Headache*, 1973, *13*, 74–76 (a).

———. Temperature feedback for the control of migraine. *Journal of Behavior Therapy and Experimental Psychiatry*, 1973, *4*, 343–345 (b).

Wolff, H. G. *Headache and other head pain* (2nd. ed.). New York: Oxford University Press, 1963.

Wolpe, J. *Psychotherapy by reciprocal inhibition*. Stanford: Stanford University Press, 1958.

———. Identifying the anxiety antecedents of a psychosomatic reaction: A transcript. *Journal of Behavior Therapy and Experimental Psychiatry*, 1971, *2*, 45–50.

Wolpe, J., & Lang, P. J. A fear survey schedule for use in behavior therapy. *Behaviour Research and Therapy*, 1964, *2*, 27–30.

7

BEHAVIORAL INTERVENTION IN REHABILITATION

Many members of the health care professions work with patients in an effort to provide a wide range of rehabilitative services. Included in the rehabilitation process are orthopedic surgeons, psychologists, psychiatrists, occupational therapists, physical therapists, nursing staff, speech therapists, social workers, and those individuals involved in vocational guidance and training. Members of the rehabilitation team are working in an ever-increasing number of health care settings, such as general hospitals, rehabilitation centers, psychiatric institutions, schools and institutions for the handicapped and mentally retarded, and geriatric facilities. The patients in these settings present many disabilities—especially cognitive, sensory, and motor deficits—as a result of chronic illnesses, accidents and injuries, and neurological and psychiatric disorders.

This chapter offers rehabilitation workers the behavioral perspective on some of the solutions to problems they must manage on a daily basis. A behavioral analysis of the rehabilitation process and components of disability behavior is demonstrated by case illustration. Finally, a number of behavioral intervention techniques are presented that have been successfully applied to management problems and physical disorders of patients seen in rehabilitation therapy.

Therapeutic goals for patients may include some of the following tasks: increasing muscle strength and joint mobility in a patient with rheumatoid arthritis, teaching typing skills to a person with peripheral neuropathy, improving the perceptual-motor skills of a child with cerebral palsy, teaching a hemiplegic patient to perform such routine activities of daily living as independent dressing skills, increasing the understandable and appropriate speech of a stroke patient with aphasia, teaching a patient paralyzed from a spinal cord injury to transfer from the bed to his wheelchair, increasing the social interaction of an elderly woman with other residents in a nursing home, instructing a patient with an amputated leg to use a prosthetic limb, and improving the task performance and productivity rate of a psychiatric patient in a sheltered workshop setting.

The Learning Process in Rehabilitation

Despite the diverse nature of these patients and the problems they present, the therapist's task is essentially the same in each case: to help the patient achieve his or her maximum capacity within the constraints of the particular disability. Rehabilitation may be defined as a process whose purpose is to "help the patient recover or to develop competence in physical, psychological, social and economic aspects of his life —competence to communicate, to make personal adaptations and relationships, to become adequate or proficient in work and recreation. . . ." (E. M. MacDonald, 1970, p. 3). The process of learning is basic to rehabilitation. Fordyce (1971b) has elaborated on this point:

> There are several reasons why rehabilitation properly emphasized learning. In the first place, learning is behavior change. When a person incurs a physical disability, there is some immediate change in his behavior potential or response repertoire. The patient, for example, who sustains injury to the spinal cord undergoes significant changes in a host of behaviors (e.g., ambulation). His disability will change what he needs to do as well as what he can do. But he will not do the new things he needs to do and is potentially capable of doing until he learns how [p. 169].

With a stroke patient, for example, gait and balance training and therapeutic exercises might be provided to teach the patient to walk again, or speech therapy might help him or her regain speech and language skills. In this case, rehabilitation involves the *relearning* of previous skills or abilities that were lost through neurological impairment. On the other hand, after assessment of the residual capacity in a patient with muscular dystrophy, rehabilitation efforts may be to help the patient *learn* to move about the house in a wheelchair and, thus, learn a compensatory skill to enable him or her to be as independent as possible, despite the loss of function.

Since rehabilitation is in essence a learning or reeducation process, the application of behavioral techniques to the various areas of rehabilitation is particularly relevant. Behavioral principles guide the therapist in teaching new behaviors and altering any existing behaviors in the patient's repertoire. Thus, rehabilitation and behavioral approaches to intervention share many basic goals and assumptions.

Teaching New Behavior

Many therapeutic goals focus on helping patients acquire new behaviors to enable them to function as independently as possible with a particular disability. Often, these necessary skills are quite complex. In addition, assessment of the patient's abilities may indicate that he or she does not currently have the sub-behaviors in his or her repertoire that make up the larger performance unit. Thus, the therapist is not in a position to wait for the patient to perform the desired behavior and reinforce it when it occurs. For instance, one should not expect a recently paralyzed patient to transfer successfully from the bed to a wheelchair on his or her first attempt as this is a difficult and unfamiliar task.

Shaping

In helping patients to perform complex behaviors in therapy, a behavioral procedure called shaping is used. The first step in applying a shaping procedure is to analyze the task that one wants to teach the patient and to break the behavior down into its several components so that they represent small, graduated steps. For example, E. M. Mac-Donald (1970) provides the following illustration of how to break down the behavior of teaching a hemiplegic patient to stand. The steps are as follows:

   1. Move forward on the seat by pulling on the arms and sliding forward or by pressing back against the chair back with the shoulders.

2. Lift the affected leg by hand to place the foot correctly.
3. Look to see if it is correct. Place the other foot correctly.
4. Place the walking aid in front and to the side of the sound foot. Put the sound hand on the chair arm, well back, and turn slightly to that side.
5. Lean forward over the sound foot, pushing the hand and foot to raise the hip from the seat. Continuing to lean forward, transfer the weight to the sound foot by straightening the arm. Gradually straighten the knee and hip to stand erect, and that of the affected leg at the same time.
6. Transfer the hand to the walking aid and check the position of the affected foot before walking [pp. 99–100].

Each step should be small enough to maximize successful performance of the behavior and to minimize failure experiences. The patient should receive sufficient reinforcement for his or her efforts at each step along the way, or it is likely that he or she will not persist in the performance of the task. Patients need early success experiences. This is particularly true of a new skill that requires the patient to engage in behaviors that are tedious and fatiguing. On the other hand, the steps should not be so small that the patient does not find the task a challenge. These rules about shaping hold true whether teaching self-care skills to a stroke patient, improving range of movement in physical therapy, or teaching a child with a developmental disorder a task requiring fine motor coordination.

A shaping procedure starts with a behavior that the patient is already capable of performing. The therapist then reinforces small steps or approximations toward the desired terminal behavior. As the patient successfully performs the behavior at each step, the criteria for reinforcement are gradually changed so that the required behavior more closely resembles the therapist's treatment goal.

Sometimes the patient has difficulty initiating a particular response, and it is necessary for the therapist to prompt or guide the behavior more directly. For example, in the case presented earlier, (teaching the hemiplegic patient to stand from a sitting position), the therapist can facilitate the patient's performance with instructions on how to move his or her body, or the therapist can model or demonstrate the various steps while the patient observes. Finally, the therapist can physically guide the patient's behavior by moving the patient's arms and legs in the appropriate manner. Gradually, the therapist fades or removes the prompts until the patient is capable of performing each step unassisted.

Positive Reinforcement and Extinction

In addition to shaping, a number of operant conditioning techniques have been used in rehabilitation settings to help patients learn a wide range of adaptive behaviors or skills. Trotter and Inman (1968) used contingent positive reinforcement to increase muscle strength through weight lifting in physical therapy. Spinal-cord-injured patients, who were confined to wheelchairs, received verbal reinforcement and encouragement from the therapist and a rest period contingent on lifting increasingly greater weights in a progressive resistance exercise program. In addition, records of the patient's progress in therapy were used as feedback to reinforce the patient's efforts. This treatment program resulted in an increase in the strength of the patient's arms and facilitated the learning of other skills that required this muscular strength, such as propelling the wheelchair, going from bed to chair, and self-care activities.

Goodkin (1966) taught patients a variety of skills in a rehabilitation center using verbal and token reinforcement of desirable behavior and an extinction procedure in which maladaptive behaviors were ignored. For example, a patient with Parkinson's disease was taught independent use of a wheelchair and to propel the wheelchair faster. In addition, operant conditioning techniques were used to teach brain injured patients such fine motor skills as learning to write faster with the nondominant hand and increasing speed on a keypunch machine. Finally, Goodkin reports the effectiveness of reinforcement procedures in increasing understandable and appropriate speech in a stroke patient with severe expressive and receptive aphasia. Similarly, Connolly (1968) gradually shaped and modified the motor responses of children through kinesthetic feedback and immediate reinforcement of correct responses. This procedure, used with normal children, suggested itself as a strategy for improving the gross and fine motor control of children with neurological disorders such as cerebral palsy.

*Electromechanical Devices as Adjuncts to
Behavior Therapy*

Several rehabilitation programs have combined the use of electromechanical devices and operant conditioning procedures to teach patients desirable behaviors and to help them compensate for behavioral deficiencies resulting from a physical disability. Berni and Fordyce (1973), for example, present the case of a woman with Parkinson's disease who frequently lost her balance in the wheelchair and would fall to the floor unless she was restrained by a belt. Because of her disability, the woman did not receive the normal proprioceptive cues to provide her with the necessary feedback to indicate that she was falling. As a result, she was unable to catch herself in time to regain her balance. To deal with this problem, an electric eye was placed on the back of the wheelchair. When her shoulders moved a short distance from the back of the wheelchair, a tone sounded, indicating that she was starting to fall. This permitted her to stop the fall by readjusting her body. This feedback procedure was effective in significantly reducing her falling behavior.

Problems with postural control were also treated by Azrin and his colleagues (Azrin, Rubin, O'Brien, Ayllon, & Roll, 1968; O'Brien & Azrin, 1970) using a similar procedure. Persons who exhibited considerable slouching behavior were fitted with a portable device to help improve their posture. When the subjects did not maintain an erect posture, an aversive noise was automatically sounded. The individual could terminate the noise by regaining an erect posture. Thus, maintaining an upright body posture was negatively reinforced. Persons who wore this device learned to maintain an improved posture. The effectiveness of this portable operant treatment device suggests that it might have considerable promise in the treatment of illnesses or injuries that result in disorders of movement or orientation of the body. Similar procedures were used by Halperin and Kottke (1968) to improve the muscular control of the neck and head posture in children with cerebral palsy, and by Birbaumer, Dworkin & Miller (1979) in treating scoliosis (which leads to excessive curvature of the spine). The latter investigators hope their unobtrusive feedback device will provide an alternative to the Milwaukee Brace. This latter device is effective if worn regularly, but it is often misused by adolescents, who are more concerned about their immediate appearance than with the long-term benefits of wearing the brace.

A frequent and potentially serious problem with spinal-cord-injured patients who are confined to wheelchairs is the development of pressure sores (decubitus ulcers). Paraplegic patients, for example, have lost all sensory awareness in their lower extremities. As a result, they are not aware of continuous pressure on a particular area of the body during prolonged sitting. If they do not periodically shift their weight to change positions, damage to the skin will occur from a reduced flow of blood to the area where sustained pressure is placed. Therefore, one of the behaviors that a paraplegic patient must learn in a rehabilitation program is to relieve pressure frequently on weight-bearing areas. This can be accomplished by training the patients to redistribute their weight by doing push-ups with their hands on the arms of the wheelchair and shifting the body to a different position. However, for most patients, this is a difficult habit pattern to learn simply through instruction or reminders from the staff, and as a result, many patients develop skin breakdowns. To increase and maintain push-up behavior in paralyzed patients, Malament, Dunn, and Davis (1975) used a conditioning apparatus that negatively reinforced the desired behavior. The device, on which the patient sat, sounded a loud tone that the patient could terminate or avoid by doing push-ups. If the patient did a push-up for a duration of at least four seconds, the tone could be postponed for ten minutes. However, if patients failed to do a push-up within a ten-minute period, the alarm sounded, and the patients could terminate the noise if they did a push-up for four seconds. Once the patient was performing push-ups at a consistent rate, the device was removed from the wheelchair. Using this procedure, these researchers were able to reduce the frequency of pressure sores in paraplegic patients who in the past had developed frequent decubitus ulcers. Furthermore, a high rate of push-up behavior was maintanined once the device was permanently removed from the wheelchair.

A treatment program to prevent pressure sores in spinal-cord-injured patients was also reported by Rottkamp (1976). Patients at a rehabilitation center were trained through demonstration, physical prompts, and social reinforcement to alter their body position on a periodic basis throughout the day. Each patient received an average of ten training sessions over approximately four weeks. Using this gradual shaping procedure and providing reinforcing consequences such as attention contingent on shifting body positions, the hospital staff members were able to increase significantly the frequencies of the patients' daily changes in their body positions. In addition, the treatment program considerably reduced the amount of assistance from the nurses previously required to insure that patients moved their bodies.

Motivating the Patient

Possibly one of the most pervasive and difficult problems that rehabilitation personnel face each day in therapy is low patient motivation. Gaining the cooperation of patients is of paramount importance since no therapy can be effective without their active participation.

There are several reasons for low motivation in the rehabilitation setting. First, rehabilitation can be a slow, difficult, and sometimes painful process. Often, the patient is faced with the task of relearning basic skills of daily living that were once taken for granted. As a result, the treatment program can acquire aversive or unpleasant properties that the patient attempts to avoid. The patient's avoidance behavior can, in turn, interfere with the goals of rehabilitation (Fordyce, 1971a). Furthermore, many patients have cognitive deficits as a result of illness or injury. These deficits may reduce both the patient's understanding of the treatment program and his or her level of cooperation. A bio-behavioral monitoring device (Goldstein et al., 1976) that prompts the patient to report data has been found to be useful in measuring rehabilitative progress.

Rearranging Environmental Reinforcement Contingencies

As noted in Chapter 3, problems of patient motivation are in fact problems of incentive or reinforcement. If the patient does not seem motivated to participate in the rehabilitation process, Michael (1970) suggests that "the basic question that should be asked is what does the patient get out of the activity?" (p. 65). The patient's environment must be arranged in such a way that meaningful consequences are provided contingent on the patient's participation in the treatment program and his or her acceptable performance in the therapeutic activities that have been established (Michael, 1970). However, a functional analysis often reveals that, in the case of disabled patients, reinforcing consequences are readily available regardless of a patient's behavior. Access to television, rest, interesting conversation, and so on are usually available without any behavioral demands being made on the patient. If motivation is low, the therapist may have to adjust the patient's environment in the patients' interest so that he or she is permitted access to these reinforcing activities and situations contingent on performance of desired treatment behaviors. Suitable reinforcers become especially critical in maintaining the patient's interest and cooperation during those times when progress is slow and the therapeutic activities are physically and mentally demanding.

In rehabilitation settings there are many naturally occurring consequences that potentially can serve as reinforcers for a particualr patient. Using the Premack Principle (Premack, 1965), discussed in Chapter 3, as a guide, effective reinforcers can be identified for each patient. A frequent consequence that follows much of a patient's behavior in health care facilities is the attention, sympathy, and concern provided by relatives, friends, and members of the treatment team. Do not underestimate the effect that attention and social approval can have on the patient's behavior. For many patients it can be a potent reinforcer! However, this social reinforcement is often not provided when the patient is engaging in the desired rehabilitation activities (e.g., exercising or dressing independently), and is instead contingent on maladaptive behaviors that are incompatible with the rehabilitation process (e.g., complaints of discomfort, refusal to participate in therapy) (Fordyce, 1971b; Michael, 1970; Trombly, 1966). Thus, although well-intentioned in their efforts, family and members of the treatment team can impede a patient's progress in the rehabilitation program by the way in which they respond to the patient's behavior. Trombly (1966) illustrates this problem in a discussion of a typical sequence of events that results when helping the disabled patient to become more independent. The therapist often provides considerable attention to the patient at times when he or she is *less* independent in an attempt to encourage the patient to become *more* independent. At the same time, when patients show signs of becoming more independent, by engaging in self-care activities, for example, they are often left alone to do more on their own. As a result, the therapist inadvertently reinforces dependent behavior instead of independent behavior on the part of the patient.

Rest and time out from therapeutic activities has also been found to be an effective reinforcer with some patients in rehabilitation settings (Fordyce, 1971b; Fordyce, Fowler, Lehmann, DeLateur, Sand, & Trieschmann, 1973; Michael, 1970). In many rehabilitation centers, the patient is permitted to terminate an activity and to rest in the therapy session when he or she is fatigued or expressing feelings of pain or discomfort. Thus, the patient is reinforced for behaviors that enable him or her to avoid engaging in the prescribed physical activity. In order to increase the frequency of such physical activity as therapeutic exercises, it is necessary to rearrange the contingencies so that rest or time out from the activity is made to follow the desired behavior. Therefore, instead of permitting rest to occur contingent on the behaviors that are incompatible with the rehabilitation process, rest is arranged to occur following a specific period of activity *before* the patient reaches the point of discomfort and fatigue. The result is that the patient is reinforced with rest *after* engaging in the desired behavior. It is important for the therapist to remember that he is not there to withdraw social privileges from the patient or act the tyrant. Plan *with* the patient a program in which reinforcers occur with a frequency equal to or, better yet, greater than before therapy. The task is not to take away but to rearrange temporal contingencies where this is possible, and so serve the patient's vital, long-term goal of rehabilitation to an active, productive life.

Reducing Fears Associated with Activity

A patient may also appear to be unmotivated to perform the desired behaviors or to be uncooperative with the therapist in the rehabilitation program as a result of specific fears that may accompany the disability. In addition, the patient may display anxiety reactions in response to specific aspects of therapy that the patient finds disturbing or distressful. These fears may interfere with the patient's progress in the rehabilitation program, and may necessitate direct intervention to facilitate the patient's participation in therapy.

This is illustrated in a case presented by Fordyce (1971b). A fifty-one-year-old patient was extremely fearful of lifting weights in physical therapy because when he attempted to lift even small weights he reported experiencing pain similar to that which he had experienced during a previous heart attack. Despite the physician's insistence that the pains were in no way related to a heart attack and that he was physically capable of lifting weights, the patient resisted participation in physical therapy as a result of his fears. He was, therefore, seen for several sessions in which systematic desensitization was used to eliminate his fears and thus enable him to engage in physical therapy. A hierarchy of items was constructed in which the patient was asked to visualize lifting increasingly larger weights for ten seconds with one hand until he experienced pain. By gradually increasing the imagined weight amount he was able to visualize up to 25 pounds without experiencing any anxiety or reporting any pain. Following systematic desensitization, he actually was able to lift the same amount of weight in physical therapy without experiencing any pain.

Systematic desensitization was also used by Di Scipio and Feldman (1971) to treat the fear of walking in a fifty-two-year-old woman with Parkinson's disease. This disorder resulted in her walking with a stiff gait that made her extremely fearful of losing her balance and falling. As a result, she confined herself to a wheelchair, and was afraid to participate in ambulation training in physical therapy. After training the patient in deep muscle relaxation, an anxiety hierarchy was constructed with items pertaining to the patient's fear of falling. For instance, some of the items were concerned with situations in which she might fall down in the presence of the hospital staff or when there were no other people around to assist her if she fell. Following seven sessions of desensitization over a three-week period, the patient was making significant progress in physical therapy. She was ambulating with a walker with minimal assistance from others, and reported fewer concerns about falling.

The following illustrates an alternative, operant approach taken in the case of a patient who voiced similar fears and refused to walk. In this patient, however, a functional analysis determined that phobic concerns were already receiving too much attention; thus, the focus was on ambulation.

CASE ILLUSTRATION 7.1

Mrs. C. is a fifty-six-year-old woman who was admitted to a rehabilitation hospital for patients with physical disabilities and chronic illnesses. She had been transferred from a general medical hospital, where she had been three weeks previously. Mrs. C. had initially been taken to the hospital following an automobile accident in which she had sustained minor injuries. When she arrived at the hospital she complained of considerable back pain and stated that she was unable to move either of her legs. In addition, she was unable to stand without assistance from others. A series of diagnostic tests and a thorough neurological examination were completed during the course of her initial hospitalization. The results of these procedures were all negative; no physical basis for her inability to walk could be found. While her back pain was diagnosed as resulting from muscles strained during the accident, her constant complaints of pain were felt to be out of proportion to the extent of the actual injury.

Mrs. C. was a woman of low-average intellectual abilities. In early childhood, she was diagnosed as having cerebral palsy; during adolescence she had had several operations involving corrective orthopedics. Thus, a model of physical disability involving back and leg complaints to gain attention was evident. Although she had always walked with a slightly abnormal gait, she had never experienced any prior difficulty in walking. It is interesting to note that about two years before this current hospitalization, her husband had been killed in an automobile accident. Since his death, she had reduced her social contacts and was described by others as being depressed. Mrs. C. had one married daughter with whom she continued to have considerable involvement. Table 7.1 summarizes the assessment and treatment procedures.

I. Defining the Target Behavior

A. BEHAVIORAL EXCESSES.   Complaints of pain from her back and legs were frequent throughout the day. When family members and friends came to visit, her conversation invariably led to a discussion of her pain and numerous somatic complaints. She expressed extreme fears of falling and complained of being dizzy whenever she was taken out of bed to stand for a few minutes each day with the assistance of the nursing staff. She would cry loudly; the nurses would respond by putting her back in bed.

The Minnesota Multiphasic Personality Inventory (MMPI) and the Fear Survey Schedule revealed obsessive concerns about disease and bodily ailments. There were also indications of concerns about expressing her opinions or revealing feelings to others. The psychologist reported that she had a "hysterical personality adjustment" and that a referral to psychiatry for a possible conversion reaction might be indicated. Regardless of the source of her inability to walk, the problem of severe muscle atrophy of her legs was a concern of her physicians. She needed to begin to walk again —that was of the most immediate importance to her health.

B. BEHAVIORAL DEFICITS.   The Beck Depression Inventory (Beck, Ward, Mendelsohn, Mock, & Erbaugh, 1961) revealed that Mrs. C. was moderately depressed. Since her husband's death, she had shown little interest in leaving her home and had significantly restricted her social life. The Gambrill-Richey Assertiveness Scale (Gambrill & Richey, 1975) indicated difficulties in effectively communicating her needs and feelings to others. This was reflected in her behavior in that she rarely initiated social interactions.

C. INAPPROPRIATE OR DEFECTIVE STIMULUS CONTROL.   There were no clear stimulus control components identified for the walking problem. However, her interactions with other people were limited to discussions about somatic complaints. She did report that fears of dizziness and falling kept her from standing up. Other people seemed to precipitate crying and complaining behavior rather than more appropriate social interaction.

D. BEHAVIORAL ASSETS.   Because of her depression, preoccupation with physical concerns, and withdrawal from social contacts, Mrs. C. evidenced few assets at the time of her admission to

Table 7.1 Treatment Program for a Nonambulatory Patient

I. Target behavior __refusal to walk_____ defined as:

   A. (too much) _crying, complaints of pain in back and legs, stayed in_
   bed at all times

   B. (too little) _walking, standing, self-care behavior_

   C. (cued by or in reaction to) _fears of falling, dizziness, other people_

   D. (strengths and skills) _interest in occupational therapy_

II. Methods of collecting information

   A. (interviews, questionnaires, test results) _interviews of patient and_
   daughter, Fear Survey Schedule, Assertiveness Inventory

   B. (overt manifestations of patient's behavior) _number of complaints to_
   nursing staff, amount of time on feet in physical therapy

   C. (what patient self-monitors and records) _number of steps taken in_
   physical therapy and on the hospital ward

   D. (lasting changes in the environment--e.g., food left over, work output)
   not applicable

   E. (physiological indices--e.g., GSR, pulse rate) _none_

III. Functional analysis of behavior

   A. (events preceding target behavior) _fear of intensifying back pain,_
   fears of falling and dizziness, wheelchair brought to bedside

   B. (events following target behavior) _attention and concern of staff and_
   other patients, daughter's frequent visits

IV. Selecting and implementing an intervention program

   A. Motivation for change

     1.(benefits of "sick-role"--e.g., attention, avoidance or responsibility)
   attention from others, avoids physical therapy, avoids self care

     2. (What would be different for patient/significant others if problem
   did not exist?) _less dependent on her daughter and son-in-law_

(continued)

B. Meaningful environmental consequences

  1. Likes <u>magazines, coffee, occupational therapy activities, visits from family</u>

  2. Dislikes <u>being ignored</u>

C. Significant others (spouse, siblings, parent, teacher) <u>daughter,</u>
<u>nurses, doctors, hospital staff</u>

D. Factors maintaining the problem <u>attention for complaining and refusing</u>
<u>to walk, fear of further pain in her back, lack of social skills</u>

E. Treatment strategies <u>physical therapy shaping program for walking, use of</u>
<u>prompts (walker), staff ignores complaints and praises progress, relaxation</u>
<u>training, thought-stopping</u>

V. Evaluation of intervention program

  A. Monitoring of treatment progress <u>nurses record frequency of complaints, physical</u>
<u>therapist records time on feet, patient self-monitors duration of walking unassisted</u>

  B. Programming for maintenance of behavior change <u>therapy with daughter,</u>
<u>volunteer work program for the patient, home visits before discharge</u>

  C. Follow-up assessment <u>(15 months after discharge) the patient was still</u>
<u>walking, a good relationship existed between mother and daughter</u>

VI. Termination (What was your treatment goal?) <u>to reestablish unassisted</u>
<u>walking and to increase patient's independence</u>

---

the hospital. In addition, she had never worked and had depended on her husband for meeting all of her needs. However, she particularly enjoyed visits from her daughter and showed some interest in craft activities in occupational therapy.

II. Methods of Collecting Information

Interviews with the patient and her daughter and several inventories and questionnaires provided a source of information about the presenting problems through self-report. The nursing staff provided behavioral observations in the form of frequency recordings of the number of times that she complained to the staff about her back pains or her legs. During the treatment program, the physical therapist also made duration recordings of the amount of time that she was able to remain on her feet. In addition, the patient was instructed to self-monitor the number of steps that she was able to take in physical therapy and while on the hospital ward.

This information was then placed on a graph and displayed on the door to her room in order to prompt remarks of praise for progress from nurses and other patients and provide a more appropriate topic of discussion.

III. Functional Analysis of Behavior

There were some indications that her fears of walking may have been exacerbated by her concern that physical movement would intensify the reported back pain. As a result, she refused to leave the bed unless absolutely necessary or to go to occupational therapy. When she did leave the bed, she was always transported in a wheelchair. Ward observations indicated that a number of reinforcing consequences followed her problem behaviors. Mrs. C. received considerable attention and concern from others for complaining behaviors and crying, whereas she was virtually ignored when quietly engaged in adaptive behaviors such as reading. In addition, Mrs. C. would discuss her complaints with the patient with whom she shared her room. This other patient, who was concerned that perhaps Mrs. C. was not receiving proper nursing care for her problems and might fall if left unattended, would in fact press the call button to summon assistance for Mrs. C. When her daughter frequently visited her in the hospital, it was also clear that this provided more opportunity for the occurrence of the problem behaviors. She brought reading material and candy, making these reinforcers obtainable without the patient's needing to walk to the gift shop.

IV. Selecting and Implementing the Treatment Program

It was clear from the assessment that Mrs. C. was obtaining considerable attention for much of her problem behavior. There were few demands placed on her to take responsibility for any of her own care or to participate actively in physical therapy programs. When she was taken to physical therapy, crying or complaints of pain resulted in her being returned to her hospital room. Since her husband was dead, she fully depended on her daughter. Her daughter, who felt guilty about her mother's living alone, reinforced her mother's frequent contacts. This led to conflict between the daughter and Mrs. C.

The treatment program was developed to reinstate walking behavior. Mrs. C. was initially trained in deep muscle relaxation and in the use of a thought-stopping technique. When she began to worry about feeling dizzy and falling, she was encouraged to visualize the word "stop" to herself in order to interfere with the bothersome thoughts. She was then instructed to engage in relaxing imagery. Following training in these procedures, a gradual shaping program was instituted to reestablish independent walking behavior. Mrs. C. could earn points for engaging in increasingly more complex walking responses. These points could be exchanged for reinforcing activities or desired items, such as time in occupational therapy, visits with family and friends, magazines, coffee, trips to the canteen, and activities within the hospital (e.g., seeing movies). The staff were also instructed to ignore her frequent crying episodes and complaints of pain, which had interfered with her attendance at physical therapy. At the same time, they were told to attend to her when she was engaging in desirable behavior (e.g., walking, self-care) and to praise her progress in physical therapy.

The shaping program began with Mrs. C.'s earning points for standing for three seconds with the aid of parallel bars. Gradually, her time was increased until she was able to stand for ten minutes without fear of falling. Next, the patient was reinforced for taking small steps while holding on to the bars. This phase continued until she was able to walk to the end of the bars. At this point, she was able to use a walker as an aid, and was required to walk the length of the physical therapy room. The walker was then removed, and Mrs. C. was rewarded for walking while holding on to the therapist's arms. The therapist then faded out his assistance until the patient was able to walk on her own. Finally, Mrs. C. was required to walk ten laps around the hospital each morning and evening. It should be noted that rest periods were used as a reward for achieving successive goals.

V. Evaluation of the Intervention Program

The treatment program was in effect for forty-three days. At the end of this period, Mrs. C. was completely ambulatory without assistance from the hospital staff. The data records indicated that crying and complaining behaviors had been nearly eliminated. In addition, Mrs. C. reported being less depressed as measured by the Beck Depression Inventory. She participated more frequently in hospital activities that were planned for the patients, including attending dances and going on shopping trips. As Mrs. C. began to make consistent progress in physical therapy, the token reinforcement program had been replaced by social reinforcement. Therefore, at the end of the program, visits with other patients and her daughter were sufficient to maintain her walking behavior.

VI. Termination of the Intervention Program

During the last two weeks of the program, Mrs. C. was given weekend passes to live at home in order to evaluate her competence for independent living. No serious problems were noted. She was able to shop and visit her daughter several blocks away. It was important, however, to help her develop interests of her own so that she would become less dependent on her daughter. Therefore, upon discharge from the hospital, arrangements were made with Mrs. C.'s consent for her to do volunteer work several days each week at a nursing care facility for the elderly a few streets from her home. The daughter was actively involved in the discharge planning and agreed that it was important for her mother to develop the necessary coping skills to deal with problems on her own. The daughter was advised what to do when her mother inappropriately expressed helplessness and dependent behavior. Fifteen months following discharge from the hospital, Mrs. C. was continuing to walk without difficulty. She was enjoying her work at the nursing home and was no longer depressed. Her daughter reported that her mother had made few inappropriate demands and that their relationship had improved considerably as a result.

The Treatment of Depression

Depression is a disturbance of mood that is extremely resistant to most therapeutic attempts. Patterns of depressive behaviors vary greatly from one person to another. The revised *Diagnostic and Statistical Manual of Mental Disorders (DSM III)* of the American Psychiatric Association (1978) has eliminated the distinction between neurotic and psychotic depressions as well as the endogenous-reactive dichotomy. Although there are three subtypes of affective disorders (i.e., episodic, chronic, and atypical), depressive features are still a part of the classification of schizo-affective disorders, senile and presenile dementia, and adjustment disorders. This may reflect the multiple etiological factors underlying depression.

Many depressive behaviors have a discernible physiological basis, originating in metabolic, enzymatic, genetic, or other biological dysfunction (Aillon, 1971). Even distinctions between subtypes of depression have been made in relation to biochemical and pharmacological influences (Depue & Monroe, 1978; Goodwin & Bunney, 1973), as in the differences between bipolar and unipolar patients. A bipolar patient is defined as a depressed patient with a prior history of mania or hypomania, whereas the depressive episode is called unipolar when it occurs in a person without a prior history of mania or hypermania. Data are presented in Depue & Monroe (1978) and Goodwin & Bunney (1973) that support the notion that these subtypes may represent differences in biological substrata and should be treated as different illnesses. In these cases, where biochemical factors can be identified, a medical-pharmacological approach is usually indicated. For example, the use of lithium in the treatment of manic-depressive disorders has been very effective (Mendels, 1975; Schlou, 1968).

Although physiological factors must be included in the clinical assessment of depressed patients, Akiskal and McKinney (1973) have suggested that depression is almost always an interaction between behavioral and physiological factors. Regardless of the neurological pathways that may be identified in future research, it is clear that many cases of depression are precipitated by environmental loss and may be understood within a behavioral framework. Depressive reactions may result from true biochemical imbalances secondary to disease, such as hyperthyroidism or Hodgkin's disease. Depression may be related to the effects of a drug, such as antihypertension medication or radiation treatment. Depression may be reactive, in response to an overwhelming life stress, such as chronic illness or the loss of a loved one. In all of these situations, the individual and his or her relatives must live with the associated depressive behavior. There is some commonality in the problems and adjustments severely depressed individuals impose on themselves and others, regardless of the biochemistry.

It is not uncommon to see such reactive depression in patients rehabilitating from illness. Many of these patients, as a result of a physical trauma or chronic disease, have lost the ability to perform many basic behaviors. They, therefore, become more dependent on others to do things for them that they were once able to do for themselves. Michael (1970) and Fordyce (1971a) have described a disability as a condition that is functionally similar to punishment. Punishment, as discussed in Chapter 2, is defined behaviorally as either the presentation of an aversive stimulus or the withdrawal of positive reinforcement contingent on a given behavior. In a similar manner, a disability can prevent a patient from having access to opportunities to obtain reinforcement in ways that were previously available prior to the onset of the disability. Thus, for example, the patient may have fewer social, vocational, and recreational opportunities because of the disability, which, in turn, restricts access to desired reinforcers. Furthermore, a patient with a disability can experience many aversive stimuli, such as pain and general discomfort, as a result of an illness or injury (e.g., amputation of a limb) or from the treatment program itself (e.g., physical activity).

It follows from this that depression can be treated by minimizing the punishing consequences that the patient experiences and increasing the patient's opportunities to obtain desired reinforcers. Therefore, the rehabilitation goals that are worked toward in therapy to help the patient adjust to the disability are in essence similar to the goals in treating a patient with depression, namely, teaching the patient the necessary skills to obtain reinforcers from the environment.

Behavioral Theories of Depression

Treatment approaches to depression are based on a wide diversity of theoretical orientations. These differ in terms of which depressive symptoms are given major emphasis. Although the theories lead to different interventions, the causality of the behavior that determines depression has not yet been evaluated. The fact that depressive behaviors are reduced given a specific treatment approach fails to provide definitive conclusions regarding the causal factors. Indeed, even depressions that have genetic or biochemical determinants can be influenced by changes in the environment or cognitive attitudes of the patients. The behavioral formulations are based on laboratory analogues as well as clinical investigations. Despite the differences in theoretical formulation, most therapies attempt to reinstate active behaviors in the patient. Whether this is attempted by altering the availability of reinforcers or changing the person's sense of control over his life depends on the theoretical background of the therapist. The most Skinnerian approach was that adapted by Ferster (1966), based on observations of the similarity between the behavior of clincally depressed individuals who showed a reduced tendency to emit behavior and that of the experimental laboratory animal analogues. It was observed that reduced frequencies of behavior occured in the bar pressing of rats under certain predictable environmental conditions:

1. when the environment requires a large amount of behavior to produce a significant change in it;
2. when aversive stimuli are present; and
3. when the controlling stimulus of behavior is suddenly removed.

It is this third condition that has been used in behavioral formulations of depressive behaviors. The theory of loss of reinforcement effectiveness (Costello, 1972) postulates that depression is a function of the amount of social reinforcement that patients receive from important people in their lives. Lewinsohn (1974) formulated a theory in which a loss of positive reinforcement leads to a reduction of activity. Cognitive theorists (Beck, 1974) place greater emphasis on the person's self-evaluative belief as the main determinant of depressive affect. If the individual has a negative self-evaluation, he or she is likely to have fewer expectations about the ability to change events in the present or future. Loss of self-esteem occurs. Seligman (1975) used a combination of the behavioral reinforcement and cognitive theories in his concept of learned helplessness. Drawing an analogy to experiments involving escape behavior in dogs, he felt that the depressed individual perceived a lack of control over his or her behavior and the consequences it was likely to produce. More recent formulations (Abramson, Seligman, & Teasdale, 1978; Miller & Norman, 1979) favor attributional models in which patients' evaluations of the reason for their helplessness affect the likelihood that they will become depressed, suffer low self-esteem, or generalize the negative expectancy about their ineffectiveness to new situations.

In the case of patients with chronic illness or injury, both the loss of reinforcer availability and the lack of a sense of control over their fate are often inevitable. The patients must cope with real limitations on their ability to adjust in everyday living situations. They may not be able to participate in activities that were previously enjoyable. There may be little medical science can offer to prevent a terminal illness. Therefore, depression is a highly probably concern for health care professionals. This section will briefly review these theories, which have led to treatments of depressive behaviors such as inactivity, mood disturbance, and feelings of unworthiness.

Loss of Reinforcement

Reinforcement is central to the model of depression presented by Lewinsohn and his colleagues (Lewinsohn, 1974; 1975; Lewinsohn, Biglan, & Zeiss, 1976). According to Lewinsohn, depression is the result of a low rate of response-contingent positive reinforcement, which can result from several factors. First, there may be few events or activities that are actually reinforcing for the patient, possibly due to the loss of effectiveness of previous reinforcers (e.g., activity now elicits pain). Second, the patient's environment may make available only a limited number of reinforcing events or activities. Finally, the patient may lack the necessary skills or abilities to obtain sufficient reinforcement. The concept of social skills, which Lewinsohn defines as the ability to perform behaviors that are reinforced by others, is of particular importance in the treatment of depression. Research has, in fact, demonstrated that depressed persons are less effective in eliciting social reinforcement from others than are nondepressed individuals (Lewinsohn & Atwood, 1969; Libet & Lewinsohn, 1973).

Since depression is conceptualized as the result of an overall reduction in the rate of positive reinforcement, it follows that the treatment of a depressed patient involves an alteration of the rate of reinforcement that the patient receives. According to Lewinsohn (1975), the primary goal in the treatment of depression is "to restore an adequate schedule of positive reinforcement for the individual through altering the level, the quality, and the range of the patient's activities and interactions" (p. 46). Lewinsohn's treatment program includes an assessment of activities or events that were pleasurable for the patient prior to the onset of the depression. This is accomplished by completion of a Pleasant Events Schedule (MacPhillamy & Lewinsohn, 1974). In addition, this schedule helps the therapist to identify currently reinforcing events for the patient and serves to point out to the patient that he or she is not engaging in many pleasant activities. Lewinsohn and MacPhillamy (1974) found that the number of pleasant activities in which depressed individuals engage and their subjective ratings of enjoyment of a number of potentially pleasant events is lower than those of other psychiatric patients or nondepressed persons.

Throughout the treatment program, patients monitor their overall daily mood and keep records of the pleasurable events or activities in which they engage. Lewinsohn's goal in the treatment of the depressed patient is to gradually increase the extent to which the patient engages in these activities. It has been demonstrated that there is a significant relationship between the daily mood changes in depressed patients and the number of pleasant activities in which they engage. Furthermore, the more the patient participates in these activities, the less depressed he or she feels (Lewinsohn & Graf, 1973).

Lack of Self-Rewarding Behavior

Another model of self-control, a variant of Lewinsohn's, assumes that depressed patients lack the skill of self-rewarding their own behaviors (Rehm & Kornblith, 1979). This treatment package includes patient's self-monitoring of positive events, daily logs of positive activities and associated mood, and self-evaluation. In the self-evaluation phase, patients select behaviors they wish to engage in more frequently and state what specific reward they will self-administer contingent upon performing the target behaviors. The studies conducted on the efficacy of this treatment (Fuchs & Rehm, 1977; Rehm, Fuchs, Roth, Kornblith, & Romano, 1979) reported improvement in patients on self-report, behavior, and the Minnesota Multiphasic Personality Inventory scale of depression greater than that achieved in social skills training, nonspecific therapy, or waiting control subjects. Unfortunately, the depressed population is comprised of outpatient volunteers solicited through advertisements. It is not established whether these patients have much in common with patients who seek help for clinical depression.

Contingency Management

Other theories have stressed the importance of selectively reinforcing behaviors that are incompatible with depressive behaviors. Rather than focusing on the patients' self-reinforcement, these programs rearrange environmental contingencies so that the patient is rewarded for adaptive behavior and verbalizations, while depressive symptoms are ignored (Burgess, 1969; Liberman & Raskin, 1971). These programs have been successful both in hospital settings and on an outpatient basis.

The use of token reinforcement for increasing self-care behaviors and improving participation in occupational and milieu therapy has been demonstrated with multihandicapped patients and neurotic depressives (Hanaway & Barlow, 1975; Hersen, Eisler, Alford, & Agras, 1973). The system developed by Williams, Barlow, and Agras (1972) for monitoring behaviors that accompany severe depression has provided a way of evaluating such programs.

The recognition that sympathy of family and significant others paradoxically increases pain and depressive behaviors has stimulated the extension of behavioral programs to teach social skills and improve marital communication. Lewinsohn, Weinstein, and Alper (1970), through use of group assertive skills programs, increased the quality of persons' interactions, thus promoting a greater potential for reinforcement from others.

Liberman and Raskin (1971) taught contingency management procedures directly to the families of depressed individuals. They demonstrated the effectiveness of instructing family members to attend selectively to and reward adaptive behaviors, while ignoring depressive ruminations. Single case reversal designs illustrated the immediate and long-term effectiveness of this approach.

Others have gone into the home; by means of observation, feedback, and contingency contracting they have improved the marital interaction with accompanying decrease in the level of the patient's depression (Lewinsohn & Shaw, 1969; McLean, Ogston, & Grauer, 1973).

Cognitive Theories

Learned Helplessness and Attribution. Seligman and his colleagues (Miller & Seligman, 1973; Seligman, 1972; 1973; 1975) have proposed a model of depression in which cognitive factors interact with specific environmental variables in the development of depressive behaviors. In earlier work with animals, it was found that after dogs had been exposed to several trials of inescapable shock by being restrained in a harness, they would not learn to escape shock when the escape response was then allowed (Seligman & Maier, 1967; Seligman & Groves, 1970). The term "learned helplessness" was coined as an explanatory construct. The recent formulation of depression involved the individual's perceived inability to control environmental events. An individual may develop this out of previous experiences in which a failure to deal with stress-inducing situations generated a negative expectancy about coping with any new stressors; or the person may have failed to learn the complex skills necessary to elicit reinforcement because he or she failed to receive reinforcement contingent on appropriate use of these skills. Research with depressed patients has supported this hypothesis (Miller & Seligman, 1973). A revised theory (Abramson, Seligman, & Teasdale, 1978) predicts how individuals will respond in any given situation depending upon where they placed blame for their previous failure. Once people perceive noncontingency, they attribute their helplessness to a cause. This cause can be unstable or stable, global or specific, and internal or external. The attribution influences the person's future expectancy of helplessness, and determines if it will be chronic or acute, broad or specific, and whether or not it will lower self-esteem. Treatment strategies that follow this theoretical formulation combine cognitive restructuring techniques with training subjects in the awareness of contingencies between their behavior and effects of the environment. Depressed subjects are shown by the use of graded tasks (Burgess, 1969) that they do have the ability to control the amount of reinforcement they receive. Miller and Norman (1979) have reviewed behavioral theory of depression within the cognitive model, and proposed an extension to attribution theory.

Negative Self-Concept. A treatment of depression that focuses on maladaptive cognitions has been developed by Beck (1967; 1974). According to Beck, depression results from a person's negative perceptions of himself or herself, of present experiences, and of the future. The depressed patient distorts his or her perceptions of events and experiences and uses faulty or illogical thinking when interpreting these experiences. For example, a study by Nelson and Craighead (1977) suggests that depressed persons may selectively attend to negative feedback from their environment and may overlook or distort positive feedback. Beck further proposes that the depressed patient manifests thoughts and attitudes about himself or herself as being in some way unworthy or inadequate. In this regard, Nelson and Craighead (1977) found that mildly depressed persons were less likely to self-reinforce their efforts and accomplishments than were nondepressed individuals. Thus, depressed persons appear to make fewer positive self-evaluations of their performance, which may, in turn, result in low "self-esteem."

Based on this formulation of depression, Beck has developed a treatment program for altering the patient's maladaptive thoughts that lead to depression. The primary focus of treatment is directed at helping patients to identify maladaptive thoughts or self-statements (such as regarding a disability as a catastrophic event about which they can do nothing, or viewing themselves as a less worthwhile individual because of the disability) and then helping the patients to evaluate and test the validity of these distorted and maladaptive assumptions. This is accomplished by teaching the patient to appraise more realistically and objectively his or her behavior and experiences. Thus, the patient is taught to challenge the basis for persistent negative cognitive patterns that lead to the depression and to replace them with more positive and realistic attitudes and assumptions.

Rush, Khatami, and Beck (1975) describe the treatment of three chronically depressed patients using the intervention strategy outlined by Beck. In one case, a thirty-seven-year-old man had been depressed for several years. The patient had been hospitalized on three occasions for the depression. Electroconvulsive therapy and antidepressant medications had provided only temporary relief from his depressive symptoms.

Cognitive-behavior therapy was conducted for twelve sessions over a four-month period. The patient and his wife were asked to keep a record of his daily activities. In addition, he was instructed to rate the degree of pleasure (on a 0–5 scale) that he derived from engaging in the various activities. These records were used to indicate to the patient that he was unrealistically evaluating his daily experiences. For instance, his assertion, "I had a terrible week," was examined in the context of his list of undertakings during that time. The list revealed substantial and, at times, rather noticeable accomplishments for which he experienced no sense of mastery or feeling of pleasure. Although he had actually accomplished a great deal, he believed that he had accomplished nothing. The patient's own data were used to demonstrate how he selectively abstracted failures and ignored his accomplishments. Using this procedure, the patient's maladaptive cognitions were clarified and more appropriate interpretations of his experiences were explored. This treatment program resulted in a considerable reduction in depressive behaviors and improvements in his ratings of mood and job satisfaction. These treatment gains were maintained at a twelve-month follow-up evaluation.

Ellis and Abrahms (1978) have applied rational-emotive therapy to alter distorted emotions in medical patients suffering from anxiety and depression related to being physically ill. They encourage the patients to reevaluate their irrational beliefs about their sickness.

Problems in Evaluating Treatment
Programs for Depression

Rehm and Kornblith (1979) have critically evaluated therapies used in the treatment of depression, including contingency management, social skills or marital treatment, imagery-based therapies (e.g., Lazarus's 1968 time projection techniques), and cognitive and self-control strategies. They concluded that the common elements within each treatment program make it difficult to evaluate the efficacy of particular components. In addition, when behavior therapies are compared with pharmacological approaches (Kovacs & Rush, 1976; Rush, Beck, Kovacs, & Hollon, 1977), the advantages are not always apparent. In patients treated for unipolar depressions on an outpatient basis, the use of tricyclic medications was just as effective as cognitive therapy. The psychotherapy patients did show less depressive symptomatology on a few scales after therapy, and the pharmacological patients returned more frequently for additional treatment.

The use of heterogeneous populations in defining "depressives" has also made it difficult to predict the most effective treatment for a given individual. The populations studied included volunteers solicited through newspaper advertisements, college students scoring high on Beck's Depression Inventory, and both unipolar and bipolar inpatients and outpatients. There is no basis on which to evaluate whether the course of depression is similar in these divergent populations. Therefore, generalizations from one population to "depressives" as a class have to be made with extreme caution. It is more appropriate to undertake an individual behavioral assessment and to delineate the area of deficit for a particular patient. If the affective state and associated low arousal is a primary symptom, a pharmacological approach may yield the quickest relief. If, instead, the patient has ineffective social skills and cannot obtain reinforcement from his environment, assertiveness training might be useful. If depressive symptoms are frequently associated with negative self-evaluations, a cognitive approach to altering the distorted emotions would be the first target. In a practical sense, a combination of these methods is likely to produce the broadest change and lead to better maintenance of the treatment benefits.

Pain Management

Another problem that many patients in rehabilitation settings present is the problem of pain. The treatment of pain is important both in its own right and because the pain can interfere with the patients' acquisition of skills that you want to teach them. That is, pain may keep the patient from actively participating in the rehabilitation program to avoid the aversive aspects of therapy. This is particularly true with chronic pain, as in patients with low-back pain or rheumatoid arthritis.

Operant Reinforcement of Pain Behaviors

Fordyce (1971b; 1976a; 1976b) has pointed out that although pain may initially be the result of some underlying organic pathology, environmental consequences can modify and further maintain various aspects of "pain behavior." Pain behavior is defined as the observable aspects of pain, such as complaining, moaning, grimacing, slow and cautious body movements, asking for pain medication, and so on. These behaviors may, in turn, be affected by their consequences. Thus, the patient's family and the rehabilitation staff may actually help the patient to learn pain behaviors by inadvertently reinforcing overt manifestations of pain. It is likely that potentially reinforcing consequences such as attention and concern from others, rest, medication, avoiding unpleasant duties and responsibilities, and other events frequently follow the maladaptive pain behavior and, as a result, hinder the patient's progress in therapy.

Based on this analysis of pain as an operant behavior, Fordyce and his colleagues (Fordyce et al., 1968; Fordyce et al., 1973; Fordyce, 1971b) have developed an elaborate treatment program in which environmental events (e.g., social attention, rest, medication) are systematically controlled and made to occur contingent on adaptive behaviors. The major goal of the treatment program is to increase behaviors such as activity level and participation in therapy, while simultaneously decreasing or eliminating pain behaviors. Members of the patient's family are actively involved in the treatment program and work closely with the rehabilitation staff. They are taught to respond to the patient's behavior in ways that reduce pain and other disability behaviors and to maximize the patient's compliance with and performance in the rehabilitation program. In essence, the patient is taught to reinterpret the sensation of pain and to tolerate it, while making more adaptive responses that will gain the attention and approval of others.

Reduction of Pain Medication

There is also a special emphasis on reducing the amount of pain medication that is frequently used by chronic pain patients. This is done in an effort to prevent addiction and habituation to the analgesic medication and to reduce the patient's general dependence on drugs. As is often the case in health care facilities, medication is provided on a p.r.n. (pro re nata: as needed) basis. That is, medication is often contingent on the very pain behavior that the rehabilitation staff would like to eliminate, such as complaints of pain, asking for medication, and so on. This may result in an increase in various pain behaviors. To deal with this problem, the delivery of medication is made contingent on the passage of time rather than on the patient's behavior. The interval between medication deliveries is gradually increased throughout the treatment program. In addition, the medication is presented to the patient in the form of a liquid that masks the taste and color of the medication. Over a period of approximately two months, the dosage level of the medication is gradually decreased until the patient is given only the liquid without an active ingredient. The patient and his or her family are informed of this medication change before or after the medication has been eliminated. This treatment program has been shown to produce a considerable decrease in the patient's complaints of pain and in the use of analgesic medication.

This operant treatment program for pain is illustrated in a case presented by Fordyce et al. (1968). The patient was a thirty-seven-year-old woman who had constant low-back pain for eighteen years. Surgery on four different occasions had failed to alleviate the pain. This problem interfered with her ability to perform her daily household activities. She reported that the pain was exacerbated by activity of any kind; as a result, she was able to tolerate movement for only twenty minutes at a time. Much of her day was spent at home in bed. Furthermore, she was taking five habit-forming pain medications each day.

The treatment program was initially conducted in the hospital, and later continued on an outpatient basis. Her medication was delivered on a time schedule rather than being contingent on pain complaints. The time interval between medication delivery was gradually increased, and the active ingredient was gradually eliminated. Hospital staff were instructed to withhold their attention when the patient was complaining of pain and to reinforce socially any attempts at participating in adaptive activities. In occupational therapy, the patient was permitted to rest only after a progressively more arduous schedule of task completion. Finally, a program was instituted to increase her walking behavior. She was given a daily assignment of walking a specified number of laps around the ward. After successfully completing the laps, she was reinforced with a rest period and praise and attention from the staff.

The patient also kept a record of the time she spent in daily activities. Information from these records was placed on a graph and served to reinforce her progress in the various rehabilitation programs.

During the seven weeks of hospitalization, this intervention program produced a significant increase in the rate and speed of the patient's walking behavior. By the end of the hospitalization, she was walking almost one mile each day. In addition, she was actively participating in occupational therapy for approximately two hours daily. The narcotic component of the pain medication was also completely eliminated by the fortieth day following her admission to the hospital. Finally, her pain complaints were virtually eliminated. Monthly follow-up visits on an outpatient basis revealed that she continued to increase her weekly activity level. Figure 7.1 illustrates the number of hours in which the patient engaged in activities during inpatient and outpatient treatment.

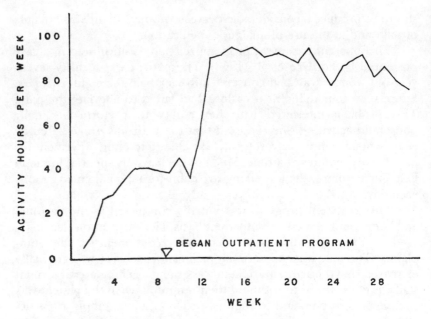

Figure 7.1   Mrs. Y.: Total hours of activity per week.

From W. E. Fordyce, R. S. Fowler, J. F. Lehmann, and B. J. DeLateur, Some implications of learning in problems of chronic pain. *Journal of Chronic Diseases*, 1968, *21*, 179–190. Copyright © 1968 by Pergamon Press, Ltd. Reprinted by permission.

Cognitive Strategies for Reducing Pain

In addition to the operant treatment approach to pain developed by Fordyce and his colleagues, there has been a recent proliferation of cognitive strategies for the management of pain (Weisenberg, 1977). While many cognitive strategies have demonstrated a capacity to bring about alterations in the perception of experimentally induced pain, there have been only a limited number of studies investigating clinical pain. Furthermore, most of these cognitive procedures have been used with acute rather than chronic pain. Despite the possible limitations in generalizing from this research to pain phenomena in clinical settings, a number of cognitive strategies have shown promising results and, therefore, warrant a brief discussion in a section on pain control procedures.

Johnson and her colleagues (Johnson & Leventhal, 1974; Johnson, Morrissey, & Leventhal, 1973; Johnson, Rice, Fuller, & Endress,

1977) have investigated the effects of providing information on helping patients to achieve cognitive control over aversive or painful medical procedures. They consistently found that accurate descriptions of the physical sensations that patients could expect to experience during an impending aversive event (such as a diagnositic medical procedure or surgery) reduced the stress and pain often associated with these procedures. The sensory information that the patient receives includes a description of what the patient will feel, see, smell, taste, and hear. For example, patients scheduled for gall bladder surgery were told that preoperative medications would make them feel "sleepy, light-headed, and relaxed," and the sensations that they would experience in the incision area were described as "tenderness, sensitive, pressure, pulling, smarting, and burning" (Johnson et al., 1977). It is assumed that providing accurate sensory information about a painful event brings patients' expectations in line with the subsequent experiences. Information about expected sensations may also reduce uncertainty for the individual (Bowers, 1968; 1971); there is evidence to suggest that when uncertainty about a noxious event is reduced, the experience of pain is also reduced (Staub, Tursky, & Schwartz, 1971).

Another method for providing information about a potentially stressful event is to expose the patient to realistic models who demonstrate the desired behaviors in that situation. A model's behavior can provide information about behavioral standards for the observer. Craig and his colleagues (Craig & Best, 1977; Craig & Neidermayer, 1974; Craig & Weiss, 1971) have shown that persons who observed models tolerate painful stimulation accepted more intense pain than did individuals who observed pain-intolerant models. Furthermore, persons who observed pain-tolerant models were themselves able to tolerate more painful stimulation, and they also rated the pain as less distressing than did individuals who either observed pain-intolerant models or who were not exposed to any models at all.

Finally, the effectiveness of several cognitive strategies has been demonstrated in which the individual performs a variety of cognitive tasks that in some way direct his or her attention away from the painful sensations. As the individual attends to stimuli that are unrelated to the pain, the person's tolerance for pain increases. Barber and his associates (Barber & Cooper, 1972; Chaves & Barber, 1974; Spanos, Horton, & Chaves, 1975) have explored the use of these various cognitive strategies in helping subjects to cope with experimentally induced pain. They trained individuals to use distracting imagery, such as imagining pleasant events, counting aloud, and attending to other stimuli in the environment (e.g., counting ceiling tiles). Subjects were also trained to selectively attend to ongoing sensations other than pain, for example, by imagining that the stimulated area is asleep or insensitive or that it has been injected with novocaine. These strategies, which provided the individual with cognitive activities that were incompatible with attending to the aversive or unpleasant stimulation, were effective in increasing the pain tolerance of the subjects.

In a clinical setting, Horan, Layng, and Pursell (1976) found that patients who were trained to imagine pleasant imagery (e.g., walking through a lush meadow or swimming in a clear blue lake) reported less pain and discomfort during dental treatment than did patients who were given no special training or who were instructed to visualize a series of two digit numbers. In a similar manner, patients who were instructed to attend selectively to more positive aspects of their hospitalization (such as relief from work responsibilities) requested less analgesic medication for postsurgery pain than did patients who were simply given presurgery information (Langer, Janis, & Wolfer, 1975).

Meichenbaum and Turk (1976) suggest a "cafeteria style" approach to training patients to cope with pain. In their training program, referred to as stress-inoculation, an individual is presented with a variety of cognitive control strategies similar to those presented earlier, from which he or she may choose when confronted with painful stimulation. To assist the patient in the use of these strategies, the authors further propose that the individual develop a plan to use when the pain becomes the most intense, and that the plan be implemented at these "critical moments."

Hypnosis in Pain Reduction

There is also a variety of experimental reports that document the capacity of hypnosis to alleviate pain (cf. Chaves & Barber, 1976; Shor, 1967, for reviews). Hilgard (1975) points out that the suggestion of a trance state plus suggested analgesia (imagining a part of the body to be numb or insensitive to pain) usually produces more substantial reduction in pain than suggestion of a trance state alone. Barber and Hahn (1962), for example, have confirmed the capacity of hypnotically suggested analgesia to alleviate pain in a laboratory setting. Hypnosis was found to produce significant reductions in self-reported pain and two psychophysiological components of the pain response (muscle tension and respiratory irregularities). Barber (1972) has provided evidence that suggestions to role-play hypnotic effects produced similar changes in pain-related behavior without hypnotic trance induction. Relief from pain by hypnosis has been noted with regard to cancer, obstetrics, surgery, and dentistry (Hilgard & Hilgard, 1975).

Sheltered Workshops and Vocational Rehabilitation

Some patients, because of a physical disability or psychiatric disorder, are unable to seek or return to independent, gainful employment in the community. For such patients, one aspect of the rehabilitation program might include vocational training in a sheltered workshop setting. Sheltered workshops provide patients with a permanent or transitional opportunity for employment in an environment that enables them to work within the limits of their disability. Furthermore, in a realistic job situation, the patient can learn adaptive work skills to become a productive employee in the sheltered workshop or, eventually, to compete for employment in the community.

Behavioral techniques are well suited for use within a sheltered workshop. The structure of these vocational rehabilitation programs permits the therapist to achieve greater control over the consequences of the patient's work behaviors. As a result, it is possible to teach appropriate and productive work skills by providing access to reinforcing consequences contingent on the desired behaviors.

Token Reinforcement

Zimmerman and his colleagues (Zimmerman, Overpeck, Eisenberg, & Garlick, 1969; Zimmerman, Stuckey, Garlick, & Miller, 1969) have used a token reinforcement program to increase the productivity of multihandicapped individuals in a community sheltered workshop. A token reinforcement program is particularly useful in such settings because it allows the therapist to reinforce immediately the desired work behavior without interfering with the ongoing performance of the individual. Thus, the therapist does not have to interrupt the very behaviors that he or she is attempting to teach the patient, in this case productive work behaviors. Zimmerman and his colleagues delivered points to the patients contingent on the completion of a specified number of work units in an assembly task. The points could later be exchanged for backup reinforcers (a variety of activities and tangible items). Using this token reinforcement system, they were able to increase significantly the productivity rates of the patients in the sheltered workshop.

Similarly, Cushing (1969) describes the effective use of contingent reinforcement with patients in a vocational rehabilitation center. Reinforcement procedures were used to deal with a number of patient behaviors that were incompatible with appropriate work behaviors, such as insufficient quality and rate of work, excessive absenteeism and tardiness, difficulty in relating to co-workers and supervisors, and poor personal appearance. One illustration of the use of reinforcement is the case of a forty-two-year-old woman who had a long history of hospitalization for a psychiatric disorder. In the sheltered workshop, her productivity rate was very low, and her interactions with her co-workers were inappropriate and highly aggressive. The treatment program consisted of providing coffee breaks and the opportunity to have her hair done in a beauty shop contingent on a minimum rate of completion of an assembly task and for interacting appropriately with the other workers. This resulted in a significant improvement in both her productivity rate and her interpersonal behavior. Eventually, the patient was able to leave the sheltered workshop and seek suitable employment in the community.

The Geriatric Patient

In 1970, approximately 10 percent of the population in the United States was 65 years old or older. This segment of the population is growing in numbers, and continues to increase each year (Bovier, 1974).

Many of the problems and principles discussed thus far in this chapter apply equally well to the elderly patient. However, in several areas, this group presents unique problems to those working in rehabilitation settings. In particular, the elderly are major utilizers of health care services. The aged occupy approximately 25 percent of the hospital beds in this country and represent 90 percent of the nursing home population. They make more visits to health care facilities, have more days with some degree of disability, and spend considerably more and longer time periods in the hospital than do younger persons (Brotman, 1974).

Rehabilitation services for the elderly are provided in a variety of settings. Following an illness or injury, many geriatric patients must be cared for in a convalescent or nursing home. For some elderly patients, institutional care is only a temporary necessity until they are able to regain sufficient physical, social, and cognitive skills to return to the community. Other elderly patients, however, remain in institutional settings for extended periods of time because of the greater extent of their disability or simply because there is no one in the community to assist in their care. Finally, where available, some of the aged can attend day care programs that provide various rehabilitation services during the waking hours and enable the individual to return to the community in the evening.

Unlike rehabilitation with younger patients, where the focus is frequently on vocational training, a major goal of rehabilitation with the elderly involves establishing more independent living skills (Heff-erin, 1968). Such therapeutic programs attempt to improve the general functioning of the individual to the point where he or she can be returned to the community, or they attempt to facilitate adjustment to the institution in order to prevent deterioration in functioning and, thus, avoid further behavioral deficits. Specifically, rehabilitation services for the elderly are directed at enhancing the patient's ability to perform activities of daily living, maintaining social contacts, and improving physical functioning.

Geriatric patients manifest a variety of problems that bring them to the attention of rehabilitation personnel. Decreased physical and cognitive activity, lower rates of social interaction, failing eyesight, poor motor coordination and dexterity, decreased motivation, fear of engaging in new and unfamiliar activities, loneliness, and feelings of helplessness are some of the problems often observed in the elderly individual. McClannahan (1973) notes that behaviors occurring infrequently seem to characterize many of the difficulties presented by the elderly. Although these problems may have a biological or physical basis for their occurrence, several investigators have proposed that the aging process and concomitant behavioral deficits are best understood as an interaction between the biological changes of the maturing individual and the environmental conditions that may modify and maintain these "aging" behaviors (Baltes, 1976; Hoyer, 1973; Hoyer, Mishara, & Riebel, 1975; Lester & Baltes, 1978; Lindsley, 1964; Rebok & Hoyer, 1977). Thus, the deficient performance of the elderly must be considered within the context of the environment in which the problem behavior occurs. From a behavioral perspective, the therapist is interested in identifying the current reinforcement contingencies that maintain the behavioral deficits frequently associated with the elderly patient (Hoyer, 1973; Hoyer et al., 1975). It follows from this conceptualization that many of the disability behaviors of the geriatric patient may be modified by changing the environmental consequences of the problematic behaviors (Cautela, 1966; Hoyer, 1973; Lindsley, 1964). This model of intervention provides a positive and optimistic approach for those who deliver rehabilitation services to the elderly. Although it may not be possible to alter biological factors, it is possible to identify and change the contingencies in the patient's environment that contribute to behavioral deficits assumed to result from growing old. Until the therapist has explored the relationship between the behavior problem of concern and environmental factors, there is no assumption that changes cannot occur in the elderly patient.

Physical Changes in Environment

Rehabilitation with the elderly through environmental intervention was first proposed by Lindsley (1964) and later elaborated upon by McClannahan (1973). Lindsley, in his discussion of behavioral intervention strategies, distinguishes between therapeutic and prosthetic environments. A therapeutic environment initiates only transitory behavior changes in the patient that must eventually be maintained by conditions outside the therapeutic setting when the individual returns to the natural environment. For example, group activities for the elderly might facilitate social interaction and maintain social skills while the individual remains in an institutional setting such as a nursing home. However, when the patient returns to the natural environment, other persons—such as the patient's family and friends—must maintain the newly acquired social behaviors. Prosthetic environments, on the other hand, continuously provide environmental conditions that consistently support and maintain adaptive behaviors and avoid the development of behavioral deficits. Changes in the physical design of the environment to help the elderly to compensate for a disability and maintain maximum performance is one example of a prosthetic environment. For instance, to help the elderly arthritic patient to compensate for any loss of mobility and motor functioning of the legs and to maintain walking behavior, handrails on walls and ramps instead of stairs could be provided in the patient's living environment. The fact that environmental constraints can inhibit positive behaviors and maintain behavioral deficits is illustrated by MacDonald and Butler (1974), who found in a nursing home that such factors as highly waxed floors and the lack of elevators tended to discourage walking behavior and reduced the overall mobility of the residents.

Social Environment

The social environment of the elderly is as important as their physical environment. Many of the behavioral deficits in the repertoire of the elderly patient are a function not simply of aging, but also of the lack of social reinforcers in the environment (Rebok & Hoyer, 1977). This is especially true for the aged person living in an institution. In addition to the loss of reinforcement by family, friends, and habitual activities, the elderly resident in institutional care frequently receives little social reinforcement from others when engaging in such adaptive, independent behaviors as self-care skills. As a result, the payoffs for behaving in an appropriate and independent manner no longer exist, and these desired behaviors, therefore, occur less often. MacDonald and Butler (1974) argue instead that institutional settings tend to reinforce dependent behaviors on the part of the elderly and that sick-role behaviors are accepted as the norm by both the staff and patients alike.

A study conducted by Lester and Baltes (1978) demonstrated that, in fact, reinforcing consequences in institutions for the elderly are often minimal or contingent on maladaptive rather than independent behaviors. For an extended period of time, they observed twenty-two residents in a nursing home and found that environmental contingencies were clearly associated with dependency in the elderly patient. The results indicated that most often positive social reinforcement was made contingent on dependent behaviors and that negative or no reinforcement occurred contingent on attempts at independent behavior. These conditions produced concomitant high rates of dependent behaviors and low rates of independent or adaptive behaviors in the nursing home residents. This study has considerable implications for those who work with elderly patients since it suggests that consequences provided by others can influence the functional abilities of the aged and are important determinants of some behavioral deficits.

Recreation programs and activities for the elderly are important to help maintain appropriate social behavior and prevent deterioration in physical abilities (McClannahan & Risley, 1975). Several investigators have demonstrated that restructuring the environment or merely providing activities can produce beneficial changes in the behavior of the elderly patient. For example, it was shown that simply rearranging chairs in the lobby of an institution for geriatric patients, so that the chairs faced each other instead of being placed in the corners of the room, resulted in a significant increase in the rate of conversation between the residents (Sommer & Ross, 1958).

In a series of studies, McClannahan and Risley (1973; 1974; 1975) found that the amount of time that elderly nursing home residents spent in productive activities could be increased simply by providing the opportunity to engage in a structured activity. Using prompts and demonstration to engage the residents initially in the use of games, puzzles, and other manipulative activities, McClannahan and Risley (1975) were able to increase the residents' use of the activity area of the nursing home from an average of only 20 percent prior to the availability of various activities to an average of 74 percent following intervention. Before the treatment program was instituted, the nursing home residents were observed to spend most of their time in their rooms, and evidenced little or no social interaction or physical activity. These results support the view that the inactivity of institutionalized elderly persons is due not necessarily to their inability or lack of interest, but to a consequence of environmental conditions. Similarly, providing a morning activity for elderly handicapped women in a nursing home (refreshments contingent on attendance at the activity) increased their participation in the activity and produced a concomitant increase in the social interaction among the residents (Blackman, Howe, & Pinkston, 1976). It should be noted that these programs did not require a significant expenditure of time or money and were instituted within the constraints of the institutional setting.

MacDonald (1972) established a pub on a hospital ward for elderly patients who were withdrawn and showed little interest in their environment. The patients were permitted to come to the pub one hour each day and to order two ounces of wine or a pint of beer. In order to use the pub, the residents were required to come independently without the assistance of the nursing staff. Several weeks after this program was introduced, there were significant increases in social interaction among the residents.

These studies suggest that activities for the elderly not only provide the opportunity for the constructive use of leisure time, but also promote social interaction among residents in institutional settings. Through environmental programming, the elderly patient can be encouraged to participate in activities that, when provided in proximity to other residents of the institution, result in an increase in the appropriate social interaction among the residents. This change in social behavior may be explained by the concept of a "behavioral trap" proposed by Baer and Wolf (1970). The notion of a behavioral trap suggests that once an initial entry response, such as physical proximity to other patients, has been shaped and reinforced, naturally occurring reinforcers in the situation continue to facilitate the acquisition of additional behavioral changes, such as increased social interaction with the peer group.

Group Therapy

Several investigators have taken a more direct approach to modifying the inappropriate or deficient social skills of elderly patients. In a group therapy format, Berger and Rose (1977) trained elderly nursing home residents in interpersonal skills using several behavioral strategies. The residents met for three one-hour sessions in which they were trained to respond to eight typical social situations that they might confront in the nursing home. Interpersonal skill training consisted of observing modeled appropriate responses by elderly persons on a videotape, role playing the various social situations, and receiving feedback and verbal praise from the therapist for responding in an acceptable manner when rehearsing the situation. As a result of this training procedure, the residents were considerably more effective in responding in the nursing home to the social situations for which they had been trained as compared to a group of residents who merely discussed the social situations or an assessment-only control group. Inprovements in the social behavior of the residents in the interpersonal skill training group were maintained at a two-month follow-up evaluation.

Also using a group therapy approach, Mueller and Atlas (1972) developed a resocialization program for regressed residents in a nursing home. In group sessions, residents were reinforced with food and tokens for interacting with other group members. This procedure resulted in increased social and verbal behavior among the residents.

MacDonald (in press) demonstrated that contingent attention from the nursing staff could shape verbal interaction among socially isolated residents. Using prompts, such as asking the residents questions and socially reinforcing their responses, MacDonald considerably increased verbal interaction among three elderly men. Following the use of this simple procedure, the men maintained a high rate of conversation with each other, despite the withdrawal of prompts from the investigator.

Self-Care Programs

Behavioral intervention programs have also been used to help elderly patients regain a variety of self-care skills to enable them to maintain some degree of independent living. These programs have reduced the impact of the aging process and maintained competent performance of the elderly individual by changing environmental contingencies.

Depression often observed in aging patients accompanies the feeling of lack of personal control over their lives. Langer and Rodin (1976) applied a self-control strategy with geriatric patients in helping them to adapt to institutionalized living.

The director of the hospital gave a talk to one group of residents which stressed the patients' right to choose between various activities and encouraged them to take responsibility for a plant and the rearrangement of their own rooms. Another group was told that they would be told which activities to attend and that the nursing staff would care for their plants. Follow-up data eighteen months later found that fewer patients in the self-control group had died as compared to the control sample where no opportunities for self-control were given (Rodin & Langer, 1977).

Geiger and Johnson (1974) used positive reinforcement to increase appropriate food consumption by elderly residents in a nursing home. Individuals selected for the treatment program had been eating less than half their evening meal. Proper eating was defined as eating the whole main course and two of three side dishes. When the residents met this criterion, they earned the opportunity to engage in a variety of reinforcing activities, such as participating in entertaining events and receiving additional attention from the staff. This program increased the average number of complete meals eaten from 12 percent prior to intervention to 84 percent following treatment. The use of special reinforcers was gradually withdrawn, and proper eating was maintained by social reinforcement such as praise from the staff. In addition to maintaining an adequate diet for the residents, the program eliminated the staff's need for coaxing and pleading with the residents to eat. It was suggested, in fact, that this attention from the staff for not eating may have reinforced and maintained the noneating behavior of the residents.

A treatment program to establish self-feeding behaviors in regressed nursing home residents was implemented by Baltes and Zerbe (1976). Physical prompts and a shaping and fading procedure were used to retrain the residents in the use of utensils and to develop independent feeding behaviors. Attention from the therapist was made contingent on gradual approximations toward self-feeding responses. The shaping strategy is presented in Table 7.2. In addition, a time-out procedure was used in which the therapist turned her back on the residents when they engaged in undesirable behaviors so as not to reinforce inappropriate responses. The effects of the treatment program were evident within a short period of time, resulting in a significant increase in self-feeding behaviors.

In order to increase the participation of elderly persons in a community-based nutritional meal program offered at a local community center, Bunck and Iwata (1978) investigated the effectiveness of a number of prompting and reinforcement procedures. The relative efficacy of four methods of recruiting new participants for the meal program was evaluated, including:

Table 7.2 Shaping Procedure for Developing Self-Feeding Behaviors

---

Step 1: Investigator's hand over subject's hand scooping up food on spoon and bringing up to the mouth of subject. Release of subject's hand after subject took a bite.

Step 2: Investigator's hand over subject's hand scooping up food and bring part way (shoulder height) up to the subject's mouth.

Step 3: Investigator's hand over subject's hand scooping up food.

Step 4: Investigator scoops food on the spoon and hands it to subject.

Step 5: Investigator hands spoon to subject.

Step 6: Investigator instructs.

From M. B. Baltes and M. S. Zerbe, Independence training in nursing-home residents. *The Gerontologist,* 1976, *16,* 428–432. Copyright © 1976 by the Gerontological Society. Reprinted by permission.

1. public service announcements on the radio,
2. home visits with prospective participants, in which the program was explained,
3. a follow-up contact, by telephone or mail, with persons who did not attend the program after a home visit, and
4. a list of fifty-eight items, mailed to persons who did not attend the program after a follow-up contact, from which the individual could select one item or activity (such as a plant or movie) or a service (such as housecleaning or yardwork) if he or she participated in the meal program.

The incentive condition was found to be the most effective in attracting new elderly participants to the meal program, and was also the most cost efficient of the four prompting procedures. In addition, incentive items were considerably more effective in maintaining attendance at the meal program than were "activity days," when a free movie or bingo game was available contingent on participation in the program.

Independent walking was the goal of treatment in a program outlined by MacDonald and Butler (1974). Two elderly residents of a nursing home were the focus of intervention; they were physically capable of walking, but had confined themselves to wheelchairs for several months. The staff had periodically transported these residents by wheelchair, and as a result, they were apparently not motivated to walk on their own even with considerable encouragement from their families and the nursing home staff. Attention from the staff was assessed as an effective reinforcer for these individuals. Physical prompts were used to initiate standing and walking behavior. When the residents made independent attempts to walk, the staff immediately praised them for their efforts and engaged them in conversation by discussing topics of interest. If the residents made no attempts to walk when requested to do so, but instead remained in the wheelchair, the staff proceeded to transport them in the wheelchair and did not verbally interact with them. By selectively attending to the desired behavior and providing contingent social reinforcement, the staff gradually increased the number of feet per day that the residents walked without staff assistance, thereby eliminating the residents' dependence on wheelchairs to move about the nursing home.

To encourage mobility and impede muscular atrophy, Libb and Clements (1969) reinforced four hospitalized geriatric patients for exercising on a stationary bicycle. Tokens were automatically dispensed from a device connected to the wheels of the bicycle, contingent on a specified number of revolutions of the wheels. The tokens were later exchangeable for a variety of consumable items. This procedure effectively increased the patients' rate of physical exercise.

Biofeedback in Rehabilitation

Biofeedback training teaches an individual to become aware of internal body sensations so that he or she can control specific internal physiological responses of the body. This is accomplished by means of highly specialized instrumentation that converts physiological activity into a bioelectric signal. This, in turn, provides the individual with continuous external feedback regarding a particular visceral response. When a person alters a visceral state so that it correctly matches a given criterion, visual or auditory feedback is immediately provided, indicating that the individual has responded appropriately.

Neuromuscular disorders such as a cerebrovascular accident (stroke), spinal cord injuries, cerebral palsy, and so on may result in the patient's inability to control muscular responses voluntarily. Electromyographic biofeedback (also referred to as EMG biofeedback) training has shown considerable promise in helping patients with neuromuscular disorders to increase the strength of their affected muscles and to regain voluntary control over them (Blanchard & Young, 1974). In this procedure, patients are provided with EMG feedback of muscular responses (e.g., feedback of the electrical potentials from skeletal muscles) to help "reeducate" paretic or spastic muscles. Much of the work in this area has been accomplished with stroke patients who exhibit paralysis or motor weakness. The goal of treatment is to help the patient to increase muscular control. A comprehensive review of this area is provided by Blanchard and Young (1974) and Keefe and Surwit (1978).

Johnson and Garton (1973) used EMG biofeedback to retrain weakened muscles in ten hemiplegic patients who wore leg braces. Biofeedback training, which was conducted during three thirty-minute sessions, was initiated in the hospital using needle electrodes inserted in the patient's foot. When the patient was discharged from the hospital, treatment continued at home with a portable feedback device using surface electrodes. This treatment program, which ranged from six to eighteen months in duration, produced increased ankle dorsiflexion in all the patients, despite the fact that they had had a stroke a year or more prior to the treatment. Half of the patients improved sufficiently to be able to walk without the aid of leg braces.

EMG biofeedback training was shown by Andrews (1964) to be effective in establishing "strong, voluntary, controlled action" of the muscular response in seventeen of twenty hemiplegic patients. Muscular control was facilitated within only five minutes of training. These patients had previously shown no return of neuromuscular function during the year since their stroke, and they had not responded to more conventional rehabilitation procedures.

Similarly, Brundy et al. (1974) enhanced muscular contractions in hemiplegic patients who previously had not benefited from conventional treatment procedures. Patients received EMG biofeedback training that was specific to the problems they presented. That is, some patients were taught to increase the strength of paretic muscles, and others were taught to decrease muscle spasticity. Training sessions were conducted three to five times each week over a two- to three-month period.

In a controlled outcome study by Basmajian et al. (1975), EMG biofeedback training was compared to standard physical therapy in the treatment of chronic footdrop in hemiplegic patients. Twenty patients were randomly assigned either to a group that received forty minutes daily of therapeutic exercises to facilitate ankle dorsiflexion or to a group that received twenty minutes of therapeutic exercises plus twenty minutes of biofeedback training. Each patient was seen in therapy for an average of sixteen sessions. Although both groups increased the strength of dorsiflexion and range of motion, the patients who received biofeedback training showed increases that were almost twice as large as the patients who received only therapeutic exercises. In addition, patients in the biofeedback group were able to maintain conscious control of dorsiflexion while walking, and a number of individuals were able to discard the short leg brace they had worn.

Finally, Woolridge and McLaurin (1976) describe the clinical application of biofeedback procedures in the physical rehabilitation of children with cerebral palsy. They present case examples that illustrate the use of biofeedback techniques with problems of head control, weight-bearing, jaw closure, and postural alignment. For example, the authors describe the use of toys that were developed to modify motor responses in young children by presenting specific feedback to them while engaged in play. Thus, a toy was used that responded to a specific motor response on the part of the child. When the child moved in the desired direction, the toy responded by moving in the same direction, thereby reinforcing a particular motor response. In this way, sitting balance could be improved in the child by providing immediate feedback regarding his or her motor behavior.

Although biofeedback procedures have shown promise in the treatment of neuromuscular disorders, more research is needed to evaluate adequately their efficacy in rehabilitation programs. It is noteworthy, however, that many patients who have not responded to other rehabilitation programs have benefited from biofeedback training procedures. These results are sufficiently encouraging to warrant additional research in this area.

Summary

Rehabilitation involves helping patients to relearn or compensate for previous skills or abilities that have been lost through impairment because of illness, injury, or the process of aging. The work of the behaviorally oriented rehabilitation specialist consists of assessing the residual capacities in these patients and teaching them compensatory skills to enable them to be as independent as possible.

The application of behavioral techniques to helping patients acquire new behaviors involves dividing complex behavior patterns into smaller components. The skills needed by these patients can then be shaped by providing immediate reinforcement for success in small, graduated steps toward the goal. Various techniques are illustrated for helping hemiplegic patients increase muscular strength required for ambulation, the use of wheelchairs, or the use of other devices to enable them to function with reduced capacities. Often, wheelchair patients need to learn to shift their weight periodically so as not to develop pressure sores, which further complicates their treatment. Behavioral techniques have been applied successfully in this area.

The problems of patient motivation are particularly evident in many of the patients seen in rehabilitation settings. Rehabilitation can be a slow, difficult, painful, and frustrating process. The treatment program itself can acquire aversive or unpleasant properties that may lead patients to attempt to avoid therapy. Therefore, the patient's environment must be arranged so that meaningful consequences are provided contingent upon the patients' participation and acceptable performance of therapeutic activities. Too often, access to television, rest, and social conversation (often sympathy) are available without any behavioral demands being made on the patient. It is necessary to reverse these contingencies so that the patient is permitted access to reinforcement activities contingent upon performance of the desired behavior. Occasionally, the patient has fears of falling or exacerbating already present pain and, therefore, resists active treatment. Systematic desensitization procedures have been applied successfully in reducing these fears.

Depression as a reaction to physical disability and chronic illness also can be treated within a behavioral framework. The patient may have fewer social, vocational, and recreational opportunities because of the disability; this, in turn, restricts access to desired reinforcers. Therefore, one of the primary goals in a behavioral treatment program is to restore an adequate schedule of positive reinforcement by altering the level, quality, and range of the patient's activities and social interactions. Patients may also become depressed through maladaptive thoughts that lead them to distort reality. The treatment program that derives from this theoretical viewpoint teaches patients to appraise their behaviors, limitations, and experiences more realistically.

The experience of pain can interfere with the patient's acquisition of skills by preventing him or her from actually participating in rehabilitation programs. Based on an analysis of pain as an operant behavior, a treatment program has been developed in which environmental events that are reinforcing for the chronic pain patient (such as rest, medication, and social attention) are made to occur contingent on adaptive behaviors. The major goal of the program is to increase such behaviors as activity level and participation in the rehabilitation therapy. Simultaneously, pain behaviors (such as complaining, moaning, and asking for medication) are decreased by being ignored. Family members are taught to respond to the patient's behavior in ways that reduce pain and other disability behaviors and to maximize the patient's compliance with the rehabilitation program. Finally, methods that have been successful in weaning patients off pain medication are described.

Evidence suggests that cognitive strategies can be used to increase pain tolerance and reduce subjective distress by having patients focus and selectively concentrate on activities that are incompatible with attending to painful stimulation. Stress inoculation training programs are suggested that help the individual acquire strategies to use at critical times when pain becomes most intense. The role of hypnosis in pain reduction needs further empirical investigation.

Token reinforcement programs to increase the productivity of multihandicapped individuals have been used in community sheltered workshops. These reinforcement procedures focus on behaviors that are incompatible with return to work, such as reduced quality and rate of work, excessive absenteeism, problems in relating to co-workers and supervisors, and poor personal appearance.

The goals of rehabilitation with geriatric patients are directed at enhancing their ability to perform activities of daily living, maintain social contacts, and improve physical functioning. Although it may not be possible to alter biological factors directly, it is possible to identify and change the contingencies in the patient's environment that contribute to the behavioral deficits assumed to result from growing old. In this regard, behavioral researchers have contributed to the field of prosthetic environments for the elderly. By restructuring the environment, the elderly may compensate for a behavioral deficit and maintain maximum functioning. Planned recreational activities are important in order to maintain appropriate social behaviors and prevent feelings of alienation and depression.

More recent technology has led to the use of biofeedback devices in rehabilitation programs, making use of electromyographic recordings to help patients with neuromuscular disorders. Patients with spastic muscles or paralysis or motor weakness resulting from a stroke have been taught to strengthen their affected muscles and regain voluntary control over them. The patient with cerebral palsy has also been able to regain postural control through the use of biofeedback training.

References

Abramson, L. Y., Seligman, M. E. P., & Teasdale, J. D. Learned helplessness in humans: Critique and reformulation. *Journal of Abnormal Psychology,* 1978, *87,* 49–74.

Aillon, G. A. Biochemistry of depression: A review of literature. *Behavioral Neuropsychiatry*, 1971, *3*, 2–19.

Akiskal, H. S., & McKinney, W. T. Depressive disorders: Toward a unified hypothesis. *Science*, 1973, *182*, 20–29.

American Psychiatric Association. *Diagnostic and Statistical Manual of Mental Disorders, Third Edition (DSM III)*, draft version. Robert L. Spitzer, Chairman, APA Task Force on Nomenclature & Statistics. January, 1978.

Andrews, J. M. Neuromuscular re-education of the hemiplegic with the aid of the electromyograph. *Archives of Physical Medicine and Rehabilitation*, 1964, *45*, 530–532.

Azrin, N. H., Rubin, H., O'Brien, F., Ayllon, T., & Roll, D. Behavioral engineering: Postural control by a portable operant apparatus. *Journal of Applied Behavior Analysis*, 1968, *1*, 99–108.

Baer, D. M., & Wolf, M. M. The entry into natural communities of reinforcement. In R. Ulrich, T. Stachnik, & J. Mabry (Eds.), *Control of human behavior—from cure to prevention*, Vol. II. Glenview, Ill.: Scott, Foresman, 1970.

Baltes, M. B. Health care from a behavioral-ecological approach. In M. Leninger (Ed.), *Transcultural health care issues and conditions.* Philadelphia: F. A. Powers, 1976.

Baltes, M. B., & Zerbe, M. S. Independence training in nursing-home residents. *The Gerontologist*, 1976, *16*, 428–432.

Barber, T. X. Suggested "hypnotic" behavior: The trance paradigm versus an alternative paradigm. In E. Fromm & R. E. Shot (Eds.), *Hypnosis: Research developments and perspectives.* Chicago: Aldine-Atherton, 1972.

Barber, T. X., & Cooper, B. J. The effects on pain of experimentally induced and spontaneous distraction. *Psychological Reports*, 1972, *31*, 647–651.

Barber, T. X., & Hahn, K. W. Physiological and subjective responses to pain-producing stimulation under hypnotically suggested and waking imagined "analgesia." *Journal of Abnormal and Social Psychology*, 1962, *65*, 411–418.

Basmajian, J. V., Kukulka, C. G., Narayan, M. G., & Takebe, K. Biofeedback treatment of a foot-drop after stroke compared with standard rehabilitation technique: Effects on voluntary control and strength. *Archives of Physical Medicine and Rehabilitation*, 1975, *56*, 231–236.

Beck, A. T. *Depression: Clinical, experimental, and theoretical aspects.* New York: Harper & Row, 1967.

———. The development of depression: A cognitive model. In R. J. Friedman & M. M. Katz (Eds.), *The psychology of depression: Contemporary theory and research.* New York: Wiley, 1974.

———. *Cognitive therapy and the emotional disorders.* New York: International Universities Press, 1976.

Beck, A. T., Ward, C. H., Mendelsohn, M., Mock, J., & Erbaugh, J. An inventory for measuring depression. *Archives of General Psychiatry*, 1961, *4*, 561–571.

Berger, R. M., & Rose, S. D. Interpersonal skill training with institutionalized elderly patients. *Journal of Gerontology*, 1977, *32*, 346–353.

Berni, R., & Fordyce, W. E. *Behavior modification and the nursing process.* St. Louis: C. V. Mosby, 1973.

Birbaumer, N., Dworkin, B., Miller, N. E. Biofeedback in scoliosis patients. Paper presented at the European Congress of Behavior Therapy, Paris, 1979.

Blackman, D. K., Howe, M., & Pinkston, E. M. Increasing participation in social interaction of the institutionalized elderly. *The Gerontologist,* 1976, *16,* 69–76.

Blanchard, E. B., & Young, L. D. Clinical applications of biofeedback training. *Archives of General Psychiatry,* 1974, *30,* 573–589.

Bovier, L. F. Demograph of aging. In S. J. W. Bier (Ed.), *Aging: Its challenge to the individual and society.* New York: Fordham University Press, 1974.

Bowers, K. Pain, anxiety, and perceived control. *Journal of Consulting and Clinical Psychology,* 1968, *32,* 596–602.

———. The effects of UCS temporal uncertainty on heart rate and pain. *Psychophysiology,* 1971, *8,* 382–389.

Brotman, H. B. The fastest growing minority: The aging. *American Journal of Public Health,* 1974, *64,* 249–252.

Brundy, J., Korein, J., Levidow, L., Grynbaum, B. B., Lieberman, A., & Friedmann, L. W. Sensory feedback therapy as a modality in central nervous system disorders of voluntary movement. *Neurology,* 1974, *24,* 925–932.

Bunck, T. J., & Iwata, B. A. Increasing senior citizen participation in a community-based nutritious meal program. *Journal of Applied Behavior Analysis,* 1978, *11,* 75–86.

Burgess, E. P. The modification of depressive behaviors. In R. D. Rubin & C. M. Franks. *Advances in behavior therapy, 1968.* New York: Academic Press, 1969.

Cautela, J. Behavior therapy and geriatrics. *Journal of Genetic Psychology,* 1966, *108,* 9–17.

Chaves, J. F., & Barber, T. X. Cognitive strategies, experimenter modeling, and expectation in the attenuation of pain. *Journal of Abnormal Psychology,* 1974, *83,* 356–363.

———. Hypnotic procedures and surgery: A critical analysis with applications to "acupuncture analgesia." *The American Journal of Clinical Hypnosis,* 1976, *18,* 217–236.

Connolly, K. The application of operant conditioning to the measurement and development of motor skills in children. *Developmental Medicine and Child Neurology,* 1968, *10,* 697–705.

Costello, C. G. Depression: Loss of reinforcers or loss of reinforcer effectiveness? *Behavior Therapy,* 1972, *3,* 240–247.

Craig, K. D., & Best, J. A. Perceived control over pain: Individual differences and situational determinants. *Pain,* 1977, *3,* 127–135.

Craig, K. D., & Neidermayer, H. Autonomic correlates of pain thresholds influenced by social modeling. *Journal of Personality and Social Psychology,* 1974, *29,* 246–252.

Craig, K. D., & Weiss, S. M. Vicarious influences on pain-threshold determinations. *Journal of Personality and Social Psychology*, 1971, *19*, 53–59.

Cushing, M. When counseling fails—then what? *Journal of Rehabilitation*, 1969, *35*, 18–20.

Depue, R. A., & Monroe, S. M. The unipolar-bipolar distinction in the depressive disorders. *Psychological Bulletin*, 1978, *85*, 1001–1029.

Di Scipio, W. J., & Feldman, M. C. Combined behavior therapy and physical therapy in the treatment of a fear of walking. *Journal of Behavioral Therapy and Experimental Psychiatry*, 1971, *2*, 151–152.

Ellis, A., & Abrahms, E. *Brief psychotherapy in medical and health practice*. New York: Springer, 1978.

Ferster, C. B. Animal behavior and mental illness. *Psychological Record*, 1966, *16*, 345–356.

Fordyce, W. E. Psychology and rehabilitation. In S. Licht (Ed.), *Rehabilitation and medicine*. Baltimore: Waverly Press, 1968.

———. Behavioral methods in rehabilitation. In W. S. Neff (Ed.), *Rehabilitation psychology*. Washington, D.C.: American Psychological Association, 1971 (a).

———. Psychological assessment and management. In F. H. Krusen, F. J. Kottke, & P. M. Ellwood (Eds.), *Handbook of physical medicine and rehabilitation*. Philadelphia: W. B. Saunders, 1971 (b).

———. Behavioral concepts in chronic pain and illness. In P. O. Davidson (Ed.), *The behavioral management of anxiety, depression and pain*. New York: Brunner/Mazel, 1976 (a).

———. *Behavioral methods for chronic pain and illness*. St. Louis: C. V. Mosby, 1976 (b).

Fordyce, W. E., Fowler, R. S., Lehmann, J. F., & DeLateur, B. J. Some implications of learning in problems of chronic pain. *Journal of Chronic Diseases*, 1968, *21*, 179–190.

Fordyce, W. E., Fowler, R. S., Lehmann, J. F., DeLateur, B. J., Sand, P. L., & Trieschmann, R. B. Operant conditioning in the treatment of chronic pain. *Archives of Physical Medicine and Rehabilitation*, 1973, *54*, 399–408.

Fuchs, C. Z., & Rehm, L. D. A self-control behavior therapy program for depression. *Journal of Consulting and Clinical Psychology*, 1977, *45*, 206–215.

Gambrill, E. D., & Richey, C. A. An assertion inventory for use in assessment and research. *Behavior Therapy*, 1975, *6*, 550–561.

Geiger, O. G., & Johnson, L. A. Positive education for elderly persons: Correct eating through reinforcement. *The Gerontologist*, 1974, *14*, 432–436.

Goldstein, M. K., Stein, G. H., Smolen, D. M., & Perlini, W. S. Bio-behavioral monitoring: A method for remote health measurement. *Archives of Physical Medicine and Rehabilitation*, 1976, *57*, 253–258.

Goodkin, R. Case studies in behavioral research in rehabilitation. *Perceptual and Motor Skills*, 1966, *23*, 171–182.

Goodwin, F., & Bunney, W. E. Jr. A psychobiological approach to affective illness. *Psychiatric Annals*, 1973, *3*, 19-53.

Halperin, D., & Kottke, F. Training of control of head posture in children with cerebral palsy. *Developmental Medicine and Child Neurology,* 1968, *10,* 249.

Hanaway, T. P. & Barlow, D. H. Prolonged depressive behaviors, in a recently blinded deaf mute. *Journal of Behavior Therapy and Experimental Psychiatry,* 1975, *6,* 43–48.

Hefferin, E. A. Rehabilitation in nursing home situations: A survey of the literature. *Journal of the American Geriatric Society,* 1968, *16,* 293–313.

Hersen, M., Eisler, R., Alford, G. S., & Agras, W. S. Effects of token economy on neurotic depression: An experimental analysis. *Behavior Therapy,* 1973, *4,* 392–397.

Hilgard, E. R. Hypnosis. *Annual Review of Psychology,* 1975, *26,* 19–44.

Hilgard, E. R., & Hilgard, J. R. *Hypnosis in the relief of pain.* Los Altes, Calif.: William Kaufmann, 1975.

Horan, J. J., Layng, F. C., & Pursell, C. H. Preliminary study of effects of "in vivo" emotive imagery on dental discomfort. *Perceptual and Motor Skills,* 1976, *42,* 105–106.

Hoyer, W. J. Application of operant techniques to the modification of elderly behavior. *The Gerontologist,* 1973, *13,* 18–22.

Hoyer, W. J., Mishara, B. L., & Riebel, R. G. Problem behaviors as operants: Applications with elderly individuals. *The Gerontologist,* 1975, *15,* 452–456.

Johnson, H. E., & Garton, W. H. Muscle re-education in hemiplegia by use of EMG device. *Archives of Physical Medicine and Rehabilitation,* 1973, *54,* 322–325.

Johnson, J. E., & Leventhal, H. Effects of accurate expectations and behavioral instructions on reactions during a noxious medical examination. *Journal of Personality and Social Psychology,* 1974, *29,* 710–718.

Johnson, J. E., Morrissey, J. F., & Leventhal, H. Psychological preparation for an endoscopic examination. *Gastrointestinal Endoscopy,* 1973, *19,* 180–182.

Johnson, J. E., Rice, V. H., Fuller, S. S., & Endress, M. P. *Sensory information, behavioral instruction, and recovery from surgery.* Paper presented at the meeting of the American Psychological Association, San Francisco, August, 1977.

Keefe, F. J., & Surwit, R. S. Electromyographic biofeedback: Behavioral treatment of neuromuscular disorders. *Journal of Behavioral Medicine,* 1978, *1,* 13–22.

Kovacs, M., & Rush, J. Cognitive-behavior psychotherapy versus antidepressant medication in the treatment of depression. In A. T. Beck (Chairman), *Current developments in the psychotherapy of depression.* Symposium at the meeting of the Eastern Psychological Association, New York, 1976.

Langer, E. J., Janis, I. L., & Wolfer, J. A. Reduction of psychological stress in surgical patients. *Journal of Experimental Social Psychology,* 1975, *11,* 155–165.

Langer, E. J., & Rodin, J. The effects of choice and enhanced personal responsibility for the aged: A field experiment in an institutional setting. *Journal of Personality and Social Psychology,* 1976, *34,* 191–198.

Lazarus, A. A. Learning theory and the treatment of depression. *Behavior Research and Therapy*, 1968, *6*, 83–89.

Lester, P. B., & Baltes, M. M. Functional interdependence of the social environment and the behavior of the institutionalized aged. *Journal of Gerontological Nursing*, 1978, *4*, 23–27.

Lewinsohn, P. M. The behavioral study and treatment of depression. In M. Hersen, R. M. Eisler, & P. M. Miller (Eds.), *Progress in behavior modification*, Vol. I. New York: Academic Press, 1974.

————. The use of activity schedules in the treatment of depressed individuals. In C. E. Thoresen & J. D. Krumboltz (Eds.), *Counseling methods*. New York: Holt, Rinehart & Winston, 1975.

Lewinsohn, P. M., & Atwood, G. E. Depression: A clinical-research approach, the case of Mrs. G. *Psychotherapy: Theory, Research, and Practice*, 1969, *6*, 166–171.

Lewinsohn, P. M., Biglan, A., & Zeiss, A. M. Behavioral treatment of depression. In P. O. Davison (Ed.), *The behavioral management of anxiety, depression and pain*. New York: Brunner/Mazel, 1976.

Lewinsohn, P. M., & Graf, M. Pleasant activities and depression. *Journal of Consulting and Clinical Psychology*, 1973, *41*, 261–268.

Lewinsohn, P. M., & MacPhillamy, D. J. The relationship between age and engagement in pleasant activities. *Journal of Gerontology*, 1974, *29*, 290–294.

Lewinsohn, P. M., & Shaw, D. A. Feedback about interpersonal behavior as an agent of behavior change: A case study in the treatment of depression. *Psychotherapy and Psychosomatics*, 1969, *17*, 82–88.

Lewinsohn, P. M., Weinstein, M. S., & Alper, T. A behavioral approach to the group treatment of depressed persons: Methodological contribution. *Journal of Clinical Psychology*, 1970, *26*, 525–532.

Libb, J. W., & Clements, L. B. Token reinforcement in an exercise program for hospitalized geriatric patients. *Perceptual and Motor Skills*, 1969, *28*, 957–958.

Liberman, R. P., & Raskin, D. E. Depression: A behavioral formulation. *Archives of General Psychiatry*, 1971, *24*, 515–523.

Libet, J. M., & Lewinsohn, P. M. Concept of social skill with special reference to the behavior of depressed persons. *Journal of Consulting and Clinical Psychology*, 1973, *40*, 304–312.

Lindsley, O. R. Geriatric behavioral prosthetics. In R. Kastenbaum (Ed.), *Thoughts on old age*. New York: Springer, 1964.

MacDonald, E. M. (Ed.). *Occupational therapy in rehabilitation*. (3rd edition). London: Bailliere, Tindall & Cassell, 1970.

MacDonald, M. J. Pub sociotherapy. *Canadian Nurse*, 1972, *68*, 30–32.

MacDonald, M. L. Environmental programming for the socially isolated aging. *The Gerontologist*, in press.

MacDonald, M. L., & Butler, A. K. Reversal of helplessness: Producing walking behavior in nursing home wheelchair residents using behavior modification procedures. *Journal of Gerontology*, 1974, *29*, 97–101.

MacPhillamy, D. J., & Lewinsohn, P. M. Depression as a function of levels of desired and obtained pleasure. *Journal of Abnormal Psychology,* 1974, *83,* 651–657.

McClannahan, L. E. Therapeutic and prosthetic living environments for nursing home residents. *The Gerontologist,* 1973, *13,* 424–429.

McClannahan, L. E., & Risley, T. R. A store for nursing home residents. *Nursing Homes,* 1973, *22,* 10–11.

———. Activities and materials for severely disabled geriatric patients. *Nursing Homes,* 1974. *23,* 19–23.

———. Design of living environments for nursing-home residents: Increasing participation in recreation activities. *Journal of Applied Behavior Analysis,* 1975, *8,* 261–268.

McLean, P. D., Ogston, K., & Grauer, L. A behavioral approach to the treatment of depression. *Journal of Behavior Therapy and Experimental Psychiatry,* 1973, *4,* 323–330.

Malament, I. B., Dunn, M. E., & Davis, R. Pressure sores: An operant conditioning approach to prevention. *Archives of Physical Medicine and Rehabilitation,* 1975, *56,* 161–165.

Marks, I. M. *Living with fear: You as therapist.* New York: McGraw-Hill, 1978.

Meichenbaum, D., & Turk, D. The cognitive-behavioral management of anxiety, anger, and pain. In P. O. Davidson (Ed.), *The behavioral management of anxiety, depression, and pain.* New York: Brunner/Mazel, 1976.

Mendels, J. Lithium in the treatment of depressive states. In F. N. Johnson (Ed.), *Lithium research and therapy.* New York: Academic Press, 1975.

Michael, J. L. Rehabilitation. In C. Neuringer & J. L. Michael (Eds.), *Behavior modification in clinical psychology.* New York, Appleton-Century-Crofts, 1970.

Miller, I. W., & Norman, W. H. Learned helplessness in humans: A review and attribution-model theory. *Psychological Bulletin,* 1979, *86,* 93–118.

Miller, W. R., & Seligman, M. E. P. Depression and the perception of reinforcement. *Journal of Abnormal Psychology,* 1973, *82,* 62–73.

Mueller, D. J., & Atlas, L. Resocialization of regressed elderly residents: A behavioral management approach. *Journal of Gerontology,* 1972, *27,* 390–392.

Nelson, R. E., & Craighead, W. E. Selective recall of positive and negative feedback, self-control behaviors, and depression. *Journal of Abnormal Psychology,* 1977, *86,* 379–388.

O'Brien, F., & Azrin, N. H. Behavioral engineering: Control of posture by informational feedback. *Journal of Applied Behavior Analysis,* 1970, *3,* 235–240.

Premack, D. Reinforcement theory. In D. Levine (Ed.), *Nebraska symposium on motivation.* Lincoln: University of Nebraska Press, 1965.

Rebok, G. W., & Hoyer, W. J. The functional context of elderly behavior. *The Gerontologist,* 1977, *17,* 27–34.

Rehm, L. P., Fuchs, C. Z., Roth, D. M., Kornblith, S. J., & Romano, J. A comparison of self-control and assertion skills treatments of depression. *Behavior Therapy,* 1979, *10,* 429–442.

Rehm, L. P., & Kornblith, S. J. Behavior therapy for depression: A review of recent developments. In M. Hersen, R. Eisler, & P. Miller (Eds.), *Progress in behavior modification,* Vol. 7. New York: Academic Press, 1979.

Rodin, J., & Langer, E. J. Long-term effect of a control-relevant intervention with the institutionalized aged. *Journal of Personality and Social Psychology,* 1977, *35,* 897–902.

Rottkamp, B. C. A behavior modification approach to nursing therapeutics in body positioning of spinal cord-injured patients. *Nursing Research,* 1976, *25,* 181–186.

Rush, A. J., Beck, A. T., Kovacs, M., & Hollon, S. Comparative efficacy of cognitive therapy and pharmacotherapy in the treatment of depressed outpatients. *Cognitive Therapy and Research,* 1977, *1,* 17–38.

Rush, A. J., Khatami, M., & Beck, A. T. Cognitive and behavior therapy in chronic depression. *Behavior Therapy,* 1975, *6,* 398–404.

Sand, P. L., Trieschmann, R. B., Fordyce, W. E., & Fowler, R. S. Behavior modification in the medical rehabilitation setting. *Rehabilitation Research and Practice Review,* 1970, *1,* 11–24.

Schlou, M. Lithium in psychiatric therapy and prophylaxis. *Journal of Psychiatric Research,* 1968, *6,* 67–95.

Seligman, M. E. P. Learned helplessness. *Annual Review of Medicine,* 1972, *23,* 407–412.

———. Fall into helplessness. *Psychology Today,* 1973, *7,* 43–48.

———. *Helplessness: On depression, development and death.* San Francisco: W. H. Freeman, 1975.

Seligman, M. E. P., & Groves, D. Nontransient learned helplessness. *Psychonomic Science,* 1970, *19,* 191–192.

Seligman, M. E. P., & Maier, S. F. Failure to escape traumatic shock. *Journal of Experimental Psychology,* 1967, *74,* 1–9.

Shor, R. E. Physiological effects of painful stimulation during hypnotic analgesia. In J. E. Gordon (Ed.), *Handbook of clinical and experimental hypnosis.* New York: Macmillan, 1967.

Sommer, R., & Ross, H. Social interaction on a geriatric ward. *International Journal of Social Psychology,* 1958, *3,* 128–133.

Spanos, N., Horton, C., & Chaves, J. The effects of two cognitive strategies on pain threshold. *Journal of Abnormal Psychology,* 1975, *84,* 677–681.

Staub, E., Tursky, B., & Schwartz, G. Self-control and predictability: Their effects on reactions to aversive stimulation. *Journal of Personality and Social Psychology,* 1971, *18,* 157–162.

Trombly, C. A. Principles of operant conditioning: Related to orthotic training of quadriplegic patients. *American Journal of Occupational Therapy,* 1966, *20,* 217–220.

Trotter, A. B., & Inman, D. A. The use of positive reinforcement in physical therapy. *Journal of the American Physical Therapy Association,* 1968, *48,* 347–352.

Weisenberg, M. Pain and pain control. *Psychological Bulletin,* 1977, *84,* 1008–1044.

Williams, J. G., Barlow, D. H., & Agras, W. G. Behavioral measurement of severe depression. *Archives of General Psychiatry,* 1972, *27,* 330–333.

Woolridge, C. P., & McLaurin, C. A. Biofeedback—background and applications to physical rehabilitation. *Bulletin of Prosthetics Research,* 1976, *27,* 25–37.

Zimmerman, J., Overpeck, C., Eisenberg, H., & Garlick, B. Operant conditioning in a sheltered workshop: Further data in support of an objective and systematic approach to rehabilitation. *Rehabilitation Literature,* 1969, *30,* 326–334.

Zimmerman, J., Stuckey, J. E., Garlick, B. J., & Miller, M. Effects of token reinforcement on productivity in multiply handicapped clients in a sheltered workshop. *Rehabilitation Literature,* 1969, *30,* 34–41.

Part III

BEHAVIORAL RESEARCH AND THE PREVENTION OF HEALTH-RELATED PROBLEMS

8

Psychological Preparation for Hospitalization

Description of the Problem

The need for psychological preparation for children entering the hospital is predicated on the belief that hospitalization and surgery are stressful and anxiety-producing experiences that can lead to transient or long-term psychological disturbances. Cassell (1965) reported slight psychological upset in as much as 92 percent of the hospitalized children studied. A number of behavior problems have been observed in children hospitalized for surgery (Chapman, Loeb, & Gibbons, 1956; Gellert, 1958), with estimates for the incidence of these problems ranging from 10 percent to 35 percent (Jessner, Blom, & Waldfogel, 1952; Prugh, Staub, Sands, Kirschbaum, & Lenihan, 1953; Schaffer & Callender, 1959).

The hospital experience itself may produce anxiety irrespective of the need for surgery (Skipper & Leonard, 1968). Anxiety-provoking experiences in the life of a young child can provide a basis for the development of healthy coping skills that can lead to mastery behaviors (Murphy, 1962). Therefore, the complete alleviation of anxiety may not be the best strategy. In fact, several authors have remarked that although preoperative anxiety may impede recovery from surgery (Dumas, 1963; Giller, 1963), anxiety at moderate levels may actually lead to more effective coping processes (Burstein & Meichenbaum, 1979; Janis, 1958; Melamed & Siegel, 1975).

The major purpose of preoperative preparation for children according to an extensive review by Vernon et al. (1965) is to provide information to the child, encourage emotional expression, and establish a trusting relationship with the hospital staff.

Methodological Problems in Research

The research studies investigating the effectiveness of various methods of preparation have yielded equivocal findings as to the differences between prepared and unprepared subjects. These studies suffer from weaknesses in experimental method that make it difficult to evaluate the data. For example, such factors as previous hospitalization experience, the age of the child, and prehospital personality, which are known to be major determinants of psychological upset, are often uncontrolled (Siegel, 1976; Vernon et al., 1965). In addition, the instruments purported to measure the children's anxiety vary considerably in validity and reliability. The use of interview questionnaires that assess parental reports or global ratings of the child's response to treatment are inadequate measures.

The distinction between state and trait anxiety is often ignored, despite data that support the findings that these are differentially affected by the hospital experience (Martinez-Urrutia, 1975; Melamed & Siegel, 1975). Kaplan and Hafner (1959) found no changes on subjects' scores on the Children's Manifest Anxiety Scale during their hospitalization for surgery. Spielberger et al. (1973) and Auerbach (1973), using the State-Trait Anxiety Inventory, provided further data indicating the stability of trait measures of anxiety with hospitalized adult surgical patients. The measures of transitory situational anxiety have been found to vary from presurgery to postsurgery assessments and again during the posthospitalization period, as would be predicted. However, the time of measurement has also varied from study to study, making further difficulties for comparison across studies.

Scope of the Chapter

Criterion of Studies Included

This review includes studies that have attempted to control for factors that have been neglected in previous research. The major emphasis is on evaluating preparation of children for elective surgery. Auerbach and Kilmann (1977) have provided a more comprehensive review of child and adult preparation for surgery. The studies presented here reflect the authors' collaborative and independent research efforts, in which criterion variables of age, sex, prehospital personality, and previous experience in hospitalization are either used as matching variables or evaluated as independent factors. The multidimensional nature of fear has been addressed by the inclusion of a wide range of measures of self-reported, behavioral, and physiological measures of anxiety. Clinical indications during recovery from surgery (such as time to first solids, frequency of postsurgical complications, nausea, and requests for pain medication) are included. In addition, both stable personality characteristics and situational measures of fear are evaluated.

The procedures described throughout this chapter follow the control group design described in Chapter 3. The issues raised are applicable to other research questions. This is illustrated by behavioral studies on the psychological preparation for childbirth. The ability to evaluate the effectiveness of any treatment package is based on clearly specifiable procedures. Control groups are necessary to substantiate the crucial elements of the treatment being evaluated. Therefore, control groups may be included for nonspecific factors that influence treatment outcome, such as expectancy for change, the therapeutic relationship of the therapist and patient, and the effect of repeated measurement. Thus, one needs to specify what it is the control group attempts to control. Some control conditions are included in an attempt to evaluate the comparative effectiveness of the therapeutic intervention against other procedures also in use for the same purpose. It is important in evaluating specific treatment components that the control group include all other possible therapeutic factors except those thought to be crucial to the treatment package in question. Likewise, the population of subjects sampled should be representative of those patients for whom the therapy is intended. Groups should be matched for all individual subject differences that might inadvertently affect the treatment outcome, such as age, race, sex, intellectual level, socioeconomic status, and previous experience in the situation.

Fear as a Multisystem Concept

In order to evaluate any treatment purported to reduce anxiety, the first task is to define how you will measure that response. Fear is a complex construct (Lang, 1968; 1977). There is an impressive body of research that suggests that measures of fear do not correlate highly with one another (Lang, Melamed, & Hart, 1970; Martin & Sroufe,

1970). This is particularly prevalent in measures of childhood anxiety (Ruebush, 1963). Therefore, it is important to sample all systems that may reflect an individual's fear. The child's self-report of subjective experience may not be congruent with how he or she actually behaves in the feared situations. The physiological response to fear-inducing stimuli may indicate increased visceral activation, while the child remains perfectly cooperative with the procedures. Which system do we believe? There is no data to suggest that any one system deserves primary consideration. In fact, different measures of behavior within a system may vary. Heart rate and sweating activity may not equally reflect arousal. Anxiety should not be inferred on the basis of a single indicator of autonomic arousal (Lacey, 1967). It is the pattern of relationships between responses that defines the meaning of fear. Individuals may differ in their tendency to exhibit certain patterns of responses in different systems or in the same systems at different times. Therefore, when group data is being evaluated, it is very important to be aware of these individual differences when reporting mean group effects. It has also been noted that desynchrony or discordance between systems may appear because of differential rates of change in the problem behaviors (Hodgson & Rachman, 1974). This implies that it is necessary to sample the behaviors at different times. The potency of the treatment effect should be evaluated by changes in particular dependent measures as well as in the observation of interrelationships between measures.

Research Strategy

Research is best guided by theoretical as well as practical considerations. Too often, programs considered to be therapeutic are applied without a careful evaluation. Some procedures for psychological preparation may in fact produce harmful effects, sensitizing the patient to unpleasant aspects of treatment. In evaluating a treatment program, it is useful to state what theoretical framework led to its development. Then, in order to test this intervention adequately, it is necessary to state the hypotheses clearly enough so that they can be defined operationally by the experimental procedures. This also enhances the likelihood that replications of the study can be done to validate their efficacy in other settings. This chapter is divided into five main sections:

1. the first presents data collected by the authors in a series of investigations designed to evaluate the efficacy of film modeling in the psychological preparation of children for elective surgery,

2. the second addresses a theoretical conception about the facilitative effect of preoperative anxiety on postoperative recovery,
3. the third evaluates the relationship between parental factors (e.g., the type of disciplinary strategy they have previously used with the child in fearful situations, the joint parent-child preparation techniques) and children's ability to cope with surgery and hospitalization,
4. the fourth illustrates how the between-groups design has been used to evaluate behavioral procedures in a different area: preparation for childbirth, and
5. the fifth reviews the necessary methodological factors in undertaking research and points the way for future studies in the area of hospital preparation.

Film Modeling to Prepare Children for Medical Procedures

There is a steadily growing body of literature regarding the therapeutic effectiveness of modeling films for the reduction of a wide variety of fears and avoidance behaviors, including small animal phobias, fears of social interactions, swimming, and so on (Bandura, 1969; Bandura, Grusec, & Menlove, 1967; O'Conner, 1969; Thelen, Fry, Fehrenbach, & Frautschi, 1979 reviewed this literature).

Applications to the preparation of children and adults for hospitalization, medical examination, and dental treatment are making their appearance (Adelson & Goldfried, 1970; Kleinknecht & Bernstein, in press; Melamed, Hawes, Heiby, & Glick, 1975; Melamed & Siegel, 1975; Melamed, Meyer, Gee, & Soule, 1976; Melamed, Weinstein, Hawes, & Katin-Borland, 1975; Melamed, Yurcheson, Fleece, Hutcherson, & Hawes, 1978; Shipley, Butt, Horwitz, & Farbry, 1978). These investigations have important implications for social learning theory and fear modification. Many of the strategies employed within the modeling film are similar to those used in other behavioral applications, such as systematic desensitization, flooding, and behavioral rehearsal. These include graduated exposure to fear-inducing stimuli through the eyes of a peer or prestige model shown coping with the stressful experience. Typically, modeling films are shown while the observer is in an aroused state, awaiting the impending procedure or operation. During the exposure to the feared situations the model may use such coping strategies as behavioral rehearsal, relaxation, pleasant imagery, or distracting tasks. If modeling demonstrates significant anxiety reduction, it can provide a sufficient and practical approach to preparing individuals for medical intervention that requires minimal amounts of professional time and can easily be adopted by hospitals, medical centers, clinics, and private practitioners. Thus, modeling is aimed not only at reducing maladaptive fear but at preventing the development of such problem behaviors. The novice patient is given information about what to expect and prototypes of how to handle these situations prior to any negative emotional experiences in the setting. It is hoped that this will allay anxiety that might generate inappropriate avoidance behaviors.

Although several films have been prepared and are currently used by hospitals in preparing patients and their families for surgery (see the end of this chapter's reference section for a list of available films), only a few have been empirically evaluated. In addition to our own investigations, Vernon and Bailey (1974) and Geidel and Gulbrandsen (1974) have systematically investigated the effect of viewing a film on actual behavior during anesthetic induction for surgery and during an ear examination.

These studies are certainly admirable from the point of view that they tested out the procedure without assuming a therapeutic benefit; however, they suffer from serious methodological problems. Vernon and Bailey (1974) found that children who observed the induction of anesthesia were rated as less anxious and less disruptive on a Global Mood scale than was a control group that did not observe any film. The authors failed to include a control for the distraction and possibly anxiety-reducing effects of showing a film prior to the stressful event. In addition, the lack of measures of self-reported discomfort or physiological responses to the stress limit the conclusions regarding the film's effectiveness.

Geidel and Gulbrandsen (1974) developed a videotape of preschool children coping with a physical examination by the doctor. They then evaluated the preparation against several control conditions, including a cartoon control film and a free play situation in a sample of twenty-four preschool children who were having physical examinations, including blood tests, inoculations, and an ear examination by the pediatrician. Unfortunately, there were several methodological flaws that make it difficult to evaluate their lack of group differences. The mothers were present at all phases of the examination, thereby mitigating what might have been greater stress on the children. Also, the children were rated as not very stressed to begin with. This reduces the likelihood that further treatment would be able to reduce stress. In addition, the children were not shown the film until after they had already received the blood test and the immunization injections. Therefore, they were "experienced" subjects even before the film's effectiveness could be evaluated during the ear examination, a procedure probably less stressful than the earlier events.

The investigation of modeling effects in our studies was designed to evaluate the overall effectiveness of the treatment package for children without previous hospital experience using those methods that were found to optimize the modeling effect. Studies conducted by the authors to identify effective components of the modeling situation are described. One must keep in mind the characteristics of the sample (sex, race, socioeconomic status, and degree of prior experience in the situation) and at what periods during the exposure to medical intervention the measures were obtained.

The following explicit questions were addressed:

1. Is the observation of a peer model effective in reducing the anxiety of children about to undergo elective surgery in the hospital, as compared to preparation procedures typically employed in children's hospitals?
2. When should children be shown the peer modeling film to produce the most effective results? Do children of different ages need different times for preparation?
3. Does the film about hospitalization reduce presurgery stress in the absence of additional preoperative preparation in the hospital?
4. Is the peer-modeling film effective in the preparation of children who have had previous hospitalization for surgery?

A special film was developed for this project (*Ethan Has an Operation,* 1974) that included all variables thought to maximize the modeling effect. Simply exposing a child to a model's behavior does not insure that the child will imitate the response. Several variables have been found to facilitate the imitation of the model's behavior. Generally, the greater the perceived similarity of the model to the observer, the greater the imitation (Bandura, Ross, & Ross, 1963; Flanders, 1968; Kazdin, 1973; Kornhaber & Schroeder, 1975; Rosenkrans, 1967). Girls have been shown to model a boy model more often than boys will model a girl's behavior (Nicholas, McCarter, & Heckel, 1971). Research on modeling and imitation in children also revealed that black subjects imitated a white model more than a black model (Neeley, Heckel, & Leichtman, 1973; Smith, 1972). Therefore, a seven-year-old white boy was used as a peer model in our study. Rachman

(1972) has postulated that models who are seen to overcome their own fear and acquire mastery in the situation are most effective in producing reductions of fear in the observer. This has been supported by research findings (Bruch, 1975; Kornhaber & Schroeder, 1975; Meichenbaum, 1971). Therefore, *Ethan Has an Operation* portrays a youngster who hesitatingly approaches the hospital accompanied by his parents. He is shown going through the admission process and the preoperative blood test, during which he displays some anxiety. The child narrates the film to enhance the likelihood of imitation. He talks with the surgeon and the anesthesiologist about what he should expect

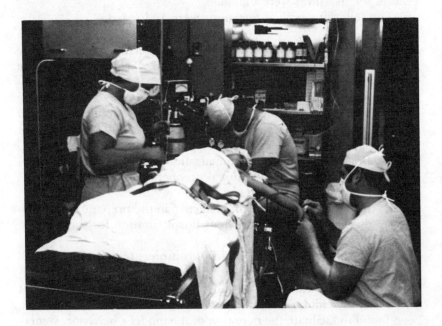

Figure 8.1   A scene from *Ethan Has an Operation,* which depicts through the eyes of a seven-year-old what happens from the time of admission to the hospital until discharge home. The scene in the operating room ends with the induction of anesthesia. The child wakes up in the recovery room and rejoins his parents shortly therafter.

From B. G. Melamed and L. J. Siegel, Reduction of anxiety in children facing hospitalization and surgery by use of filmed modeling. *Journal of Consulting and Clinical Psychology,* 1975, *43,* 511-521. Copyright © 1975 by the American Psychological Association. Reprinted by permission.

during surgery. The anesthesia induction in the operating room is depicted since the child, though premedicated, is awake (see Figure 8.1). He wakes up with some discomfort in the recovery room, but is tended by a caring nurse. His parents are at his bedside when he returns from surgery. His departure from the hospital is the final scene. Other children are in the playroom and describe their own experiences to Ethan before his operation; this incorporates the potential benefits from using multiple models (Bandura, 1969). The decision to give specific information about the depicted procedures was based on research reporting that patients receiving preoperative preparation of a specific, rather than general, nature showed less postoperative anger, depression, and negative effects than did those with inadequate information (DeLong, 1970; Johnson & Leventhal, 1974).

The decision to show children the film at the time of admission to the hospital was based on findings that modeling is most effective immediately prior to the impending event (Flanders, 1968). A second study (Melamed, Meyer, Gee, & Soule, 1976) more specifically addresses this question of the optimal time for preparation, given age as a factor.

An unrelated film, *Living Things Are Everywhere* (1974) was chosen because it featured a preadolescent white boy who takes a nature hike by himself and learns new things. It controlled for interest value, length of time, and the use of a peer model coping with new experiences. Although instructional, it deals with behaviors unrelated to the hospital.

Study 1: Film Modeling

Hypothesis. Children who view a peer-modeling film related to the hospital experience will show less anxiety than will children who observe an unrelated film, even when both groups of children receive additional psychological preparation by the hospital staff.

Method

Subjects

In each of the following studies, the characteristics of our sample remain essentially the same. The children chosen were between the ages of four and twelve years and were admitted with no prior history of hospitalization and scheduled for either tonsillectomies, hernia repairs, or urinary-genital tract surgery. The length of stay in the hospital ranged from two to three days. In the first study, thirty subjects were randomly assigned to the experimental and control groups. These groups were equivalent for age, sex, race, and type of operation. An equal number of mothers in both groups stayed overnight with their children. Regardless of which film was observed, all children received the same standard preoperative preparation once they were admitted to the hospital. This consisted of talks with the surgeon and/or anesthesiologist, a playroom visit with the child-life worker, demonstrations of the masks, anesthesia induction procedures, and observation of a photograph album depicting other children at various stages of their hospital experience. Therefore, the film's potency had to be evaluated against preparation for surgery already considered valuable, but not previously evaluated.

Measures of Trait Anxiety

In order to assess the multidimensional nature of anxiety, several indices of the child's emotional behavior were employed, including self-report, behavioral, and physiological measures. Four measures were used to assess "trait" anxiety of the long-term effects of the hospital experience.

  1. The first measure was the Anxiety Scale (Klinedienst, 1971). The thirty items that make up this scale were rationally derived from the Personality Inventory for Children (Wirt & Broen, 1958). Items on the scale, which the mother rates as true or false about her child, are intended to measure more chronic and stable anxiety.

  2. The Children's Manifest Anxiety Scale (Castaneda, McCandless, & Palermo, 1956) was a second measure of the long-term effects of the hospital experience.

  3. The Human Figure Drawing Test (Koppitz, 1968) was the third index of trait anxiety. Koppitz has developed a set of norms for thirty "emotional indicators" that were used to score the subjects' drawings. Average inter-rater agreement for independent raters who scored the drawings was 97 percent.

  4. The Peterson Behavior Problem Checklist was filled out by parents (Quay & Quay, 1965). This reveals the degree of behavior problems that the child exhibited in the four weeks prior to the hospital experience.

Measures of State Anxiety

Situational or "state" anxiety was assessed by the Palmar Sweat Index, the Hospital Fears Rating Scale, and the Observer Rating Scale of Anxiety.

1. The Palmar Sweat Index (Thomson & Sutarman, 1953; Johnson & Dabbs, 1967) is a plastic impression method that permits enumeration of active sweat gland activity of the hand. Since sweat glands of the hand are primarily affected by emotional factors and not by such other variables as temperature, the number of active sweat glands provides a measure of transitory physiological arousal. The Palmar Sweat Index was recorded from the index finger of the child's left hand. Rater reliability for two persons independently scoring the same area of the print was .93 as determined by the Spearman-Brown reliability coefficient.

2. The second measure of situational anxiety was the Hospital Fears Rating Scale. This is a self-report measure consisting of eight items from the subscale "Medical Fears" that was factor analyzed from the Fear Survey Schedule for Children (Scherer & Nakamura, 1968). Another eight items having face validity for assessing hospital fears were also included. These sixteen items, along with nine unrelated "filler" items form the Hospital Fears Rating Scale. Each subject rated his degree of fear for each item on a "Fear Thermometer" having a scale that ranged from 1 (not afraid at all) to 5 (very afraid). The sum of the ratings on the sixteen medical fear items was the subject's score for this measure.

3. The Observer Rating Scale of Anxiety was developed because no other relevant measures for children existed at that time. This behavioral observation scale was composed of twenty-nine categories of verbal expressions and skeletal-motor acts thought to represent behavioral manifestations of anxiety. A time-sampling procedure was used in which an observer indicated the presence or absence of each response category during three intervals of time in a nine-minute observational period. Examples of items indicative of anxiety include "crying," "trembling hands," "stutters," "talks about hospital fears, separation from mother, or going home." The frequency of responses observed during the total period of observation was the subject's score on the Observer Rating Scale of Anxiety. Rater reliability was assessed throughout each phase of the experimental procedure. Average inter-rater reliability, which was computed by dividing the number of observer agreements by the total number of categories of behavior that were observed, was 94 percent.

Procedure

The measurement periods were:

1. before the film, at the time the child was being hooked up for physiological measurement by a "doctor" (*prefilm*),

2. after the film, immediately following the hospital-relevant or control film (*postfilm*),

3. before the operation (assessment took place the evening before surgery after the children had already been given preoperative instruction and had received preoperative medical procedures, including blood test, urinalysis, and any other procedures if required) (*preoperative*), and

4. immediately prior to the postoperative examination three to four weeks after discharge, at which time the child returned to see the surgeon (*postoperative*).

The trait measures of anxiety were assessed only at the first and last measurement times as previous research predicted that these measures would not reflect change over a short time period. All other measures were sampled at the four time periods by raters unaware of the experimental hypothesis and assigned conditions. Variation in the time and type of premedication made assessment during preoperative induction impractical. Also, since some of the children were discharged prior to full recovery from anesthesia and pain medication, the effect of immediate recovery from the operation was obtained on a global postoperative recovery questionnaire evaluating time of first liquids, solid food, nausea, vomiting, and amount of pain medication.

Results

The state measures of anxiety consistently reflected differences between the hospital-relevant and control film groups. Differences were also noted between the pre- and posthospital parental ratings of the degree of behavior problems.[1] As predicted, the measures of trait anxiety did not demonstrate treatment effects.

Since there were no differences in anxiety levels between groups at the initial assessment, the findings can be clearly interpreted as determined by the intervention. Figure 8.2 illustrates the statistically significant difference in palmar sweating between the groups at various measurement times. The night before surgery, the children who viewed the hospital film showed lower levels of sweat gland activity than did those who had been exposed to an unrelated control film.

[1]Analyses of variance for repeated measures were used in evaluating the results. Statistically significant results reported in this section achieved an α level beyond $p < .05$. Readers should review Winer (1962) if they want a more extensive understanding of the analyses.

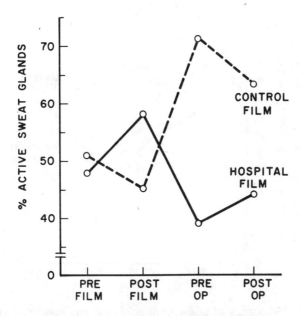

Figure 8.2 Percent of active sweat glands for the experimental and control groups across the four measurement periods.

From B. G. Melamed and L. J. Siegel, Reduction of anxiety in children facing hospitalization and surgery by use of filmed modeling. *Journal of Consulting and Clinical Psychology,* 1975, *43,* 511-521. Copyright © 1975 by the American Psychological Association. Reprinted by permission.

This significant group difference was still in effect four weeks postsurgery, when the children returned to the hospital for an examination by the surgeon. The effects across time periods further revealed that children who viewed the hospital film showed an immediate increase in sympathetic arousal after the film, which was significantly reduced at both preoperative and postoperative assessments. On the other hand, the control group subjects showed significant increases in palmar sweating from postfilm to preoperative and postoperative assessments. The unrelated film they viewed did not significantly alter their arousal level.

Similar results are found between groups for the Observer Rating Scale of Anxiety. The group that viewed the hospital film exhibited significantly fewer anxiety-related behaviors than did the control group at both preoperative and postoperative assessments (see Figure 8.3).

The hospital-film group showed decreases in the frequency of

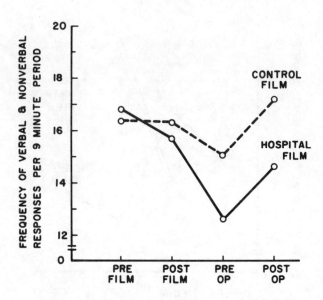

Figure 8.3   Frequency of observer-rated verbal and nonverbal anxiety responses for the experimental and control groups across the four measurement periods.

From B. G. Melamed and L. J. Siegel, Reduction of anxiety in children facing hospitalization and surgery by use of filmed modeling. *Journal of Consulting and Clinical Psychology,* 1975, *43,* 511-521. Copyright © 1975 by the American Psychological Association. Reprinted by permission.

anxiety-related behaviors from both prefilm and postfilm to preoperative measurement. Although the four-week follow-up showed a significant increase in anxiety-related behaviors over the preoperative assessment, this was still significantly lower than the prefilm level at the time of initial hospitalization. The control group subjects showed a significant increase in observer-rated anxiety from preoperative to postoperative assessment, even though they received standard preparation from nurses and child-life workers.

The self-report measures of hospital fears showed a significant effect of age. Regardless of the film conditions, younger children reported greater medical concerns. However, the children seeing the hospital peer-modeling film reported fewer medical concerns than did those viewing a control film the night before surgery and at the post-hospital examination (see Figure 8.4).

The postoperative recovery questionnaire revealed a tendency for the hospital-film subjects to exhibit fewer postsurgical complications

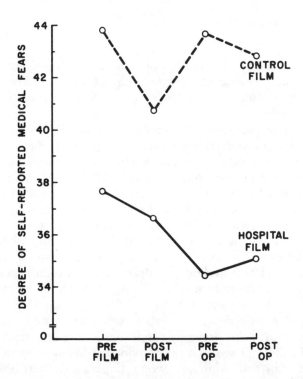

Figure 8.4 Degree of self-reported medical fears for the experimental and control groups across the four measurement periods.

From B. G. Melamed and L. J. Siegel, Reduction of anxiety in children facing hospitalization and surgery by use of filmed modeling. *Journal of Consulting and Clinical Psychology*, 1975, *43*, 511-521. Copyright © 1975 by the American Psychological Association. Reprinted by permission.

than the control subjects. Fewer experimental subjects (21 percent) received pain medication after release from the recovery room than did those who had not viewed the hospital film (30 percent). Whereas 37 percent of the latter children exhibited nausea with vomiting, only 17 percent of the experimental subjects vomited. In fact, 54 percent of the children receiving the hospital-film preparation were able to eat solid food on the same day of the operation as compared to only 26 percent of the control group sample.

Although these results were in the expected direction, the differences obtained may have been due to random fluctuation. These measures also may reflect individual physicians' preferences to prescribe analgesics, rather than the child's recovery.

Discussion

These results support the efficacy of using a film to prepare children for the hospital experience. The fact that treatment differences persisted at the postoperative examination indicates generalization of preparation effects.

The increase in arousal level for the hospital-film group immediately after it was observed lends support to Janis's (1958) contention that a moderate amount of arousal might facilitate response to stress in those facing impending surgery. The fact that behavioral indices of anxiety increased at the return visit to the hospital supports the notion that this type of preparation is most effective at the time immediately preceding the experience. Also, more specific information regarding what to expect in the hospital was shown in the film, whereas the posthospital examination itself was not portrayed. This is consistent with Vernon's (1973) finding that differences between experimental and control subjects were smallest during those phases of anesthesia induction which were not portrayed by the modeling film.

The failure of trait anxiety tests to discriminate between groups is consistent with the previous results indicating the absence of a change of children's scores on the Children's Manifest Anxiety Scale during their hospitalization for surgery (Kaplan & Hafner, 1959). This finding is also consistent with research on adult surgical patients (Auerbach, 1973; Spielberger et al., 1973). The adult studies did report similar patterns of changes on anxiety state measures from presurgery to postsurgery and posthospital assessments. There is a decline from presurgery to 48 hours after surgery, and a marked decline in the convalescent period.

Trait anxiety as assessed by the Peterson Behavior Problem Checklist in this study revealed a marked increase in parents' report of behavior problems during the month after hospital discharge for the children who did not have the opportunity to view the preparatory film. This is most noteworthy in view of the fact that both groups of children received preoperative preparation during their hospital stay by the nursing staff and child-life workers. It would, therefore, appear that the film had greater impact than just conveying information about what to expect. In fact, more recent data (Melamed, Yurcheson, Fleece, Hutcherson, & Hawes, 1978) indicated a greater effectiveness of peer modeling than a demonstration of the same dental procedures.

Study 2: Time of Preparation and Age of the Child

Hypothesis 1. Children over seven years of age will benefit from seeing the peer-modeling film a week in advance of admission for surgery, whereas younger children will show less anxiety if they view the film at the time of the impending surgery.

Hypothesis 2. Children who view a peer-modeling film will show reduction of anxiety, even in the absence of standard inhospital preparation.

The second experiment (Melamed, Meyer, Gee, & Soule, 1976) followed from the findings of the first project. There were some age differences, with the degree of medical concerns and prehospital trait anxiety being greater among younger children. This, together with research suggesting that younger children need a different amount of time to incorporate preparation, led us to consider the interaction of time of preparation and age. Therefore, in this experiment, we varied the time prior to actual hospital admission during which the children would view the film. In one group, children viewed the film five to nine days prior to surgery; in the second group, the film was shown on the day of admission. This latter strategy repeated our previous work.

It was predicted that there would be a greater reduction of anxiety for older children (seven years and older) given the opportunity to see the film in advance of their hospitalization, as compared to younger children. This was based on speculation that older children might benefit from a longer interval between preparation and the occurrence of the procedure. Mellish (1969) has suggested that younger children, particularly very anxious ones, need only a few days of preparation since longer intervals may only increase anticipatory anxiety. Heller (1967) suggested that:

> older children will need a more detailed and lengthy preparation. The younger child, because of shorter attention span, can be prepared much closer to the actual time of hospitalization . . . A few days for the younger child and several days and weeks for the older child would seem reasonable.

There are differences between researchers, however; the optimal preparation time for children of different ages has not yet been determined. Dimock (1960) has recommended that preparing a child too early may lead to an increase in fear. But just how early is too early? An extensive review of literature failed to find comparative studies of the effectiveness of preparation at different times.

One study (Newswanger, 1974) used a two-day preparatory period in preschool children prior to hospitalization for tonsillectomy and adenoidectomy. Home visits were made by a nurse-teacher, who demonstrated various procedures that would happen to the child. The control group members were also visited at home, but they were read an unrelated story by the nurse-teacher. The observational data taken during stressful medical procedures was very elaborate and demonstrated significantly more mastery behaviors by children receiving the preparation. There were also significantly fewer behaviors classified as negative or passive among the hospital-relevant prepared group. Although preschoolers benefited during their hospital experience from a two-day advance period of preparation, there was a lack of behavioral difference between the prepared and unprepared children two weeks after discharge.

In Study 2, we were also concerned about whether the film by itself would effectively reduce anxiety. Many hospitals have neither the facilities nor the staff to incorporate preoperative teaching on a large scale. General hospitals often treat the young child in a manner similar to the adult patient. We were concerned about the possible sensitizing effect the film might have if it was observed by a child who then did not have access to supportive staff or if medical procedures differed to a large extent from those depicted in the film. The previous research on the effectiveness of modeling in the reduction of fears even with a single, brief exposure encouraged us to assume that the film might be potent in the absence of further preparation. Thus, a group of children who saw the film were not given the standard inhospital preparation. Only minimal staff interaction about specific procedures was given; this was restricted to the time the procedure took place, and occurred only if the child requested it (see Table 8.1).

Subjects met the same requirements as stated in Study 1. The battery of measures used was identical, with the exception of an additional measurement period at admission time for those receiving film preparation one week in advance of hospital admission. This made it possible to evaluate whether or not the benefits of early preparation were seen at that time.

The results of this study replicated our previous research findings. The children all showed marked reduction on self-reported medical

Table 8.1 Design Table for Study 2: Time of Preparation and Age of the Child

		Time of Film Viewing	
		Day of Admission	5-9 days Prior
Type of In-hospital Preparation	Minimal Preparation	n = 8	n = 8
	Standard Hospital Preparation	n = 8	n = 8

concerns and were rated by observers as showing fewer disruptive behaviors from prefilm to preoperative assessment.

The children who were prepared by viewing the film one week in advance of hospitalization reported fewer medical concerns on the Hospital Fears Rating Scale at the time of admission. This advanced preparation group also tended to have lower physiological arousal at the preadmission assessment. However, by the night prior to surgery there was no advantage for the early preparation group; both groups were low in preoperative anxiety.

The time of preparation was not a major factor influencing stress reduction in children. The age of the child as well as the time of assessment needed to be considered. The younger children exhibited a significant increase in anticipated medical fears from preoperative to postoperative assessment, whereas the older children showed an over-all reduction in self-reported medical concerns regardless of when they viewed the film. The highest report of medical concerns occurred in the young children viewing the film at the time of admission to the hospital. These results are based on a small sample, and thus, can only serve to generate additional hypotheses to be tested.

However, it is interesting that older children viewing the film a week in advance show remarkably similar physiological data as was obtained in the first study (Melamed & Siegel, 1975). They showed an immediate increase in physiological arousal upon viewing the film, with decreases from postfilm to preoperative assessment. On the other hand, the younger children who viewed the film a week in advance showed a steady increase in arousal, whereas the younger children who viewed the film at the time of hospital admission showed a pattern similar to that of children viewing the hospital film in Study 1. An increase of palmar sweating after seeing the film was followed by a decrease the night before surgery.

These data suggest that the age of the child must be considered in deciding on the optimal time for film preparation of children about to have surgery. Younger children did not benefit from preparation too far in advance of the actual stressful event. Older children, on the other hand, may benefit by prior exposure to information regarding the event. They showed less physiological arousal the night prior to surgery than older children who did not view the film one week in advance. It would be useful to know what the children were thinking between the early film exposure and the day of admission.

With regard to the second hypothesis of the film's effectiveness in the absence of extensive inhospital preparation by the staff, some exploratory data is available. There were no significant group differences in this experiment between groups receiving minimal preparation (excluding demonstrations and talks with child-life workers) and those children receiving extensive hospital preparation. It would be premature to conclude from these data that the film alone had an overriding effect. The particular quality of inhospital preparation varies markedly from one hospital to another, and even differs depending upon which staff are involved.

A more conclusive comparison, supportive of the effectiveness of the film alone, is the comparison between the group viewing the film with minimal preparation and the control group of Study 1, who received the extensive hospital preparation but viewed an unrelated film. The group viewing the hospital film showed lower preoperative anxiety on both the Hospital Fears Rating Scale and Observer Rating Scale of Anxiety than did the control group receiving only the standard hospital preparation without viewing the hospital film. Of course, this finding needs to be cross-validated in other hospital settings in studies that vary the amount of preoperative preparation with and without the hospital film.

Study 3: Effects of Film Modeling for Children Who Have Had Previous Operations

Hypothesis 1. Children who view a hospital peer-modeling film prior to surgery will show a reduction of anxiety as compared with children viewing an unrelated control film. (This is a replication of Study 1.)

Hypothesis 2. Those children having had previous hospitalization for surgery will not benefit (reduce anxiety) as much as will children who have not had previous hospitalization.

Little research attention has been devoted to variables that indicate which subjects will respond the most favorably to therapeutic modeling. Melamed and her colleagues (Melamed, Yurcheson, Fleece, Hutcherson, & Hawes, 1978) have demonstrated the differences in the effectiveness of modeling films when the previous experience of the subject was evaluated. Children who had already had previous restorations did not reduce their disruptiveness more after viewing the modeling film than a group who saw an unrelated film. Furthermore, there were interactions between the child's history of previous experience and the length of preparatory film and whether or not a peer model was depicted.

Children with no previous experience were sensitized by viewing a demonstration of the impending procedure that did not show a peer model. Siegel (1977) conducted a study that addressed this issue. It demonstrated the complexities in assuming that the hospital film preparation would be equally effective with all children. Children with one or more hospital experiences may react differently from children with no previous hospital experience, such that modeling would not produce similar treatment effects. This study investigated the effects of prior history of hospitalization and exposure to the peer-modeling film on anxiety-related behaviors in children undergoing elective surgery. Procedures were the same as in the Melamed and Siegel 1975 study; however, history of previous surgery was included as a between-groups factor.

Children aged five to twelve who were admitted to the hospital for elective surgery were assigned to treatment groups based on whether this was the first or second hospital experience. If this was the second admission for surgery, the first surgery had to have taken place after the age of five. (This restriction was to control for varying recall capacity of younger children.) All children observed either the peer-modeling (*Ethan Has an Operation*) or the unrelated control film. There were four conditions in this 2 X 2 factorial design (see Table 8.2.).

In general, the results of the modeling film's effectiveness replicated the previous findings in that those who viewed the film prior to admission for their first elective surgery showed reduced emotional behaviors. Figures 8.5, 8.6, and 8.7 show the similar pattern of results. The fact that this finding was cross-validated lends further credence to

Table 8.2 Design Table for Study 3: Effects of Film Modeling for Children with Previous Operations

		Level of Previous Experience	
		No Previous Operation	Previous Operation
Type of Film Preparation	Hospital Peer-Modeled	n = 12	n = 12
	Unrelated Film	n = 12	n = 12

the potency of film preparation for children without previous experience. The setting and procedures at the University of Missouri Medical Center were not depicted in the hospital film, which was developed at Case Western Reserve University. However, the film tended to have no significant effect on children seeing it immediately prior to a second hospitalization for surgery. Figures 8.5 and 8.7 indicate that these

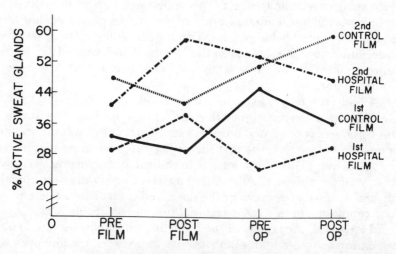

Figure 8.5 Percent of active sweat glands for the experimental and control groups across the four measurement periods in children having their first or second operations.

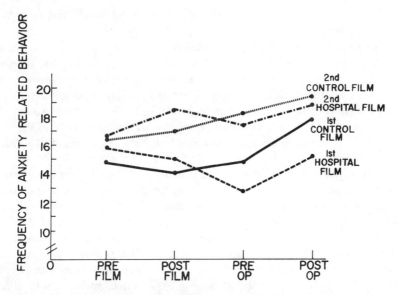

Figure 8.6 Frequency of anxiety-related behavior in the experimental and control groups across the four measurement periods in children having their first or second operations.

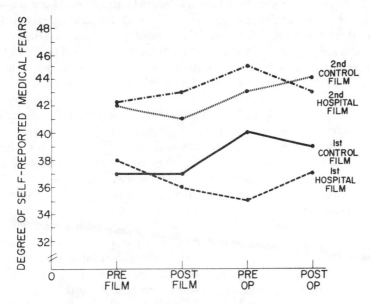

Figure 8.7 Degree of self-reported medical fears for the experimental and control groups across the four measurement periods in children having their first or second operations.

children did have high prefilm levels of anxiety on the self-report and physiological arousal measures. These results suggest that the second hospitalization may have been more anxiety evoking for these children. In addition, children with previous hospital experience tended to be significantly more anxious the evening prior to surgery (controlling for initial level effects) than were children in the hospital for the first time (physiological and self-reported fear), regardless of the film intervention.

Interpretations of these results within a learning theory framework would suggest that subjects entering the hospital for the second surgery have had prior exposure to unconditioned pain and discomfort stimuli associated with hospital conditions and personnel. With a second exposure to the conditioned stimuli brought about by viewing the modeling film, sensitization rather than habituation or extinction occurred. In this experienced group, fear behaviors have been reinforced through the prior conditioning experience, and it is more difficult to extinguish their arousal levels since they start out at higher levels of arousal than do the children with no prior experience. These treatment differences may be accounted for by the fact that children with a previous history of surgery may have been too highly aroused to attend adequately to the film at the time of admission. There is some evidence for this in that, immediately following this film, subjects in the second-time surgery group were significantly more aroused than were children seeing it before their first hospital experience. The modeling film consistently assisted the children with no previous hospitalization to modulate and reduce their anxiety levels. In these children, anxiety has not already been additionally reinforced by the real-life experience. Their anxiety levels show habituation during the remaining hospital experience as compared to children viewing an unrelated film.

Given these results, future research should investigate multiple exposures to a preparatory film. Children may require repeated exposures to the film to overcome the negative emotional response that has been conditioned by previous hospital experience. Similar findings with adults suggest the need for different types of videotape modeling depending upon prior experience. Adults prepared for their first endoscopy examination by repeated exposure to the videotape reduced their stress as compared with unprepared patients (Shipley, Butt, Horwitz, & Farbry, 1978). However, when the study was repeated (Shipley, Butt, & Horwitz, 1979) using patients who had previously undergone one or more endoscopy examinations, there was little benefit from videotape exposure. When the patient's repression-sensitization coping styles were taken into account, however, the data suggested that individuals who are vigilant about threat-related events (i.e., sensitizers) did show a decrease in anxiety as a function of the number of exposures to preparation videotapes, whereas those who characteristically avoid information pertinent to their lives (i.e., repressors) showed increase in arousal (heartrate) with repeated showings. The influence of cognitive processes and coping styles as mediators of anxiety are examined in the next section.

Prestress Levels of Anxiety and Coping Behavior

Janis's (1958) curvilinear model of the relationship between preoperative anxiety levels and postoperative recovery has stimulated a great deal of research in adults and has interesting implications for the preparation of children. This theory predicts that a moderate level of anxiety prior to surgery is predictive of satisfactory postsurgical adjustment. At a moderate level of arousal, thoughts and fantasies about the forthcoming operation are elicited. It is thought that in experiencing these surgery-related images, the patient begins to develop a more realistic view of the stressors to be encountered. Coping strategies could then be invoked. In this way, the patient engages in the constructive "work of worrying." Although there have been many studies generated by this theory, they are far from conclusive. The difficulties lie in the lack of a consensus of how to define anxiety. Janis used retrospective and global self-reports. Others use more specific physiological indices. The criterion for "moderate level" is not specified. Auerbach (1973) employed the Spielberger (1972) State-Trait Anxiety Inventory, and found some evidence that the A-State was curvilinearly related to postoperative adjustment.

Several studies have found results that directly challenge Janis's main assumptions (Johnson, Leventhal, & Dabbs, 1971; Levy, 1945; Martinez-Urrutia, 1975; Vernon, Foley, & Schulman, 1967). Another study (Vernon & Bigelow, 1974) found no evidence that cognitive preparation among adult hernia-repair patients was related to anticipatory fear or the work of worrying. On the other hand, a study by Egbert et al. (1964) using adults hospitalized for abdominal surgery found that group differences in the amount of pain medication requested postsurgery and the length of the hospital stay were related to instructions given to the experimental group regarding what to expect in terms of postsurgical pain and the intensity and duration of pain. These patients were also instructed in how to cope with this discomfort by relaxation suggestions and reassurances about the normalcy of the pain as a consequence of the surgery and the availability of pain medication if the level became intolerable. They were much less anxious than unprepared subjects, and required less pain medication. The methodologic flaw of this study was that the manipulation to facilitate the "work of worrying" was repeatedly given to the experimental treatment group throughout the convalescent period, whereas no similar interaction with staff occurred in the control group. There may have been subtle experimenter bias in persuading subjects to tolerate the pain without medication.

Other investigators (Fenz & Epstein, 1967; Shipley, Butt, & Horwitz, 1979; Speisman, Lazarus, Mordkoff, & Davison, 1964; Wolff, Friedman, Hofer, & Mason, 1964) have found that subjects' defensive disposition and prestress anxiety level were predictive of how successfully they coped with a stressful situation. The Janis model predicted that highly defensive patients tend not to experience presurgical anxiety. The absence of preoperative anxiety leaves the patient unprepared for the distress of surgery, and consequently leads to a poorer postsurgical adjustment.

The influence of preoperative information on recovery in surgical patients has been found to interact with individual differences in preferred mode of dealing with stress. In two studies (Andrew, 1970; DeLong, 1971), patients were classified as "copers," who preferred vigilant or sensitizing defenses, or "avoiders," who preferred denial-type of defense or nonspecific preferences. Among hernia-repair patients, copers showed the best recovery from surgery, deniers showed the poorest—particularly if they received specific information about the risks of surgery prior to their operations (Andrew, 1970). In a similar study, DeLong (1971) found that individuals given specific information had less complicated recoveries, particularly if they were classified as "copers." The avoiders showed the poorest recovery, regardless of whether they received specific information about surgery or general hospital information.

The internal-external locus of control dimension has been used widely as a correlate of the patient's response to stressful events. The most popular scale (Rotter, 1966) used to measure the generalized expectancy of individuals regarding the causes for their experiences has twenty-three items that classify individuals as to their belief in their own control over events. Those scoring high on internal locus of control hold the belief that outcomes of interactions between persons and events that befall them are, at least in part, determinable by the acts of those persons. An external locus of control, on the other hand, refers to the belief that events occur for reasons that are irrelevant to a person's actions and thus are beyond attempts at controlling them. The locus of control orientation has accounted for individuals' adjustment to oral surgery. In a study that evaluated the effects of locus of control on the patient's anxiety regarding oral surgery (Auerbach, Kendall, Cuttler, & Levitt, 1976), the internal-oriented individuals recovered much better after being prepared by specific information about surgery and postoperative care, whereas the external-oriented subjects did better with more general information about the setting, dentists, and general procedures. In a different study (Seeman & Evans, 1962) it was found that hospitalized tuberculosis patients classified as internals knew more about their illness and pursued information relevant to their illness more often than did those patients who were classified as externals.

Wallston et al. (1976) have now developed a health-focused locus-of-control scale. Hypertensive patients with internal beliefs that they themselves are responsible for their health are more apt to seek information about their illness. A child version of the health-focused locus-of-control scale has begun to be validated (Parcel & Meyer, 1978).

Findings in the research just discussed demonstrate the necessity for developing intervention techniques most appropriate for individuals who differ in their typical mode of dealing with stress. However, the results are not always clear. Cohen and Lazarus (1973) investigated sixty-one adult surgical patients classified into three groups based on whether they showed avoidance, vigilance, or both kinds of coping behavior concerning their surgical problem. The five recovery variables included days in the hospital, number of pain medications, minor medical complications, negative psychological reactions, and the sum of these. The results showed that the vigilance group had the most complicated postoperative recovery, although only two recovery variables (days in the hospital and minor complications) were statistically significant. Coping dispositions, anxiety, and life stress showed no clear or consistent relationships with recovery.

A study of female patients aged eighteen to sixty-eight undergoing abdominal surgery (Sime, 1973) investigated the Janis-Leventhal (1968) hypotheses regarding the relationship of preoperative fear level, extent of information seeking, and amount of information received about surgery. There was no consistent support for a curvilinear relationship between level of preoperative fear and favorable recovery in the moderate fear group. Amount of information was related to postoperative negative affect.

The effectiveness of two stress-reducing strategies was assessed in allaying the anxiety of adult patients about to undergo major surgery (Langer, Janis, & Wolfer, 1975). The first strategy entails coping by the cognitive reappraisal of anxiety-provoking events, calming self-talk, and cognitive control through selective attention. The second strategy consists of supplying information about the threatening event, along with reassurances for the purpose of producing emotional inoculation. Subjects were exposed to either the coping device, the preparatory information, both strategies, or neither. The prediction that the coping device would effectively reduce both preoperative and postoperative stress was confirmed. An analysis of nurses' ratings of preoperative stress showed a significant main effect for the coping device, as well as one of the postoperative measures (number of pain relievers requested and proportion of patients requesting sedatives). The preparatory information, however, did not produce any significant effects on these postoperative measures. This study attempted to parcel out the separate contributions of coping strategy and information. This variable of information is often confounded in psychological preparations and must be studied separately in order to judge the effectiveness of the psychological preparation above and beyond the information given.

The predictions from Janis's model may not be directly relevant in young children. Many authors have mentioned that children are likely to have distorted ideas about hospitalization and illness and that such ideas may contribute to psychological upset. Freud (1952) emphasized that the response of the child to surgery does not depend upon the type or seriousness of the operation but on the type and depth of fantasies aroused by it. Children's conceptions range from fantasies of punishment, mutilation, and castration to fears of abandonment (Deutsch, 1942; Freud, 1952; Gips, 1956; Erikson, 1958). Gellert (1958), in a controlled study investigating 102 hospitalized and nonhospitalized children four to sixteen years of age, found that two-thirds of her subjects attributed illness partially or entirely to transgressions against rules or to the omission of recommended acts. Given these descriptions, one must inform children about the impending hospital experience by alleviating the misinformation or distorted views that they have. Thus, it is suggested that psychological preparation must be specific and age appropriate to allay rather than enhance upset. Plank (1971) further stated that some children need their defenses during an acute hospitalization.

In the literature concerning children, Prugh and his collaborators (Prugh, Staub, Sands, Kirschbaum, & Lenihan, 1953) and Jackson, Winkley, Faust, and Cermack (1952) suggest that preparatory communications can have a marked influence in preventing depressive reactions and other adverse sequelae of surgery and hospitalization in young children. In these studies, unfortunately, the communications were confounded with other important variables, such as the fact that some mothers were present at the time of distressing events. Raters were also aware of the experimental treatment manipulation. Moran (1963) attempted to improve on this by specifically presenting the preparatory communications to both parents and children awaiting tonsillectomies. He found fewer signs of emotional disturbance during hospital convalescence and at home in these children than in a matched control group receiving only standard hospital care. In our own investigations, we have avoided showing the film to parents and have matched our samples for number of parents remaining with the child overnight. The variable of separation may also have different effects depending upon the age of the child, the parent-child relationship, and the length of separation. This is carefully reviewed in Vernon et al. (1965).

In a study of children's stress reactions to cast removal, a relationship was found between the type of preparatory communication and distress ratings of the children during the procedure. The study (Johnson, Kirchhoff, & Endress, 1975) found that children who received a taped message about the sensations that would accompany cast removal (including the sound of the saw) had fewer observed signs of stress than a control group that had not received such preparation. A group that received general instructions about the procedure did not differ significantly from the control group. In addition, pulse rate increased significantly from the waiting room to fifteen to thirty seconds into the cast removal in the control group and general procedure group but not in the group that had received information about sensations. The sensory preparatory information had its greatest effect on the reduction of distress for those children who admitted some fear of the impending procedure.

Burstein and Meichenbaum (1979) attempted to test Janis's theory more directly with children. They compared children expecting minor surgery on relative preference for hospital-relevant or nonrelevant toys one week prior to, immediately after, and one week following surgery. The study is mostly correlative; the measures of anxiety and defensiveness leave much to be desired. However, they found that a low level of anxiety before hospitalization is marginally associated with a high level of anxiety following hospitalization, which parallels Janis's findings with adults. Children rated high in defensiveness spent much less time with stress-relevant toys in the prehospitalization group. Most of the other relationships failed to support the theory.

A study employing the Palmar Sweat Index (PSI) was used to evaluate the effectiveness of preoperative preparation of puppet therapy for children aged five to nine who were admitted for minor surgery (Johnson & Stockdale, 1975). Although there was an immediate reduction of arousal as measured by PSI immediately after puppet therapy, there was an increase in PSI from the posttreatment measurement to the evening prior to surgery. The authors interpret this as caused by the children's greater knowledge, compared to control subjects, about hospital operative procedures they would encounter. This was seen as a temporary increase, in that the later postsurgery measure found those children who had been exposed to puppet therapy were less anxious than were control subjects the evening after surgery. This may be interpreted as supportive of the Janis hypothesis.

In our own research, there are some findings supportive of the Janis position. In the first experiment and in the replication (Study 3), children who saw the film showed a significant increase in arousal immediately after viewing it. However, at the preoperative and postoperative assessments, not only were they lower in physiological arousal, but they also expressed fewer medical concerns and showed less anxiety than those children seeing an unrelated film. Further tests are needed to tell whether this implies that the film allowed the children to prepare more effectively for surgery or simply that the relevance of the film led to more interest or attention that was reflected in palmar sweating. However, the film conveys realistic information regarding the procedures they will undergo and the pain that will occur after surgery. The vicarious experience that viewing *Ethan* evokes in the viewer through his statements of his fears and by his cooperation with the procedures may contribute to the film's effectiveness.

The second study presented here also supported the theory that arousal facilitates the handling of the stress. The older children who showed an increase in physiological arousal upon seeing the film one week in advance of their hospitalization showed a significant decrease in physiological arousal at the preoperative assessment. In addition, they decreased their report of medical concerns from preoperative to postoperative assessment (four weeks after discharge from the hospital). The younger children benefited more from film preparation on the day of admission than from advanced preparation. They also showed an immediate postfilm increase in arousal, followed by a decrease the night prior to surgery and at the posthospital assessment, whereas younger children viewing the film one week in advance showed progressive increases in palmar sweating throughout their hospital experience.

Parent-Child Relationships in Children's Adjustment to Surgery

Effects of Disciplinary Techniques

Although it is a widely held view that the child with a poor prehospital adjustment is especially vulnerable to psychological upset, there have been few research studies that have specifically investigated this area. Case studies by Richter (1943) suggested that children suffering severe emotional disturbances during and following illness were subservient, docile, perfectionistic, nonaggressive, and/or repressed prior to illness.

Jessner, Blom, and Waldfogel (1952) were among the first systematically to investigate children's reactions during their hospitalization for surgery. They found that children with previous neurotic tendencies showed the most severe postoperative disturbances regardless of the type of preparation received. They reported interesting shifts in the anxiety concerns of children of different ages. Children younger than five showed the greatest fear of hospitalization and separation; children aged five to seven were most afraid of hospitalization and the operation; children aged seven to ten were afraid of the hospitalization, the operation, and the anesthesia; and children aged ten to fourteen were afraid mostly of the anesthesia and the accompanying threat of loss of self-control and consciousness. This suggests that age must be considered a factor in assessing the degree of severity of the child's reaction. Many children older than seven can inhibit aggressive and immature reactions during the hospital experience, only to show a posthospital period of maladjustment.

The manner in which poorly adjusted children manifest their reactions to surgery has also been addressed. Several authors (Jackson, 1942; Prugh et al., 1953; Senn, 1945) have suggested that prehospital symptoms are intensified by hospitalization because they are related to the child's personality structure and represent characteristic patterns of adaptation. Thus, it is felt that the child with phobic tendencies prior to hospitalization will show an increase in phobic concerns following the experience.

In part, the development of fear is related to children's modeling of the fearful behaviors of others. The development of fear is also associated with the manner in which they themselves learn to master other fearful situations, such as getting a haircut, going to school for the first time, staying away from home overnight, and so on.

To investigate the relationship between how parents have handled a child's past reactions to potentially stressful situations and how well the child has coped with the stress of hospitalization, a retrospective investigation was conducted on children who had participated in our earlier studies (Zabin & Melamed, in press). A questionnaire was developed to assess the use of different reinforcement strategies used by parents with their child in fearful situations. The parents' responses to this questionnaire were then correlated with their child's anxiety during hospitalization for elective surgery in the Melamed and Siegel (1975) study. The questionnaire contained fourteen items representing hypothetical situations in which children often become fearful or refuse to engage in the feared act. These items included having a haircut, an injection, an operation, or a tooth drilled, approaching a puppy, fear of thunder and lightning, and being teased. Both parents were asked to respond individually to each of these items regarding how they would deal with each situation with their child if it came up at the present time. Each item had five response alternatives representing the use of either positive reinforcement, punishment, physical force, reinforcement of dependency, or the use of modeling and reassurance. The option of describing another alternative response to the problem situation was also given. A total score was obtained representing the frequency with which each parent used each of the techniques represented. In addition, both a combined score and a score representing the disagreement between mothers and fathers were calculated.

Parents of the children who participated in the Melamed and Siegel (1975) project were invited by mail to fill out this "Child Development Questionnaire" as it related to their child who had been hospitalized. This data was gathered eight to twelve months after the surgery. Responses to the questionnaire were received from 80 percent (N = 36) of the mothers and 67 percent (N = 30) of the fathers in the forty-five cases contacted.

The results revealed that parents who tended to use positive reinforcement, modeling, and reassurance were more likely to have children with lower anxiety scores on several of the measures assessed during and following the hospital experience. On the other hand, children with high anxiety (across all measures) at all assessment periods were more likely to have parents who used a high proportion of punishment, force, and reinforcement of dependent behaviors in the management of potentially stressful experiences.

These results, because of their correlational nature, do not necessarily reflect causality. However, they do suggest that when children come from a home in which positive reinforcement for approaching feared situations has been used consistently, they will most likely exhibit greater coping behaviors with less associated anxiety during their hospital experience. The results further suggest that when fathers use punishment to threaten children for their reluctance to face threatening events, their children are most likely to exhibit anxiety-related behaviors when facing a new, fearful situation. On several measures of anxiety, the parental use of reinforcement for dependency was associated with greater reports of stress in the child during the hospital experience. Thus, it seems that modeling and reassurance in dealing with fear was more often related to a child's ability to cope with the stress of the hospital experience.

Importance of Joint Parent-Child Preparation

In a series of well-controlled studies, Mahaffy (1965), Skipper, Leonard, and Rhymes (1968), Wolfer and Visintainer (1975), and Visintainer and Wolfer (1975) investigated the effect of preparing the mothers of children having minor surgery. This is based on the emotional contagion hypothesis (Campbell, 1957; VanderVeer, 1949), which holds that a parent's emotional state may be transmitted to a young child, and on the clinical observation that emotionally upset or uninformed parents are often unable to assist their children in coping with stress. The Wolfer and Visintainer studies best meet the research requirements of this review, and are elaborated on here. They hypothesized that children and parents who received special psychological preparation and continued supportive care, in contrast to unprepared control children and mothers, would show less behavioral upset and better coping and adjustment as indicated on the following ten dependent variables:

1. observer ratings of the children's upset behavior and cooperation with procedures at five potential stress points,
2. pulse rates at admission, and before and after the blood test and preoperative injections,
3. resistance to anesthesia induction,
4. recovery room medications,
5. ease of fluid intake,
6. time to first voiding,
7. posthospital adjustment on Vernon et al. (1965) Posthospital Behavior Questionnaire,

8. mothers' self-ratings of anxiety at potential stress points throughout the hospitalization,
9. mothers' rated satisfaction with various aspects of the nursing and medical care they received, and
10. mothers' ratings of adequacy of information they received.

The experimental condition was a combination of psychological preparation and supportive care for mother-child dyads that was provided at six stress points:

1. admission,
2. shortly before the blood test,
3. late in the afternoon the day before the operation,
4. shortly before the preoperative medications,
5. before transport to the operating room, and
6. upon return from the recovery room.

The preparation with the mothers was intended to explore and clarify their feelings and thoughts, to provide accurate information and appropriate reassurance, and to explain how the mother could help care for her child. The child component of the "stress point nursing care" included information, sensory expectations, role identification, rehearsal, and support. The results of the study supported the hypothesis that children and parents who received systematic psychological preparation and continued supportive care, in contrast to those who did not, would show less upset behavior, more cooperation in the hospital, and fewer posthospital adjustment problems. The experimental group had significantly lower mean upset ratings and higher mean cooperation ratings at each of the stress points than the control group. Children in the prepared condition demonstrated somewhat greater ease of fluid intake, significantly lower heart rates after the blood test and before and after the preoperative medication, significantly lower incidence of resistance to anesthesia induction, and significantly lower posthospital adjustment scores. Younger children (aged three to six) showed greater upset and less cooperation than older children (aged seven to fourteen). Parents in the experimental group had significantly lower self-ratings of anxiety, higher ratings of the adequacy of the information received, and greater satisfaction with the hospital care than parents in the control group. Thus, there seemed to be support for beneficial effects of systematic preparation and support for hospitalized children as well as their parents.

However, several methodological problems in this study are apparent:

1. observer bias was introduced in that the nurse-rater occasionally observed the nurse-researcher in the act of preparation,
2. parents who were given specialized attention by the nurse may have felt obligated to rate their satisfactions higher, and
3. because only one nurse-researcher was used in preparation, it might have been the warm, trusting relationship she developed, rather than the specific preparation, that was responsible for the results,
4. although no children had been hospitalized within the past year, there was no indication that the groups were matched for prior hospital experience.

In another study, Visintainer and Wolfer (1975) attempted to parcel out the specific treatment contribution of the supportive relationship, information alone, or information in combination with a supportive relationship. Therefore, the addition of a single preparation was not significantly different from the supportive care condition, during different stressors. An additional control for placebo effects of the supportive relationship was examined by continuing support throughout the hospital experience.

The results indicated that the general trend was for children in the stress-point preparation and single-session preparation conditions to have lower upset, higher cooperation, and higher ease-of-fluid-intake ratings than those children in the supportive care and control groups. When the single session preparation was compared separately to the supportive care and control conditions, it was significantly more effective only for blood test upset, cooperation ratings, and the nurses' preoperative medication cooperation rating. The consistent supportive care group was significantly more cooperative than the control group during the blood test and when given the preoperative medication. Thus, on these behavioral ratings, only the stress-point preparation was consistently superior to the other treatment conditions, except when contrasted to the single-session preparation. This would support the important role of information in anxiety reduction. In terms of posthospital adjustment, however, the single session preparation was not significantly different from the supportive care condition, which, in turn, was not significantly different from the control condition. Parents in the stress-point preparation group were less anxious, more adequately informed, and more satisfied with the care they received than were the parents in the other three groups. Thus, the benefit of combining information with the opportunity of a supporting relationship with a nurse at particularly stressful points during the hospital experience was demonstrated. Additional research is needed to examine more clearly the role played by parent preparation. Ideally, one must compare parent preparation alone, child preparation alone, and concurrent parent and child preparation in order to evaluate clearly the effectiveness of joint preparation.

Evaluation of Behavioral Approaches in Preparation for Childbirth

The between-groups evaluation of therapeutic effectiveness can be applied to other problem areas. Two excellent studies (Condas & Scenticka, 1972; Frazier, 1974) compared behavioral treatment for childbirth with more traditional natural childbirth preparation, such as Lamaze (1970) training. This research area presents a problem in terms of the subject variable, in that control groups of unprepared patients are misleading. The woman who chooses not to receive any preparation for childbirth is probably quite different in her attitudes, fears, and motivation for education regarding the birth process. In addition, it is probably unethical to deny a couple the opportunity for childbirth preparation so that the researcher can have an "unprepared" sample upon which to compare treatment effectiveness. The birth experiences of a new mother are quite different from those of a multipara, both physiologically and psychologically. It is important, therefore, to distinguish between these two subtypes in any research population. The popularity of natural childbirth in this country and others must indicate that some reinforcing experiences occur as a couple shares the preparation and birth experience. Many of the current strategies, such as Lamaze and Childbirth Without Pain, share behavioral components. They discuss the importance of information about the impending event, and often provide modeling experiences, either through films or actual sharing between couples about delivery experiences. There is emphasis on being relaxed and employing breathing exercises for the transition phase of labor, at which point the child's progress out of the birth canal can be hindered if muscle tension accompanies the contractions of the uterus. The woman and her assistant (usually the child's father) practice a coping strategy to be used later in the actual situation. This behavioral rehearsal includes anticipation of phases of contraction with progress in labor and techniques to use in conjunction with the physiological demands at this time. They practice a variety of distraction procedures or associated responses incompatible with fear (relaxation and breathing exercises) that become conditioned to the cues that will most likely occur during labor.

It is difficult to evaluate which component of this prepared childbirth—the togetherness, the relaxation, or the information—affects the subjective experience. There have been a few attempts to evaluate this by comparison with control groups that contain a combination of these elements. Condas and Scenticka (1972) compared systematic desensitization with prophylactic training typically employed in prepared childbirth classes. They selected forty pregnant women (primiparas and multiparas) who had chosen to be prepared for childbirth. These women were also selected because they received high scores on the Taylor Manifest Anxiety Scale (TMAS). The patients were matched on age, parity, education, and anxiety level, and were assigned to either systematic desensitization or traditional prophylactic training. The desensitization group constructed hierarchies related to stressful aspects of labor and delivery. The results indicate tht both procedures reduced anxiety (TMAS); however, this was even greater for women in the systematic desensitization group. In addition, the length of labor was significantly shorter in these latter subjects, even when the data were analyzed separately for primiparas and multiparas. Finally, the women in the systematic desensitization group were rated by the obstetrician as experiencing less pain and less restlessness than women in the psychoprophylactic group. These findings are impressive given that the women in the control group also received training. It would be interesting to have a group of untreated women who would have undertaken such training, but for whom no opportunity was available at that particular setting.

The effectiveness of biofeedback-assisted relaxation (electromyograph or galvanic skin response) has also been found to facilitate labor and delivery (Frazier, 1974). The thirty volunteers received either relaxation training or no treatment. However, 96 percent of both groups had had previous Lamaze training. The treatment subjects had a minimum of two biofeedback-assisted relaxation sessions, and were told to practice at home between sessions. The subjects all had delivered before. The biofeedback training group had significantly shorter first stages of labor, experienced more rapid cervical dilation and fetal descent, and used less analgesic medication than the control subjects.

Although neither of the two research projects described is definitive in terms of what the effective component was, the fact that the addition of the behavioral treatment (systematic desensitization or biofeedback) affected meaningful clinical indices during the birth process argues for the importance of future research.

Methodological Considerations for Future Research

Although much useful information has come from the many studies reviewed in this chapter, it is difficult to present a simple list of general conclusions. This is primarily because of the differences between experimenters in theoretical orientation and the many conditions that vary between studies. Thus, the following discussion attempts mainly to outline the primary variables that must be taken into account before proceeding with an assessment of hospital preparation strategies.

Definition of Patient Characteristics

The review has pointed out the necessity of matching patients under consideration in different treatment groups on variables of age, sex, race, prehospital personality, and previous hospital experience to control for influences that markedly reflect the individual's response to the hospital experience, regardless of the type of preparation received.

Measures Used to Assess the Reduction of Fear

There is considerable evidence that much of the lack of convergence across studies is caused by a broad range of responses measured with very little consistency. The use of multidimensional analysis in our series of studies allowed for the replication and clarification of treatment effects. The use of broad therapeutic strategies, such as modeling, may have their effect by concurrently altering behaviors that encourage emotional expression, rewarding approach behaviors toward potentially stressful events, and reinforcing the child for coping with new stresses. It is more likely that these approaches will also reduce physiological upset and promote cooperative behavior during the hospital experience.

Time of Measurement

Retrospective report, or observation only during the actual period of hospitalization, limits the interpretation of the long-term effects of preparatory treatment. The research strategy that includes both pre-hospital experiences and posthospital recovery permits a more complete evaluation. Our own research strategy has focused on obtaining information about prehospital experiences that may affect the child's adjustment, such as the parents' predisposition toward medical procedures or their reinforcement of the child's coping strategies in other fearful situations. The assessment of the child's base level of anxiety may also be important in evaluating the responsiveness to any treatment preparation. The research on the prestress level of anxiety as it relates to postsurgical recovery is not definitive and requires careful assessment of the chronic and situational anxiety that the child brings with him or her. During the hospital experience, it is important to sample children's behaviors during specific stress-related experiences such as the blood test, anesthetic induction, or recovery period. Finally, to determine the lasting effects of the treatment manipulation, it is important to reevaluate the child's behavior, attitudes, and somatic arousal responses in a posthospital situation that has some components similar to that of the original stress experience. In our surgery project, we have routinely reassessed the children at the surgeon's one-month follow-up examination, which occurs in the hospital and often involves the removal of sutures and a physical examination. A number of studies have merely repeated the assessment procedures in the home, where many factors and diverse experiences make it difficult to evaluate the persistence of the effects of the hospital experience on the child. Therefore, whenever possible, posthospital measures should include some medically related situation.

Hospital Practices in Effect during the Investigation

Investigators assessing the potency of a psychological preparation usually present it in the context of procedures already being used. In our research, we made sure that all children had the same degree of staff preparation prior to our preoperative evaluation. At that time, the only difference that could contribute to group differences was the fact that a hospital-relevant film had been observed. Once the staff is convinced of the efficacy of the therapy, they might allow you to evaluate this intervention in the absence of other variables that might affect it. If one develops an intervention program that involves staff in the formulation, but only minimally involves their time in its implementation and evaluation, it is more likely to receive the necessary cooperation.

Complexity of Treatment Variables

Many of the studies reviewed in this chapter failed to give a precise definition of the procedures used. The use of compound treatments, in which information and support were given, makes it difficult to parcel out the effective components. The use of film modeling guarantees that the procedures employed with each patient are identical. Editing capability makes videotape ideal for separating out components of treatment and evaluating them by devising different versions of the therapeutic tape.

It is also important that the treatment be evaluated with regard to a homogeneous problem. For instance, children with several surgical experiences who repeatedly undergo complicated procedures should not be lumped together with those undergoing minor elective surgery.

Lack of Statistical Evaluation

The use of global measures is difficult to quantify in such a way that parametric statistics can be applied. Research in the area of hospital preparation has suffered by a marked lack of concern with the establishment of reliability and validity of the measures used. The importance of observers' being unaware of group assignment or experimental hypotheses should not be overlooked. One way to minimize observer bias is to include a sample of children who are also observed but are not exposed to any of the treatment procedures.

Need for Future Investigations

In addition to the need to refine measures of stress in children undergoing hospitalization, the development of behavioral measures that would be sensitive to changes even in sedated children is necessary for evaluating the immediate postsurgical period.

There is a lack of longitudinal investigation on children; we have little data about the vulnerability of children to the hospital experience. In addition, long-term follow-up data on patients who received hospital preparation might reveal the influence of these procedures on the patients' future response to medical procedures, attitudes toward health care professionals, and future health-seeking behavior. Vernon et al. (1965) appropriately concluded that there is a neglect of the psychological benefits that may accrue to individuals through their experience in mastering their distress during hospitalization. Most studies measure failures in dealing with stress. There is a great need for research evaluation to include measures of the patient's competence.

Summary

The need for psychological preparation for hospitalization has led to the use of multiple treatment preparations. This has made it difficult to assess the relative contribution of the specific procedures used.

Our own studies, which were designed to answer specific questions regarding the efficacy of filmed modeling in hospital preparation, have yielded findings that are consistent with previous research and are used throughout the chapter as illustrations of research methodology.

The relationship between the amount of arousal precipitated by film preparation and the degree of later stress reduction has implications for Janis's contention of the facilitative effect of a moderate amount of preoperative anxiety. However, the interpretation of this data awaits further systematic experimentation. The increased autonomic activation may indicate the observer's identification with the film model, a true increase of anxiety, or merely some nonspecific attention factor. Other studies that bear on the Janis hypothesis were reviewed.

The vulnerability of children to hospitalization may depend on previous successful coping experience and may be influenced by their parents' handling of their stress in relation to earlier childhood experiences. It was found that parents who typically used positive reinforcement in encouraging their children to approach new situations and concurrently used modeling and reassurance had children who coped more effectively with their hospital or dental experiences than if force, threat, or reinforcement of dependency were the primary approaches used. Mothers who themselves reported the most general fears had children who were most anxious on measures of chronic anxiety during the posthospital experience. These findings point up the need for joint preparation of parents and children when hospitalization is indicated. The studies reviewed indicated that this would be worthwhile. Individual differences in the parents' ability to prepare children must be studied. Since the general trend is to encourage the parents to remain with their children throughout the hospital stay, an available population for the evaluation of the relative contribution of joint preparation of child and parent exists. The age of the child and the particular type of preparation must be considered within this context.

To illustrate another application of the between-group design to other health care practices, two studies evaluating behavioral treatments for natural childbirth were presented. The subject and measurement problems unique to the area were discussed.

In conclusion, the area of research into the psychological preparation of individuals for hospitalization has been one in which behavioral researchers have already made notable contributions. The study of preparation for hospitalization is a fertile naturalistic setting for asking more general questions about the nature of fear, its measurement and reduction. Research in this area has only begun to yield significant findings. The clinical questions need to be asked more clearly. Research designs that compare treatment procedures must carefully control other pertinent variables that also affect reaction to hospitalization. A greater concern with the reliability of measures and common usage of these across studies would provide information about the validity of the measurement instruments.

References

Adelson, R., & Goldfried, M. R. Modeling and the fearful child patient. *Journal of Dentistry for Children,* 1970, *37,* 476.

Andrew, J. Recovery from surgery, with and without preparatory instruction for three coping styles. *Journal of Personality and Social Psychology,* 1970, *15,* 223–226.

Auerbach, S. M. Trait-state anxiety and adjustment to surgery. *Journal of Consulting and Clinical Psychology,* 1973, *40,* 264–271.

Auerbach, S. M., Kendall, P. C., Cuttler, H. F., & Levitt, N. R. Anxiety, locus of control, type of preparatory information, and adjustment to dental surgery. *Journal of Consulting and Clinical Psychology,* 1976, *44,* 809–818.

Auerbach, S. M., & Kilmann, N. Crisis intervention: A review of outcome research. *Psychological Bulletin,* 1977, *84,* 1189–1217.

Bandura, A. *Principles of behavior modification.* New York: Holt, Rinehart & Winston, 1969.

Bandura, A., Grusec, J. E., & Menlove, F. L. Vicarious extinction of avoidance behaviors. *Journal of Personality and Social Psychology,* 1967, *5,* 16–23.

Bandura, A., Ross, D., & Ross, S. A. Imitation of film-mediated aggressive models. *Journal of Abnormal and Social Psychology,* 1963, *66,* 3–11.

Bruch, M. Influence of model characteristics on psychiatric inpatients' interview anxiety. *Journal of Abnormal Psychology,* 1975, *84,* 290–294.

Burstein, S., & Meichenbaum, D. The work of worrying in children undergoing surgery. *Journal of Abnormal Child Psychology,* 1979, *7,* 121–132.

Campbell, E. Effects of mothers' anxiety on infants' behavior. Unpublished doctoral dissertation, Yale University, 1957.

Cassell, S. Effects of brief puppet therapy upon the emotional responses of children undergoing cardiac catheterization. *Journal of Consulting Psychology,* 1965, *29,* 1–8.

Castaneda, A., McCandless, B. R., & Palermo, D. S. The children's form of the Manifest Anxiety Scale. *Child Development,* 1956, *27,* 317–326.

Chapman, A. H., Loeb, D. G., & Gibbons, M. J. Psychiatric aspects of hospitalization of children. *Archives of Pediatrics,* 1956, *73,* 77–88.

Cohen, F., & Lazarus, R. Active coping processes, coping dispositions, and recovery from surgery. *Psychosomatic Medicine,* 1973, *35,* 375–389.

Condas, O., & Scenticka, B. Systematic desensitization as a method of preparation for childbirth. *Journal of Behavior Therapy and Experimental Psychiatry,* 1972, *3,* 51–54.

DeLong, R. Individual differences in patterns of anxiety arousal, stress-relevant information and recovery from surgery. Unpublished doctoral dissertation, University of California, Los Angeles, 1970. *Dissertation Abstracts International,* 1971, *32,* 554B.

Deutsch, H. Some psychoanalytic observations in surgery. *Psychosomatic Medicine,* 1942, *4,* 105–115.

Dimock, H. G. *The child in hospital: A study of his emotional and social well-being.* Philadelphia: Davis, 1960.

Dumas, R. G. Psychological preparation for surgery. *American Journal of Nursing,* 1963, *63,* 52–55.

Egbert, L., Bartlett, G., Welch, C., & Bartlett, M. Reduction of postoperative pain by encouragement and instruction of patients. *New England Journal of Medicine,* 1964, *270,* 825–827.

Erikson, F. Reactions of children to hospital experience. *Nursing Outlook,* 1958, *6,* 501–504.

Fenz, W., & Epstein, S. Gradients of physiological arousal of experienced and novice parachutists as a function of approaching jump. *Psychosomatic Medicine,* 1967, *29,* 33–51.

Flanders, J. A review of research on imitative behavior. *Psychological Bulletin,* 1968, *69,* 316–337.

Frazier, L. M. Using biofeedback to aid relaxation during childbirth. *Birth and Family Journal,* 1974, *1,* 4.

Freud, A. The role of bodily illness in the mental life of children. *The Psychoanalytic Study of the Child,* 1952, *7,* 69–80.

Geidel, S., & Gulbrandsen, M. Use of videotape as a modeling tool for reducing stress in preschool children having a physical examination. Unpublished master of science in nursing thesis. University of Wisconsin, 1974.

Gellert, E. Reducing the emotional stress of hospitalization for children. *American Journal of Occupational Therapy*, 1958, *12*, 125–129.

Giller, D. W. Some psychological factors in recovery from surgery. *Hospital Topics*, 1963, *41*, 83–85.

Gips, C. How illness experiences are interpreted by hospitalized children. Unpublished doctoral dissertation, Columbia University, 1956.

Heller, J. A. *The hospitalized child and his family.* Baltimore: The Johns Hopkins Press, 1967.

Hodgson, R., & Rachman, S. Desynchrony in measures of fear. *Behaviour Research and Therapy*, 1974, *12*, 319–326.

Jackson, E. B. Treatment of the young child in the hospital. *American Journal of Orthopsychiatry*, 1942, *12*, 56–62.

Jackson, K., Winkley, R., Faust, O. A., & Cermack, E. The problem of emotional trauma in the hospital treatment of children. *Journal of the American Medical Association*, 1952, *149*, 1536–1538.

Janis, I. L. *Psychological stress.* New York: Wiley, 1958.

Janis, I. L. & Leventhal, H. Human reaction to stress. In E. Brogatta and W. Lambert (Eds.), *Handbook of personality theory and research.* Boston: Rand McNally, 1968.

Jessner, L., Blom, G. E., & Waldfogel, S. Emotional implications of tonsillectomy and adenoidectomy in children. In R. S. Eisler (Ed.), *The psychoanalytic study of the child.* New York: International Universities Press, 1952.

Johnson, J. E., Kirchhoff, K., & Endress, M. P. Altering children's distress behavior during orthopedic cast removal. *Nursing Research*, 1975, *24*, 404–410.

Johnson, J. E., & Leventhal, H. Effects of accurate expectations and behavioral instructions on reactions during a noxious medical examination. *Journal of Personality and Social Psychology*, 1974, *29*, 710–718.

Johnson, J. E., Leventhal, H., & Dabbs, J. M. Contribution of emotional and instrumental response processes in adaptation to surgery. *Journal of Personality and Social Psychology*, 1971, *20*, 1, 55–64.

Johnson, P., & Stockdale, D. Effects of puppet therapy on palmar sweating of hospitalized children. *Johns Hopkins Medical Journal*, 1975, *137*, 1–5.

Johnson, R., & Dabbs, J. M. Enumeration of active sweat glands: A simple physiological indicator of psychological changes. *Nursing Research*, 1967, *16*, 273–276.

Kaplan, A. M., & Hafner, A. J. Manifest anxiety in hospitalized children. *Journal of Clinical Psychology*, 1959, *15*, 301–302.

Kazdin, A. Covert modeling and the reduction of avoidance behavior. *Journal of Abnormal Psychology*, 1973, *81*, 87–95.

Kazdin, A. The effect of model identity and fear-relevant similarity on covert modeling. *Behavior Therapy*, 1974, *5*, 624–635.

Kleinknecht, R., & Bernstein, D. Short-term treatment of dental avoidance. *Journal of Behavior Therapy and Experimental Psychiatry,* in press.

Klinedienst, J. K. Relationship between Minnesota Multiphasic Personality Inventory and Personality Inventory for Children data from mothers of distrubed children. Unpublished doctoral dissertation, University of Minnesota, 1971.

Koppitz, E. M. *Psychological evaluation of children's human figure drawings.* New York: Grune and Stratton, 1968.

Kornhaber, R., & Schroeder, H. Importance of model similarity on extinction of avoidance behavior in children. *Journal of Consulting and Clinical Psychology,* 1975, *43,* 601–607.

Lacey, J. I. Somatic response patterning and stress: Some revisions of activation theory. In M. H. Appley & R. Trumbull (Eds.), *Psychological stress: Issues in research.* New York: Appleton-Century-Crofts, 1967.

Lamaze, F. *Painless childbirth, psychoprophylactic method.* (L. R. Celestin, trans.) Chicago: Regnery, 1970.

Lang, P. J. Fear reduction and fear behavior: Problems in treating a construct. *Research in Psychotherapy,* 1968, *3,* 90–102.

Lang, P. J. The psychophysiology of anxiety. In H. Akiskal (Ed.), *Psychiatric diagnosis: Exploration of biological criteria.* New York: Spectrum, 1977.

Lang, P. J., Melamed, B., & Hart, J. Automating the desensitization procedure: A psychophysiological analysis of fear modification. *Journal of Abnormal Psychology,* 1970, *76,* 220–234.

Langer, E., Janis, I., & Wolfer, J. Reduction of stress in surgical patients. *Journal of Experimental Social Psychology,* 1975, *11,* 155–165.

Levy, D. M. Psychic trauma of operations in children. *American Journal of Diseases of Children,* 1945, *69,* 7–25.

Living Things Are Everywhere, Encyclopaedia Britannica Educational Corporation, 425 North Michigan Avenue, Chicago, Ill., 60611, 1974.

Mahaffy, P., Jr. The effects of hospitalization on children admitted for tonsillectomy and adenoidectomy. *Nursing Research,* 1965, *14,* 12–19.

Martin, B., & Sroufe, L. A. In C. G. Costello (Ed.), *Symptoms of psychopathology.* New York: Wiley, 1970, pp. 216–259.

Martinez-Urrutia, A. Pain and anxiety in surgical patients. *Journal of Consulting and Clinical Psychology,* 1975, *43,* 437–442.

Meichenbaum, D. Examination of model characteristics in reducing avoidance behavior. *Journal of Personality and Social Psychology,* 1971, *17,* 298–307.

Melamed, B. G., Hawes, R. R., Heiby, E., & Glick, J. The use of filmed modeling to reduce uncooperative behavior of children during dental treatment. *Journal of Dental Research,* 1975, *54,* 797–801.

Melamed, B. G., Meyer, R., Gee, C., & Soule, L. The influence of time and type of preparation on children's adjustment to hospitalization. *Journal of Pediatric Psychology,* 1976, *1,* 31–37.

Melamed, B. G., & Siegel, L. J. Reduction of anxiety in children facing hospitalization and surgery by use of filmed modeling. *Journal of Consulting and Clinical Psychology,* 1975, *43,* 511–521.

Melamed, B. G., Weinstein, D., Hawes, R., & Katin-Borland, M. Reduction of fear-related dental management problems with use of filmed modeling. *Journal of the American Dental Association,* 1975, *90,* 822–826.

Melamed, B. G., Yurcheson, R., Fleece, E. L., Hutcherson, S., & Hawes, R. Effects of film modeling on the reduction of anxiety-related behaviors in individuals varying in level of previous experience in the stress situation. *Journal of Consulting and Clinical Psychology,* 1978, *46,* 1357–1367.

Mellish, R. W. P. Preparation of a child for hospitalization and surgery. *Pediatric Clinics of North America,* 1969, *16,* 543–553.

Moran, P. Experimental study of pediatric admissions. Master's report, Yale School of Nursing, 1963.

Murphy, L. *The widening world of childhood.* New York: Basic Books, 1962.

Neeley, J., Heckel, R., & Leichtman, H. The effect of race of model and response consequences to the model on imitation of children. *Journal of Social Psychology,* 1973, *89,* 225–231.

Newswanger, A. Hospital preparation of pre-school children as related to their behavior during and immediately following hospitalization for tonsillectomy and adenoidectomy. Unpublished master of science in home economics thesis, University of Delaware, May, 1974.

Nicholas, K., McCarter, R., & Heckel, B. Effects of race and sex on the imitation of television models. *Journal of Social Psychology,* 1971, *85,* 315–318.

Nowlis, V. Research with the mood adjective check list. In S. S. Tomkins and C. E. Izard (Eds.), *Affect, cognition, and personality.* New York: Springer, 1965.

O'Connor, R. D. Modification of social withdrawal through symbolic modeling. *Journal of Applied Behavior Analysis,* 1969, *2,* 15–22.

Parcel, G. S. & Meyer, M. P. Development of an instrument to measure children's health locus of control. *Health Education Monographs,* 1978, *6,* 149–159.

Plank, E. N. *Working with children in hospitals.* Cleveland: Case Western Reserve University Press, 1962 (2nd ed., 1971).

Prugh, D. G., Staub, E. M., Sands, H. H., Kirschbaum, R. M., & Lenihan, E. A. A study of the emotional reactions of children and families to hospitalization and illness. *American Journal of Orthopsychiatry,* 1953, *23,* 70–106.

Quay, H., & Quay, L. Behavior problems in early adolescence. *Child Development,* 1965, *36,* 215–220.

Rachman, S. Clinical application of observational learning, imitation and modeling. *Behavior Therapy,* 1972, *3,* 379–397.

Richter, H. G. Emotional disturbances of constant pattern following nonspecific respiratory infections. *Journal of Pediatrics,* 1943, *23,* 315–325.

Rosenkrans, M. Imitation in children as a function of perceived similarity to a social model and vicarious reinforcement. *Journal of Personality and Social Psychology,* 1967, *7,* 307–315.

Rotter, J. B. Generalized expectancies for internal versus external control of reinforcement. *Psychological Monographs,* 1966, *80,* (Whole No. 609).

Ruebush, B. K. Anxiety. In H. W. Stevenson (Ed.), *Child psychology*. The sixty-second yearbook of the National Society for the Study of Education. Chicago: University of Chicago Press, 1963.

Schaffer, H. R., & Callender, W. H. Psychological effects of hospitalization in infancy. *Pediatrics*, 1959, *24*, 528–539.

Scherer, M. W., & Nakamura, C. Y. A fear survey schedule for children (FSS–FC): A factor analytic comparison with manifest anxiety (CMAS). *Behaviour Research and Therapy*, 1968, 173–182.

Seeman, M. & Evans, J. W. Alienation and learning in a hospital setting. *American Sociological Review*, 1962, *27*, 772–783.

Senn, M. J. E. Emotional aspects of convalescence. *Child*, 1945, *10*, 24–28.

Shipley, R. H., Butt, J. H., & Horwitz, B. A. Preparation to reexperience a stressful medical examination: Effect of repetitious videotape exposure and coping style. *Journal of Consulting and Clinical Psychology*, 1979, *47*, 485–492.

Shipley, R. H., Butt, J., Horwitz, B., & Farbry, J. Preparation for a stressful medical procedure: Effect of amount of prestimulus exposure and coping style. *Journal of Consulting and Clinical Psychology*, 1978, *46*, 499–507.

Siegel, L. J. Preparation of children for hospitalization: A selected review of the research literature. *Journal of Pediatric Psychology*, 1976, *1*, 26–30.

————. Therapeutic modeling as a procedure to reduce stress associated with medical and dental treatment. Paper presented at the Association of Advancement of Behavior Therapy, Atlanta, 1977.

Sime, A. The relationship of preoperative fear, coping, and information to recovery from surgery. Unpublished doctoral dissertation, University of Minnesota, 1973.

Skipper, J., & Leonard, R. C. Children, stress and hospitalization: A field experiment. *Journal of Health and Social Behavior*, 1968, *9*, 275–287.

Skipper, J., Leonard, R. C., & Rhymes, J. Child hospitalization and social interaction: An experimental study of mothers' feelings of stress, adaptation and satisfaction. *Medical Care*, 1968, *6*, 496–506.

Smith, S. M. The effect of race, prestige, and vicarious reinforcement on imitative behavior, altruistic, motor and verbal. *Dissertation Abstract International*, 1972, *32(10–A)*, 5898.

Speisman, J., Lazarus, R., Mordkoff, A., & Davidson, L. Experimental reduction of stress based on ego defense theory. *Journal of Abnormal and Social Psychology*, 1964, *68*, 367–380.

Spielberger, C. D. Anxiety as an emotional state. In C. D. Spielberger (Ed.), *Anxiety: Current trends in theory and research*. New York: Academic Press, 1972.

Spielberger, C. D., Auerbach, S. M., Wadsworth, A. P., Dunn, T. M., & Taulbee, E. S. Emotional reactions to surgery. *Journal of Consulting and Clinical Psychology*, 1973, *40*, 33–38.

Thelen, M., Fry, R. A., Fehrenbach, P. A., & Frautschi, N. N. Therapeutic videotape and film modeling: A review. *Psychological Bulletin*, 1979, *86*, 701–720.

Thomson, M. L., & Sutarman, M. The identification and enumeration of active sweat glands in man from plastic impressions of the skin. *Transactions of the Royal Society of Tropical Medicine and Hygiene,* 1953, *47,* 412–417.

VanderVeer, A. The psychopathology of physical illness and hospital residence. *Quarterly Journal of Child Behavior,* 1949, *1,* 55–71.

Vernon, D. T. Use of modeling to modify children's responses to a natural, potentially stressful situation. *Journal of Applied Psychology,* 1973, *58,* 351–356.

Vernon, D. T., & Bailey, W. C. The use of motion pictures in the psychological preparation of children for induction of anesthesia. *Anesthesiology,* 1974, *40,* 68–72.

Vernon, D. T., & Bigelow, D. Effect of information about a potentially stressful situation on response to stress impact. *Journal of Personality and Social Psychology,* 1974, *29,* 50–59.

Vernon, D. T., Foley, J. M., & Schulman, J. L. Effect of mother-child separation and birth order on young children's responses to two potentially stressful situations. *Journal of Personality and Social Psychology,* 1967, *5,* 162–174.

Vernon, D. T., Foley, J. M., Sipowicz, R. R., & Schulman, J. L. *The psychological responses of children to hospitalization and illness.* Springfield, Ill.: Charles C. Thomas, 1965.

Visintainer, M., & Wolfer, J. Psychological preparation for surgical pediatric patients: The effect on children's and parents' stress responses and adjustment. *Pediatrics,* 1975, *56,* 187–202.

Wallston, B. S., Wallston, K. A., Kaplan, G. D., & Mardes, S. A. Development and validation of the Health Locus of Control Scale. *Journal of Consulting and Clinical Psychology,* 1976, *44,* 580–585.

Winer, B. J. *Statistical principles in experimental design.* New York: McGraw-Hill, 1962.

Winnett, R. L. The effect of modeling and play therapy techniques on children's adjustment to brief hospitalization and surgery. Paper presented at the Rocky Mountain Psychological Association Convention, Las Vegas, April, 1979.

Wirt, R. D., & Broen, W. E. Booklet for the Personality Inventory for Children. Minneapolis: Authors, 1958.

Wolfer, J., & Visintainer, M. Pediatric surgical patients' and parents' stress responses and adjustment as a function of psychological preparation and stress-point nursing care. *Nursing Research,* 1975, *24,* 244–255.

Wolff, C. T., Friedman, S. B., Hofer, M. A., & Mason, J. W. Relationship between psychological defenses and mean urinary 17-hydroxycorticosteroid excretion rates. *Psychosomatic Medicine,* 1964, *26,* 576–591.

Zabin, M., & Melamed, B. G. The relationship between parental discipline and children's ability to cope with stress. *Journal of Behavioral Assessment,* in press.

Films about Hospital Preparation

A Two Year Old Goes to the Hospital, University Film Library, New York, 1952.

Christine Has an Operation (audiotape filmstrip), W. B. Saunders Co., Philadelphia, Penn., 19105, 1974.

Ethan Has an Operation, Health Sciences Communication Center, Case Western Reserve University, Cleveland, Ohio, 44106, 1974.

Linda: Encounters in the Hospital (Cardiac Surgery), University of California, Extension Media Center, Berkeley, Calif., 94720, 1975.

Scott Goes to the Hospital, Alfred Higgins Productions, Inc., Los Angeles, Calif., 90069, 1973.

To Prepare a Child, Media Center, Children's Hospital, National Medical Center, Washington, D. C., 1976.

We Won't Leave You, Edward A. Mason, M.D., Mental Health Training Film Program, 58 Fenwood Road, Boston, Mass., 02115, 1975.

When a Child Enters the Hospital, Polymorph Films, Boston, Mass., 02115, 1975.

You're Going to Have an Operation, Learning Resources Center, University of Florida College of Medicine, Gainesville, Fla., 32610, 1977.

9

Management of Dental Patients

In the management of patients, dentists and their auxiliaries face several major behavioral problems that can impede or prevent delivery of quality treatment. This chapter focuses on specific instances in which behavioral techniques have proven effective in:

1. insuring that the patient will come in for his appointments and keep coming back for routine reexamination,
2. achieving cooperation from the patient during actual dental restorative procedures, including acceptance of anesthetic injections, good chair behavior, and tolerance of some discomfort,
3. teaching the patient to carry out on a regular basis oral hygiene practices that promote healthier teeth and gums,
4. treating special pain-related dental problems such as bruxism, temporomandibular joint dysfunction, and adjustment to fixed and removable prosthetic devices.

The specific treatment examples given here are meant to serve as guides. They can be adapted to fit various settings and help improve the efficiency of dental treatment. A more extensive critical review of the clinical and experimental literature has been provided elsewhere (Melamed, 1979). This chapter is a translation of research findings into practical recommendations for immediate use.

Psychology in Dentistry

All dental personnel practice psychology to some extent in the management of their patients. Several books have been written on this subject (e.g., Ayer & Hirschman, 1972; Wright, 1975). Behavioral principles are often employed without awareness and are therefore not always used in the most effective manner. For instance, the child may be rewarded at the end of treatment with a trinket from the "treasure box" in the hope that he or she will look forward to the next visit. From a learning standpoint, this is not a very effective strategy for teaching the child how to behave during treatment. It is a noncontingent reinforcer in that receiving a toy does not depend on the child's behavior. A better procedure would be to provide feedback or praise during treatment, when the child is making cooperative responses.

Dentists usually treat siblings independently of one another. Research shows, however, that older siblings can be used as models to promote better cooperation (Ghose, Giddon, Shiere, & Fogels, 1969). In a review article, Epley (1974) points out that pain also can be better tolerated in the presence of a reassuring adult. Yet mothers are usually excluded from the operatory.

The dentist, hygienist, or assistant usually emphasize flossing and brushing techniques. Modeling techniques and the use of "disclosure wafers" have facilitated the learning of these behaviors. However, feedback on how the patient is handling plaque control is critical to the effective use of a new toothbrush and brushing instructions. In a similar sense, dental appliances must be worn regularly to achieve the desired outcome. Reinforcement principles have been used to maintain the patients' compliance with braces, dentures, and other appliances. The orthodontist motivates his patients to wear elastic bands on their appliances, reinforcing them for coming in with them on (White, 1974). Unfortunately, this does not necessarily guarantee that they are worn between sessions. Specific shaping procedures can be used to increase the compliance outside the office.

Dentists may also be involved in the care of patients who suffer from pain associated with bruxism or more broadly defined temporomandibular joint pain dysfunction (Melamed & Mealiea, in press). Even when all has been done to resolve dental occlusal disharmony, including surgical intervention, many of these patients still suffer pain. Often, anxiety triggers the external pterygoid masseter muscle, which exacerbates this condition. Occasionally, the problems persist as strongly learned habits that need to be unlearned. Behavioral strategies such as EMG biofeedback, relaxation, and counterconditioning procedures work. Simple shaping procedures have been used to increase the patient's adjustment to dental prosthetics that often produce gagging and complaints from the patient. These procedures are not very time-consuming and make it more likely that the patients will be comfortable and use the appliances as recommended.

Why Do Patients Fail to Come for Treatment?

It is annoying when patients do not show up for their appointments. Yet many patients come to dentists only when they are in real pain and none of their own remedies have alleviated the problem. This pain may condition a negative emotional response whenever dental images are aroused. It may lead to future avoidance behavior. Generally, people expect dentists to do things *to* them, not with them. The uncomfortable feeling of sitting in the dental chair with a mouth full of mechanical devices, not knowing when a session will end, and not even being able to complain may lead to fears about loss of control or claustrophobic anxiety.

Description of the Problem

It has been estimated that 12 million Americans avoid dental treatment each year because of psychological concerns (Friedson & Feldman, 1958). Dental anxiety may include fears of:

1. criticism for poor oral health,
2. loss of control,
3. pain,
4. anesthetic injection, and
5. the sound and feel of the drill.

A survey by Kleinknecht, Klepac, and Alexander (1973) found several areas related to fear of dentists, dental stimuli, and past contact with fearful friends or family members. This suggested to them that it is useful to view fears of the dental situation as learned responses to stimuli inherent in dental treatment. This is an important finding since what has been learned can be unlearned.

Behavioral Treatment of Dental Fears

It is important to make a distinction between the persistent avoider and the hesitant dental patient. For the former, the answer is not very easy. If we cannot get the patient into the dentist's office, there is no opportunity to teach him or her to cope with fear in order to experience successful treatment. In some cases, the persistent avoider may need adjunctive treatment in relaxation, systematic desensitization, or biofeedback (see Chapter 2) prior to undertaking necessary dental treatment. A few may come in if promised nitrous oxide, premedication, or general anesthesia. In most cases, it is appropriate to refer them to a behavior therapist or a dentist experienced in the handling of phobic patients.

Systematic Desensitization

Gale and Ayer (1969) successfully treated a patient who had previously been traumatized during extractions and had avoided the dentist for several years. Systematic desensitization was chosen as the treatment most likely to be accepted by this patient, as it involved graded exposure to the unpleasant situations. With the patient's assistance, an anxiety hierarchy was developed that ranged from low-anxiety items ("thinking about going to the dentist," "getting in your car to go to the dentist") to higher-level anxiety situations ("having a tooth pulled," "getting two injections," "hearing the crunching sounds as your tooth is being pulled"). The patient was trained in deep muscle relaxation. He then visualized these scenes in a relaxed state, beginning with the lower-level items, until they no longer evoked anxiety. After eight sessions, this patient was able to make and keep appointments with the dentist to complete all necessary treatment.

Research does indicate that systematic desensitization reduces patients' anxiety and gets them *into* the office. Shaw and Thoresen (1974) and Krop, Jackson, and Mealiea (1976) worked with patients who had avoided dental treatment for over three years. They found that both systematic desensitization and other stress management techniques were very successful in reducing fears. A sample of an individual's hierarchy is included in Table 9.1.

In the construction of an anxiety hierarchy, it is important for the patient to give a rating to each item (on a seven- or nine-point scale from "completely relaxed" to "terror") to insure that their own sub-

Table 9.1   Dental Fear Hierarchy

1. You are picking up the phone and calling the dentist for an appointment.

2. You are getting out of the car and looking at the outside of the dentist's office.

3. You are walking into the receptionists' area of the dentist's office, and you tell one of the receptionists that you're here for your appointment.

4. You have been sitting in the reception area of the dentist's office for about five minutes.

5. You have been waiting in the office for your turn about twenty minutes.

6. You are sitting in the dental chair in an upright position.

7. You are getting a novocaine shot for numbness.

8. The saliva ejector is placed into your mouth.

9. You have your mouth open while the dental assistant stands over you and places her hand inside your mouth.

10. You hear the noise from the dentist's drill (both fast and slow speed).

11. You are sitting in the dental chair in a full reclining position.

12. You are having stitches removed from your gum.

13. You have been in the dental chair for about forty-five minutes.

14. You feel the pain after having teeth pulled.

15. You feel the numbness of the novocaine wearing off and the full, tingly feeling as it is happening.

16. The dentist is putting moist material in your mouth to make a mold, and you keep your mouth closed for one minute.

17. You have your mouth open while the dentist and the assistant stand over you and place their hands inside your mouth, forcing you to breathe through your nose.

---

jective anxiety is used as the basis for ordering the situations. Temporal considerations (closeness to the time of the appointment) involve only one dimension. Patients may be anxious about being criticized and having others watch them being treated as well as fearing specific instruments, sounds (drilling), and procedures. Pain tolerance has been increased by desensitization (Klepac, 1975).

Modeling

Exposure of the patient to an actual or filmed restorative session in which another patient is observed allows the patient:

1. to find out what will happen,
2. to see a prototype for how the patient can cope with stress, and
3. to experience vicariously what it may feel like.

One of the earliest studies was by Corah and Pantera (1968). They demonstrated that videotaped simulation of a dental procedure involving amalgam restoration, employing either a third person patient model or an eyeview perspective, yielded higher ratings of anxiety than a control film unrelated to dentistry. They found that there was a corresponding increase in skin conductance of highly anxious subjects while watching the first-person version of the film. Highly and mildly anxious subjects gave different ratings to these dental simulation videotapes.

In a validation study, Corah and Salmonson (1970) found that when using the first-person (eyeview) videotape, greater anxiety was induced by the simulation if it was shown in face of an impending dental appointment than if it was shown right after an appointment. Self-ratings of discomfort supported this finding. However, the significant physiological arousal on both skin conductance and percent change in finger pulse volume showed significant increases both before and after appointments.

This discordance between fear measures is not unusual in anxious adult dental phobics (Kleinknecht & Bernstein, 1978) and implies that the dentist should define fear not only by what the patient says or does, but also in terms of somatic arousal (see "Pinpointing Fear," below).

The clinical use of modeling with children has been widespread; however, few studies have been done with dental phobic adults. Shaw and Thoresen (1974) demonstrated that in adult patients who had avoided dental treatment for a mean of 3.7 years, videotape modeling (including relaxation training and imagery) produced results equivalent to systematic desensitization in much less time (6.1 vs. 8.3 hours).

A recent clinical application (Kleinknecht & Bernstein, 1979) used a combination of symbolic modeling (watching another patient overcome fear), graduated exposure (sequential videotape exposure to dental situations), and self-paced in vivo practice (sitting in the dental chair without receiving treatment). Two patients who had avoided treatment for thirteen and six years, respectively, were able to see their dentist and other doctors (endodontist) after only three and one-half hours of therapist contact time.

Environmental Control

The dental office may be arranged to lessen anxiety. If soft music masks the sound of the drilling and if the patient has visual releases, such as open-window views, ceiling art, and gurgling fishtanks, he or she may tolerate the session more comfortably. Corah, Gale, and Illig (1979) demonstrated reduced reports of discomfort in patients who played a video game or listened to relaxation tapes during the restorative session.

Maintaining Cooperative Patient Behavior in the Operatory

Dentists often underestimate their value as socializing agents in our society. How dentists teach youngsters to cope with their stress in the office may be critical to the individual's future ability to handle new, potentially stressful situations. More important, it will influence how cooperative a patient he or she will be in the future. Therefore, in scheduling appointments and in the relationship dental personnel establish with the patient, it is important to consider the influence of procedures on enhancing cooperation and reducing fear. This section deals with suggestions derived from the research literature.

Scheduling Appointments

It is important to schedule appointments so that the patient is not left to wait very long. Opton (1969) found that this waiting period enhances the anxiety. Schedule minimal activities for initial visits (e.g., oral examination, X-rays, home-care instructions), thereby eliminating the association of unpleasant events with the dental setting. A friendly interaction with the dental assistant outside the operatory has been shown to be effective in allaying fear (Sawtell, Simon, & Simeonsson, 1974). It is useful to permit patients to become familiar with the dental personnel and sights and sounds of the equipment during prophylaxis or radiographic sessions (White & Davis, 1974). In fact, there is evidence that children respond with less anxiety if they are initially interviewed away from the operatory and are subsequently treated in an operatory where dental apparatus is kept out of sight (Swallow, Jones, & Morgan, 1975). Once treatment has begun, one may then judge patients' tolerance and use short time periods until they appear more comfortable. Finally, it is beneficial to give children control over the proceedings, such as a signal for a rest stop (Corah, 1973).

Establishing a Trusting Relationship

As in any situation, the confidence that the patient acquires in the dentist enhances his or her trust and, thereby, facilitates cooperation. The traditional use of the tell-show-do technique (Addelston, 1959) with children also proves invaluable with hesitant adults. This simply involves taking the time to tell them what is about to be done, showing how it will be done, and telling them what sensations they can expect to hear and feel and when the procedure will be over. Corah (1973) demonstrated that if the child patient has some control over the progress of the treatment by initiating rest periods, he or she reports less fear and seems better controlled. However, giving adults a similar signaling device did not produce clear results (Corah, Bissell, & Illig, 1978). Dentists' ratings of patient anxiety were equivalent for these patients with "perceived control" and a control sample of patients treated in the typical fashion. In fact, the patients in the group with the signaling device had more autonomic arousal (spontaneous galvanic skin responses) during the anesthesia injection and during high-speed drilling than did subjects without this device. The relationship between GSR and anxiety is not necessarily reflected in this situation. Other research does indicate that subjects given perceived control over aversive events become more aroused (Averill, 1973). It was noted that, in the dental study, few patients actually used the signal to stop treatment. Adults already have some controlling responses, such as grunts, groans, and pleading eye movements, and it is possible that another signal is unnecessary. Patients should be encouraged to participate actively in their treatment. This may be accomplished, for example, by permitting them to hold the suction tube or mirror. Giving them something to do with their hands also limits the possibility that they will make a movement that will disrupt treatment. Allowing patients brief rest intervals after they have tolerated some discomfort may reinforce their cooperative behavior. Recent studies revealed better cooperation in response to guided instructions by the dentist than in response to either a permissive or an evaluative dentist (Melamed, Fleece, Hutcherson, & Fox, 1978; Wurster, Weinstein, & Cohen, 1979).

How Do You Recognize Fear in Patients?

Pinpointing Fear

Anxiety and cooperative behavior are frequently interrelated. To achieve cooperation, the patient's fear must be recognized. By becoming a careful observer of specific signs—verbal, behavioral, and somatic—one can recognize when patients are afraid or uncomfortable.

Fear is a complex phenomenon. It may not be clearly reflected in any one system. A person may say he is afraid, but may fail to show avoidance behaviors or to exhibit visceral arousal in the fear situation. Thus, a three-systems approach is recommended in which somatic indices (pulse rate, flushing, sweat, irregular breathing), self-reports of anxiety or discomfort, and observations of behavior or motor acts (fainting, fidgeting) are evaluated. Research involving dental fears has indicated low intercorrelations between fear responses (Kleinknecht & Bernstein, 1979; Melamed, Weinstein, Hawes, & Katin-Borland, 1975; Melamed, Hawes, Heiby, & Glick, 1975; Venham, Bengston, & Cipes, 1977).

Self-Report

Pay attention to the patient's self-report. Statements such as, "When will it be over?" "Will it hurt?" "I want my Mommy," or "I've got to go to the bathroom" may indicate fear.

Some questionnaires are also available that provide some advance information regarding the extent of fear presented by a patient. The Children's Fear Survey Schedule, modified for dental items, has been found to be predictive of the degree of disruption in the dental chair (Melamed, Weinstein, Hawes, & Katin-Borland, 1975). The questionnaire for adults developed by Kleinknecht, Klepac, and Alexander (1973) provides an index of a patient's pattern of fear reaction to specific components of the dental situation. When patients have an opportunity to complete these questionnaires in the waiting room, and thereby voice their concerns at the outset, it is possible to evaluate the need for special preparation.

Behavioral Measures

Behavioral observations that relate to fear in the dental chair have been studied, particularly in children. The Behavior Profile Rating Scale reproduced in Table 9.2 illustrates some patient behaviors that have been found to correlate with dentists' ratings of anxiety, self-reports of fear, and sweating activity (Melamed, Weinstein, Hawes, & Katin-Borland, 1975). In adults, fear responses are more subtle since there is more expectancy for appropriate compliance. Grunting, wincing, or excessive fidgeting may signal discomfort. Kleinknecht and Bernstein (1978) failed to find significant relationships between fear level and postural status, general activity, or specific movements in adult dental patients. Highly anxious patients moved around more in the waiting room, but this movement was markedly reduced when they were in the chair under treatment. This reaction may be a more cautious fear response. Thus, with adults, more subtle behavioral indices, such as frequently coming late or canceling appointments, may reveal a fearful patient.

Physiological Arousal

Observable physiological cues may also be used, such as irregular breathing, breath holding, redness in the face, excessive perspiration, or pupillary dilation. Heart rate (pulse rate) has also been found to be a predictive measure of anxiety in both adult and child patients. It is less responsive to random environmental changes than galvanic skin response, and appears to be a valid indicator of dental anxiety.

Meldman (1972) employed heart rate response to tape-recorded sound of a dentist's drill as a predictive measure of dental anxiety. Patients were tested before their scheduled appointments. Increased heart rate was found in subjects who reported fear of dentists and drilling. This Dental Drill Phobia test, as it is called, is proposed as a useful quantifiable measure of the patient's experience of fear. It may be a useful predictive measure of persons who need special preparation. If valid, this measure would also provide a way to evaluate patient's responses to behavioral therapy programs designed to modify this type of fear.

A more sophisticated analysis was done by Gang and Teft (1975), who found that heart rate and Multiple Adjective Checklist (Nowlis, 1965) responses of hostility, depression, and anxiety varied directly with the subjects' experience of the sound of the high-speed drill in an analogue study. Heart rate was found to be more accelerated in subjects who had less experience with the dental drill and who rated

Table 9.2   Behavior Profile Rating Scale

	Successive 3-minute observation periods									
	1	2	3	4	5	6	7	8	9	10
Separation from mother										
(3) Cries										
(4) Clings to mother										
(4) Refuses to leave mother										
(5) Bodily carried in										
Office behavior										
(1) Inappropriate mouth closing										
(1) Choking										
(2) Won't sit back										
(2) Attempts to dislodge instruments										
(2) Verbal complaints										
(2) Overreaction to pain										
(2) White knuckles										
(2) Negativism										
(2) Eyes closed										
(3) Cries at injection										
(3) Verbal message to terminate										
(3) Refuses to open mouth										
(3) Rigid posture										
(3) Crying										
(3) Dentist uses loud voice										
(4) Restraints used										
(4) Kicks										
(4) Stands up										
(4) Rolls over										
(5) Dislodges instruments										
(5) Refuses to sit in chair										
(5) Faints										
(5) Leaves chair										

From B. G. Melamed, D. Weinstein, R. Hawes, and M. Katin-Borland, Reduction of fear-related dental management problems using filmed modeling. *Journal of the American Dental Association,* 1975, *90,* 822–826. Copyright © 1975 by the American Dental Association. Reprinted by permission.

the acoustic stimulus as more unpleasant. These subjects also scored higher on the affective scales. The sample had particular peculiarities in that dental hygiene students were selected as the familiar group and their associations to the sound of the drill might be more impersonal than the control sample.

Lewis and Law (1958) demonstrated the feasibility of using polygraphic recordings of heart rate, hand and face temperature, and galvanic skin response to study children's emotional responses during dental treatment. They evaluated the effect of parental presence, and found no difference in heart rates with or without parents. Kominek and Rozdovcova (1966) found increased heart rate in children to words preceding anesthetic injection such as "Nurse, the hypodermic please."

Providing Information to Reduce Stress

Knowing What to Expect

As previously discussed, the tell-show-do technique (Addelston, 1959) gives the patient some sense of being able to anticipate events. It is also important to teach the patient how he or she is to behave during treatment. This can be accomplished in a variety of ways.

Modeling

The use of modeling with children having no prior experience with the actual dental setting is based on the assumption that information about what to expect and how to behave reduces anxiety. Research has demonstrated the effectiveness of such preparatory videotapes (see Figure 9.1) (Adelson & Goldfried, 1970; Melamed, Hawes, Heiby, & Glick, 1975; Melamed, Weinstein, Hawes, & Katin-Borland, 1975). A controlled study (Ghose, Giddon, Shiere, & Fogels, 1969) demonstrated the use of the older sibling in reducing the fear in the younger child who observes him during treatment. Fear of specific procedures (such as the injection) have also been dealt with through modeling and a similar procedure of emotive imagery (Ayer, 1973; Christen, 1972). The use of behavioral rehearsal and imagery initiating mouth openings have been used. Christen (1972) had the children imagine and practice what would take place.

The use of modeling procedures for children who have already had dental treatment is still being investigated. Melamed, Yurcheson, Fleece, Hutcherson, and Hawes (1978) presented data that suggest

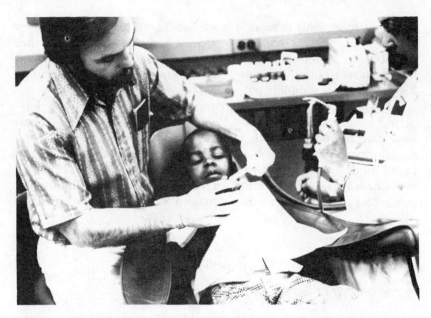

Figure 9.1   A child is prepared for dental treatment. The dentist explains what
he will do in advance and shows the child the instruments that will
be used. This is typical of a scene depicted in a film used in a
study by Melamed, Weinstein, Hawes, and Katin-Borland (1975).
From B. G. Melamed, D. Weinstein, R. Hawes, and M. Katin-Borland,
Reduction of fear-related dental management problems using filmed
modeling. *Journal of the American Dental Association,* 1975, *90,* 822–
826. Copyright © 1975 by the American Dental Association. Reprinted by
permission.

that children who have had previous treatment benefit from viewing
the entire treatment through the eyes of the peer model. Children
without prior experience respond better after seeing a peer model
undergoing the anesthetic injection or after seeing a demonstration of
the entire procedure. Modeling effects are reduced with prior experience (Klorman et. al., 1980).

Cognitive Manipulations (Self-Control Strategies)

Meichenbaum (1975) and others suggest, particularly with adults
undergoing dental procedures, that the individual should self-instruct
coping verbalizations to remain calm. Other coping mechanisms involve opening eyes, counting, imagining oneself in a more pleasant
environment, planning a party, constructing a grocery list, or deciding
whom to invite to one's next gathering. For some patients, rehearsal
in their imagination of successfully getting through the session is use-

ful. Dentists have devised other distractions, such as listening through headphones to music or audioanalgesic masking noises. However, this does impede communication with the patient, and there is no systematic research demonstrating the efficacy of this strategy as a pain-reducing device. Corah, Gale, and Illig (1979) compared relaxation tapes, perceived control, a distraction video game, and a control session as to the stress reaction of adult dental patients during the restorative session. Both relaxation and distraction were effective in reducing self-reported discomfort during operative dental procedures. Patients liked playing the video game best.

Horan, Layng, and Pursell (1976) used emotive imagery to reduce self-reported dental discomfort in adults undergoing prophylaxis. The patients reported less discomfort when instructed in pleasant emotive imagery as compared to a silent period or being instructed to imagine neutral letters. Heart rate, however, did not differ under these conditions.

In a study conducted by Siegel and Peterson (in press), several brief intervention strategies for reducing anxiety and facilitating cooperation were investigated with low-income preschool children with no previous dental experience. Children were randomly assigned to one of three groups:

1. coping skills group—children were taught to use several coping techniques, such as relaxation, distracting imagery of pleasant events, or calming self-talk;
2. sensory information—children were told what to expect at the dentist's office, including sights, sounds, and sensations; they also heard tape-recorded sounds of the dental equipment, such as the drill, and
3. no-treatment control—children were read a story unrelated to the dental visit.

The intervention strategies were provided approximately one-half hour before the dental session.

Using behavioral observations and independent ratings of the dentist and an observer, the investigators found that during the restorative session, which included injection of anesthetic medication, children in both the coping skills and sensory information groups were less disruptive. In addition, both treatments had children who were rated as less anxious than children in the no-treatment control group. The treatment groups did not differ from each other on any of these measures. Finally, after restorative treatment, the coping skills group and the sensory information group had lower pulse rates than the control group.

Dentist Reinforcement

The dentist also needs to explore what reinforcers are available in maintaining the patient's cooperation. Does the patient have the necessary skills to cooperate? Do others in the environment play a significant role in maintaining the problem behavior?

Most people like to please others. As a result, the dentist's approval of their cooperation is rewarding. Specifically, the patient can be reinforced for compliance with the dentist's instructions (e.g., "That's very good, Bobby, you held your mouth open wide when I asked"). Patients do not like to be criticized. Research has demonstrated that criticizing children induces anxiety and increases disruptive behaviors (Fleece, 1979).

Shaping. Another method for facilitating cooperation is controlling the length of the dental session. Allowing rest periods for better cooperation is quite useful. In addition, starting with briefer sessions and gradually increasing these as the individual is able to tolerate longer time periods in the chair can be very effective.

Research with hard-to-manage or other atypical patients, such as the retarded, the hyperactive, and the physically handicapped, has indicated that such behavioral treatment strategies as positively rewarding specific behaviors (e.g., reinforcement for keeping the mouth open) reduces the need for restraints, enhances patient cooperation, and diminishes the amount of time needed for the procedure. The patient's behavior is shaped by the use of specific reinforcement strategies (Horner & Keirlitz, 1975; Kohlenberg, Greenberg, Reymore, & Hass, 1972). Wurster, Weinstein, and Cohen (1979) have found that directive guidance, including feedback, facilitated cooperation.

Punishment. Several authors have cautioned against the use of aversive techniques (Drash, 1974; Hill & O'Mullane, 1976; Wright, 1975). They suggest that there is a risk of traumatizing the patient resulting in a dental phobia. In addition, emotional responses may be disruptive of desirable behavior. Punishment may even enhance aggressive behaviors. Many dental schools suggest the use of a stern voice or physical restraint with disruptive patients. These techniques are often used because they do, in fact, work. At least, they may temporarily suppress interfering behaviors so that dental treatment can be completed. Levitas (1974) supports the use of Craig's (1971) hand-over-mouth technique when the child is verbally capable of understanding the command (three to six years of age) and is out of control in the chair. Empirical data is lacking on the effectiveness of different behavioral strategies. Research with pedodontic patients suggests that different reinforcement strategies produce different results (Melamed, Fleece, Hutcherson, & Fox, 1978). If the aim of the program is to increase cooperation, objective measures of success may include the ease with which the procedures can be completed, the number of teeth restored, the percent of the session during which the patient complied with instructions, decreased indices of anxiety, and the reduced degree of disruptive behaviors. The ultimate test of a strategy's effectiveness comes in successive dental sessions. Has the patient learned how to behave? Does he or she appear less anxious? Does he or she return for recall visits?

Promoting and Maintaining Oral Hygiene

Patients who neglect oral hygiene practices are prone to periodontal disease, and may require frequent restorative treatment or have a displeasing appearance. For the patient, the motivation for learning and performing daily oral hygiene, such as toothbrushing, flossing, and proper diet, should be a reduction of dental visits and costs along with improved physical appearance and self-perception. Unfortunately, there is a delay in time that serves to reduce the likelihood that these daily habits are reinforced. Biting into a sweet is more immediately rewarding than thinking of the decay that may be building up. These behaviors must be learned as habits early in life. Often, oral hygiene practices are part of parents' program to educate their children in self-care behaviors. Advice from the dentist about appropriate brushing technique and proper diet is often insufficient, by itself, in getting children to comply with the recommended procedures. Reinforcement procedures used to gain patient cooperation, such as shaping and token economies, have been equally effective in establishing and maintaining good oral health practices (Lund & Kegeles, 1979). Some parents have a chart on which the child records his toothbrushing behavior on a daily basis. A weekly allowance or some other incentive (e.g., trip to the movies or a TV show) may be contingent upon the regularity of performing this function. An elaborate school program (Martens, Frazier, Hirt, Meskin, & Proshek, 1973) found that the use of tokens, social praise, group projects, and individual attention from the dental hygienist facilitated toothbrushing behavior in second graders. Other programs to increase flossing behavior have focused on breaking down the required behaviors into motor learning chains and using reinforcement for corrective imitation of each response (Thornburg & Thornburg, 1974). This is especially useful with retarded individuals (Troutman, 1977). Although flossing is considered important, this procedure is not consistently practiced by most adults.

Another approach in getting adults to practice good oral hygiene has been studied by Evans and his colleagues (1970). This involved giving information and fear-arousing messages about consequences of not brushing and flossing. They found that the level of fear arousal was not as crucial as whether or not specific procedural information was available. The use of the "disclosing wafer" as immediate feedback regarding the effectiveness of oral hygiene practices was valuable both as an assessment device and as a motivating factor. Many dentists routinely rinse the mouth with dye (a disclosing solution) to point out to the patient the areas that are being missed during brushing.

Pain-Related Dental Problems

There are at least three conditions that result from the interaction of psychological stress and actual dental dysfunction:

1. the problem of bruxism (tooth grinding) has recently been addressed as an example of a disorder in which emotional factors exacerbate the problem (Glaros & Rao, 1977);
2. patients suffering from temporomandibular joint dysfunction (TMJ), also called myofacial pain dysfunction (MPD), are prone to anxiety, depression, and pain often unalleviated by dental procedures;
3. the wearing of removable and fixed prosthetics is often uncomfortable for patients with gag reflexes or problems in oral-musculature control or inappropriate swallowing.

There are proven procedures based on behavioral principles that may be explored with the patient.

Bruxism

If bruxism is conceptualized as a response to generalized or environmentally specific stress, teaching a subject to relax may be an effective means of reducing or eliminating bruxism. Jacobson's (1938) progressive relaxation technique, which involves learning how to locate tension by contracting various muscle groups and then relaxing them, has been shown in some cases to reduce physiological concomitants of muscular tension. There are other exercises and massages specifically for the masticatory muscles that have been reported to be effective (Ackerman, 1966; Maslanka & Kwapanski, 1974). Hypnosis has also been used (Goldberg, 1973). Procedures involving the use of EMG biofeedback, in which the patients increase their awareness of muscle tension involved in mastication, have also been found useful in the treatment of bruxism (Solberg & Rugh, 1972).

Another approach that has yielded success with nocturnal bruxists includes a device (Heller & Strang, 1973) worn during sleep that wakes the patient up with a loud noise if the rate of grinding of the teeth exceeds his or her base level. Ayer and Gale (1969) reported that massed practice, through having a patient grind his teeth for one minute and relax for one minute over a period of several trials, reduced the bruxing behavior of a twenty-six-year-old patient whose wife complained that his bruxing disrupted her sleep. There are, however, contradictory research findings as to the effectiveness of this massed-practice approach (Ayer & Levin, 1975; Heller & Forgione, 1975).

Bruxing in children has not been studied as thoroughly. Reding, Rubright, and Zimmerman (1966) have reported that in the three- to seventeen-year-olds they have surveyed, 15 percent had a history of nocturnal tooth grinding. In a sample of 196 children ranging from 10.7 to 13.1 years, Lindquist (1971) reported that 14.9 percent of the parents had heard their children grind their teeth. It has been found that children with brain damage, mental retardation, and cerebral palsy brux significantly more than normal children (Lindquist & Heijbel, 1974; Siegel, 1960; Swallow, 1972). Thumbsucking in children has been treated with both positive and aversive conditioning techniques as well as the use of fixed dental appliances. However, it is generally agreed that these habits are unlikely to result in permanent damage to the dentition, particularly if they are abandoned by the ages of four to five.

Temporomandibular Joint Dysfunction

This condition can lead to serious problems if left untreated. Many patients complain of pain even after a dentist's best efforts at correcting malocclusion. These intractable-pain patients do benefit from some of the above-mentioned behavioral treatment approaches. Biofeedback training, in particular, has been found useful for such patients (Budzinski & Stoyva, 1973; Carlsson & Gale, 1976; Dohrmann

& Laskin, 1976; Gessel, 1975; and Olsen, 1977). Gessel (1975) found that older individuals who suffered severe depression did not benefit from biofeedback or antidepressants. The dentist must recognize that psychological factors may play a role in their pain complaints. In these cases, the sick-role may be inadvertently reinforced by sympathetic relatives, the ability to avoid work situations, and the avoidance of interpersonal conflict (see Chapter 4). Rugh and Solberg (1976) have suggested that treatment should deal less with finding the cause of pain and more with providing patients with the skills to tolerate their pain in order to lead more productive lives.

Gagging and Difficulty in Maintaining Dentures

The problem of the gag reflex is a major one in that it may interfere with ongoing dental treatment or prevent patients from wearing partial or full dentures or orthodontic appliances. A shaping program was undertaken with a thirty-year-old woman who would not wear her dentures because of gagging. This procedure was successful after ten brief treatment sessions carried out by the patient at home. She was instructed to insert her plates, to count aloud from a column of numbers, and to remove the dentures prior to gagging. Over a period of days, she was able to wear her dentures while reading passages and engaging in household activities, and ultimately, during an entire meal (Stoffelmayr, 1970).

Another form of behavioral therapy—called myofunctional therapy—also has been used to facilitate the use of dentures. This procedure trains the denture patient in mouth-muscle control so that the prosthesis can be worn comfortably (Plainfield, 1977).

Specific applications of providing contingencies to maintain the wearing of orthodontic headgear and elastic bands are described by White (1974). He used a token-reinforcement program to maintain compliance with orthodontic treatment. Adolescent patients meeting their set criteria earned time listening to a jukebox or enjoyed special reading material before their dental appointment.

Summary

This chapter has reviewed behavioral principles applied to a number of dental problems, including getting patients to come for treatment, facilitating cooperation during treatment, decreasing fears, maintaining appropriate oral hygiene, and reducing the unpleasant sensations associated with bruxism, temporomandibular joint dysfunction, and the wearing of removable and fixed prosthetics.

The approach of systematic desensitization has worked well in decreasing fear in both child and adult patients and in increasing their cooperation during needed treatments. The approaches of gradual exposure to the dental operatory and advanced preparation by watching a sibling or a film involving a peer model undergoing restorative treatment has increased cooperative behaviors in children. The use of specific positive reinforcement procedures is recommended for the shaping of cooperative behavior in hard-to-manage patients, such as the mentally retarded or physically handicapped. Dentists are cautioned against the use of criticism and aversive techniques until more systematic research is provided. The application of reinforcement principles in teaching oral hygiene has emphasized the use of consistent incentives during early childhood training and immediate feedback regarding the effectiveness of habit in prevention of dental caries.

References

Ackerman, J. B. A new approach to the treatment of bruxism and bruxomania. *New York State Dental Journal*, 1966, *32*, 259.

Addelston, H. Child patient training. *Fortnightly Review of the Chicago Dental Society*, 1959, *38*, 17.

Adelson, D., & Goldfried, M. Modeling and the fearful child patient. *Journal of Dentistry for Children*, 1970, *37*, 476–488.

Ayer, W. A. Use of visual imagery in needle phobic children. *Journal of Dentistry for Children*, 1973, *40*, 125.

―――. Thumb, finger-sucking and bruxing habits in children. Paper presented at Conference on Oral-Motor Problems in Dentistry. Washington, D.C., May, 1979.

Ayer, W. A., & Gale, E. N. Extinction of bruxism by massed practice therapy. *Journal of the Canadian Dental Association*, 1969, *35*, 492.

Ayer, W. A., & Hirschman, R. *Psychology and dentistry*. Springfield, Ill.: Charles C. Thomas, 1972.

Ayer, W. A., & Levin, M. P. Elimination of tooth grinding habits by massed practice therapy. *Journal of Periodontology*, 1973, *44*, 569.

―――. Theoretical bases and application of massed practice exercises for the elimination of tooth grinding habits. *Journal of Periodontology*, 1975, *46*, 306.

Averill, J. Personal control over aversive stimuli and its relationship to stress. *Psychological Bulletin*, 1973, *80*, 286–303.

Budzinski, T., & Stoyva, J. An electromyographic feedback technique for teaching voluntary relaxation of the masseter muscle. *Journal of Dental Research*, 1973, *52*, 116–119.

Carlsson, S. G., & Gale, E. N. Biofeedback treatment for muscle pain associated with the temporomandibular joint. *Journal of Behavior Therapy and Experimental Psychiatry*, 1976, *7*, 383–385.

Christen, A. Improving the child's dental behavior through mental rehearsal. *Northwestern Dentistry*, 1972, *51*, 223–225.

Corah, N. Effects of perceived control on stress reduction in pedodontic patients. *Journal of Dental Research*, 1973, *52*, 1261–1264.

Corah, N., Bissell, G. D., & Illig, S. Effects of perceived control on stress reduction in adult dental patients. *Journal of Dental Research*, 1978, *57*, 74–76.

Corah, N., Gale, E. N., & Illig, S. J. Psychological stress reducing during dental procedures. *Journal of Dental Research*, 1979, *58*, 1347–1351.

Corah, N., & Pantera, R. Controlled study of psychologic stress in a dental procedure. *Journal of Dental Research*, 1968, *47*, 154–157.

Corah, N., & Salmonson, R. Psychological response to a simulated dental procedure as a function of proximity to an actual dental appointment. *Journal of Dental Research*, 1970, *49*, 438–441.

Craig, W. Hand over mouth technique. *Journal of Dentistry for Children*, 1971, *38*, 387–389.

Davison, G., Tsujaimoto, R. N., & Glaros, A. G. Attribution and maintenance of behavior change in falling asleep. *Journal of Abnormal Psychology*, 1973, *82*, 124–133.

Dohrmann, R. J., & Laskin, D. M. Treatment of myofascial pain dysfunction syndrome with EMG biofeedback. *Journal of Dental Research*, 1976, *55B*, 249.

Drash, P. New tools for use in pediatric dentistry with the handicapped child. *Dental Clinics of North America*, 1974, *18*, 617–631.

Epley, S. W. Reduction of the behavioral effects of aversive stimulation by the presence of companions. *Psychological Bulletin*, 1974, *81*, 271–283.

Evans, R., Rozelle, R., Lasseter, R., Dembroski, T., & Allen, B. Fear arousal persuasion, and actual versus implied behavioral change: New perspective utilizing a real life dental program. *Journal of Personality and Social Psychology*, 1970, *16*, 220–227.

Fleece, E. L. Contingency management as a method of reducing children's disruptive behaviors during dental treatment. Unpublished Ph.D. dissertation. Case Western Reserve University, 1979.

Friedson, E., & Feldman, J. The public looks at dental care. *Journal of the American Dental Association*, 1958, *57*, 325–335.

Gale, E., & Ayer, N. M. Treatment of dental phobias. *Journal of the American Dental Association*, 1969, *73*, 1304–1307.

Gang, M., & Teft, L. Individual differences in heart rate responses to affective sound (dental drill). *Psychophysiology*, 1975, *11*, 423–426.

Gessel, A. Electromyographic biofeedback and tricyclic anti-depressants in myofascial pain-dysfunction syndrome: Psychological predictors of outcome. *Journal of the American Dental Association,* 1975, *91,* 1048–1052.

Ghose, L., Giddon, D., Shiere, F., & Fogels, H. Evaluation of sibling support. *Journal of Dentistry for Children,* 1969, *36,* 35–49.

Glaros, A. G., & Rao, S. M. Bruxism: A critical review. *Psychological Bulletin,* 1977, *84,* 767–782.

Goldberg, G. The psychological, physiological and hypnotic approach to bruxism in the treatment of periodontal disease. *Journal of the American Society of Psychosomatic Dentistry and Medicine,* 1973, *20,* 75–91.

Heller, R. F., & Forgione, A. G. An evaluation of bruxism control: Massed negative practice and automated relaxation training. *Journal of Dental Research,* 1975, *54,* 1120.

Heller, R. F., & Strang, H. R. Controlling bruxism through automated aversive conditioning. *Behaviour Research and Therapy,* 1973, *11,* 327.

Hill, R., & O'Mullane, D. A preventive program for the dental management of frightened children. *Journal of Dentistry for Children,* 1976, 30–34.

Horan, J. J., Layng, F. C., & Pursell, C. H. Preliminary study of effects of "in vivo" emotive imagery on dental discomfort. *Perceptual and Motor Skills,* 1976, *42,* 105–106.

Horner, D., & Keirlitz, I. Training mentally retarded adolescents to brush their teeth. *Journal of Applied Behavior Analysis,* 1975, *8,* 301–309.

Jacobson, E. *Progressive relaxation.* Chicago: University of Chicago Press, 1938.

Kleinknecht, R., & Bernstein, D. The assessment of dental fear. *Behavior Therapy,* 1978, *9,* 626–634.

———. Short-term treatment of dental avoidance. *Journal of Behavior Therapy and Experimental Psychiatry,* 1979.

Kleinknecht, R., Klepac, R., & Alexander, L. Origins and characteristics of fear of dentistry. *Journal of the American Dental Association,* 1973, *86,* 842–848.

Klepac, R. K. Successful treatment of avoidance of dentistry by desensitization or by increasing pain tolerance. *Journal of Behavior Therapy and Experimental Psychiatry,* 1975, *6,* 307–310.

Klorman, R., Hilpert, P., Michael, R., LaGana, C., & Sveen, O. Effects of coping and mastery modeling on experienced and inexperienced pedodontic patients. *Behavior Therapy,* 1980, *11,* 156–168.

Kohlenberg, R., Greenberg, D., Reymore, L., & Hass, G. Behavior modification and management of mentally retarded dental patients. *Journal of Dentistry for Children,* 1972, *39,* 61–67.

Kominek, J., & Rozdovcova, E. Psychology of children's dental treatment. *International Dental Journal,* 1966, *16,* 1–29.

Krop, H., Jackson, E., & Mealiea, W. Effects of systematic desensitization and stress management training in reducing dental phobia. Paper presented at the meeting of the Association for the Advancement of Behavior Therapy, Washington, D.C., 1976.

Levitas, T. HOME-hand over mouth exercise. *Journal of Dentistry for Children,* 1974, *42,* 178–182.

Lewis, T., & Law, T. Investigation of certain autonomic responses of children to specific dental stress. *Journal of the American Dental Association,* 1958, *57,* 769–777.

Lindquist, B. Bruxism in children. *Odontologisk Revy,* 1971, *22,* 413–424.

Lindquist, B., & Heijbel, T. Bruxism in children with brain damage. *Acta Odontologia Scandinavica,* 1973, *32,* 255–259.

Lund, A. K., & Kegeles, S. Cognitive and behavioral strategies for children's preventive dental behavior. *Journal of Dental Research,* 1979, *58,* 132.

Maslanka, T., & Kwapinska, W. Rehabilitation of masticatory muscles by means of active exercises. *Czopismo Btomatolgiczne,* 1974, *27,* 731–735 (English Abstract).

Martens, L., Frazier, P., Hirt, K., Meskin, L., & Proshek, J. Developing brushing performance in second graders through behavior modification. *Health Services Report,* 1973, *88,* 818–823.

Meichenbaum, D. Self-instructional methods. In F. Kanfer & A. Goldstein (Eds.), *Helping people change.* New York: Pergamon, 1975.

Melamed, B. G. Behavioral approaches to fear in dental settings. In M. Hersen, R. M. Eisler, & P. M. Miller (Eds.), *Progress in behavior modification,* Vol. 7. New York: Academic Press, 1979.

Melamed, B. G., Fleece, L., Hutcherson, S., & Fox, L. Contingency management by dentists to reduce disruptive behavior in patients. *Journal of Dental Research,* 1978, *57,* 117.

Melamed, B. G., Hawes, R., Heiby, E., & Glick, J. The use of filmed modeling to reduce uncooperative behavior of children during dental treatment. *Journal of Dental Research,* 1975, *54,* 797–801.

Melamed, B. G., & Mealiea, W. L., Jr. Behavioral intervention in pain-related problems in dentistry. In J. M. Ferguson and C. B. Taylor (Eds.), *A comprehensive handbook of behavioral medicine.* Jamaica, N.Y.: Spectrum Publications, in press.

Melamed, B. G., Weinstein, D., Hawes, R., & Katin-Borland, M. Reduction of fear-related dental management problems using filmed modeling. *Journal of the American Dental Association,* 1975, *90,* 822–826.

Melamed, B. G., Yurcheson, R., Fleece, L., Hutcherson, S., & Hawes, R. Effects of film modeling on the reduction of anxiety-related behaviors in individuals varying in levels of previous experience in the stress situation. *Journal of Consulting and Clinical Psychology,* 1978, *46,* 1357–1367.

Meldman, M. The dental-phobia test. *Psychosomatics,* 1972, *13,* 371–372.

Olson, R. E. Biofeedback for MPD patients nonresponsive to drug and bite-plate therapy. *Journal of Dental Research,* 1977, *56B,* 40.

Opton, E. Psychological stress and coping processes in the practice of dentistry. *International Dental Journal,* 1969, *19,* 415–429.

Plainfield, S. Myofunctional therapy for complete denture patients. *Journal of Prosthetic Dentistry,* 1977, *38,* 131–137.

Reding, G. R., Rubright, W. C., & Zimmerman, S. O. Incidence of bruxism. *Journal of Dental Research,* 1966, *45,* 1198–1204.

Rugh, J. D., & Solberg, W. K. Psychological implications in temporomandibular pain and dysfunction. *Oral Sciences Review*, 1976, *7*, 3–30.

Sawtell, R., Simon, J., & Simeonsson, R. The effects of five preparatory methods upon child behavior during the first dental visit. *Journal of Dentistry for Children*, 1974, *41*, 37–45.

Shaw, D., & Thoresen, C. Effects of modeling and desensitization in reducing dental phobia. *Journal of Counseling Psychology*, 1974, *21*, 415–420.

Siegel, J. Dental findings in cerebral palsy. *Journal of Dentistry for Children*, 1960, *27*, 233–238.

Siegel, L. J., & Peterson, L. Stress reduction in young dental patients through coping skills and sensory information. *Journal of Consulting and Clinical Psychology*, in press.

Solberg, W. K., & Rugh, J. D. The use of biofeedback devices in the treatment of bruxism. *Journal of the Southern California Dental Association*, 1972, *40*, 852–853.

Stoffelmayr, B. The treatment of retching responses to dentures by counteractive reading aloud. *Journal of Behavior Therapy and Experimental Psychiatry*, 1970, *1*, 163–164.

Swallow, J. Dental disease in handicapped children—An epidemiological study. *Israel Journal of Dental Medicine*, 1972, *21*, 41–51.

Swallow, J., Jones, J., & Morgan, M. The effect of the environment on a child's reaction to dentistry. *Journal of Dentistry for Children*, 1975, *42*, 43–44.

Thornburg, H., & Thornburg, E. The motivational aspects of teaching patients dental home care. *Journal of the American Society of Preventive Dentistry*, 1974, *4*, 14–20.

Troutman, K. Behavioral management of the mentally retarded. *Dental Clinics of North America*, 1977, *21*, 621–635.

Venham, L., Bengston, D., & Cipes, M. Preschool child's response to sequential dentist visits. *Journal of Dental Research*, 1977, *56*, 454–459.

White, L. Behavior modification of orthodontic patients. *Journal of Clinical Orthodontics*, 1974, *8*, 501–505.

White, W., & Davis, M. Vicarious extinction of phobic behavior in early childhood. *Journal of Abnormal Child Psychology*, 1974, *2*, 25–32.

Wright, G. *Behavioral management in dentistry for children*. Philadelphia: W. B. Saunders, 1975.

Wurster, C. A., Weinstein, P., & Cohen, A. J. Communication patterns in pedodontics. *Perceptual and Motor Skills*, 1979, *48*, 159–166.

Afterword

Beyond the Bedside

Behavior therapy has been a major catalyst in the emergence of this rapidly growing new field of research and practice, which we call Behavioral Medicine. The notion of applying behavioral science knowledge to medicine is, of course, not new. Courses in behavioral science have been taught in most medical schools for many years, yet for just as many years the impact of such courses seems to have been less than optimal. The reason for this may be that medicine is ultimately a practical venture, and that until quite recently most of the behavioral science applications were descriptive in nature—they pointed up problems in medical care, but offered little in the way of practical guidance to the health care worker enmeshed in the day-to-day complexities of patient care. Such approaches have left many health care workers with the distinct impression that the behavioral sciences are impractical and that their interventions are ineffective. While much has yet to be learned about behavior and behavior change, applied psychology has now developed a large body of research detailing interesting and effective applications to many conditions, and this has been the theme of this informative book.

Behavioral medicine, however, has other roots than these new approaches to behavior change. These roots comprise the basic work underlying our understanding of behavior and how to change it. They include knowledge about overt behavior, cognitive processes, and psychophysiology; as well as the descriptive and experimental studies from a variety of disciplines that have advanced our understanding of the problems involved in the delivery of health care, of the limitations involved in the medical treatment of certain problems, and of the various risk factors underlying health problems such as cancer and

cardiovascular disease. Thus a set of problems and a developing intervention science and technology have emerged together, and it is the
beginning interactions between problems and solutions that has generated the new field.

Medicine today is faced with two different and equally complex
problems. On the one hand, curative medicine has increased its power
by taking advantage of the recent advances in basic science and technology. On the other, there is a growing realization that many of the
ills that beset modern man are in part a product of the remarkable
changes that have taken place in our environment over the past fifty
years, bringing major changes in our life style that in turn have
changed the incidence and prevalence of many diseases. This realization has strengthened efforts to alter life style (or factors that impinge
on life style) to prevent disease. Behavior problems are, of course,
found in both curative and preventive medicine.

Highly developed diagnostic and therapeutic procedures often
arouse fear and may call for difficult behavior changes on the part of
the patient. Clearly, the applied behavioral sciences have a role here
in helping patients understand, cope with, and alter their behavior as
they become involved in one aspect or another of the health care
system. But one might ask who is going to apply this behavioral science
knowledge in the real world. Health care professionals are busy people. A recent survey (Noren, Frazier, Altman, & De Lozier, 1980)
found that family practitioners spend an average of thirteen minutes
with each patient, while internists spend about eighteen minutes.
Health education was provided by internists in less than one quarter
of the visits and by family physicians in only 16% of visits. Given the
complexities of medical diagnosis and management, obviously little
time is left to provide health information let alone counseling devoted
to behavior change. Some of the slack will undoubtedly be taken up
by other health care workers such as nurses, dietitians, rehabilitation
counselors, and so on. Here, there is a need for such professionals to
acquire the new knowledge and skills detailed in this book. The way
has, however, also been opened for the psychologist to move beyond
the traditional concern with mental health problems, and to become
a more active member of the general health care team—a collaboration
that will undoubtedly result in a more sophisticated approach to the
behavior problems of patients, which, for lack of time or lack of skill
presently go unrecognized or are ignored.

Beyond the bedside, the behavioral sciences can provide help in
areas that do not directly involve patient care. The delivery of health
care often involves a complex organization within which patient ser-

vices are delivered. It is becoming clear that the way in which the staff of such clinics is organized, is trained, and works has profound implications for the quality of health care provided to patients. At the extreme, poorly organized clinics with badly trained personnel will offer inferior services. But many of the problems are more subtle than this and will call for the development of an active research endeavor into the functioning of the health care environment, a development which in my opinion would be most useful to modern medicine.

So far we have been dealing with patients and those who care for them. But for most of our lives we are not patients; yet health should be of vital concern to us. The applications of behavioral science expertise to optimize health and thus prevent the occurrence of illness will undoubtedly comprise one of the most exciting parts of behavioral medicine. Some research has already begun to identify ways in which information can be brought to large populations to help individuals change their behavior and thus positively affect their health. The Stanford Three Community Study (Farquhar, Maccoby, Wood et al, 1977) demonstrated that a media campaign aimed at helping individuals change their diet, stop smoking, and exercise more resulted in a decrease in the risk of coronary artery disease in the populations to which the campaign was addressed as compared with a control population. Moreover, the risk reduction was maintained over the three years of the campaign. While the risk reduction obtained with a group who participated in a face-to-face counseling program was greater, a concentrated media campaign alone was useful. These findings combined with others suggest that mediated procedures including the printed word have an effect upon behavior, although less strong than that of therapist-intensive approaches. From a public health point of view, even small changes in behavior that lead to small changes in risk factors for a given disease can be important. For example, a community in which weight remained stable with increasing age would be expected to have an advantage over communities in which the more usual increases in weight might be observed.

Applying what we now know would undoubtedly have a considerable impact upon the health and comfort of both individuals and communities. It is, however, to future research that we must look for the greatest benefits. Here many exciting and challenging opportunities exist. Obviously we have much to learn about the process of behavior change in many different situations; this knowledge in turn might lead to more effective ways of handling the many problems encountered in the daily practice of medicine, or in prevention both at a personal and the community level. In particular, we desperately need to understand how to maintain behavior change over the long term. In addition, exciting work is beginning to appear in more traditional areas such as understanding the mysterious placebo effect so that we can harness its curative potential. The rapid advances in electronic technology now give us the potential to move out of the laboratory and study many aspects of behavior in real life—where, as they say, the real action is. This, we hope, will allow the progressive accumulation of knowledge needed to increase our understanding of the behavioral side of health and illness and to develop a technology to influence such behaviors for the benefit of all. Without the necessary research development, however, the field will not deliver on its potential promise.

Stewart Agras, M.D.
Stanford University
School of Medicine

References

Farquhar, J. W., Maccoby, N., Wood, P. D., Alexander, J. K., Breitrose, H., Brown, B. W., Haskell, W. L., McAlister, A. L., Meyer, A. J., Nash, J. D., & Stern, M.P. Community education for cardiovascular health. *Lancet* 1977, 1192-1195.

Noren, J., Frazier, T., Altman, I., & De Lozier, J. Ambulatory medical care: A comparison of internists and family practitioners. *New England Journal of Medicine* 1980, 302:11-16.

APPENDIX

Appendix Table A.1   Treatment Program Outline

I.   Selecting and defining target behavior(s)

    A. Behavioral excesses
    B. Behavioral deficits
    C. Inappropriate or defective stimulus control
    D. Behavioral assets

II.   Methods of collecting information

    A. Self-report measures
    B. Behavioral observations
    C. Patient self-monitoring
    D. Permanent product measures
    E. Physiological measures (instrumentation)

III. Functional analysis of behavior

    A. Antecedent events
    B. Consequences

IV.   Selecting and implementing an intervention program

    A. Motivation for change
      1. Patient (secondary gains)
      2. Significant others
    B. Assessment of available reinforcers
    C. Availability and cooperation of significant others and staff
    D. Factors maintaining the problem
      1. Skill deficit
      2. Lack of incentive (insufficient reinforcement)
      3. Excessive or insufficient arousal (anxiety, anger, depression)
    E. Treatment strategies

V.   Evaluation of the intervention program

    A. Continuous monitoring of progress during treatment (use of feedback to modify program as indicated)
    B. Programming for maintenance of behavior change (transfer to real life)
    C. Follow-up assessment (Is reinstatement of treatment program necessary?)

VI. Termination of the intervention program (What was your treatment goal?)

Appendix Table A.2   Treatment Program Guide Form

I.   Target behavior _____ defined as:

    A. (too much) _____

    _____

    B. (too little) _____

    _____

    C. (cued by or in reaction to) _____

    _____

    D. (strengths and skills) _____

    _____

II. Methods of collecting information

    A. (interviews, questionnaires, test results) _____

    _____

    B. (overt manifestations of patient's behavior) _____

    _____

    C. (what patient self-monitors and records) _____

    _____

    D. (lasting changes in the environment--e.g., food left over, work output)

    _____

    E. (physiological indices--e.g., GSR, pulse rate) _____

    _____

III. Functional analysis of behavior

    A. (events preceding target behavior) _____

    _____

    B. (events following target behavior) _____

    _____

(continued)

Appendix Table A.2   (continued)

IV. Selecting and implementing an intervention program

    A. Motivation for change

        1.(benefits of "sick-role"--e.g., attention, avoidance or responsibility)

        _____

        _____

        2. (What would be different for patient/significant others if problem

        did not exist?) _____

        _____

    B. Meaningful environmental consequences

        1. Likes _____

        2. Dislikes _____

    C. Significant others (spouse, siblings, parent, teacher) _____

        _____

    D. Factors maintaining the problem _____

        _____

    E. Treatment strategies _____

        _____

        _____

V. Evaluation of intervention program

    A. Monitoring of treatment progress _____

        _____

    B. Programming for maintenance of behavior change _____

        _____

    C. Follow-up assessment _____

        _____

VI. Termination (What was your treatment goal?) _____

    _____

_____

INDEXES

Subject Index

Author Index